China beyond the Headlines

China beyond the Headlines

**edited by Timothy B. Weston
and Lionel M. Jensen**

ROWMAN & LITTLEFIELD PUBLISHERS, INC.
Lanham • Boulder • New York • Oxford

ROWMAN & LITTLEFIELD PUBLISHERS, INC.

Published in the United States of America
by Rowman & Littlefield Publishers, Inc.
4720 Boston Way, Lanham, Maryland 20706
http://www.rowmanlittlefield.com

12 Hid's Copse Road
Cumnor Hill, Oxford OX2 9JJ, England

British Library Cataloguing in Publication Information Available

Library of Congress Cataloging-in-Publication Data

China beyond the headlines / edited by Timothy B. Weston and Lionel M. Jensen.
    p.   cm.
    Papers presented at a symposium at the University of Colorado in 1997; many of them revised.
    Includes bibliographical references and index.
    ISBN 0-8476-9854-8 (alk. paper) — ISBN 0-8476-9855-6 (paper: alk. paper)
    1. China—Social conditions—1976– 2. China—Economic conditions—1976– 3. China—Relations—United States 4. United States—Relations—China. I. Weston, Timothy B., 1964– II. Jensen, Lionel M.

HN733.5.C4285 2000
306'.0951—dc21   99-050294

Printed in the United States of America

I dedicate this volume to my parents, Burns H. Weston and Hanna B. Weston. Their interests and concerns have fired my own.

T. B. W.

For the laboring peoples of China and the United States with the earnest hope that in their daily industry they will work free of the national stereotypes that limit prospects for ecumenism.

L. M. J.

Contents

Chronology   ix

Table of Equivalents and Measures   xi

Foreword: Between the Lines and beyond the Text
    Geremie Barmé   xiii

Preface and Acknowledgments   xix

Map: The World and China   xxiii

Map: China   xxiv

Introduction: LEAD STORY—Favored Nations, Intertwined Fates
    Timothy B. Weston and Lionel M. Jensen   1

Part One   Above the Fold

1   Big Bad China and the Good Chinese: An American Fairy Tale
    Jeffrey N. Wasserstrom   13

2   Everyone's a Player, but the Nation's a Loser: Corruption in Contemporary China
    Lionel M. Jensen   37

3   China's Many Faces: Ethnic, Cultural, and Religious Pluralism
    Susan D. Blum   69

4   Promoting Human Rights in China: An Activist's Perspective
    Xiao Qiang   97

5   China's Road to a Democratic Society: Perils and Prospects
    Wei Jingsheng   113

6 Beyond Exceptionalism: China's Intellectuals from Tragic Heroes to
U.S. Allies
Timothy Cheek   121

7 Identity and Diversity: The Complexities and Contradictions of
Chinese Nationalism
Tong Lam   147

8 China's New Economic Reforms: Replacing Iron Rice Bowls with
Plastic Cups
Henry Rosemont, Jr.   171

Part Two   Below the Fold

9 Development and Destruction: The Dimensions of China's
Environmental Challenge
Vaclav Smil   195

10 Marketing Femininity: Images of the Modern Chinese Woman
Harriet Evans   217

11 China's Labor Woes: Will the Workers Crash the Party?
Timothy B. Weston   245

12 Reading Out-of-Print: Popular Culture and Protest on China's
Western Frontier
Jay Dautcher   273

13 China's Market Reforms: Whose Human Rights Problem?
Tim Oakes   295

14 Border Crossings: Chinese Writing, in Their World and Ours
Howard Goldblatt   327

Afterword: EXTRA—Headlines Obscure the Full Story
Timothy B. Weston and Lionel M. Jensen   347

Index   355

About the Editors and Contributors   363

Chronology

1898	100 Days Reform Movement
1911	Xinhai Revolution—the collapse of the Qing dynasty and the founding of the Republic of China
1912	Founding of the Nationalist Party (Guomindang/Kuomintang)
1921	Founding of the Chinese Communist Party
1945–49	Chinese Civil War (Communists versus Nationalists)
1949	Communist Revolution—Mao Zedong (1893–1976) becomes the leader of China; founding of the People's Republic of China (PRC)
	Nationalist Party retreats to Taiwan, reestablishing the Republic of China
1966–76	Great Proletarian Cultural Revolution
1975	"Four Modernizations" are proclaimed
1976	Mao Zedong dies
1978	Deng Xiaoping (1904–1997) becomes "paramount" leader; beginning of the Four Modernizations (agriculture, industry, science and technology, national defense)
1978–79	The Democracy Wall Movement
	Wei Jingsheng's "The Fifth Modernization—Democracy"

1979	"Normalization" of PRC–U.S. relations
	Formation of Special Economic Zones (SEZs)
1981	"Socialism with Chinese Characteristics" is officially proclaimed the national goal
1989	Tian'anmen "Democracy" protests; June 4th Massacre
1992	Deng Xiaoping's "Southern Tour"—reaffirms commitment to capitalism
1997	Deng Xiaoping dies—Jiang Zemin becomes president
	Return of Hong Kong
	President Jiang Zemin pays state visit to the United States
	Collapse of Asian financial markets
1998	President Bill Clinton pays state visit to China
1999	Premier Zhu Rongji pays state visit to the United States
	NATO destroys Chinese embassy in Belgrade
	Chinese protesters attack U.S. embassy in Beijing and ignite the U.S. consulate in Chengdu
	U.S. Congressional Report reveals Chinese theft of U.S. nuclear secrets
	China celebrates the Fiftieth Anniversary of the Founding of the People's Republic
	Portuguese entrepôt of Macao returned to Chinese sovereignty
2000	Original projected date for the realization of the Four Modernizations (revised in 1994 to 2047)

Table of Equivalents and Measures

Renminbi (rmb): lit. "peoples money," national currency of China
    8.24 Chinese Dollars (*yuan*, ¥) = 1 U.S. Dollar
    7.77 Hong Kong Dollars = 1 U.S. Dollar

centimeter (cm):	.39 inch
gram (g):	.035 ounce
Gigatonne (Gt):	one billion metric tons
hectare (ha):	2.47 acres
kilogram (kg):	2.2 pounds
square kilometer (km^2):	.38 square mile
megatonne (Mt):	million metric tons
meter (m):	3.28 feet
square meter (m^2):	10.76 square feet
cubic meter (m^3):	35.31 cubic feet
microgram (μ):	1/1,000,000 gram
milligram (mg):	1/1,000 gram, .015 grains
millimeter (mm):	1/1,000 meter, .1 cm
mu	.667 acre
tonne (metric ton, t):	1,000 kg; 2,205 pounds

Foreword

Between the Lines and beyond the Text

Geremie R. Barmé

There's a school of thought that argues that China is a story just waiting to happen. The headlines have been written, the outcome preordained. The only thing that's missing is copy from the frontlines of the breaking media event, information that will fill in the fine detail, add a touch of local color here, a dab of poignancy there. For any marketable description of the endgame requires a dimension of personal tragedy and a measure of bathos that makes any good story just that.

All too often in the West, particularly in the United States, China doesn't seem to have much of a chance; it barely even has a present. But it does have a future. If you restrict your media consumption to glib sound bites and headline one-liners, it's a future that is the past of the Soviet Union or could just as well be the past of a swath of Eastern European nations. It's supposed to be the future of all the defunct autocratic one-party police states that held sway during the twentieth century.

China's tomorrow is, as they say, its yesterday. Or, as the Russian philosopher Mikhail Epstein put it when considering the denouement of the Soviet empire: "The 'communist future' had become a thing of the past, while the feudal and bourgeois 'past' approaches us from the direction where we had expected to meet the future."

Caught between the dire historical fate of European totalitarianisms and the seemingly impossible future of Chinese socialism and communism, the present itself disappears, or at best becomes a stopgap diversion that keeps the progress of history on hold. The headlines from that frontline are about a story waiting to be told. Epstein calls this particular condition "postfuturism, insofar as it is not the present that turns out to be behind us, but the future itself."[1]

In the 1980s and 1990s popular characterizations of mainland China readily invoked a grand narrative that told a story about that last bastion of recalcitrant one-party rule being undermined by economic reforms and the liberating pressures of technology, social change, and global markets. It was a view that presented us with an inexorable logic: market diversity will result in increased commercialization; the growth and strengthening of new social forces as well as of a general liberalization will in turn engender political, social, and cultural pluralism. While it is all too common to encounter Chinese thinkers and writers who gloat to Western analysts and observers that China and its politics are simply "too complex" *(tai fuza)* and beyond the ken of outsiders to truly understand, Western masters of whither China scenarios are equally confident in their privileged knowledge about the globalized future of the world. For their part they argue that everything is really "very simple" *(hen jiandan)*. They reason that the mainland will inevitably go the way of Taiwan and sooner or later become a pluralistic market democracy. Their confidence is based on a linear view of historical change; they believe they've seen the future, and they claim it works, at least for them.

This comfortable Euro-American consensus is promoted variously by political pundits, economists, and media savants. It holds that eventually a regimen of international good sense will prevail, and as a result countries everywhere will fall into line as they promote free speech and democratic elections; everywhere prosperous multinationals will blossom to produce benign market-driven cultures.

It is beyond these headlines of a homogeneous and untroubled vision of the world that the authors of this book seek to delve. They are scholars and writers whose divergent experience and insight comes, as does the best professional journalism about China, from a wide-ranging and continuous conversation with people both in China and elsewhere. This book is an invitation to listen in to that conversation, to understand how a more nuanced and diverse kind of dialogue within China and among those concerned with that vast and complex territory and its population can be meaningfully taken up in the new century.

The essays in this book discuss the mechanisms whereby the headlines about China are produced and offer readers a broader context in which to consider the issues of Chinese politics, thought, and society today. In particular they share insights into the lively and complex discussions that have been and are being conducted within the Chinese-language world about that country and, through their guided introduction and broad range of scholarly insight, they construct a framework for an exchange between interested and informed American readers and interlocutors in China whose voices are not heard often enough on these shores.

China beyond the Headlines is a book that engages with and speaks to a particular environment of information and public perception. For the mass media, the inside source with privileged insight or some startling revelation that makes sense of everything that happens in China is a prized find. This hierarchy of information matches the hierarchy of publishing sources. We only have to scan the elite media of Manhattan for examples of the clutch of cognoscenti who hold sway over much opinion-making about the mainland. In general, half a dozen experts run the gamut of China opinion from A to B (*pace* Dorothy Parker). With a few exceptions, this boutique opinion ranges from the alternative views to the polished salon experts who conceal a deeply ideological, and at the same time commercially viable, stance behind their promotion of those ideas and individuals who are supposed to represent the real China, or at least the potential of a future China; the one, of course, that is our past.

Many of these experts or informed cultural tourists and brokers you have been exposed to are as deeply ideological and committed to their cause as any Maoist; you could say they are market democrats with a Marxist-Leninist mindset. Their logic is simple and they preach a counter-revolution that is a form of progressive privatization. It offers a crude revolutionary practice in verso: our enemy's enemy is our friend. This was once the line pursued by Chairman Mao Zedong, but now it plays well among media anti-Maoists. It is a line that argues that whatever individuals, social forces, organizations, or events militate against the present regime, undermine its purchase on power, and hold on the people's minds are both positive and worthy of support.

In this book the academics—historians, anthropologists, literary translation specialists, geographers, philosophers, and political scientists—as well as journalists and human rights activists, are engaged in a debate that argues against any simplistic or morally disengaged judgment on China. As the editors point out, the men and women talking in and through these chapters are keenly aware that China is not some object for disinterested analysis but a reality as well as a field of knowledge that engages us in the most basic and powerful dilemmas of contemporary thought and life: the individual and society, the market and politics, the local and the global, the past and the future. These are issues not of mere arcane academic concern; they are of vital public interest and immediacy.

Conversations that cut across and confound stereotypes run into difficulties no matter what the geopolitical environment. In China, reasoned and self-reflexive analysis among popular writers and academics are all too often stymied not only by the fiat of publishers but also by mass sentiment. Perhaps that is why the West, that is Euro-America, often doesn't appear to have much of a chance in China either. For as the script there goes, the United States is the sole surviving global hegemon in a unipolar world; it is the policeman of the planet that is in cahoots with NATO and the European Economic Union. The monolithic power of U.S. Inc. will go to any lengths to impose its will on others, especially those who would dare challenge its international claims to authority. In the name of national security it succors a commercial empire and furthers the imperial domination pursued by its multinational companies and regional minions.

Nor, according to this populist story, does the United States have a future; it can only replicate the past of other doomed empires and colonial powers. A strong and unified China is conceived as being a beacon of postcolonial struggle, the self-appointed head of a revenant Third World. With its vast human resources, massive economy, autonomous ideology, and tradition of militant independence, the People's Republic of China tells itself that it is the greatest countervailing force to the bullying North American superpower in the international arena. The Third World dream of the dispossessed nations united under the leadership of an anti-imperialist China will be realized in a new millennium inaugurated by the Asia-Pacific century.

This conflict of caricatures, be it found in China or the United States, Asia or Euro-America, infiltrates and mediates the mainstream and streamlined "China story" at every turn. As I have said elsewhere, it is a simple turn of mind that generates a style of reporting that rejects the messy gray zones of complex realities and nuanced scenarios. Media propagandists on both sides of the geopolitical divide delight in broad brushstrokes and knowing, expert prognostication. They proffer an apocalypse-now version of *realpolitik* thinking for mainstream news consumers. It is reporting that advertises itself in the name of national interest and makes a show of being aimed at a concerned and informed public. Moreover, in its purview historical mission is usually wedded to national interest by writers who argue that what is good for the United States is good for everyone else. In such writing, the Other (China or the United States, depending on where you stand, either literally or metaphorically) is demonized and, above all, depicted as a malevolent and purposeful polity set on a course of economic expansion and regional domination.[2]

The storyline that all-too-often has China, not to mention the United States, in its grip is one of Manichean simplicity. The Communist apparatus of China (both in its bureaucratic machinations and ideological pronouncements) is readily cast as being hide-bound, out-of-touch, in decay, and incapable of adjusting to the fast pace of economic change or the unsettling and pluralistic realities of its own society. How can the creaky Marxism-Leninism of early modernism cope with the frenetic pastiche of the postmodern age, it is asked. "China on the verge" is a conceit that feeds off narratives determined by the Brezhnev-era Soviet Union of the 1970s, a country of permanent political and economic stagnation that was the yesterday of Russia's today. In this view of the Far East, the notion of an unchanged and challenged autocracy conflates neatly with abiding mythologies about oriental despotism, eternal Cathay, and political Chinoiserie. For China, no matter how one makes concessions to its rapid transformation, complex social reality, and restive economy, is a country caught up in over two centuries of stereotypes. The People's Republic today is never very far from a realm in which cutesy Maoism is forever frozen as if on a piece of "old china," a topos that brings to mind Charles Lamb's 1823 description of painted scenes on export porcelain from the Qing empire where "those little, lawless, azure-tinctured grotesques, that under the notion of men and women float about, uncircumscribed by any element, in that world before perspective. . . ."[3]

The editors and authors of *China beyond the Headlines* not only challenge accepted views of unchanging China and present readers with a complex reality, they question and reflect on the ways in which we think we know China or how we should think about knowing China. They help us interrogate unconsidered assumptions not only about that country but also about this country; they consider anew the process of academic and media knowledge and consider the crucial question of scholarly accountability and engage with the need for public dialogue. The value of this book is not that it provides easy answers to questions related to the global future and the place of the Sino–U.S. relationship within it, but rather that it helps us to think about new ways to ask questions about that future, and that is a future that is in nobody's past.

NOTES

1. Mikhail N. Epstein, *After the Future: The Paradoxes of Postmodernism and Contemporary Russian Culture*, translated by Anesa Miller-Pogacar (Amherst: University of Massachusetts Press, 1995), xi.

2. See Geremie Barmé, *In the Red: On Contemporary Chinese Culture* (New York: Columbia University Press, 1999), 367.

3. Charles Lamb, "Old China," in *Elia, 1823* (reprint; New York: Woodstock Books, 1991).

Preface and Acknowledgments

China beyond the Headlines originated in the spring of 1997 when Timothy B. Weston participated in a debate on the pros and cons of renewing Most Favored Nation (MFN) status with China. That debate, held in Fort Collins, Colorado, and organized by U.S. Congressman Bob Schaffer, was structured in a way that militated against the recognition of shared challenges and the need for cooperation between the United States and China. Indeed, in their efforts to produce winning debate speeches and campaign soundbites, panelists such as the far-right conservative Tom Tancredo (subsequently elected U.S. Congressman in the November 1998 elections) reduced both countries to mere caricatures. The debate format forced the participants to speak in either/or terms and worked against conversation about more nuanced policy choices in line with the complex realities and challenges faced by China, and by China and the United States together. It was patently clear that the debate itself had grown formulaic. Those who called for the revocation of MFN status referred to China as "Red China," employing outmoded Cold War terminology that reflected little understanding of the momentous changes that have taken place in the world in recent decades. These people argued that China must accept our values with regard to human rights, abortion, and democracy—as though U.S. citizens easily agree as to what those are—and that until it does so, the United States cannot have a mutually respectful relationship with that country.

On the other hand, those who called for the renewal of MFN status invoked the tremendous business opportunities that China offers and argued that increased trade between the United States and China will result in a China that is more like us. Here again was the idea that it is the United States' responsibility to change China. Because virtually all debaters accepted this basic premise, only disagreeing about the means of change, there was little room for discussion of China on its own terms and no chance of critical reflection on the politics and culture of the United States. This was a great pity, for the people who comprised the audience at the "debate" in Fort Collins, like most citizens across the U.S. heartland, were clearly very interested in China and Sino–U.S. relations. All of this persuaded Weston that U.S. public awareness of China must be both better informed and well nurtured. This collection of essays represents an effort in that direction. As such, it is best understood as an experiment.

The initial phase of this experiment was the convening of a symposium at the University of Colorado at Boulder in the fall of 1997. The symposium brought together an unusual group of people: China specialists from many fields (history, anthropology, geography, philosophy, political science) journalists, and human rights activists. The purpose in bringing this diverse array of people together was not narrowly academic but rather was to provoke wide-ranging discussion among experts and between experts and the public. We hoped that it would occasion reflections on our own role as teachers about China and about the various points with which we disagree in regard to China. As an event that was open to the general public, the organizers insisted that all participants prepare presentations that were highly accessible and that were morally engaged. By "morally engaged," we meant that scholars could not obey the instinct to act simply as technicians of knowledge about China but instead had to reason through the ethical dilemmas posed by being experts in a field so thoroughly politicized and in the public light. It is our belief that intellectuals must play a public role in the United States and that their "expertise" is not only the product of scholarship. Their authority must derive from mastery of knowledge, its effective communication, and, above all, the moral agency inherent in their role (in this instance) as interpreters of a foreign culture. Each of the symposium participants has spent considerable time in China, in many cases for the purpose of doing research on his or her academic specialty, and none of them could help but reflect on the present China in which they lived and worked.

Invited participants, for the most part, succeeded in meeting the challenge we put forward and the most obvious result of their self-reflexivity was an animated discussion among panelists and members of the public. The symposium was divided into three panels, each devoted to a topic certain to facilitate the kind of interchange we sought from panelists and the public: "Thinking about the Headlines: High Politics, Social Change, and

Diplomatic Difficulties" (David Shambaugh, Jeffrey N. Wasserstrom, Timothy B. Weston, and Xiao Qiang); "Beyond the Headlines: Local, Cultural, and Social Issues Too Often Ignored" (Susan D. Blum, Timothy Cheek, Lionel M. Jensen, and Tim Oakes); "China in the American Mind: Tensions, Opportunities, and (Mis)Representations in the Media" (Richard Bernstein, Henry Rosemont, Jr., Peter Van Ness, Jeffrey N. Wasserstrom, and William Wei). Heated exchanges took place between some of the panelists and between audience members and panelists on subjects such as human rights; the sources of political tension between the United States and China; the relationship between economic freedom and democracy; who is entitled to judge whom, and on what grounds?; the contemporary plights of women and minorities in China and the United States; and the global threat of China's ecological adversity, among others. This persuaded us that these issues need further discussion and that they are deeply felt by many Americans, and also that there is a need for such convocations, where experts learn from the audience as well as the other way around. We were generally quite pleased with the symposium, especially that it opened a great number of conversations and closed very few. The two of us found that this experiment in scholarly accountability and public dialogue raised more questions than we could have imagined and therefore concluded that it would be beneficial to invite more people to participate in the discussion and to explore the idea of publishing the products of our interchange. In order to assure more thorough (but by no means total) coverage of contemporary issues, we solicited several papers from individuals working in such fields as nationalism and identity (Lam Tong), ecology (Vaclav Smil), minority studies (Jay Dautcher), women's studies (Harriet Evans), contemporary Chinese literature and translation (Howard Goldblatt), and democracy and human rights (Wei Jingsheng). In the year following the convocation, the conversation became more intense and the issues more salient—the expected result of our decision to increase the range of topics covered and the variety of voices involved in the discussion. Because these matters are as significant as they are unresolved, we readily admit that this book represents a dialogue in progress.

With an experiment as unconventional and wide-ranging as this one, we have incurred a great number of institutional and personal debts. Inspiration for the symposium from which this volume developed came from a series of conversations with Howard Goldblatt. Thereafter, the office of John Buechner, president of the University of Colorado at Boulder, provided a generous grant from its humanities fund that served as the foundation for the convening of the symposium. Additional, substantial financial assistance was provided by the Offices of the Chancellor, the Associate Vice-Chancellor for Research and Creative Activities, the Vice-Chancellor for Academic and Student Affairs at the University of Colorado at Denver and the Center for International Business and Economic Research. The Graduate Committee on the Arts and Humanities at University of Colorado at Boulder covered the costs of participant travel. The departments of history at the Boulder and Denver campuses, as well as the Asian studies program (Boulder) and the program in Chinese studies (Denver), contributed ancillary funds. The national and regional maps of China that appear in certain chapters are the fine work of Carola Hiltawsky, a gifted and courageous cartographer from the department of geography, University of Colorado at Denver. Indexing was accomplished through the inspired and untiring labors of Mark Barnhouse and William Gayhart, for which we and the book's readers are very grateful.

Generous thanks are also due to: Jeff Wasserstrom for his recommendations and introductions; Susan Jakes, who was the cheerful conduit for messages to and from Wei Jingsheng; Wang Ping for her translation help with Wei Jingsheng's article; Dr. Louis C. Liley Jr. (whose street scene graces the book's cover) and Mark Henley for their photographs; James S. Cannon for generously sharing his scholarship on China's environmental crisis; Hal Aqua of Aqua Design, who produced the aesthetically compelling brochures and posters for the symposium; Franc Shelton for his recommendations at the planning stage of the symposium and for his assistance on a number of logistical matters thereafter; Elisa Holland for drawing up the survey distributed to the audiences; and Erika Kuenne and Michael Jacobsen for serving as rapporteurs whose notes proved valuable in our retrospective deliberations.

At Rowman & Littlefield, the book's expeditious and expert production was overseen by Karen Johnson. Moreover, Matt Hammon's careful and exacting interventions ensured successful production. We are especially indebted to the ever-perspicacious and encouraging Susan McEachern, our editor, for her belief that the symposium would make a good book and for her endlessly good-natured recommendations for revisions of the manuscript's content.

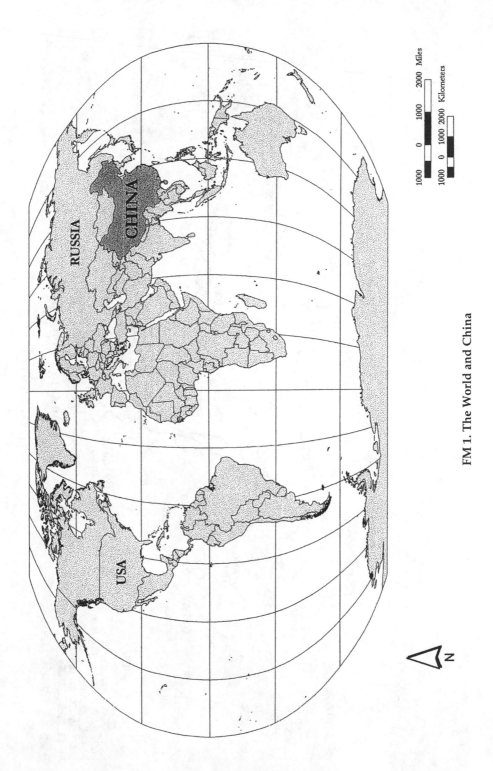

FM 1. The World and China

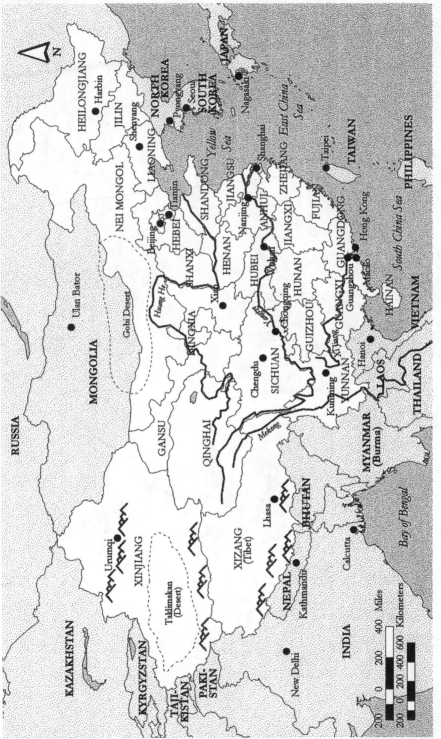

FM 2. China

Introduction

LEAD STORY—Favored Nations, Intertwined Fates

Timothy B. Weston and Lionel M. Jensen

Chinese and Americans have been regarding one another for over two hundred years yet they still do not see one another clearly, and sometimes they even misunderstand one another terribly. This is no wonder. China and the United States are both big countries, and U.S. history, though short, is quite complicated. As for China, its culture and traditions have evolved over thousands of years and, factoring in the influence of modern political ideas (some are not ideas, but prejudices), this has produced a particular perspective on foreigners, especially Americans. As a result, while it is true quite a few things are well understood, misunderstandings nevertheless still abound. To look at a people, at a country and its people, is not simply to look in a "Western mirror." The [mistaken belief that it is] is frequently the reason why the two countries' sentiments diverge and why their policies are so difficult for the other to comprehend. Rapidly, misunderstandings produce very serious consequences. As China and the United States have sought to manage their relations, misunderstandings have arisen from these causes; history is replete with examples.

In relations between the two countries it is very important that one side have an understanding of the other, but this is not an easy thing. . . .

> —Wang Xi, "Congshu zhubian qianyan" (Series Editor preface),
> in Yang Yusheng, *Zhongguoren de meiguoguan: yige lishi de kaocha*
> (Chinese Views of America: A Historical Interpretation), 1997

This book, like the symposium that gave rise to it, is a product of the politics of the present as seen through the eyes of scholars of China. Throughout the world today, consciousness and anxiety about China are on the rise. The receding of the Soviet Union and the ensuing collapse of the Cold War bilateral international political complex have left many with the feeling that China has become one of the greatest challenges of the present era

1

and the coming century. The sense of China as a threat to a great degree derives from its growing economic might and unapologetic refusal to disavow the Communist Party, despite the collapse of communism throughout the world. While eastern and central European satellites of the USSR underwent largely peaceful revolutions against communism in 1989, China held fast and indignantly to the omnipotence of the Party-state and ordered a military crackdown against its own people. In the decade since the bloodshed at Tian'anmen Square and elsewhere in China, the United States in particular has witnessed a growing apprehension of economic competition and inevitable military conflict with China, as evidenced in the welter of articles in the popular press and a scattering of scholarly works on these subjects. At the same time an equal but opposite fear in China of the United States as political and economic hegemon has become increasingly evident in the last several years. It seems, then, that the respective perception of both nations is governed by conflict.

However, conflict is but one way to view the growth in the Chinese global presence and it is clear some policy makers in Washington are now inclined to perceive China as a partner rather than an adversary, as was demonstrated by the two countries' announcement of a "strategic partnership" in 1998. The most obvious symbolic confirmation of the mutuality of this partnership came during President Bill Clinton's state visit to China in June 1998 when President Jiang Zemin[1] announced the Party's decision to redirect his nation's nuclear warheads away from the United States. There are many—scholars, politicians, pundits, and citizens—who remain distrustful or suspicious of this approach and insist that the United States must see China as an implicit adversary, indeed one bent upon global dominance. The persistence of this adversarial view is signaled by the issuance of the report of the House Select Committee on U.S. National Security and Military/Commercial Concerns with the People's Republic of China (the Cox report) that the Chinese had been stealing U.S. nuclear intelligence for more than two decades. This inquiry was provoked by the revelation in the winter of 1999 that a Chinese-American scientist at Los Alamos National Laboratory in New Mexico had downloaded legacy codes containing the history of U.S. nuclear weapons development.

More ominous than the report's "findings" was its frequent suggestion that the Clinton administration had long been aware of the espionage and thus was complicit in this breach of national security. Nevertheless, the signal lack of hard evidence was made clear by Attorney General Janet Reno's announcement on May 27, 1999, that the FBI determined that there was no evidence to prove the chief suspect, Wen Ho Lee, was guilty as alleged. Moreover, upon investigation of the likelihood that the Chinese were producing nuclear warheads based upon purloined information, the CIA found that it was "impossible to tell how much had been obtained through espionage rather than dogged research."[2] As well, the Natural Resources Defense Council asserted in June 1999 that the purported stolen information about nuclear technology had already been made public.

Nevertheless, the U.S. political tendency to demonize China persists, as became evident in late September 1999. In a Washington press conference, Senator Arlen Specter (R-PA), chairman of a Senate oversight committee, the charge of which is to review recent FBI activities, identified the issue of Chinese espionage as his primary concern. Above all, we and the other contributors believe that neither China nor the United States must be demon to the other. While we accept that it is likely that both countries spy on one another and have been doing so for decades, it now seems that the current round of charges against China are driven by short-term political objectives rather than by genuine threats to U.S. national security. Our purpose in collecting these essays is not to assume partisanship in this intensely fluctuating debate over China. Ours is an interest in offering for public view the largely unrepresented complexity of China, something that is always lost when scholars and the media refuse to imagine China in a manner other than that required by the bipolar political complex that continues to color U.S. thinking about geopolitics.

This volume focuses primarily on China itself, and by design many of the articles also make comparisons between China and the United States. We do not, however, believe that China and the United States can be considered independent of the rest of the world. We consider this volume to be an experiment in rethinking the principal paradigms by which China and its place in the world have been understood. Thus, we must at the outset declare our signal lack of interest in defending or attacking China as friend or foe. Instead, we propose a dialogue, a conversation if you will, between scholars of China and between such scholars and the larger U.S. public. The fundaments of conversation, in China as well as in the West, are mutual respect, openness, and self-reflexivity between interlocutors of equal status.

Establishing such a dialogue is difficult now that China has become so much a part of the instinctual U.S. political geography. Indeed, many people believe that they know enough about China to make informed judgment against it. They "know," for example, that: it has a "Great Wall"; it has the world's largest population; it is one of the world's greatest human rights offenders; it is the world's fastest growing economy; it is an aspiring superpower; it is a perpetual violator of international copyright; it has one of the world's most stringent birth control policies; it is an unflinching authoritarian state; it is a country that trafficks internationally in arms sales and seeks to interfere in the politics of other nations, including the United States. The headlines are replete with information about these matters and yet there is a great deal about China, perhaps the most important things, that people in the United States cannot know unless they make a concerted effort to get beyond the headlines.

Likely to know about China only what is available in our print and broadcast media, U.S. citizens lack reliable knowledge and so cannot easily resist the temptation to fear or demonize China. Thus, all too often they neglect opportunities to consider the possibilities for cooperation. The present volume, we hope, may alleviate such instinctual fears by casting contemporary China in a spectral light. A curious thing happens in the brighter light released when one exercises the choice to get beyond the headlines—China begins to resemble the United States in very startling ways. This similarity is not that of competitive superpowers bent on each other's elimination for the satisfaction of an outmoded bipolar worldview. Above all, what the two countries share is an instinctive exceptionalism: a sense of uniqueness and a special destiny that are the products, proudly held, of distinct national, historical experiences and achievements. The Chinese take pride in the richness of their civilization, the success of their modern revolution, the recent exponential growth of their economy, the diversity of their peoples, the world's largest population, and their prominent place in contemporary international politics. When Chinese people reflect on their country's current status and future role, they instinctively compare China to the United States. The United States as well values its history, the success of its revolution against colonialism, its democratic tradition, its cultural diversity, its global economic strength, and its cultural influence throughout the world. In short, each country perceives itself as the world's most favored nation.

While the achievements of each are admirable, China and the United States also bear many of the burdens of late-twentieth-century modernity: decline in national spending on education and welfare, increasing illiteracy, overweening national pride, growing alienation from politics, an increasing commercialization of values, political corruption, growing problems with narcotics and sexually transmitted diseases, a stark inequality of income and opportunity, a sharpening tension between community and individual welfare, and a pervasive sense of moral drift.

This commonality has become more evident in recent years as U.S. citizens have begun paying greater attention to China. Plenty of opportunities exist, since all over the country business groups, church groups, students, teachers, and journalists are convening meetings to talk about China. Furthermore, in the last decade, travel to China and from China to the United States has become easier and more frequent, so that some segments of U.S. society have considerable familiarity with Chinese people. Yet these Chinese are almost entirely students, intellectuals, middle-class business people, and government officials from coastal, urban China, representing their nation's new elite, not the vast majority of the rural and urban working population. Recognizing this greater intercultural interchange, we remained suspicious of the depth of the "knowledge" gained from it and raised a number of questions that might mark the limits of contemporary U.S.–Chinese understanding—questions such as: To what extent are the contemporary situations of China and the United States comparable and/or intertwined? Do China and the United States have a defensible right to question one another's domestic politics? In what ways does capitalism—or more broadly, the economic relationship between the two countries—define the nature of our respective paths and interactions? What are the international responsibilities of China and the United States in an age of diminishing bipolarity and increasing "globalization"? With these thoughts uppermost in our minds, we directed symposium panelists to revise their presentations for this book.

As a result, the principles that brought about effective post-symposium discussion have been adhered to in the papers in this anthology. Many but not all of the articles are reworked versions of papers given at the symposium, and it is hoped that they reflect its dialogical character and the sense of China's rapid change and fluidity. The benefits of this dialogue will be evident to the extent that readers recognize the new conceptual framework provided by the book's give-and-take on a selective but significant number of contemporary concerns. Our wish is that this collection will inspire readers to think about China and its place in the world from a variety of new perspectives. Readers are not expected to come away from this volume believing any one thing in particular; the subjects addressed are highly complex and offer no simple solutions. The authors of the various articles, and indeed the two of us as editors as well, have differing views on a number of issues.

For example, while we agree that China's present situation is ominous in its "lawlessness," political cynicism, and accelerating economic inequality, we disagree on the role the Chinese Communist Party (CCP) should play in solving these matters. Weston does not believe the collapse of the CCP would necessarily bring about a positive outcome. He cautions that there is as of now no developed political alternative to the Party and that such a collapse could bring about even greater chaos. While Weston, like Jensen, is critical of the CCP for many things, he does not believe (potentially violent) change, especially revolutionary change spurred on by the actions of foreign governments, is likely to bring about a healthier and more prosperous China in the short term.

Jensen, on the other hand, considers the CCP to be the greatest obstacle in the path of China's millennial remaking of itself as an international power, in large part because it has lost all legitimacy in the eyes of the people. Although much of what is wrong in contemporary life may not be the responsibility of the Party, most Chinese instinctively identify the government as an agent of great evil. Moreover, Jensen contends, the government's violation of the state constitution in its efforts to limit freedom of assembly and freedom of speech have intensified popular disaffection and stifled the development of native institutions and instincts of a nascent democratic character. Recognizing our conflict of opinion, we encourage readers to regard this book as a starting point for their thinking about China, not as a conclusive statement containing authoritative answers.

The essays have been arranged under two principal headings, both playing on the headlines theme: "Above the Fold," which includes essays that we believe address subjects commonly understood to be newsworthy both in China and beyond—that is, subjects likely to appear on the upper half of the front page of the newspaper. The final six essays comprising part 2, which we call "Below the Fold," concentrate on lesser-known subjects that are equally newsworthy but, to the detriment of our understanding China, ordinarily do not make it above the fold. This arrangement of the essays into two main parts—the public and acknowledged, on the one hand, and the commonly experienced but publicly unacknowledged, on the other— parallels the informal but nevertheless ubiquitous division of Chinese social life into matters discussible in the official press available on the *qiantai,* or front stage, and those that ordinarily only get discussed on the *houtai,* or backstage. As everyone knows, it is absolutely essential to listen in on the whispered discussions of the backstage of any society if he or she wishes to gain a reliable understanding of the dramas being played out on the front stage and in the headlines.

Beyond American headlines are Chinese headlines, and they portray a very different world. The contributors to this volume are well aware of the difference between U.S. reporting and Chinese reporting, an awareness that results from research and residence in China. The substantial differences between the coverage of the NATO bombing of the Chinese embassy in Belgrade in U.S. and Chinese media are due to more than transparent national interest. The news reports of both countries do not reflect the conplexity of the domestic forces that shaped these polar reactions.

Another concrete example of this disparity in worldviews: Tibet. For consumers of the U.S. media, Chinese policy in Tibet is unequivocally a symbol of Beijing's disregard for a minority people and their historical culture. Simply speaking, for most U.S. citizens—those who do and do not drive cars emblazoned with "Free Tibet" bumper stickers alike—Tibet is a human rights problem, one that could be resolved by China withdrawing its military forces and permitting Tibet to preserve and celebrate its religious and cultural traditions, symbolized so effectively in the person of the Dalai Lama. For consumers of the Chinese media, Xizang (Tibet) is an autonomous region within the People's Republic of China; it is a province and has historically been so since the seventeenth century. Most Han Chinese, to the extent that they even think about Tibet, believe that it has been liberated from slavery and feudal superstition by the Chinese communist revolution. The average Chinese person gives no more credence to Tibetan aspirations for greater control over their lives than the average U.S. citizen does to native Hawaiians' movement for independence.

As should now be clear, we believe it behooves us to acquire knowledge of China and its headlines, thereby taking into account the view of the world they describe as we read our own newspapers. This contemporary "double vision" is necessary today, particularly when relations between China and the United States are strained by the irresolute deliberations of the World Trade Organization concerning the admission of China, the tensions wrought by NATO's bombing of Yugoslavia and China's embassy there, accusations that for twenty years China has been stealing U.S. nuclear secrets, and so on. The year 2000 promises to be marked by mutual distrust and suspicion as well, since U.S. presidential aspirants—who always talk in tough, general terms on the campaign trail—will compete to show which of them has the strongest line on China. The candidates will not be making up tensions with China where there are none, but they will undoubtedly frame their visions in terms of what is good for the United States, ignoring the fact that China has legitimate interests of its own that cannot and should not be denied.

This collection of articles is not intended as an apology for everything that China stands for, any more than it is intended as a condemnation of the United States for all that it does. Rather, to repeat: we believe China needs to be understood in more complex terms than the vast majority of U.S. media presentations permit, that it is necessary to move beyond the headlines. Bold-print, surface-level knowledge is not enough, in large part because it limits us to a circumstance in which we are trying to take a photograph of a fast-moving vehicle without an adequate understanding of the direction it's coming from or the forces that propel it forward. The value of this collection lies not in its being an up-to-the-minute snapshot; rather, it is an experiment in offering new formulae for the analysis of China and of relations between China and the United States. The effectiveness of such an experiment depends largely upon the respective authors' abilities to take in the journalistic particulars of this rapidly changing society while at the same time offering a larger paradigmatic context that places the details in a richer and deeper framework that militates against simplification and demonization. Mutual sympathy and respect are absolutely essential if China and the United States are to work together to address their many interrelated social, economic, and cultural problems, and the principal purpose of these essays is to encourage thinking in this direction. Demonizing each other may serve immediate political interests in China and the United States, but it is unlikely to lead to responsible decisions about the long term.[3] Little is to be gained from one-dimensional understanding of the other, for this is mostly based on the very ignorance that the essays in this book seek earnestly to counter. It is our express conviction that a continued disinclination of the two nations to understand each other will prove perilous to the planet. We believe the information and range of perspectives contained in this collection will assist in the process of rethinking the meanings of "China," the "United States," and their increasingly intertwined relations so that the twenty-first century will be one that is notable for Sino–U.S. cooperation rather than conflict.

NOTES

1. The U.S. media habitually identifies Jiang Zemin as the "president" of China because he is the figurative head of the Chinese state. The title is a close approximation rather than a literal translation of his place in Chinese officialdom. In the Chinese press, Jiang is most commonly referred to as *Guojia zhuxi* (State Chairman). This title, which neither exists in the Communist Party hierarchy nor is replicated in any Western political office, is a rough equivalent of our "president." The Chinese term for president, *zongtong*, has been used increasingly as an official honorific for Jiang, perhaps reflecting the international media recognition of him as president. Nevertheless, it is critical to remember that as state chairman/president Jiang Zemin is not an elected official and that the political warrants for his "presidency" (and his real power) derive from his roles as general secretary of the Chinese Communist Party and (like Deng Xiaoping before him) chairman of the Central Military Commission. The frequency with which Jiang is identified as president in China does suggest a growing emphasis on the civilian rather than the Party or military significance of the Chinese head of state.

2. Lars-Erik Nelson, "Washington: The Yellow Peril," *New York Review of Books*, July 15, 1999, 6. Nevertheless, with conservative Republicans in the U.S. Senate blocking passage of the Comprehensive Test-ban Treaty, Lee, a naturalized U. S. citizen originally from Taiwan and employed for more than two decades in U.S. weapons labs, was indicted by a federal grand jury in New Mexico on December 10, 1999. He was charged with 59 counts of removing classified data on design, construction, and testing of nuclear weapons. Yet, Lee was never accused of espionage, perhaps because an ongoing investigation of personnel at Los Alamos and a search of his home and possessions yielded no concrete evidence of his having transferred information to anyone. At the time of the indictment, Dr. Lee was deemed by federal prosecutors to be a "flight risk," and as this book goes to press, he is being held without bail, awaiting trial.

3. A recent scholarly paper by Peter Van Ness compels us (China and the United States) to reconsider and to abandon the Cold War bipolarity of our political judgment. Peter Van Ness, "How to Avoid a Cold War with China, Part One— Coping with China: The United States' Policy Debate," a paper presented at the International Studies Association, Toronto, Canada, March 1997.

Part One:

Above the Fold

There is only one streetscene in China worth remembering in Western eyes. That is the scene of the man and the tank, shot on Beijing's Avenue of Eternal Peace at the height of the "troubles" in 1989. It is the streetscene that constitutes the mind's-flash image of the Western world . . . The representation is so powerful that it demolishes all other understandings. This streetscene, this time and this event, have come to constitute the compass point for virtually all Western journeys into the interior of the contemporary political and cultural life of China. . . . History stopped at this point, and so too did the analytical diversity of Western historians, sociologists and cultural critics. From this time onward, most accounts of things Chinese would be retold through the lens of the man versus the tank.

—Michael Dutton, *Streetlife China*, 1998

Big Bad China and the Good Chinese:

An American Fairy Tale

Jeffrey N. Wasserstrom

In the long history of our associations with China, these two sets of images [of a wondrously civilized and brutally barbaric place] rise and fall, move in and out of the center of people's minds over time, never wholly displacing each other, always coexisting, each ready to emerge at the fresh call of circumstance [evoking in turn] emotions about the Chinese [that] have ranged between sympathy and rejection, parental benevolence and parental exasperation, affection and hostility, love and a fear close to hate.
—Harold Isaacs, *Scratches on Our Minds: American Views of China and India*, 1958

In many countries, public debates on diplomatic policy are routinely distorted by factors that have little or nothing to do with the foreign nations involved. The United States is no exception. Political struggles in Washington between Democrats and Republicans often spill over into the international arena, coloring arguments about the best way to treat a foreign power. More generally, praise or criticism of a distant government is frequently inspired by dreams and nightmares rooted in visions we have of our country's place in the world. This can lead to the promotion of the notion that residents of a foreign land yearn to be just like us—or to darker imaginings, in which the same people or their leaders come to stand for all we abhor.

It is the interplay between these sorts of China-related fantasies that Harold Isaacs analyzed so skillfully in the work from which my epigraph is taken—a work written more than four decades ago that, regrettably, remains all too relevant today. I say this because in the spring and summer of 1999, U.S. citizens once again had dreams and nightmares about China, which tell us more about ourselves than about the Chinese, coloring policy and shaping headlines in the United States. This, at least, is my reading of the media commentary and public debates that accompanied the April 1999 visit to Washington of Premier Zhu Rongji and have continued in the aftermath of his meeting with President Clinton, growing more aggressive in coverage of the Cox report on Chinese theft of nuclear secrets. Again and again, the word *China* appears in news stories, editorials, and political speeches, paired with highly charged negative phrases (such as "nuclear espionage"), in a way that is meant to suggest that the greatest concern of Beijing is to undermine our way of life. Simultaneously, however, we are presented by the media and some politicians with an image of the People's Republic of China (PRC) as a country filled with good people (including some "reformist" leaders) determined to steer it in the right direction—that is, "Americanize" it. There is now, in sum, as there has often been before, a tension between two radically different kinds of morality tales about China, one of which demonizes and the other of which romanticizes the Chinese people.

It is worth noting, of course, that neither the kind of tension nor types of stories alluded to here are unique to the Sino–U.S. context. U.S. tales about China have analogues within other lands, where people also have been known to swing between admiring and despising the Chinese.[1] Moreover, the tales people of the United States tell about China are similar in many ways to those we have told in the past or continue to repeat about different countries.[2] It is not enough, however, to treat the phenomenon as just one more case of "Orientalism" and then move on—even if one is impressed, as I certainly am, by how much Edward Said's controversial analysis of that topic has to offer.[3] The problem is that, while Said's critique of Western presumptions about Asian "others" works very well at a high level of generalization, it misses some of the nuances of some specific cases—including this one. This is because there is something distinctive as well as generic about the misconceptions that have continually shaped and distorted the way people of the United States (a particular group of Westerners) have thought about the Chinese (residents of a specific Asian country). There is more than a generic form of "Orientalism" at work in the interplay of what, borrowing from a useful terminology developed by urban theorist Mike Davis, I sometimes refer to as the "sunshine" and "noir" versions of the U.S. story-line about China.[4] The tension between these two variations on the common theme of U.S. fantasies about Chinese difference is, moreover, one that may have many parallels but is not quite like any other.

SUNSHINE AND NOIR IN 1999

Returning to these specifics, the latest manifestation of the tension I have in mind came through clearly in a speech given by President Clinton in April 1999 and Republicans' reactions to Zhu Rongji's visit. Speaking on the eve of his first face-to-face meeting with the Chinese premier in Washington, Clinton referred to the recent promotion within this nation of the idea "that China is a country to be feared." He mentioned that a "growing number of people say it is the next great threat to our security and well-being." Clinton then distanced himself from such noir visions, with their undertones of menace and paranoia, warning that they were fostering a "climate of distrust" that could damage Sino–U.S. relations for years to come. More specifically, he said, invoking a favorite sunshine theme—namely, that exposure to our ways will inevitably convey the attractiveness of "Americanization" to the Chinese—this climate was counteracting the positive influence of "the exchanges that are opening China to the world." Steve Forbes, one of those campaigning to be the Republican Party's next presidential candidate, countered immediately by saying Clinton seemed ready to "kow-tow" again to China—a loaded term suggesting obeisance to an unjust and tradition-bound ruler—in a "distasteful" manner. Editorials and political cartoons echoed these themes. So it goes. And so it has gone, albeit always with minor variations and shifts of emphasis, for many decades.[5]

Why have sunshine and noir stories about China remained so popular for so long in the United States? What gives each the ability to remain, as Isaacs put it in 1958, potent protean forces ever "ready to emerge at the fresh call of circumstance" in a new yet familiar guise? One reason is that, although they may originally be based on fantasies, widely accepted fairy tales about foreign lands can become so deeply embedded in a culture as to assume a real presence and substance—lives of their own. This is because pundits, journalists, policy makers, the creators of works of popular culture, and even scholars, caught up in a particular fantasy, can end up working together (albeit in most cases unconsciously) not just to create but also to bolster the hold of illusory utopian or dystopian visions. The process works especially well (or, rather, particularly badly, in that it always distorts reality) when the foreign country in question is located at a great cultural as well as physical distance from the United States. In such cases, the creators and consumers of these sunshine or noir morality tales can end up thinking that unnuanced pictures of an "Other" stand for reality. That is, they can end up treating them as apt representations of the outside world, not just chimeras conjured into being from within our own psyches and our own culture.

A different way of saying all this is simply that we should always remember that tracking U.S. foreign policy debates may tell us more about our own country than about the other nations involved, but that this is especially true in certain cases. It is especially true when the foreign country in question is not just far-off in physical or symbolic terms but is also one that U.S. citizens have a long tradition of admiring or despising with particular passion. It is especially true in the case of countries whose relations with the United States are typically seen as centrally important due to concerns associated with trade or security. And it is especially true as well in the case of countries that tend to be thought of as among the largest or strongest in the world. China is one of the relatively few countries that registers as significant on all three of these different scales. It is hardly surprising, then, that debates over U.S. relations with China are particularly prone to distortion and oversimplification.

China is, after all, a large and strategically important country with which U.S. citizens have had a complex ongoing love–hate relationship. A landmark early study of this phenomenon was, as already suggested, *Scratches on Our Minds*, a work based largely on a series of interviews about images of the Chinese and the people of India that its author, a journalist and former resident of China, conducted with 181 relatively well-educated individuals in the United States. The author's main conclusion regarding the Chinese of the U.S. imagination has already been summarized earlier as the creation of the interplay of two sets of images. One set, according to Isaacs, was linked to a "cluster of admirable qualities," which included such things as "high intelligence, persistent industry, filial piety, peaceableness, stoicism," and courageousness in the face of adversity. The other set was tied to an equally evocative vision of "cruelty, barbarism, inhumanity; a faceless, impenetrable, overwhelming mass" that had the potential to create, not stand proud in the face of, disaster.

A number of more recent works have picked up on the themes Isaacs introduced, noting continuities well beyond the 1950s of the processes he described four decades ago. Isaacs himself wrote several such works, including the special introductions he provided to the various new editions of his 1958 classic that were periodically issued in the 1960s and 1970s. The fact that there never seemed a compelling reason to rework the main body of that text is, I think, a telling sign in and of itself.

There are a variety of other works in this vein that could be discussed, but here I will just note two particularly interesting ones from the early 1970s and early 1990s, respectively, which take forms quite different from *Scratches on Our Minds* but add weight to its basic argument. One of these is a fascinating CBS documentary, "Misunderstanding China," which was made at the time of President Nixon's famous first visit to the PRC in 1972. This documentary makes a particularly memorable case for the interplay-of-images idea developed by Isaacs, since the medium of film allows it to combine commentary with visual texts. Particularly noteworthy is the effective use made of footage from Hollywood movies from the 1920s–1960s that presented U.S. audiences (and those in other countries) with demonized or romanticized images of China.

The second text worth special mention is sociologist Richard Madsen's *China and the American Dream: A Moral Inquiry.* This study, written in the immediate aftermath of the protests of 1989 and the June 4th Massacre of that same year but published in 1995, argues clearly and convincingly for the continued relevance of familiar dreams and nightmares about China in the post–Cold War era. It shows that the struggles of 1989 were, like various previous Chinese phenomena, viewed by many in the United States through a strange distorting prism, which reduced complex confrontations to simple stand-offs between forces of pure good and unadulterated evil. Though he uses different terms, Madsen demonstrates that the basic contours of the sunshine and noir story-lines remained essentially intact despite the various transformations that affected China in first the Maoist and then the early post-Mao periods. His study is also particularly effective at mapping the changing contours of missionary dreams of transforming China through some kind of conversion—either to foreign religions or to secular ideologies.[6]

The tension between demonizing and romanticizing impulses that these and many other works describe can be traced back as far as the opening decades of the nineteenth century. This was when some U.S. citizens first became entranced with visions of a time when the "oldest" and "youngest" of countries would find common ground. It was also then, however, that some of these dreamers' compatriots began to worry that when the "dragon woke," the shock waves would reach across the Pacific.

New technologies and the rise and fall of regimes in China have added novel glosses to these hopes and fears, but the basic contours of the sunshine and noir tales have remained essentially the same.[7]

Giving added power to these fantasies has been the tendency of U.S. politicians and pundits to single out China as a key real or potential trading partner, as well as an important real or potential strategic ally. So, too, has the fact that, due in part to the sheer size of its population and in part to its periodic efforts to assert its claim to be taken seriously as a military power, China has long been viewed as a land with which all major countries must reckon. To sum up, for many reasons, it is just the type of country that is most likely to be misrepresented in the U.S. media and handled badly in U.S. political discourse. And this is just what has happened and continues to happen today.

How can we best go about thinking through and placing into context this general phenomenon and the specific ways that recent U.S. debates about and coverage of Washington's China policy and Chinese internal affairs have been distorted? Here, I think, three interrelated developments are particularly worth singling out as sources of concern. The first is attempts by some of the most vocal supporters and critics of President Clinton's approach to the PRC, as well as the mainstream media covering their interchanges, to reduce complex policy choices to simple binary oppositions. A related tendency has been for commentators to divide China specialists into just two camps as well, on the basis of how they stand on the supposed dichotomy between "engagement" and "containment" strategies. The assumption operating here seems to be that there are only two ways to answer questions such as that posed in the title of the lead article of a special issue of *Time* magazine, issued just before Clinton set off for Beijing in June 1998: "How Bad Is China?" One can choose "really awful" (hence, it must be contained) or "not so terrible" (hence, engagement is desirable). Or, to borrow from the stark terminology Steve Forbes recently employed, one can either "kow-tow" or refuse to do obeisance to Beijing and its representatives.

The second worrisome development is the emergence as a major force of a new sort of China-bashing that defies familiar political categories and in this sense is a distinctive product of the post–Cold War era. There have been ongoing moves during the past several years by a peculiar alliance of different sorts of demonizers. Some of the current bashers are former Cold War hawks (like U.S Senator Jesse Helms, R-NC) but others are people whose political affiliations are much harder to categorize (indeed, some tend to take positions on the left on many issues). The goal of this loosely configured alliance seems to be to convince policy makers and the public that the current Chinese regime is as bad as any that has ever existed—not just in China but in any part of the world. As a result, according to members of this group, anything short of an unqualified hard line toward the Chinese Communist Party (CCP) amounts to "coddling" tyrants.

The third noteworthy development, which sometimes takes the form of a backlash against the second, involves moves to breathe new life into the enduring fantasy of a China that is about to undergo or is already undergoing rapid "Americanization." Here, opponents of demonization tap into the same rich sunshine tradition that once inspired religious missionaries. The only difference is that now it is conversion to free markets and open elections as opposed to Christianity that is thought of as what is needed to allow China to fulfill its destiny—always presumed to be that of becoming a land just like our own. The assumption is that China's people, when left to their own devices and shown the light, will spontaneously exhibit a strong desire to see this sort of change take place. The only things that are imagined to have held them back have been a combination of stultifying traditions (be they "Confucian" or Communist) and hostile regimes (be they housed in the Forbidden City or the CCP's Zhongnanhai complex).

Fantasies of an "Americanizing" China pick up steam whenever commentators can find signs on the horizon of traditions losing their hold or when leaders emerge who seem to be interested in pushing the country in a bold new direction. In its most recent form, which crystallized during Clinton's 1998 trip to the PRC, the signs of imminent "Americanization" that have fascinated the U.S. media have included everything from the increase in Chinese access to the Internet to the growing importance of stock markets in China. Comments about the proliferation of McDonald's restaurants in the PRC and the rising popularity of bowling as a form of recreation were among the favorite sound bites of television news crews covering Clinton's trip.

Jiang Zemin's calls for privatization of state industries in 1997 and then agreement to hold a joint televised press conference with Clinton in 1998 made him a perfect candidate, in some eyes, to lead the PRC through a period of "Americanization." Such a period is thought to have begun already, with burgers, bowling, and village elections as the key symbols. The idea seems to be that now the way is clear for the Chinese to move steadily from there toward demanding and getting televised multi-party campaigns for president. Zhu Rongji has sometimes shared the spotlight with Jiang as the "reformer" who can make all this possible, but it is mainly the spontaneous desire to become more like us, which is imagined to be strong among ordinary Chinese people, that is seen as fueling the drive for "Americanization."

All three of the interrelated trends outlined previously should be a cause for concern for the same reasons. First, because they hinder public understanding of a major foreign power. Second, because they make it harder than it already was (and it has never been easy) for socially concerned citizens of this country to figure out how best to respond to a changing China. Third, because they make it more difficult to design effective government approaches to the PRC.

PARALYZING POLARITIES

To understand how the process of mystification sketched out previously works, let us begin with the issue of binary oppositions, the notion that there are only two possible positions to take on China, a hard one and a soft one, and only two sorts of China specialists. It is foolish to imagine that the only way to view Sino–U.S. policy is either to embrace the particular sort of soft line that has been pursued by the Clinton administration (and has sometimes been supported as well by certain Republican luminaries, including Henry Kissinger and Newt Gingrich) or to advocate the much harder one that has been supported by the White House's most virulent critics (including the *New York Times* "liberal" columnist Abe Rosenthal and syndicated conservative pundit George Will). After all, it is possible to view favorably some things Bill Clinton has done (like his moving toward a resumption in the late 1990s of the sorts of high-level exchanges suspended after the June 4th Massacre) while remaining critical of others (such as his willingness to greet Jiang enthusiastically in Manila in 1997 and then pull out all stops in honoring the Chinese leader during his first summit meeting in Washington, even before a single major concession on human rights had been made by Beijing). One can say that the time was right for the president of the United States to have direct meetings again with his Chinese counterpart but that the first of these should have been handled in a more tentative and less enthusiastic manner. Similarly, one can say that Clinton did many of the right things when he was in Beijing in 1998, including speaking out forcefully about human rights issues, but has generally failed at setting an appropriate tone for high-level meetings in the United States. Here, one can argue, he has too often allowed a concern for photo opportunities to overshadow a concern with moving forward on contentious but essential issues.

When it comes to experts, it is equally foolish to imagine that there are only two types. There are certainly some who think economic development will magically turn the PRC into a liberal democracy. There are definitely others who view China as an increasingly powerful but otherwise unchanging totalitarian state, shaped by the same dangerous mixture of indigenous despotic traditions, imported Marxist-Leninist ideas, and nationalistic dreams that fueled high Maoism. There are, however, many academic China specialists in the United States (such as many of the contributors to this book—myself very much included) who are deeply skeptical of both these positions. The people I have in mind, as well as our counterparts in Europe and Australia and other parts of the world, are not a clearly defined group with an unambiguous agenda, and we often disagree with each other on many things about China. What we share are serious doubts about the business lobby's claims concerning the "naturalness" of the link between free trade and democratization, as well as a sense that the PRC is currently weaker, its future more uncertain, than those who warn of a mounting "China Threat" insist.

We see problems, in other words, with both the noir vision of a vicious and monolithic CCP impervious to real change and the patronizing sunshine fantasy of a simple road leading from burgers and bowling to a fully "Americanized" China. We see little point in continually reposing questions such as "How Bad Is China?" and "When Will the Good Chinese People Get to Live Just As We Do?" And those of us who are interested in Sino–U.S. relations tend to try to stake out positions on this subject that are neither completely in accord with nor diametrically opposed to those of the Clinton administration.

Unfortunately, you would never know that in-between positions, complex questions, or ambiguous feelings about the accomplishments and real costs of revolution and reform could even exist, if you only paid attention to the voices shouting loudest and being amplified most effectively in the mainstream U.S. media. The press has been busy dividing up policies and experts into neat piles, and it now seems incapable of considering the border areas lying betwixt and between—even though it is in these areas that many scholars who spend their careers studying China feel at home.

DREAMS, NIGHTMARES, AND POPULAR PERCEPTIONS

The other two worrisome tendencies alluded to previously are what, along with partisan politics, have obviously been driving the binary framing of the China debate. What gives this polarization its punch is that positively and negatively charged images of China and the Chinese have such a well-established place within U.S. political discourse and popular culture. It is important to resist both the vilification and the "Americanization" paradigms, as each inhibits understanding of what is going on in China. This is, moreover, a moment when it seems that news stories custom-made to reinforce demonizing trends (such as, most recently, reports of spies leaking nuclear secrets to Beijing and illegal campaign contributions making their way into Democratic Party coffers) are continually emerging and vying for our attention. And so, too, are ones well suited to serve the purposes of romanticizers (such as, again most recently, reports of Zhu and Jiang's recent visits to the United States that stress their credentials as open-minded pragmatic reformers determined to "Americanize" China's economy).

A case could certainly be made for the idea that neither the demonizing nor romanticizing paradigms is as clearly in vogue just now as one or the other has tended to be during many previous moments in the history of Sino–U.S. relations. It was easy in the mid-1980s, when Deng Xiaoping was being hailed as "Man of the Year" by *Time* magazine and otherwise glorified in the U.S. media, to say that the sunshine approach to China was dominant. Conversely, in the immediate aftermath of the June 4th Massacre, for obvious reasons, stories that put forth a noir vision of China were most prevalent. The current moment is a more ambiguous one. Nonetheless, looking back over the last five years or so as a whole, the darker imaginings seem on balance to have been more pervasive. They seem at least to have tended to prove the more dangerous of the two types of illusions, where the framing of sensible approaches to Sino–U.S. relations are concerned, and also to have made a deeper imprint on the U.S. popular imagination. For this reason, in the pages that follow, noir fantasies as opposed to sunshine ones will receive the lion's share of attention; demonization will be the focus, romanticization will be dealt with only in passing.

It is crucial to note, where demonization is concerned, that there are always more and less restrained types of it with which the analyst must reckon. When taking a relatively moderate form, as in *The Coming Conflict with China*—a book discussed in more detail later in this chapter and in

Tong Lam's contribution to this volume—attempts to play up the Chinese threat simply distort our understanding of an important issue. In its more unbridled manifestations, such as sensationalist magazine covers that use graphics and text to try to convince us of the magnitude of the Chinese menace, the latest noir discussions of China do much more than this. In such works, the proliferation of which reached a peak recently early in 1997, visions of the China Threat breathe new life into old stereotypes of the Yellow Peril and the Red Menace that should by now be long dead and well buried. The sensationalist cover of the March 10, 1997, issue of *The New Republic*, which showed a fierce dragon crushing people beneath its talons while being supplicated by Uncle Sam, was bad enough. Still more disturbing was the March 24, 1997, cover of *The National Review*, which dubbed the president a "Manchurian Candidate" and included racist caricatures of Al Gore and both the Clintons, complete with slanted eyes, buck teeth, and stereotypically Asian garb.

The trend toward demonization slowed a bit toward the end of 1997, as news of the CCP's privatization plans sparked a round of comments celebrating the fact that Jiang and company were "changing course" and "embracing capitalism," but it picked up steam again at the very end of that year. One thing contributing to its renewal was the release of three Hollywood movies that cast the PRC in a negative light. These were *Seven Years in Tibet* (starring Brad Pitt), *Kundun* (a film about the Dalai Lama's childhood), and *Red Corner* (which presented Richard Gere as a U.S. lawyer imprisoned on false charges in Beijing).

Movies provide a fanciful, but nonetheless effective, point of departure for taking up the general issue of demonizing trends. In particular, I am not thinking of the release of the films just mentioned—though that was certainly an interesting event in the history of U.S. popular culture relating to China. Instead, what I have in mind as a framing device for discussion is the early 1997 re-release of a quite different trio of movies. These are films that actually have nothing to do with Asia at all but rather are set long ago in a galaxy far, far away.

I should note, before proceeding, that there is a long and venerable tradition among commentators on Sino–U.S. affairs to use Hollywood movies to probe popular understanding or misunderstanding of the Chinese. In *Scratches on Our Minds*, for example, the contrast between positive and negative cinematic portrayals of the Chinese, in romanticized films such as *The Good Earth* and demonizing movies such as the *Fu Manchu* serials, is used to drive home the book's argument about the bipolar nature of U.S.

opinions. Many films besides *The Good Earth* contributed to the romantic image, including such influential ones as Frank Capra's *Battle for China* segment in the *Why We Fight* World War II propaganda series. In some of these, in fact, the Chinese people are presented as being superior to the people of the United States, at least in certain specific ways, such as the developed nature of their spirituality. This theme re-emerges in a sense in *Seven Years in Tibet* and *Kundun*, though obviously with Tibetans being celebrated as more in touch than are European or American citizens with the truly sacred. Many films without "Fu Manchu" in their title, meanwhile, as the documentary *Misunderstanding China* shows so effectively, contributed to the demonization motif. There were, for example, Cold War period pieces such as *Fifty-Five Days in Peking*, in which audiences were expected to cheer as Charleton Heston led the U.S. cavalry and other foreign troops against Chinese Boxers who looked and acted suspiciously like the "savage" Indians in John Wayne movies.

In light of all this, it is tempting to simply update here the cinematic framework developed in works such as *Scratches on Our Minds* and *Misunderstanding China* and use it to analyze all the recent Hollywood China films. This could help us place into a familiar context not just *Seven Years in Tibet* and *Kundun* but also *Red Corner*, and maybe even the animated Disney film *Mulan*. This is because Richard Gere's character in *Red Corner* is shown fighting against great odds, much as Heston was in *Fifty-Five Days*, to put an end to a form of madness in Beijing. And there are scenes in *Mulan* that present the hold of "tradition" as all that is keeping the Chinese from behaving just as we would like them to act.

As tempting as such an updating of the framework developed by Isaacs and *Misunderstanding China* might be, my use of cinematic allusions here will follow a different path. This is one that will seek to place recent China-bashing movies into a distinctively post–Cold War framework. This is why the specific films that I will use as a starting point are, as already indicated, not ones that are about any part of Asia but are instead the first three installments of the *Star Wars* saga released to theaters.

DARTH VADER AND THE DEMONIZATION OF CHINA

It is worth remembering that, when the original series of three *Star Wars* movies presented theatergoers of two decades ago with a cinematically ambitious vision of an epic struggle between good and evil, the U.S. audiences attending the films had worldviews that were structured around Cold War polarities. They found it natural, therefore, to equate Luke Skywalker and the other heroic "Rebels" with the Free World alliance led by the United States and to see in the tyrants of the "Dark Side" science-fiction counterparts of the Soviet leaders. Just to make sure that the public made these connections, Ronald Reagan and others took to calling the USSR the "Evil Empire" and hailed the need for a "Star Wars" defense system to combat Moscow.

When the trilogy returned to the theaters in 1997 for a special twentieth-anniversary run, the audiences who came to watch were living in a changed world. It was unclear whether, in this post–Cold War environment, there would be any kind of consensus, even among conservatives, about the contemporary power that new generations of viewers should be encouraged to identify with the Evil Empire of the films. It seemed possible to speculate, in fact, that if there was a new consensus, it might be that there was no longer any totalitarian and expansionist regime that could aptly be described as representing the special threat to U.S. interests and world peace that earlier generations of U.S. citizens had associated first with the Axis powers and then the Soviet Union. Had we finally entered an epoch, some wondered hopefully, in which there was no terrestrial regime that needed to be viewed as being as dangerous as the extraterrestrial one of Darth Vader?

This question certainly remains an open one, but a concerted effort has been made by influential U.S. pundits and politicians (most but by no means all of them firmly on the right) to convince us that China fits the bill, and in doing so they have demonstrated a fondness for linking the current leaders of the PRC to everyone from Genghis Khan and Fu Manchu to Hitler and Stalin. Presenting their view as the only serious alternative to the kind of "constructive engagement," with little talk of messy issues like human rights, that is being advocated by pro-China business interests and the political establishment—an approach that the new demonizers brand "appeasement"—these touters of "The China Threat" have been making their presence felt for some time now. Several years ago, for example, a couple of Republicans in Congress were trying to convince us that aborted human fetuses were routinely sold for food in the PRC. Then, during the presidential campaign of 1996, we had Abe Rosenthal using his *New York Times* columns to invoke memories of Hitler, lambasting both Clinton and Dole for behaving like "Chamberlains" instead of "Churchills" toward the PRC. Others revived anti-Soviet Cold War rhetoric, calling for "containment" strategies to neutralize the supposedly unbounded territorial ambitions of Beijing.

Even though it was not, even at that point, a novel part of the political landscape by any means, the demonizing trend definitely intensified early in 1997, as noted earlier. Not only did prominent pundits such as George Will jump on the bandwagon, but contributors to special "China Threat" issues of periodicals, such as the February 24 edition of *The Weekly Standard*, even began making explicit references to the PRC as a new "Evil Empire" to be feared and resisted. Growing concern about the transfer of sovereignty over Hong Kong and domestic scandals associated with Asian and Asian-American campaign contributions—these were but two of many factors that have added new polemical force in 1997 to the demonization of China and the reproduction of the old polar opposition.

Take, for example, the China issue of *The Weekly Standard* mentioned previously. In it we find Congressman Chris Smith characterizing the "fundamental basis of the disagreement" in the United States on Sino–U.S. relations as a simple division between those foolish enough to think that "the men who rule China are more like businessmen" and those sensible enough to realize that "they are more like Nazis." Others draw lines between those who do and do not take seriously the rising tide of Chinese nationalism, and those who are and are not willing to "sell out" the cause of dissidents "in order to sell a few more Big Macs." Contributors to 1997 issues of *The New Republic* also invoked related binary oppositions. In the issue of March 10, 1997, one contributor claimed that Chinese-Americans fell into two basic camps: some care about human rights and side with dissident Harry Wu, who wants a "Holocaust museum-style memorial" built to honor those incarcerated in PRC labor camps; others focus only on business and call for a soft line toward Beijing. The April 21, 1997, issue suggested in its cover story that there are only two types of experts: a majority who mistakenly claim that "China is marching toward democracy" and a minority who realize it remains in the grips of a crippling form of totalitarianism.

One of the most interesting illustrations of how complexities have at times been reduced to simple oppositions by the new demonizers, as well as of how familiar divisions between the "left" and the "right" have become muddied in the process, is provided by the aforementioned *The Coming Conflict with China*. Written by a pair of journalists and longtime China watchers, Richard Bernstein and Ross H. Munro, who were represented in the February 24, 1997, issue of *The Weekly Standard* by an essay entitled "PLA Incorporated," this book is a mixture of careful and even at times insightful commentary, interesting but sensationalized detail, and alarmist analysis. For our purposes here, what is most interesting about it is the claim by Bernstein and Munro that China experts can be divided up into two groups.

The first type of specialists, they class as belonging to the New China Lobby, a catch-all for academics and nonacademics who minimize the threat to U.S. interests of the PRC and downplay the value of pushing hard on human rights issues. Some of the people in this group are so naive as to believe economic development always leads to democracy and freedom. Others, such as the Democratic and Republican former policy makers turned businessmen and consultants belonging to the Kissinger Associates firm, who have large investments in China to protect and clients with even larger stakes in the Chinese market, are motivated by a less naive belief: namely, that engagement means profits. Still others are part of a small band of unnamed "senior scholars of China" who "write useful articles on Chinese politics," in part because they are able to "maintain excellent contacts" with top leaders, but who know that in order to gain the access on which they depend they must "remain silent" or "flatter" the regime on "certain subjects," such as human rights and Tibet.

The specialists described by Bernstein and Munro as being on the opposite side of the fence from the New China Lobby are the small handful of journalists and academics who have been denied permission to go to or at least had trouble getting visas for the PRC. *The Coming Conflict* suggests that, if we want to find people whose opinions about Beijing can be trusted, we should look to the members of this politically eclectic group. It includes both Ross Terrill (who had an article on Deng's death in *The National Review* issue with the racist cover) and Orville Schell (whose pieces appear in *The Nation* from time to time). Interestingly, in a *New York Review of Books* essay on *The Coming Conflict with China*, Jonathan Mirsky (a U.S. journalist who is now based in London and who has had some trouble of his own getting into China lately) used a similar criteria for supporting his claim that Bernstein and Munro deserve to be believed. He cited, as evidence that their arguments about the PRC had struck home, the fact that the official *Xinhua* (New China) news agency had denounced their writings as "racist" scribblings that support the reassertion of American "hegemony" in Asia. Mirsky's comment hints at a very important aspect of the Sino–U.S. relations equation that is beyond the scope of this chapter but is taken up elsewhere in this book by Tong Lam. This is that, on the Chinese side, there are also intense positive and negative images of the other country involved that need to be taken into account, since they often end up distorting and over-simplifying discussion of major issues. Regardless of this, Mirsky's comments do not prove the validity of *The Coming Conflict's* main arguments.[8]

BEYOND THE POLARITIES

There are all sorts of problems with the China-bashing trend sketched out previously, the "Americanization" fantasy counter-trend alluded to in passing, and the dichotomous references to experts that fill so many U.S. commentaries on Chinese affairs. Most generally, these trends work together to create yet another situation in which U.S. foreign policy is being tossed between the Scylla of condescending romanticization and the Charybdis of dehumanizing demonization—perils that Isaacs described so well in his discussion of *The Good Earth* and "Fu Manchu" imagery and perils that are made all the more treacherous because of the various ways that Chinese domestic politics can distort the view of the United States of those looking across the Pacific from Beijing. One result of all this is that, as in the past, the option of treating China as an equal power, with which the United States has very serious areas of disagreement and also common interests, ends up getting short shrift.

It is very difficult for the many academic China specialists who have neither business investments nor top-level contacts in the PRC, yet who have also not had trouble getting visas despite speaking out as their consciences direct them against things the Beijing regime has done, to be heard in the current debate or even to find a place from which to speak. We are not included when commentators divide the experts into just two groups, since many of us have been bitterly disappointed by some of Beijing's actions and feel that the U.S. government should look for more effective ways to express anger over human rights abuses, but we also feel that it is misleading to describe the current Chinese regime as analogous to that of the Nazis or Stalin.

Many in this in-between camp, who are trying to stake out various sorts of intermediary positions between the demonizing and romanticizing wings in the China debate, are convinced that the PRC has changed and continues to change in fundamental ways and that the quality of life of many ordinary Chinese was improved in the Maoist and Dengist eras—yet we still find much to criticize about how the country was run in both periods. We are concerned as well about how it is governed today, in part because of the current regime's continuing failure to make good on the CCP's long-standing promises of pursuing gender equality and putting an end to official corruption—issues discussed in more detail in the chapters by Harriet Evans and Lionel Jensen. Many of us in this loosely defined group feel that it is imperative for the Communist Party to make bold moves toward opening up cultural and political life and yet were not optimistic about the plans Jiang announced in 1997 to begin transforming all state enterprises into private ones. This was due in part to our awareness of the side-effects these moves were likely to have on those who would end up with neither secure jobs nor a developed social welfare safety net.

On the one hand, many of us do not feel that the business lobbyists and romanticizers are right when they insist that investment and industrialization always leads to a pure form of freedom—Singapore and other cases suggest that authoritarianism and development can and often do go hand-in-hand. In fact, one thing that worries us about contemporary China is the suffering produced by the increasing inequalities of wealth that are in part results of economic growth—a phenomenon described well by both Tim Oakes and Timothy Weston in their contributions to this volume. Another is the reconfiguration of patriarchy that has come in the wake of marketization, which is discussed insightfully in Harriet Evans's chapter. We do not think it makes sense to present China as an unchanging despotism, in short, since much has in fact been changing in the PRC, for the better as well as for the worse.

Another basic factual problem with the polar oppositions is that they minimize the sense people in the United States have of the range of opinions that are being expressed by the Chinese themselves and the complexity of the developments occurring in China these days. How can one speak blithely of being for or against "the dissidents," when there are important divisions among those considered part of this ill-defined group? Harry Wu, a former resident of the gulag, may call for both a hard line and consumer boycotts of goods produced by prison labor, but Wang Dan, a history student at Beijing University and one of the leaders of the 1989 protests, has argued strongly for the desirability of foreign powers engaging with, rather than trying to isolate, the Beijing authorities. The latter even expressed approval of Clinton's controversial decision to take part in a state ceremony at Tian'anmen Square in 1998. There are doubtless some within the dissident community who are in favor of consumer boycotts yet approve of the Clinton line toward China, as well as some who objected to the president going to Tian'anmen but do not think consumer boycotts appropriate. When it comes to nationalism, there are dissidents who have continued to try to use and dissidents who have sought to distance themselves from the symbolism of *jiuguo* (national salvation). Such symbolism played a key role in the protests of 1989 but was also invoked by the government to defend the massacres that put an end to that struggle. Some statements by the Dalai Lama, meanwhile, indicate that, in contrast to the new demonizers, he views the current CCP regime as one that is undergoing important changes that could even lead in the not-too-distant future to a breakthrough on Tibet. Xiao Qiang, finally, while making a thoughtful and powerful case for one important vision of the current state of human rights in China in his chapter for this volume, says some things with which a variety of dissidents would disagree.

Clearly, the main thing we should do in order to "side with the dissidents" is to start listening more carefully to the range of their opinions, as well as to those of people in China who have taken independent stands on certain issues, while refusing at the same time to sever completely their ties to the regime (something also recommended by Timothy Cheek in his essay on intellectuals). One key theme that some independent-minded establishment intellectuals and dissidents alike have focused on in recent years is that the current leaders in Beijing are more sensitive to outside influence on some issues than on others. For example, though they remain determined that no political parties able to compete with the Communists should be allowed and are unwilling to entertain any thoughts of freeing Tibet or giving up on dreams of reunification with Taiwan, many within the current leadership do seem to care about (at least being perceived as) moving their country toward the rule of law. This has even allowed some ordinary people (and intellectuals) to sue the government for mistreating them (as the controversial muckraking journalist Dai Qing did at one point), without being thrown in jail or killed, as one would imagine happening in a PRC ruled by Darth Vader.[9]

Developments such as these have important implications when it comes to strategies for bringing pressure on Beijing to improve its human rights record. Rather than alternating between presenting the Chinese authorities with laundry lists of abuses and simply being silent on human rights, as recent U.S. administrations have tended to do, it might be helpful for policy makers to draw a distinction between general practices that are part of PRC state policy but with which the U.S. government disagrees (such as the occupation of Tibet), on the one hand, and things that the regime has done that violate China's constitution (which guarantees a certain amount of free expression, for example) or that break promises that were made to foreigners or Chinese citizens. By concentrating most of their attention on the latter type of abuses, while not necessarily ignoring completely the former, U.S. officials might be able to bring some much needed consistency to the human rights dimension of our relations with Beijing. Retroactively, this would have meant being more assertive when Wang Dan and Liu Xiaobo were re-imprisoned in 1996 for engaging in activities that are supposed to be legally protected in the PRC but being less energetic when Harry Wu was detained for doing things that may have been admirable but that even he admits involved breaking laws.

With Beijing's ongoing interest in using high-level summits to legitimate the power of leaders such as Jiang and Zhu, we continually have appropriate moments to make the same basic point: in order for the United States to take a foreign power seriously in issues of trade or diplomacy, it needs to know that the regime can keep its word. The president could make it very clear that the continuing upturn in Sino–U.S. relations needs to be held hostage, not to vague and shifting criteria or even (as good as it was that Wei Jingsheng and Wang Dan were both released) to the occasional granting of asylum to a high-profile dissident in a noblesse oblige fashion, but rather to the Chinese regime's ability to establish a pattern of keeping promises, both to the United States and to residents of the PRC. By doing this, the U.S. government would make the point that it prefers to deal with foreign powers on a basis of equality and is ready to try to move beyond condescending to or demonizing the PRC, but it can do so only if Beijing begins to demonstrate more effectively that it can abide by the rules it makes for itself.

Perhaps the largest overarching problem with the trend toward framing the debate on China in polarizing terms is that we are prevented from focusing on the main challenge that lies before all people who want to understand the PRC—the challenge of making sense of a regime that is not quite like any that has ever existed before, either in China or elsewhere, and that is undergoing a strange mixture of unprecedented and in many ways contradictory changes. It is difficult but important to figure out how best to think about a Chinese ruling party that is still powerful but battle-scarred, internally divided but unlikely to fall as long as there is no organized opposition to challenge it. We are just not used to thinking realistically about a regime with the following characteristics:

1. It is based on a Leninist organization that has managed to maintain its monopoly on power despite being beholden to an official ideology that is discredited in the eyes of many, including more than a few top members of the governing elite itself.
2. It retains its Leninist cast in many matters yet is quite ready to experiment with market reforms and even allow some room for local innovation and experimentation in the political realm, including village elections in which independent candidates more than occasionally win.
3. It clings to symbols and rituals developed by earlier charismatic revolutionary leaders and yet is now headed by very different sorts of people, including some who believe quite sincerely (though often as much for pragmatic as moral reasons) that it is important for China to move toward the rule of law.
4. It runs an enormous country that is rapidly becoming less cohesive and more decentralized, yet at the very same time is also more fervently nationalistic than ever in certain ways.

What all this means is that, if we want to make sense of China today, we need new modes of thinking about a country that is transforming itself and being transformed in novel ways. The Chinese regime is not a "Red Dynasty" just like an imperial ruling house of old, if for no other reason than that succession issues are settled in radically different ways. It is not just like that which ran Nazi Germany, if for no other reasons than that Beijing's current leaders are much less popular with the citizens of the PRC than Hitler was with ordinary Germans in the late 1930s and the CCP is not trying to exterminate any ethnic group. The regime is not just like that which held power in Moscow in the days of Stalin, if for no other reason than that there is a great deal more individual freedom in many aspects of private and public life in the PRC now than ever existed in the Soviet Union, at least before Gorbachev's day. The current regime is not just like that which ran China during the period of high Maoism, if for no other reason than that it is less committed to ideals of economic equality. In addition, when today's leadership singles out a person for political persecution, it is usually because they claim that this individual has done something inappropriate, not just that he or she was born into the wrong class or is related to the wrong person. The present regime is not even just like that which ran China in the mid-1980s, if for no other reason than that the role of state-run industries in national economic life is much different than it was before. This is a phenomenon with complex ramifications for workers and the government, some of which Timothy Weston sheds light on in his contribution to this volume.

The present moment is a potentially dangerous time in many areas of world politics, including that of Sino–U.S. affairs, and our failure to have a ready-made cognitive slot into which to place the current CCP regime makes the situation all the more difficult to address thoughtfully. In such a time of uncertainty, there is a pressing need to find new ways of thinking and of crafting policy toward a major world power. Clearly, we need something better, at least, than the scattershot approach to China that has characterized the policies of both of the last two administrations, each of which has sent Beijing erratic signals and chosen strange times to make or withhold gestures of conciliation. When a new approach is needed, as any Hollywood director knows, doctoring old scripts and clinging to the favored imagery of an earlier generation of scriptwriters is not the thing to do. It is not enough to update the "Americanizing" imagery of Frank Capra's World War II propaganda films, substituting visions of Jiang Zemin and Bill Clinton at the stock market for Chiang Kai-shek and Franklin D. Roosevelt calling for joint military efforts against Japan. The world of *Star Wars*, meanwhile, may be a wonderful one to revisit in the theaters, but it is a dangerous and disturbing one to try to recreate in the real world, no matter which foreign leader is cast in the Darth Vader role.

NOTES

Several people and institutions provided me with opportunities to try out and get public reactions to some of the ideas presented in this chapter. In particular, I am grateful to the editors of this volume, Lionel Jensen and Timothy Weston; to Ronald Edgerton of the University of Northern Colorado; and to George Wilson of Indiana University's East Asian Studies Center. I would also like to thank several colleagues who commented on drafts of this essay as it evolved. Particular gratitude is due to Harriet Evans, Marilyn Young, Stanley Rosen, and Nicholas Cullather, each of whom read more than one draft; and also to Michael Curtin, Sue Tuohy, Jeffrey Gould, Michael Schoenhals, Jeffrey Isaac, and Elizabeth Perry. A special thanks is due to the editors of *Dissent*, and Michael Walzer in particular, for working with me on pieces that appeared in the summer 1997 and fall 1998 issues of their periodical and then allowing me to draw heavily on those essays in this chapter. Last but not least, I am grateful to Jim and Adrian McClure and my son Sam for helping me refine my use of *Star Wars* analogies.

1. For an idiosyncratic, but often insightful and always elegantly written, recent overview of some of the varied images of China that have captured the imaginations of Westerners living in differing lands in varied periods, see Jonathan D. Spence, *The Chan's Great Continent: China in Western Minds* (New York: W. W. Norton & Co., 1998).

2. Of particular relevance here is the case of U.S. visions of Japan. This is not just because there are many similarities as well as some differences between U.S. images of China and Japan, but also because there is a complex relationship between the two. The subject is far too big to explore here, but suffice it to say that it has often been the case that when China is being most intensely romanticized in the United States (e.g., during World War II), Japan is being demonized. The reverse is frequently true as well: e.g., the U.S. media's glorification of Deng Xiaoping as an "Americanizing" reformer in the mid-1980s coincided with an intense wave of the Japan-bashing. For a lively introduction to U.S. images of Japan, which is particularly good on issues associated with popular culture, see Sheila K. Johnson, *The Japanese through American Eyes* (Stanford: Stanford University Press, 1988).

3. Edward Said, *Orientalism* (New York: Viking, 1979). The principal and enduring argument of the book is that the "Orient" was a product of the European colonial imagination, specifically the imagination coexistent with the conquest of the Middle East by the British and the French. Said argues that it was this imagination that belittled the native culture as quaint and exotic while valorizing the dominant white other responsible for its domination and misrepresentation.

4. Mike Davis, *City of Quartz: Excavating the Future in Los Angeles* (New York: Verso, 1991). Davis uses "sunshine" and "noir" to refer to the competing positive and negative "city myths" associated with L.A., but the optimistic connotations of the former term and sinister overtones of the latter seem evocative and appropriate here as well.

5. "Clinton Urges China Foes Not to Stoke a New Cold War," *Washington Post*, April 8, 1999, A2; see also, for another use of terms similar to that of Steve Forbes, Michael Kelly, "Zhu Zings; Clinton Kow-tows," *New York Post*, April 14, 1999, 29.

6. Harold R. Isaacs, *Scratches on Our Minds: American Views of China and India* (New York: John Day, 1958); reissued with new prefaces in 1972 (New York: Harper's) and 1980 (Armonk, N.Y.: M. E. Sharpe); Richard Madsen, *China and the American Dream: A Moral Inquiry* (Berkeley: University of California Press, 1995). For additional discussion of the way discussions of 1989 conformed to recurrent patterns relating to Sino–U.S. misconceptions, see Jeffrey N. Wasserstrom, "History, Myth, and the Tales of Tiananmen," in *Popular Protest and Political Culture in Modern China*, 2d ed., Jeffrey N. Wasserstrom and Elizabeth J. Perry, eds. (Boulder, Colo.: Westview Press, 1994), 273–308. For a thoughtful and interesting general discussion of Isaacs and his book, see Andrew J. Rotter, "In Retrospect: Harold R. Isaacs's Scratches on Our Minds," *Reviews in American History*, vol. 24, no. 1 (March 1996): 177–188.

7. An excellent survey of recent trends in U.S. press coverage is Carolyn Wake-

man, "Beyond the Square," in *Covering China*, a special issue of *Media Studies Journal* (Winter 1999): 58–67.

8. Jonathan Mirsky, "Peking, Hong Kong, and the US," *New York Review of Books* (April 24, 1997).

9. One useful place to turn for recent discussions of some relevant issues by a range of different sorts of Chinese dissidents and critical voices within the non-dissident community, is *Hong Kong Goes Back*, a special issue of *INDEX on Censorship* (January 1997). An excellent up-to-date account of some of the main fissures within communities of Chinese intellectuals and artists is Geremie R. Barmé, "The Revolution of Resistance," in *Conflict and Resistance in Contemporary China*, Elizabeth J. Perry and Mark Selden, eds. (London: Routledge, 1999).

SUGGESTED READINGS

Covering China, a special issue of *Media Studies Journal* (Winter 1999).

Hong Kong Goes Back, a special issue of *INDEX on Censorship* (January 1997).

Harold R. Isaacs, *Scratches on Our Minds: American Views of China and India*, 3d ed., with a new preface by the author (Armonk, N.Y.: M. E. Sharpe, 1980).

Richard Madsen, *China and the American Dream: A Moral Inquiry* (Berkeley: University of California Press, 1995).

Elizabeth J. Perry and Mark Selden, eds., *Conflict and Resistance in Contemporary China* (London: Routledge, 1999).

Edward Said, *Orientalism* (New York: Viking Press, 1979).

Jonathan D. Spence, *The Chan's Great Continent: China in Western Minds* (New York: W. W. Norton & Co., 1998).

James C. Thomson, Jr., Peter W. Stanley, and John Curtis Perry, *Sentimental Imperialists: The American Experience in East Asia* (New York: Harper, 1981).

2

Everyone's a Player, but the Nation's a Loser:

Corruption in Contemporary China

—*Lionel M. Jensen*

In 1994, officials of China's Supreme People's Procurator told two Western political scientists that that agency alone had received an average of 1,250,000 reports by citizens of official corruption each year during the last few years. From 1988 to 1993, the Discipline Inspection Committee of the National People's Congress investigated more than 870,000 official violations at various levels, 730,000 officials were disciplined, and 150,000 expelled from the Communist Party.

—Cheng Li, *Rediscovering China,* 1997

The crackdown on corruption must be combined with encouraging justice. The majority of our cadres are good, honest, and dedicated to their duties. In the process of the anti-corruption struggle, the advanced units who are efficient, honest, hard-working, dedicated, selfless, and courageous in fighting corruption in various localities and departments should be publicized.

—Li Peng, "Resolutely Wage
Struggle against Corruption," 1993

For most of the last decade the Chinese government has been engaged in a rearguard action to mitigate a notable tendency among its officials to misappropriate public funds and property for private advantage. According to China's criminal statutes and administrative regulations, as well as its most recent revised constitution (1982), malfeasance of this order is a grave offense punishable by heavy fines, lengthy imprisonment, or even execution.[1] Though such "corruption" is not the exclusive province of officials—indeed, it is endemic in contemporary life—the Chinese Communist Party (CCP) is considered by the public to be the principal source of this peculiar form of felonious behavior. At the same time, other than the occasional instance of corporal punishment (execution, incarceration), the primary means of reducing the growth in China's profit-push corruption is reeducation and moral reform through appeal to the principles and practices of "clean government." This is not an effective solution but a symbolic one that harkens back to the moral teachings common to the catechism of the revolution. Education in public virtue, the Communist Party has long believed, always trumps private self-aggrandizement. Though this may have been true in the past when the CCP was the guarantor of a successful revolution, today it no longer possesses the moral authority of its revolutionary heyday and popular disillusionment is so widespread that the recurring appeal to morality as counter to corruption's illegality (visible in the epigraph from Li Peng) has little effect.

So, the previous epigraphs frame the difficulty of China's dilemma with corruption: increasing instances of graft are disciplined by the moral advocacy of model emulation. However, the language of a repetitive ethical formula cannot rid daily life of its specific, multiple manifestations of corruption, which may explain why moral suasion is paired with punishment exacted according to "rule by law." Perhaps this is why, spurred on by growing evidence of popular discontent as well as concern within its own ranks with the abuse of privilege by upper-echelon Party officials, the CCP launched a frontal assault on such corruption in the summer of 1998 by the public sentencing to sixteen years in prison of one of its highest ranking officials, Chen Xitong.

The celebrity of Chen's case was such that it received significant coverage in the daily papers of most U.S. cities and, in this way, the topic of corruption was added to a discrete list of keywords by means of which we make sense of China. Indeed, along with human rights, international copyright violation, industrial espionage, and protectionism, corruption has become one of the several windows from which we view (and, quite often, castigate) contemporary China. The national prominence of this problem in China has ensured its representation in the Western press, where corruption has become a frequently cited consequence of Chinese business and politics. In the United States talk of corruption in China has focused especially on the insidious, corruptive qualities of *guanxi* (relations, relationships, social connections, networking) and how the business of Chinese business and politics is accomplished through a welter of banquets, favors, gifts, and, of course, the vigorous flow of a broad, deep current of cash. However, in order to move away from these increasingly familiar journalistic portraits and stereotypes toward the meaningfulness of corruption on Chinese ground, it is helpful to explore first the complex web of significance spun from the case of Chen Xitong. An examination of the complicated political, legal, and symbolic aspects of this illustrative case provides insight into the reasons for the nation's lingering corruption crisis.

CORRUPTION: THE HARVEST OF GOVERNANCE

The facts of Chen's case, specifically the implication of family members as well as a great number of political associates and cronies, tend to confirm the instinctual linkage of corruption and social connections. However, this conventional interpretive association is dissolved in the swamp of complicity surrounding Chen Xitong. The 1998 trial of Chen, former mayor of Beijing, Beijing Communist Party secretary, influential member of the Politburo, and long-time ally of the late vice-premier, Deng Xiaoping, was the first open sentencing of a Politburo member since the trial of the infamous "Gang of Four" in 1980.[2] Chen was found guilty of "corruption and dereliction of duty" and charged with removing 2.2 billion yuan from the Beijing city treasury. His son, Chen Xiaotong, figured prominently in the case and had already been convicted and sentenced to twelve years for accepting bribes and for misuse of public funds. More than forty officials were implicated in a complex scheme of bribery, embezzlement, investment fraud, and influence-peddling.

Some of those involved were Wang Baosen, former executive vice-mayor and treasurer of Beijing in charge of foreign investment, Zhou Beifang, chairman of Shougang Concord Holdings, Inc., and his father, Zhou Guanwu, chairman of Shougang (Capital Iron and Steel Corporation) and one of China's most powerful industrial tycoons as well as a close friend of Deng Xiaoping. Speculative official estimates of the collective theft of property and funds range between 24 billion and 38 billion yuan, the lion's share of which was obtained through foreign speculation and the sale of planning permissions and construction permits in Beijing. The volume of the excess became clear within moments following Wang's death by self-inflicted gun-shot wound on April 4, 1995. His suicide, most agree, set the scandal in motion. Within a few weeks Chen Xitong (April 28) had resigned his position as Communist Party secretary of Beijing and

Guangdong Province's Party newspaper *Nanfang zhoumo* (Southern Weekend) had published an investigative report alleging that Chen Xiaotong abetted the escape of his father's mistress to Hong Kong and regularly demanded more than $90,000 to secure audiences with high-ranking government officials.

According to the legal statutes governing corruption, the sheer magnitude of this scandal, the exorbitant amount of money involved, and the unconscionable flouting of public trust should have earned the Chens' and the Zhous' death. This had been the earlier, widely publicized fate of Shen Taifu, president of Great Wall Machinery and Electronic High-Technology Industrial Group, who was found guilty in April, 1994, of bribery and embezzlement in the amount of $375,000. The case brought against him in the summer of 1993 involved more than 100 other officials and the total value of his theft far exceeded the $375,000 for which he was held accountable. It was reported that Shen led 100,000 Chinese to purchase $172 million-worth of "high-yield" (24 percent) bonds to support cutting-edge research on power generation. No research was conducted; Shen and his associates simply pocketed the cash. Mere weeks following the verdict, Shen was executed and only a single CCP official, the minister of science and technology Li Xiaoshi, was arrested.

The contrast in both the crimes and the punishments of Shen Taifu and Chen Xitong and his associates casts in relief the politics of the Chinese legal system while demonstrating that such matters of corruption are not entirely about profiteering and peddling influence. Shen, a prominent but politically less-well-connected new-age Chinese capitalist, was dispatched less than a year after his investment fraud was revealed, whereas Chen, prominent and exceedingly well-placed politically, was put under house arrest for two years and incarcerated for a year before the public announcement of his sentencing for having "accepted and embezzled a large number of valuable items . . . [and] squandered a large amount of public funds to support a corrupt and decadent life."[3]

Indeed, Chen was guilty of malfeasance, but he was, as well, a victim of Party politics, in particular the sudden loss of protective patronage and of an aggressive post-Deng assertion of Shanghai cliquism by President Jiang Zemin. Chen's sentencing—the public act, its timing, and the penalty—conveys other meanings not immediately evident to the unschooled reader of the daily text of Chinese politics. In this light of intra-Party venality, corruption appears as a political tool that may be employed to call attention to the illegal (yet much too common) excesses of one's political enemies while the complainant eludes legal retribution under a cloud of virtue. This delicate dynamic helps account for the individuals charged and for the deliberate pace of the state's resolution of the case.

By the time of the Chinese New Year celebrations of 1998, nearly four years after the initial finding against Chen, the principal target of the investigation had yet to be tried and the public had grown restive with the Party's hesitancy in trying one of its own. It was not until February 27, 1998, that Chen was formally accused of "corruption and dereliction of duty" and, nearly three years after being placed under house arrest, on March 10, Party authorities closed the investigation. The inquiry, following adjudication by Beijing's intermediate and higher courts, culminated in an official report calling for charges of embezzlement and dereliction of duty and a maximum sentence of seven years. It was believed that "corruption" would be very hard to prove because most of the offenses governed by the relevant articles of the criminal code were conducted by Chen's second son and his personal secretary. Only twenty-two gifts totaling 550,000 yuan—"eight gold and silver products, six deluxe watches, four expensive pens, three cameras, and one video camera"—which Chen had received as a representative of the state, formed the unassailable core of the case made against him for "dereliction of duty." The report was presented for adoption by the National People's Congress later in March 1998; however, only 55 percent of China's largest political body voted in favor of adopting the initial report against Chen Xitong.

China's National People's Congress (NPC) functions predominantly as a rubber-stamping agency for the decisions of the Political Bureau of the Chinese Communist Party (Politburo) and so when policy is put to a vote, it is generally greeted with unanimous acclaim. Not in this instance, however. The NPC majority considered the recommended sentence too lenient and so rejected this first report against Chen. Because his crimes were egregious and widely publicized and because the Party had always tried to shield its highest malfeasant officials from judicial inquiry or to consent to the merest punishment for their offenses, it was important that the government signal the sincerity of its anti-corruption campaign by giving Chen a healthy dose of jail time. Thus, the near rejection of the Party's official report led to the more strenuous finding against Chen at the end of July 1998.

In the course of negotiations between Chen and the Party's officials who brought the indictments, Chen allegedly defied the government's consideration of execution as a proper punishment, warning, "If you sentence me to death, you can get 300 coffins ready." An ominous promise, to be sure, and one offering an obvious conclusion: even the authorities prosecuting the corrupt are themselves corrupt. It appears that in exchange for not disclosing the crimes of other Party luminaries, Chen received a more lenient sentence. Another interpretation of the sentencing emerges from consideration of the crime itself. The practice of selling planning approvals and construction permits to the highest bidder was widespread in 1990s Beijing; Chen Xitong, as chief municipal authority, merely rode the crest of this wave until political fate no longer favored him—that is, when his powerful patron, the most powerful man in China, passed away and the leadership of Jiang Zemin grew from the fertile soil of Deng Xiaoping's demise.

Nonetheless, as each of these more publicized cases of illegality and wantonness are paraded before the Chinese public in an effort to rectify Party errors, reinforce "rule by law," and proffer an uplifting moral challenge, the government loses more ground to a doubting citizenry tired of the contradiction between the government's admirable words and abominable deeds. This is perhaps the defining legacy of the hybrid political economy Deng termed "socialism with Chinese characteristics"—a moral confusion wrought by a contradictory ideology. How else can one make sense of the essential commonness of official excess in the national, provincial, and local strata of daily life and of the reflexive incapacity to rectify it? For example, in the fall of 1998 in Guangdong, China's most economically prosperous province, a provincial committee uncovered extensive wrongdoing by senior officials: Wu Shihua, former chief of the Jiangmen City Judicial Bureau, embezzled nearly 2 million yuan in a hotel construction scam while also withdrawing more than 3.5 million yuan from public funds for house and chauffeured limousine expenses; Guangdong People's Congress Standing Committee vice-chairman, Yu Fei, used the privileges of his office and the offices of a holding company run by his two daughters and his son-in-law to buy cheap and sell dear (to the tune of 28 million yuan in profit) the use rights for about 1,000 acres of very desirable land in the Daya Bay Development Zone. An investigative report on fiscal impropriety in Guangdong released by the Central Committee for Financial Work revealed that the Guangdong Branches of the Industrial and Commercial Bank of China had made 222 billion yuan in bad loans, a great portion of which were irretrievable. Moreover, another inquiry, this one into provincial corruption and filed by the Organization Department of the CCP Central Committee and the Ministry of Public Security in October 1998, reported that:

of the families and children of Guangdong's three leading bodies of the provincial party committee and provincial government, the provincial People's Congress . . . 47 percent are now engaged in business and are working in China-invested companies or jointly-invested companies in Hong Kong and Macao . . . while those engaged in business or [who] are working in financial, securities, and trading companies inside the country account for about 45 percent of the total.[4]

The sum of 92 percent of the families and children of provincial officials involved in highly profitable enterprise conveys the appalling degree of graft in Chinese life.

Still, such provincial detail, along with Chen's sentencing and several other cases of official misconduct that have been brought to light since 1995, makes it evident to Chinese and U.S. observers alike that corruption in China is simply about the abuse of privilege by the powerful few. This is not the only meaning of corruption, to be sure, but the reader may ask: other than confirming a suspicion that China is a nation despoiled by its leaders, what is the value of exploring the plural phenomena of corruption? What can we learn of China through a reflection on this particular national problem? In response, I would offer that corruption is an effective measure of the condition of contemporary Chinese society for it conveys much about the critical space between moral ideals and real life. Corruption is as much about language as it is about politics—specifically, how words in China, especially the highly formalized instructions of the Party, seek to bring about a desired outcome in the world. Corruption in China is most explicitly about the collapse of CCP integrity, the unseemly compromising of its ideals, and the concomitant squandering of public weal (all of which are evident in the essays by Oakes, Smil, and Weston in this volume). All of this is, of course, unfortunate—a fate that befalls many altruistic political experiments; however, it is the implicit significance of how this misfortune has released most Chinese from the obligation to believe the government and, even worse, to flout a fledgling legal establishment arrayed against corruption that I find most worthy of our attention.

To grasp the import of this claim, we must proceed in order attending to four types of detail. First, we must examine the lack of fit between our understanding of corruption and that of the Chinese. Second, with an appreciation of the many Chinese contexts of corruption, ranging from the sensational to the everyday, we will clarify the popular Western mistake of equating social connections (*guanxi*) and those illegal practices that fall under the rubric of "corruption." Third, we will re-conceive corruption as a key symbol of Chinese life, as a reflection of that nation's ambition and the consequent struggle to reconcile this with its revolutionary legacy; we will thereby learn much about the promise and peril of China's national identity. Fourth, we will consider the curiously parallel dilemmas of the United States and China with corruption and the loss of public trust.

In the context of an intercultural dialogue conducted through corruption, it should be clear that the meaningfulness of this phenomenon is found in the effort to cross boundaries and in a necessity of judgment eloquently described by Andrew Nathan in *Chinese Democracy:*

> I am not a believer in the kind of analysis of other societies that tries to avoid value issues on the grounds that different societies' values are not the same. Discussing another society's values is a sign of respect, not cultural arrogance. Not to do so means either pretending that differences do not exist or— disrespectfully to our own values—acting as if we do not consider them important.[5]

It is the task of the present essay to effect such a respectful inquiry into the values of contemporary Chinese society, and it begins with a recasting of corruption in a more clarifying light by way of a question: What is it?

CORRUPTION: A LINGUISTIC CONSIDERATION

Corruption is a common moral and social flaw of developing economies and may be broadly defined as "the abuse of a public position of trust for private gain." So defined, corruption is visible in most parts of the world, particularly prominent in those national economies recently converted to market capitalism. For citizens of the United States and China corruption is easily defined, both in word and deed. In English, it connotes a change from good to bad in manners or morals and has cognate associations with the impairment of integrity or moral principle, depravity, decay, and decomposition. A definition for us would include: inducement to wrong by bribery or the departure from what is pure or correct. Etymologically, corruption is derived from the Latin *corruptus/corrumpere*, bearing the meaning of the English "to reave" or break. As for the politics of corruption, it is more often than not an unpardonable but unpunishable offense.

In U.S. political life there is comparatively little legal talk about corruption as an offense, though many United States citizens believe that their politicians are corrupt. Cases of influence-peddling, bribery, extortion, abuse of office, and embezzlement that involve politicians and business executives do not seem to achieve the nefariousness and national prominence signaled by "corruption" in China. Save the recent case of former Clinton administration agriculture secretary, Mike Espy, corruption as a punishable offense in U.S. life is usually associated with the Mafia and is governed by the federal racketeering statutes.[6]

Similar connotations of decline from a former state or transgression are found in China in the principal terms reserved for such action: *tanwu, fubai,* and *fuhua.* The most common Chinese term for corruption is *tanwu,* literally, "greed" and "dirt." It carries the same implicit moralistic injunction as the Latin *corruptus* and for this reason the current campaigns to eliminate corruption have emphasized the Party's commitment to "clean government." As a rather general category of malfeasance it has a specific, distinctly ethical significance that only recently has reached beyond the cloistered walls of China's political elite. The term *tanwu* conjures a different association in the popular mind, to wit the abuse of privilege by members of the Party and their descendants, collectively referred to as the princelings (*taizidang*), whose excesses are supremely evident in the previously mentioned widespread provincial nepotism found in Guangdong.

The growth in the number and sophistication of greed/dirt categories suggests, moreover, that the common example of official abuse of privilege, combined with the Party's ideological emphasis on the pursuit of profit and self-aggrandizement in the name of modernity and nationhood, has ensured the proliferation of corruption beyond the morally disestablished Communist Party and its descendants. In fact, the term *tanwu* itself has proven inadequate to the task of representing contemporary excess and has been superseded by a new coinage, *guandao*—*guan,* "official," and *dao,* "turning." The greater specificity of the term suggests a refinement of the popular argot that identifies officials as the perpetrators of corruption, once exalted figures who have fallen from grace. For this reason, official turning is frequently paired with a statement of the moral depravity of the offender—in other words, sexual excess, drinking, carousing, and so on—backed by evidence, as in the recent bribery scandal involving Hubei vice governor Meng Qingping, also known as "Hubei's Wang Baosen," who allegedly lived a "dissolute life, trading power for women" in acquiring a number of mistresses, yet also visiting prostitutes.

"Official inversion," or turning, carries forward the altruistic implication of official status, in that it is the crime of officials who have turned away from the warrants of their role. The term's ambiguity is only overcome in Chinese context, where *guandao* may also be understood as the "official turnaround" wherein "officials . . . arrange to procure raw materials or commodities at the fixed price and then 'turn around' to reap large, illicit profits by selling on the private market."[7] Though it might be clever to gamble public chips on a high-stakes private game of profit, the frequent failures of such a risk must be attributed to a character flaw, not to a larger malfunction of the political and economic system.

Social connections (*guanxi*) may play a role in this pattern of official abuse of public weal, but only because in such instances social connections themselves have been corrupted. Official turning, however, is not a consequence of social connections, principally because it bears the moral significance corrupt official practices lack. Social connections may be observed in the webs of deceit and profiteering spun by Chinese officials, but I would suggest that these practices are nepotism, not networking, and are usually referred to in Chinese as *tequan*, "special powers," common to powerful families and complexes of association who exercise privilege to line their pockets. In stark contrast, networking, or social connections, is a traditional lattice of face-to-face relations with kin and non-kin that underwrites individual identity and is repeatedly sustained through diverse rituals of sentiment such as weddings and funerals, being a host or a guest, and giving gifts. Most important, this "complex network of social support and sentimental attachment,"[8] as Andrew Kipnis has described it, stands in diametric opposition to the practices of Party politics and indeed constitutes an effective deterrent of state capitalist advance. The association of corruption with social connections is incidental rather than intentional and the confusion of their separateness is the consequence of a subtle subversion of the everyday in China wherein law, the executor of the state's intention, aims to curb social connections, thus freeing the community of individual laborers to abandon the rhythms of family, field, and forefathers for the throbbing pace of the market.

CORRUPTION PAST AND PRESENT: MORALITY AND THE LAW

One scholar of the global phenomenon of corruption in developing countries has elegantly linked it to the growing marketization of the world economy, writing that "corruption is the illegitimate reminder of the values of the market place (everything can be bought and sold) that in the age of capitalism increasingly, even legitimately, permeate formerly autonomous political and social spheres."[9] The characterization seems especially apt for China now, where the formerly exclusive sphere of national politics is influenced by considerations of profit.

Nothing demonstrates the thoroughness of this capitalist permeation more convincingly than a partial inventory of excesses listed in a recent work report of the Central Discipline Inspection Commission responsible for the investigation and prosecution of corruption. The report was issued following a five-year program to increase "party discipline and punish corrupt elements" and produced voluminous evidence of malfeasance among a staggering number of national and regional officials: smuggling, bribery, bribery in exchange for omission of action, fabrication, prostitute visits, illegal fund raising, illegal release of smuggled goods, armed resistance to the anti-smuggling squad, arbitrary imposition of service charges, collection of illicit fees, random installation of highway checkpoints, using public funds for tourism in foreign countries, unwarranted fees in elementary and middle schools, and kickbacks for the purchase or sale of medical and pharmaceutical products.[10]

Though corruption is grandly displayed on the stage of contemporary Chinese life, it has lurked in the shadows of the national polity since its founding. As a crime it has had a curious history in the nearly half-century of Communist Party rule, almost exclusively referring to the misdeeds of Party members. A glance at post-liberation Chinese legal history, specifically the statutes drawn up in the wake of the Three Anti Campaign of the early 1950s,[11] shows that corruption was a matter of concern very early on.

It was first legally defined in the 1952 Statute of Penalties for Corruption, wherein several different kinds of violation were specified: accepting bribes, embezzlement, extortion, fraud, speculation, misappropriation, seizure of property, and theft. The statute offered a national articulation of crimes produced as a result of improper cadre attitudes, such as *difang zhuyi* ("localism") and *benwei zhuyi* ("departmentalism"), in contrast to concerns for the greater good and which could be remedied through reform and reeducation. In the beginning phases of socialist construction, corruption took the form of bribes tendered to local officials by peasants desirous to reduce their tax obligations to the state, appropriation (often theft) of public grain by cadres for personal use, and the use of state monies for private expenditures to employ servants or to purchase supplies. The most common violation under this category of greed/dirt was a generic one: the appropriation of public property. These several categories of the original criminal taxonomy have required adjustment and modification in more recent decades, as reflected in subsequently emended legal codes. In 1979, with the inception of the economic and political reforms that provided the groundwork for China's recent "economic miracle," the Chinese Communist Party specified in a newly updated criminal code that such offenses as the seizure of public property by officials for personal profit would be punished with criminal detention of not more than five years.[12]

Nine years later definitions of corruption were more finely articulated. The 1988 Supplementary Regulations Relating to Corruption and Bribery legally discriminate between the misappropriation of public and private property; consequently, "corruption" in this instance refers to appropriation (*taoqu*) of any property (by public officials) for private gain.[13] What these stipulations disclose is that criminal corruption was originally understood within the scope of a collective social system where cadres and Party could exert influence to appropriate public goods. China has diverged significantly from this paradigm in the last two decades and so the legal formulations of corruption have grown even more complex. Moreover, the change in corruption's meaning, as reflected in the growing number of criminal statutes addressing it, says much about the consequences of a socialist experiment that in recent decades has acquired "Chinese characteristics."

Now, with the increasing privatization of economic incentive under the "responsibility system," wherein individual households and local enterprises receive no income from the state and are responsible for both profit and loss, the singular definition of corruption as appropriation (or, rather, misappropriation) has given way to multiple specifications of "economic crimes." Over the last several years the further emendation of the legal code to reflect new permutations of abuse (and which has occurred in tandem with the increasing privatization of the economy) dramatizes the endemic quality of corruption in contemporary society—a concern of far greater moment for the government than the excesses of high-ranking officials.

For example, one of the most striking features of the recently revised and amended PRC Criminal Law is its Part II, "Special Provisions," the largest portion of the entire criminal code. Chapter III of Part II is comprised of eight sections and is devoted to "Crimes Undermining the Order of the Socialist Market Economy." The first five sections read: Crimes of Manufacturing and Selling Fake and Shoddy Goods; Crimes of Smuggling; Crimes of Disrupting the Order of the Company and Enterprise Administration; Crimes of Undermining the Order of Financial Management; Crimes of Financial Fraud, and adumbrate a horizon of violations inclusive of both citizens and Party members. Chapter IV of these Special Provisions details the offenses and punishment for "Crimes Infringing upon the Rights of Private Citizens" and reveals the extent to which the legal mind of Chinese socialism has drifted toward bourgeois considerations. Now, armed with an elaborate criminal code, a Central Discipline Inspection Committee (CDIC), headed by Wei Jianxin, works in concert with provincial party organs to ferret out corruption and to prosecute reform through moral reeducation or, if such efforts fail, through corporal punishment and incarceration. However, it is very clear from Party initiatives and press reports that punishment even more than moral suasion is the common mechanism of reform.

What is illegal, in the case of corruption, is also unethical because law under a socialist state works to reinforce the moral narrative of human emancipation through revolution and administrative personnel shoulder the greatest burden of labor in demonstrating commitment to this myth. The normative impulse definitive of China's socialist experiment is also explicit in the numerous administrative regulations, such as the "Provisional Regulations on the Penalties for Corruption and Bribery of State Administrative Personnel" (1988), which supplement the frequently emended criminal code. Thus, the legal language of prescription and proscription found in the nation's statutes and in administrative regulations is designed to effect a moral outcome, as can be seen in a recent work report detailing the Party's progress in battling corruption:

Party committees and commissions for discipline inspection at all levels have conscientiously organized the great masses of party members and cadres to study Marxism-Leninism-Mao Zedong Thought, and particularly Deng Xiaoping Theory of building socialism with Chinese characteristics. They also have conducted an education in the Party constitution. They have conducted educational campaigns to promote party spirit, work style and discipline with emphasis on the requirement of paying attention to study, politics, and righteousness. They have launched extensive propaganda activities to help people learn from advanced models . . . [14]

In the face of the widening reach of corruption's tide, serial citation of the successes of reeducation in the cardinal virtues of socialism with Chinese characteristics is troubling rather than reassuring, for it makes explicit the inefficacy of legal sanction in a society whose members feel little obligation to follow the laws of a government that has succeeded in so thoroughly flouting public trust. A legal culture is only now taking shape in China, but, unfortunately, it is occurring in an environment where political and economic power are coupled at every level, and in such circumstances a more enthusiastic embrace of party ideology or "correct thought" cannot possibly repress the rapacious desire of the powerful for profit. This may explain why the state constitution and its many revisions often refer to "rule by law" instead of "rule of law," yet it also helps account for the growing sophistication of the Chinese legal code and for the increasing tendency of Chinese citizens to turn to the law in defending themselves from corruption.

CORRUPTION: AN ANGULAR VIEW

Thus, the concerned observer must look beyond the present salience of greed and graft to discern a recurrent pattern—that Party corruption, even more than its dictatorship's avowed opposition to pluralist democracy, has provided the background hum of popular protest. For example, in the heady days of late spring 1989, the most vociferous cries of students, workers, and countless other Chinese citizens were those against official corruption and for a proper legal system. It was the materialistic excesses of Party members and their associates, especially prominent officials, that provoked public outrage, an outrage exaggerated by a hopelessness consequent upon the knowledge of the inefficacy of law in deterring official graft. Student protesters pontificated against the nepotism of the politically prominent, citing the practices common among them of: sending their children (the *taizidang*) to the finest U.S. colleges and universities, placing them at the head of new corporations, and granting them expensive foreign cars and palatial residences.

So what is familiar to us as the Democracy Movement or the Tian'anmen Square demonstrations, that portrait of a citizenry desirous for democracy and arrayed against tyranny, was underwritten by a pervasive concern with the ideological fraud explicit in the Chinese Communist Party's private enrichment at public expense. The protests were muted by murder, as was the cry for substantive reform. Now, more than a decade later, corruption, nepotism, and illegality are more salient and more troubling, particularly because material acquisitiveness and self-aggrandizement have overtaken many of the Chinese who previously inveighed against such habits among Party members.

But even as, or because, the seeds of corruption have spread among the larger population, for the last six years, it seems almost continuously, China has been in the throes of country-wide anti-corruption campaigns. In speeches before Party multitudes and on television and radio, national and provincial leaders alike have called for its elimination. Standing before the Party faithful at the Fifteenth National Congress in September 1997, President Jiang Zemin gave a lengthy state of the nation report in which he identified the fight against corruption as a "grave political struggle vital to the very existence of the Party." He underscored the importance of the struggle by saying that if corruption cannot be mitigated, "the Party will lose the confidence and support of the people."[15] (Parenthetically, I must note that this sober assessment of the gravity of the problem and the consequences if it is not solved was proffered only in the final minutes of President Jiang's address in the closing lines of its last section, titled "The Communist Party of China Facing the New Century.") Of course, one could argue that it is precisely because it has long lost "the confidence and support of the people" that the CCP and its many operatives have enriched themselves at the public's expense. Indeed, this is the contention of Wei Jingsheng in his essay in chapter 5 of this volume.

The commonness of corruption is a national embarrassment for the Party, something very evident in the moralistic injunctions of the laws against it and the even more righteous public posturing of its luminaries. Take, for instance, the government's own figures, offered in support of its prosecution of corruption cases: between October 1992 and June 1997, "discipline inspection organs nationwide have resolved more than 670,000 cases out of over 731,000 investigated crimes, with over 669,300 people being sanctioned by the party and the governments, of whom 121,500 people lost their party membership, and 37,492 were criminally punished."[16] In 1995 alone when 2,262 senior Party officials were prosecuted for corruption, there were numerous national scandals from all parts of the country involving prominent Party figures and industrial executives accused of embezzlement and fraud. In fact, corruption defines China's state capitalist political economy and as a "social disease requiring constant vigilance," the Party's fight against it is, according to Li Peng, "a matter of life and death for the nation."

There is good reason for leaders to hold forth righteously against the advancing evil of official malfeasance. Even with the much heralded success of the nation's economy, public trust in the Party is eroding precipitously. In fact, China's economic growth, rather than mitigating the adverse political consequences of Party corruption, has dramatized them. The nation's accelerated prosperity engendered expectations of material benefit that have come to grief as economic growth has stalled, urban incomes have declined, and the income gap between rich and poor has widened to frightening proportions, all trends that have been exaggerated by the larger Asian economic collapse (see Henry Rosemont's essay in chapter 8). By 1994, according to a recent article by Liu Binyan and Perry Link, "the disparity between rich and poor was already greater in China than in the United States. In that year the richest 20 percent of the U. S. population owned 44.3 percent of the country's wealth, whereas in China the richest fifth owned 50.2 percent; the poorest fifth in the U.S. owned 4.6 percent of the wealth, in China 4.3 percent."[17] Today the disparity is even more graphic.

In essence, as anti-corruption laws proliferate, so do the varieties of corruption. And, as China witnessed its most exponential growth in corruption between 1992 and 1997, over the same period its economy became increasingly more skewed to the benefit of a privileged few. He Qinglian, a Beijing intellectual, has recently concluded that the increase in domestic economic disparity and advancing Party corruption are not coincidence but the consequence of a willful enterprise of "reform" (gaige), "in which power-holders and their hangers-on plundered public wealth." Furthermore, she adds, "the primary target of their plunder was state property that had been accumulated from forty years of the people's sweat, and their primary means of plunder was political power."[18] These are the most damning of corruption's consequences and they are the reason why, in a poll of 2,500 urban residents conducted in the fall of 1995 by a market research firm in Beijing, 71 percent of respondents were dissatisfied with the integrity of officials and more than half urged the government to do more to eliminate corruption.[19]

Yet it is hardly difficult to imagine how dissatisfaction becomes indignation among the Chinese citizenry when in August 1999 the auditor general of China, Li Jinhua, reported that 14.2 billion dollars (117.4 billion yuan), one-fifth of the nation's yearly tax revenue, had been "misappropriated." The total sum is astonishing, but what is appalling are the manifold abuses hidden within the figure. Tactfully recounting in the euphemistic style of Party proclamation the results of his eight-month audit of the Finance Ministry, Li affirmed that *all* of China's eighteen provincial treasuries under investigation were guilty of "loose auditing practices . . . [having] pocketed central government revenues into their own accounts."[20] In addition, tax officials had "exceeded their power to reduce and relieve taxes" and customs agents had "reduced tariff rates in violation of state regulations." Given the historic flooding that ravaged northern and southern China in the summers of 1998 and 1999, the most damning of Li's revelations was that the Ministry of Water Resources had collected substantial funds, not for building dams and dikes as was their charge, but for erecting luxury office buildings. The social connections that bind China's working masses offer no inhibition to such gargantuan entitlement of district, provincial, and national officials who, instead of serving the people (*wei renmin fuwu*), now "serve the people's money" (*wei renminbi fuwu*).[21]

SNAPSHOTS OF EXCESS

The ripples from these reports are slow to make their way to us in the West, but when they do we are accustomed to include them within a widening circle of corruption wrought by greedy Chinese officials through their social connections. However, from the U.S. vantage the Chen Xitong case is less salient on our corruption register than is another recent event. For us, a particularly egregious case of Chinese "corruption," in the sense of the breaking of a trust, occurred a few years ago with the Beijing government's repossession of an attractive parcel of commercially zoned real estate upon which a McDonald's restaurant had been built and was in operation. Shortly after serving the fast-food conglomerate a summary notice of eviction, the city announced that the property was being sold to a prosperous Hong Kong real estate tycoon. The value of the tract had increased substantially in the interval between its original acquisition by McDonald's and the declared commercial acquisitiveness of the Hong Kong developer; thus, it made little sense to permit the large, foreign corporation to retain it. The cost/benefit calculus underwriting the revocation was sound: much more money could be made by evicting the present tenants and making the property available to a higher, "better connected" Chinese bidder.

Moreover, because all land in China is technically "owned" by the Party, the legal repercussions for the state of the violation of a contract—whether for construction, occupancy, or commercial use—are virtually nil. Charges of contract violation, illegality, fraud, and corruption were made by the offended party, but McDonald's never regained the site. Let the buyer beware. While this specific incident might enrage us, it would not be seen as an instance of corruption by Chinese; indeed, it is nothing more than the expected consequence of an aggressive capitalist spirit. It reeks of corruption to us, but it is not a punishable offense in China, as is most of what is officially designated as corruption. Though unfair, the government's action was defensible in the context of an aggressive calculus of profitability. What is missing here in the incredulity engendered by the incident is exactly what we presume is behind corruption—social connections. McDonald's is a multinational corporation headquartered in the Chicago suburbs, whereas the higher bidder was Chinese and connected.

The contemporary varieties of Chinese graft are remarkable and provide a broad, spectral display of human ingenuity. In ongoing efforts to curb, and even deny, these market-inspired acts of cunning, official news reports and Party announcements have revealed: bogus stock schemes, insurance scams, extortion, bribery, copyright violation, false advertising, tax farming, sex slavery, sale of body parts, and many permutations of the timeless stock-in-trade of the petty capitalist—bait and switch.

A recent and extraordinary case of the last of these occurred in Heilongjiang (in China's far northeast) in 1990. Town officials had colluded with the experimental farm of the Dongbei Agricultural Institute to sell two-year-old corn seeds with a 65 percent sprouting rate at the retail price for seeds with a 90 percent sprouting rate. Following an unexpectedly small harvest, the peasants sought redress before the district people's court in Harbin, the province's capital, and were awarded a judgment equal to their losses, approximately 135,000 yuan. What was extraordinary was that the case involved 709 peasant households that filed a class-action suit against the town government of Taiping and a local seed company. The provincial radio report of the case and its outcome provides evidence of the efficacy of the State Compensation Law at the same time that it reveals the workings of "official corruption" of the sort most familiar to Chinese.[22] In U.S. dollars the settlement totaled $23,664, which, when doled out to the hundreds of offended households, came to $33 each, or 267 yuan: paltry perhaps but, in principle, astonishing.

In this historic circumstance—the first ever collective legal action taken by peasants—the responsible parties were punished and the "legal rights and interests" of the peasant households were "safeguarded." Yet one must understand that such legal redemption, though increasingly common, is far from the norm and is most intelligible when considered as one aspect of a political culture of illegality. Justice of this sort remains rare, though the excesses of Party officials are not; the results of their enterprise at the public's expense can be fatal.

A story I was told by an urban official in southwestern China several years ago cast into relief the local, lethal consequences of profiteering by public officials. He reported that in southern Yunnan in 1994 a group of rural township officials confiscated the land of several peasant families in order to sell it to Japanese developers. The officials seized the land and negotiated its sale, merely informing the peasant landholders of their imminent eviction but not before the victims of the scheme sought, and obtained, vengeance by beating the schemers to death. The land was returned to the families and, in turn, the peasants who were convicted of the officials' murder were executed.

These unfortunate actions are underwritten by a rapacious drive for profit, something that was first celebrated by Deng Xiaoping himself more than a decade ago when he proclaimed a new national motto, "to get rich is glorious." Profit is the prime mover of contemporary Chinese society, no less a force for officials than it is for individual citizens, orphanages, and universities, perhaps because wealth brings freedom from the normal political constraints of daily life. Furthermore, since Deng's dramatically over-celebrated *nanxun* ("southern tour") in 1992, the Party's advocacy of a rapid accumulation of profit as the solution to China's economic backwardness, as well as its need for democracy and the rule of law, means that the aggressive pursuit of wealth amounts to an admirable compliance with state directives to enrich oneself. With money, you can easily acquire a passport, you can travel widely within the country, you can barter access to the wider world of information, and you can, in certain respects, escape the long arm of Chinese law. But it is in this latter respect that obsessive aspiration for affluence can make the issue of corruption particularly ominous.

THE OMNIPRESENT FACE OF LOCAL CORRUPTION

Recollections from two periods of residence in southwest China during the last seven years can illustrate the kinds of practices that are identified as corrupt by Chinese and permit us to explore similarities with our contemporary situation. Moreover, these observations suggest that China, not unlike the United States, is in the pervasive throes of a moral drift wherein the only guide for meaningful action is the maximal interest of the singular self. In order to protect the innocent and to shield myself from the guilty, I have imposed a certain anonymity on these written reflections.

The Costs of Achievement

A few years ago a graduate student in English at a modest Chinese institution of higher learning received an international fellowship from a foreign university. The fellowship honored "distinguished students in developing countries" and offered its recipients the opportunity to continue their graduate education toward the Ph.D. on its campus in the South Pacific. The fortunate student, who had been serving as an instructor of English, informed his department supervisor that he had received the fellowship in question and inquired about applying through his university work unit (*danwei*) for a passport. Though the department was honored by his achievement, an answer to his inquiry was not forthcoming. From the supervisor's perspective, his English instructor's opportunity, if honored, would be experienced as a loss—to wit, the loss of a faculty member who taught a great number of courses unwanted by his older, stationary colleagues. He was told that approval of his leave was conditional upon compensation of his work unit. Furthermore, he had to understand that his leaving might result in the eviction of his extended family from the faculty housing that the work unit had provided. The necessary paperwork for the passport was completed and submitted to provincial government authorities but not without requiring the graduate student to repay the cash value of his entire education through the M.A.—at the cost of 30,000 yuan— which he still managed to do with a salary of 80 yuan per month. In this instance, the graduate student's social connections—a network of family, friends, and well-wishers, turned over their savings to meet the bribery demands of university and party officials. The student, now the possessor of a Ph.D., and his immediate family live and work in the South Pacific and make reimbursement payments to family and friends at home.

Benefits of Public/Private Ambiguity

As China moves from state socialist to state capitalist organization, the ambiguity of local fiscal responsibility and/or legal accountability for such expenses as taxis, banquets, private cars, and buses provides endless opportunity for abuse. Banqueting at public expense is another gray area just beyond the reach of China's expanding system of law and it is probably the most commonly practiced. Elaborate banqueting by officials is a common focus of CCP denunciation and though the Party refrains from identifying it as corruption—calling it instead "an unhealthy tendency"— it is clear that most Chinese citizens do consider it willful misappropriation of public funds. Former Premier Li Peng denounced banqueting at public expense as the "abuse of power for private gain," by this referring to the excessive practice common to officials. However, as an unhealthy tendency banqueting is widely observed and practiced by Chinese in the countryside and the city. For restaurant owners, for example, the work unit, or business-hosted, banquet is distinguished in terms of expense from a dinner party hosted by an individual for family and friends. The latter form of largesse is less common and always costs less for the same menu. I was once told that a banquet I was intending to host for my students would cost my work unit in excess of 300 yuan per table; however, when I insisted that the financial burden was entirely my own, I was told the cost would be approximately 100 yuan per table.

In China when one takes a taxi and asks for a receipt (*fapiao* or *shoushu*) for the fare, the driver presumes that its issue is critical to reimbursement of the rider by the work unit. The amount of such a trip, under such assumed circumstance, may be revised upward for the benefit of driver and rider. Taxi rides for which one spends 10 or 15 yuan are "receipted" at 25 yuan. The same is true of the individual purchase of goods in a store. The total value of snacks, soft drinks, cigarettes, chocolate, toilet paper, and so forth, is inflated on the receipt so that the purchaser may be compensated by the work unit in excess of the purchase. Hence, while the Party is ripping off the people, the people at the same time are exploiting the Party—a destructive and unrepentant mutual parasitism.

Perhaps such behavior can be deemed "corrupt," but it is not far removed from the U.S. business lunch and is founded on an identical presumption: somebody else will pick up the tab, as when the administrative officers of a large U.S. state university charged a $1,200 bill for steaks and drinks at an exclusive restaurant to "operating expenses." Familiar to us as the rational choice of maximizing one's prospects for gain, this world of mutual mistreatment is the antithesis of an earlier era when the Party was the consummate provider for and caterer to the rural and urban Chinese masses.

CHINESE CORRUPTION AND THE FAILED PARADISE

If such behavior may be deemed "corrupt," then corruption touches virtually everyone in China as one may see in a quatrain of popular doggerel
(*shunkouliu*) that succinctly renders one view of the lamentable moral condition of the Chinese nation:

> The Central Committee is busy with factional warfare.
> Provincial officials are hunting for overseas airfare.
> Urban officials are eating and drinking up a storm.
> In the villages and townships, gambling is the norm.[23]

These rhyming couplets conjure a telescoping image of deviation and dis-
cord perpetrated by both public official and private citizen. The joke is not
about lawlessness per se so much as excess: an exaggerated political com-
bativeness; an excess of Party privilege that permits, among many other
perquisites, international travel and excessive banqueting at public expense.
It presumes the widespread quality of the practices against an unstated
backdrop of moral probity. What is intriguing about this quatrain (and this
could be said of any number of similar limericks now legion) is how the joke
works. The humor turns on the implied portrait of descent from a state of
grace, one of the principal connotations of corruption in English and Chinese, as noted previously. And it is this implicit moral valence that offers just
the least vestige of an earlier constitution of Chinese self and society.

Chinese officials are never supposed to better themselves at the public's
expense, especially a public that can only accept the leadership it is given.
Perhaps that is why "communist morality" has always been understood
as puritanical self-sacrifice and zealous struggle against corruption. And
the contemporary state of a morally disestablished Party will stand out
dramatically against the backdrop of the celebrations of the founding of
the PRC. Comparisons will naturally be drawn, and all to the detriment of
the government of China's "socialist spiritual civilization," for the morality of self-sacrifice was the hallmark of the earlier revolutionary party and
the obsession of its luminaries and was never stated better than by China's
former vice-chairman of the Central Committee, Liu Shaoqi (1898–1969),
in his work *How to Be a Good Communist*:

The Communist Party represents the proletariat which is itself exploited but
does not exploit others, and it can therefore carry revolution through to the

end, finally abolish all exploitation and sweep away all the corruption and rottenness in human society. The proletariat . . . through the Party and this [democratic] state apparatus . . . is able to lead the masses of people in waging unrelenting struggle against all corruption and rottenness and in ceaselessly weeding out of the Party and the state organs all those elements that have become corrupt and degenerate (whatever high office they may hold), thereby preserving the purity of the Party and the state apparatus.[24]

Liu's proud celebration of the solidarity of communist and worker raging against the machine of corruption was nothing more than a mythical map, one now shredded by the unrestrained impulse toward the pursuit of wealth. The good communist is an ideal, not unlike our own nation's model of citizenship, the meaning of which resides in the moral context of a politicized struggle narrative of the ceaseless contest between good and evil.

Carried through city and countryside on giddy tongues, the ironic quatrain quoted previously had been circling through the streets, alleyways, and neighborhoods of China for several years before Li Peng addressed the varied political problems of such abuse of privilege in a speech before the Central Committee and the State Council in late September 1993. By this time the ideological coherence of an overly heroized ethic of Party probity was gone and the fragments of the good communist tale were only useful as burlesque. Moreover, as Li addressed his comrades, the rivalrous national struggle for human betterment through material acquisition (that lesson with which citizens of the United States still wrestle mightily) had become a popular obsession. With the spread of this obsession, the implicit moral contrast of corruption had become less visible as the face-to-face relations of human community once nurtured through social connections were jettisoned in favor of a utilitarian strategy of self-enlargement.

Titled "Resolutely Wage Struggle against Corruption," Li's stylistically coded remarks provide a prosaic but illustrative counterpoint to the poetry of popular sentiment as they subtly recall the moralistic formulations of *How to Be a Good Communist*:

The most acute problem of corruption at present is the exchange of power for money and the abuse of power for private gain. . . . It must be understood that, in some government departments and among some personnel working in those departments, as well as among leading cadres, the phenomenon of corruption exists and is rather serious in some cases. Some people have neglected or failed to fulfill their duties, have perverted justice for bribes, have offered and accepted bribes, have resorted to blackmail and extortion, have become corrupt and decadent, and have already committed crimes. . . . The masses of the people are looking to us, as are lower-level departments; they have pinned high hopes on the anti-corruption struggle . . . [25]

The "anti-corruption drive" is the proffered remedy for this systemic ailment in its promotion of the "building of socialist spiritual civilization." The message here, however, is one of punishment and constraint, without even the weakest gesture toward a moral contrast narrative of the sort implicit in the heroism of the Party. Instead, there is "rule by law."

Yet one can understand the exertion of punitive reflex in light of the absurdly elevated standards of probity and accomplishment to which the Party still holds itself. A cursory review of Articles 12 through 28 of the constitution, just like the common citation of corruption reform successes, conveys rather eloquently the grandiosity of the government's self-concept: the state "protects socialist public property," "protects the rights of citizens to own lawfully earned income, savings, houses and other lawful property," "continuously raises labor productivity, improves economic results and develops the productive forces by enhancing the enthusiasm of the working people, raising the level of their technical skill, disseminating advanced science and technology," "properly apportions accumulation and consumption, pays attention to the interests of the collective and the individual," "develops socialist educational undertakings and works to raise the scientific and cultural level of the whole nation," "promotes the development of the natural and social sciences," "develops medical and health services," "develops physical culture and promotes mass sports activities to build up the people's physique," "promotes the development of literature and art, the press, broadcasting and television undertakings, publishing and distributing services, libraries, museums, cultural centres and other cultural undertakings," "trains specialized personnel in all fields who serve socialism," "strengthens the building of socialist spiritual civilization through spreading high ideals and morality, general education and education in discipline and the legal system, and through promoting the formulation and observance of rules of conduct and common pledges by different sections of the people in urban and rural areas," "promotes family planning," "protects and improves the living environment and the ecological environment," "maintains public order and suppresses treasonable and other counter-revolutionary activities."

Taken together, these many tasks represent a Sisyphean endeavor. How could any political administration hold itself to such standards, or rather, how could strictly maintaining the achievement of such altruistic objectives as legal necessity not lead to disaster? Tethering morality to legality may be effective in small groups, but it has proven utterly useless as a political solution to corruption in China writ large.

And herein lies the problem: only the coercive force of the state can ensure success in the struggle against corruption. Model emulation of the sort that governed earlier visionary political experiments such as the Cultural Revolution is ineffective, but in this battle to find a solution the Party is in fact divided against itself. If profit enables China to attain its "goal of being prosperous and strong," and the exemplary cases of prosecuted corruption are brought against those who have been exceedingly successful in reaping a profit, then the national battle to eliminate corruption cannot succeed. Such campaigns must be prosecuted in the interest of maintaining the credibility of Party rule and preserving the public perception that politics is necessary to national improvement. And it is on this internal but productive contradiction—a metaphorical hinge—that our attention easily turns from China to home, where political and economic power are no less mutually reinforcing.

"CORRUPTION" U.S. STYLE

Of course, cash is king in U.S. politics as well and there is more than enough of the kind of distorted social connections associated with Communist Party corruption. Former government officials become lobbyists and peddle influence and connections with the politically powerful for the benefit of the corporations that pay them. And, such lobbyists are paid handsomely. Significant contributors to campaigns are rewarded by the newly elected official with sinecures, and friends and business associates are given high-level government appointments. The manner and volume of these enabling transactions is obscure for most United States citizens or at least those not privy to the political culture of the "Beltway"; however, it is in the realm of national campaigns and the corporate behemoths of the Democratic and Republican National Committees that the average citizen has become very familiar with the dominant role played by money and influence. That there is good reason for concern about private threats to public trust is explicit when President Clinton is seen in a videotape segment of a recent Public Broadcasting System (PBS) *Frontline* program, telling a group of Democratic contributors that "not only does your money buy you access, it buys you influence." So, the political bog of China's market socialism against which we hold forth is only different in kind from the crisis in which we are enmeshed. U.S. public life is beset by similar problems, as is instinctively clear to observers of the hearings on "campaign finance reform."

For much of 1997 and 1998, our nation's representatives were embroiled in lengthy, irresolute Senate and House hearings on campaign finance reform that yielded startling evidence of the extent to which obscene sums of private money influence public policy. Both parties were guilty of reliance upon massive amounts of "soft money" in running their national campaigns in 1996: the Republicans $138.2 million and the Democrats $123.9 million. The Federal Election Commission FEC, following a year-long investigation, declared that the Republican and Democratic Presidential Campaign Committees had to return more than $24 million. Even with this knowledge, it is impossible to be sanguine about the final sum spent, which, according to the FEC, exceeded $2.7 billion!

The Democratic Party in particular suffered the brunt of the criticism and not merely because of the Republican majority in both houses of Congress, but because of inappropriate and illegal dealings with political operatives linked to unscrupulous Asian investors and to the defense establishment of the People's Republic of China. In the course of the hearings it became clear that the Clinton administration took every opportunity to raise cash, from arranging for the use of the Lincoln Bedroom of the White House, to scheduling coffees with the president and vice president. One witness before the Senate committee, Roger Tamraz, was painfully ingenuous in stating how one brokers political connections by testifying that he had donated $300,000 to the Democratic National Committee for the chance to meet with President Clinton and exhort him to favor the construction of an oil pipeline from the Caspian Sea through Central Asia. He believed that such generosity would influence policy outcomes in a manner favorable to his interests and when this did not happen, he baldly asserted (before the committee) that he would have gladly donated $300,000 more for a "more private meeting"!

Even more arresting is how little has been done to remedy the problem, as an overwhelming number of U.S. citizens have demanded political reform. A March 1997 *New York Times* poll revealed that nine out of ten U.S. voters wanted "comprehensive finance reform." According to Common Cause, a more recent Melman Poll yielded an 80–90 percent affirmative response on the issue of campaign finance reform. Campaign reform bills have been stalled in committees, riders have been attached to them, and neither house of Congress has been able to put it to a vote. The campaign finance debacle is no doubt understood by high-level Chinese leaders, which may explain why U. S. complaints against Chinese corruption create little obligation to recognize them as serious.

Money commands enormous significance, whether in the politics of democracies or dictatorships. In the late 1990s the ideals of both of our polities—Chinese and U.S.—have been commoditized. Notions like one man, one vote or freedom of speech stand as ideals in tension with which our political and social lives are lived. The Bill of Rights is not an indefeasible possession of U.S. citizens but a contractual complex for the exercise of politics, not unlike the guidelines for the good Communist. That public trust has eroded in the United States is clear from figures measuring a mere 45 to 50 percent of registered voters who ever exercise their privilege in national elections; indeed, most polls indicate that a great majority of U. S. voters eschew politics. Political outcomes appear to average voters to be driven by wealth, thus persuading them of the superfluity of their vote. A declining public confidence is highlighted by the disparity between citizen sentiment and political action. Taking advantage of a population that has the vote but declines to exercise it and elected officials' ignorance of public concern resembles the Chinese Communist Party's defiance of China's citizenry.

CONCLUSION

Jiang Zemin, China's president and Communist Party general secretary, began his official state visit to the United States in the fall of 1997 with a stop in Hawaii. During his brief stay in the fiftieth state he was photographed swimming, inelegantly though competently, in the waves off Waikiki. After his one-hour swim, he commented on the warmth and translucence of the waters and stated that "back at home" he tries to swim some everyday. Jiang's aquatic habits were the focus of media attention for a time, insofar as they provided a contrastive image of the hard-line leader pleasurably cavorting in the surf—a regular guy. Upon seeing photographs of the event, I could not repress an instinctual visual association with Mao Zedong's choreographed swim across the Yangzi River in 1966, nor could I stop thinking of the chairman's oft-quoted figurative phrasing of the Communist Party's natural legitimacy: "the Party is to the masses, as a fish is to water." Viewing footage of Jiang's labored negotiation of the waves, I wondered if the water might rise or grow sufficiently turbulent to provoke a physical memory of the mass line dictum—anything that might bring China's president face-to-face with the genuine fount of his authority.

Though his penchant for swimming may garner U. S. appreciation, such antics remind Chinese back home of the ocean-wide space separating them from their self-appointed leaders and the greatest corruption of all—the fraud of the Party-state. The overwhelming majority of Chinese do not, because they cannot, swim. Thus, in a very odd way, the behavior of China's president suggests a greater commonality with U.S. residents than with Chinese, and if so, then we have grounds to note the chasm between leaders and the led and to emphasize the comparability of our situations.

Now that relations between China and the United States have changed in such a way as to challenge the manner in which each has long understood the other, U.S. citizens are keenly aware of China. With a joint declaration in June 1998, the two countries formed a "strategic partnership" for the twenty-first century, the greater mutual, political intimacy of which has made the business of one the business of the other. China and, all subjects related to it, is news in the United States and, in a comparatively brief time, U.S. citizens have learned a great deal about their former international adversary. What we can recognize, now that the ideological mystifications of the past have dissolved somewhat, is that China and the United States have much in common and the sensationalist aspects of the former's corruption scandals must not blind us to our definitive points of comparability.[26] Yet, even with respect to the specific behaviors that qualify as political corruption, both nations are close rather than far.

In order that the invocation of China's national concern with corruption not be misunderstood as a self-righteous Western criticism, I am asserting that we can—no, we must—speak respectfully across our differences, understanding as we do that no one nation holds the norm of norms and that the consequences for believing so are globally catastrophic. This, in the end, is what makes China's ominous national problem as meaningful for us as it is for them.

NOTES

I am an intellectual historian of China, a text scholar who, in the course of his researches and language training, has lived a few years in China and Taiwan. Thus,

I am not a "Chinahand" and so it is with a measure of hesitancy that I venture into the world of contemporary Chinese politics by offering some thoughts on the meaning of corruption. Nonetheless, there is much that the informed observer can glean from experience of the everyday in China and from the Chinese government's tireless documentation of the causes and consequences of its national problem. For this reason I consider my observations and judgments about corruption in China to be the impressions of an interloper. By way of these impressions I hope to provide greater insight into Chinese corruption and to provoke reflection on its curious resonance with contemporary U.S. political culture. In preparing this chapter I have benefited from the careful criticisms and wise counsel of Timothy Weston, Susan McEachern, and, especially, Susan Blum. Students from my History 4612/5612 course, "Sex, Freedom, and Economy in Contemporary China," also offered needed insight. The essay's strengths reflect the generous and creative intervention of all of my readers and critics, while its remaining weaknesses and shortcomings are entirely my own.

1. "The People's Republic of China Criminal Law" (FBIS-CHI-97-056: Beijing, March 17, 1997).

2. The Gang of Four (*Siren bang*)—Jiang Qing, Mao Zedong's second wife, Yao Wenyuan, Wang Hongwen, and Zhang Chunqiao—were identified in the official Party history published in 1980 as the individuals responsible for the excesses of the Great Proletarian Cultural Revolution (1966–1976). Filmed excerpts of their trial were shown on national television and all were found guilty of crimes against the state.

3. "Former Beijing Party Chief Chen Xitong to Get 15 Years," *Inside China Today* Web page. ⟨http://www.insidechina.com⟩, August 12, 1998, 2.

4. "China: Guangdong: Main Cadres under Investigation," *Hong Kong Cheng Ming*, November 1, 1998 (FBIS-CHI-98-315), 3.

5. Andrew Nathan, *Chinese Democracy* (Berkeley: University of California Press, 1985), viii.

6. A recent example of such unethical or illegal official misconduct was the case of the former agriculture secretary who was charged with thirty counts of malfeasance, including bribery and corruption.

7. Liu Binyan and Perry Link, "A Great Leap Backward?," *New York Review of Books*, vol. 45, no. 15 (October 8, 1998): 20.

8. Andrew B. Kipnis, *Producing Guanxi: Sentiment, Self, and Subculture in a North China Village* (Durham, N.C.: Duke University Press, 1997).

9. John Girling, "Preface," *Corruption, Capitalism and Democracy* (London and New York: Routledge, 1997), vii.

10. This is an incomplete catalogue of the types of corruption encountered in the course of the recent campaigns to establish clean government, distilled from "Work Report Delivered by the CPC Central Commission for Discipline Inspection to the 15th CPC National Congress, Approved at the Ninth Plenary Session of the

Central Commission for Discipline Inspection on September 9, 1997" (Beijing: Xinhua Domestic News Service, September 24, 1997), (FBIS-CHI-97-267), 2–5, and Gao You, "Display New Achievements and Usher in the 15th National People's Congress: Jilin Achieves Substantial Results in Anticorruption Work," *Changchun Jilin Ribao,* August 13, 1997 (FBIS CHI-97-245: Changchun, September 2, 1997).

11. The *Sanfan* (Three Anti) campaign of 1951–52 was aimed at local cadres and their three objectionable practices: corruption, waste, and bureaucracy.

12. See *The Criminal Law and the Criminal Procedure Law of the People's Republic of China* (Beijing: Foreign Languages Press, 1984).

13. This practice was a consequence of the pre-revolution, extra-legal right of officials to *nuoyong,* meaning to draw from public funds for private needs on the condition that such monies were returned. See the illuminating discussion in Julia Kwong, *The Political Economy of Corruption in China* (Armonk, N.Y.: M. E. Sharpe, 1997), 9–21.

14. "Work Report Delivered by the CPC Central Commission for Discipline Inspection to the 15th CPC National Congress," 4.

15. "Jiang Zemin's Report at the 15th National Congress of the Communist Party of China," 29.

16. "Work Report Delivered by the CPC Central Commission for Discipline Inspection to the 15th CPC National Congress," 3.

17. Liu and Link, "A Great Leap Backward?," 21.

18. He Qinglian, *Zhongguo de xianjing* (Hong Kong: Mingjing chubanshe, 1998), as quoted in Liu and Link, "A Great Leap Backward?," 19.

19. Min Qi and Li Wei, "Dalu shimin zhengzhi taidu diaocha" (An Investigation of the Political Attitudes of Mainland Citydwellers), *Zhongguo Shibao* (China Daily), October 15–21, 1995, 48–49.

20. "Auditor Uncovers $14 Billion Misuse of Public Money," *Agence France Presse,* Beijing, August 17, 1999.

21. This modification of the celebrated Maoist axiom was first heard in the late 1980s among Beijing's alienated youth and is discussed in the context of the emergent culture of rock music by Andrew F. Jones, *Like a Knife: Ideology and Genre in Contemporary Chinese Popular Music,* Cornell East Asia Series, no. 57 (Ithaca, N.Y.: Cornell University East Asia Program, 1992).

22. "Peasants Win Lawsuit against Town Government," *Heilongjiang Provincial Radio Service,* Harbin, Heilongjiang Province, *FBIS,* December 21, 1990, as quoted in *China since Tiananmen: Political, Economic, and Social Conflicts,* Lawrence R. Sullivan, ed. (Armonk, N.Y.: M. E. Sharpe, 1995), 111–112.

23. Marlowe Hood, "Political Jokes Mock Chinese Leadership," *South China Morning Post,* December 7, 1991, 5, as quoted in Sullivan, *China since Tiananmen,* 108.

24. Liu Shao-chi (Liu Shaoqi), *How to Be a Good Communist* (Lectures Delivered at the Institute of Marxism-Leninism in Yenan [Yan'an], July 1939) (Boulder, Colo.: Panther Publications, 1967), 8–9.

25. Li Peng, "Resolutely Wage Struggle against Corruption," *Renmin ribao,* September 27, 1993, *FBIS,* September 30, 1993.

26. This is the rather admirable conceptual approach taken by Thomas Metzger and Ramon Myers in their recent policy work, one that I hope will be heeded by politicians in the course of the primaries for the 2000 national election. See Thomas A. Metzger and Ramon H. Myers, *Greater China and U.S. Foreign Policy: The Choice between Confrontation and Mutual Respect* (Stanford: Hoover Institution Press, 1996).

SUGGESTED READINGS

Geremie R. Barmé, *In the Red: On Contemporary Chinese Culture* (New York: Columbia University Press, 1999).

Richard Bernstein, "China-Basher Bashes Bashing," *New York Times,* Sunday, June 29, 1997, 16.

Michael Dutton, *Streetlife China* (Cambridge: Cambridge University Press, 1998).

W. J. F. Jenner, *The Tyranny of History: The Roots of China's Crisis* (London: Penguin Books, 1994).

Chalmers Johnson, *Nationalism and the Market: China As a Superpower* (Cardiff, Calif.: Japan Policy Research Institute, Working Paper no. 22, July 1996).

Andrew B. Kipnis, *Producing Guanxi: Sentiment, Self, and Subculture in a North China Village* (Durham, N.C.: Duke University Press, 1997).

Julia Kwong, *The Political Economy of Corruption in China* (Armonk, N.Y.: M. E. Sharpe, 1997).

Liu Binyan and Perry Link, "A Great Leap Backward?," *New York Review of Books,* vol. 45, no. 15 (October 8, 1998).

Richard Madsen, *China and the American Dream: A Moral Inquiry* (Berkeley: University of California Press, 1995).

Thomas A. Metzger and Ramon H. Myers, *Greater China and U.S. Foreign Policy: The Choice between Confrontation and Mutual Respect* (Stanford: Hoover Institution Press, 1996).

Andrew J. Nathan, *Chinese Democracy* (Berkeley: University of California Press, 1985).

Henry Rosemont, Jr., *A Chinese Mirror: Moral Reflections on Economy and Society* (LaSalle, Ill.: Open Court, 1991).

Lawrence R. Sullivan, ed., *China since Tiananmen: Political, Economic, and Social Conflicts* (Armonk, N.Y.: M. E. Sharpe, 1995).

Ezra Vogel, ed., *Living with China: U.S.–China Relations in the Twenty-First Century* (New York: W. W. Norton & Co., 1997).

Wei Jingsheng, *The Courage to Stand Alone: Letters from Prison and Other Writings* (New York: Viking, 1997).

3

China's Many Faces:

Ethnic, Cultural, and Religious Pluralism

Susan D. Blum

The noblest countries, England, France, and Italy, are those where the blood is the most mixed. . . . The fact of race, which was originally crucial . . . thus becomes increasingly less important. Human history is essentially different from zoology, and race is not everything, . . . and one does not have the right to go through the world fingering people's skulls, and taking them by the throat saying "You are of our blood; you belong to us!" Aside from anthropological characteristics, there are such things as reason, justice, the true, and the beautiful, which are the same for all. . . . What we have just said of race applies to language too. Language invites people to unite, but it does not force them to do so. . . . There is something in man which is superior to language, namely, the will. . . . Can one not have the same sentiments and the same thoughts, and love the same things in different languages? . . . Th[e] exclusive concern with language, like an excessive preoccupation with race, has its dangers and its drawbacks. Such exaggerations enclose one within a specific culture, considered as national; one limits oneself, one hems oneself in. . . . Religion cannot supply an adequate basis for the constitution of a modern nationality either. . . . A nation is a soul, a spiritual principle. Two things, which in truth are but one, constitute this soul or spiritual principle. One lies in the past, one in the present.
—Ernest Renan, "Qu'est-ce qu'une nation?," 1882

Americans most often receive news of China through three basic images: First is Political China, where everyone is preoccupied with the intricacies of political organization—who is premier, prime minister, party secretary, minister of this and that. Visually, this looks like a row of grim, late-middle-aged men either standing or seated, dressed in military garb or

Fig. 3.1. The many faces of China. (Photos by Susan Blum)

increasingly natty Western-style suits, listening to speeches or marching in a political ritual. The second image is the Big Bad Chinese State in all its manifestations: human rights violations, political prisoners, censorship, the Communist Party's fierce ideological grasp on people's beliefs, successfully promulgating the Party line about Chinese civilization. This one looks like prisoners on their way to execution, tanks threatening lone protesters in Tian'anmen Square, monks beaten in Tibet. The third image is Business China, the most commonly portrayed China since the late 1980s. This image focuses on money making—joint ventures (preferably with American companies), factories, housing projects, and so forth. One sees it portrayed in shiny coastal buildings, in cellular-phone-toting, motorscooter-riding, well-dressed and permed young people or in close-ups of the merchandise now available in the glittery department stores of China's cities. A fourth image is little seen now—that of Poor China, the one we pitied when we were children, forced to eat our vegetables because "children are starving in China." Bold journalists occasionally remind their readers that this China has not disappeared, and acute photojournalists note the contrasts between the increasing wealth of China's fortunate and the increasing misery of those who fall through the wide cracks.

Still, despite the existence of some variety in the Chinas presented to American viewers, the China that emerges recalls the image I have when I visit friends who live just outside Washington, D.C. The centers of their world are largely contained within the Beltway, like a New Yorker's view of the United States, where everything west of the Hudson River fades off into inconsequentiality. But just as one gets a different view of the United States from Colorado or from visiting Haitian vodou (voodoo) organizations in Brooklyn, so there are alternative views of China.

I am a cultural anthropologist who has spent most of my time in China in the city of Kunming, which is near Burma, in southwest China. This chapter relies on my own field experience as well as the research of other scholars. I will challenge any assumptions about China's uniformity, introducing three aspects of China's pluralism, though there are, of course, others that one could adduce as well. (My choice of three, both in the initial images and in my corrective, is arbitrary, though the folklorist Alan Dundes has provided a fascinating psychoanalytic discussion of Americans' use of three to list things: red, white, blue; lions, tigers, bears; the good, the bad, and the ugly; and so forth.)[1] The China that exists beyond the big three images is one that even visitors to the country might miss if they did not

Fig. 3.2. Yunnan Province

have an introduction to it. The first subject is one that may be a bit startling to Americans who can scarcely distinguish Japanese from Chinese (on the basis of appearance).

ETHNIC DIVERSITY

My first subject is China's ethnic diversity. China is often believed to be ethnically quite homogeneous, with black-haired Chinese-speaking people constituting the majority known as Han. Indeed, the percentage of people officially classified as Han is extraordinarily high—about 92 percent (though falling). That, of course, still leaves 8 percent of 1.2 billion—96 million, or larger than the population of Mexico—who do not claim Han identity. I cannot discuss here the problematic aspects of the category "Han," except to suggest that, like a "generic American," it is hardly without a history and evolution.

My concern here is with the 8 percent, or 96 million people, classified by the Chinese state as *minzu*, a category halfway between "nationality" like in the former Soviet Union and "ethnic group" like in the United States. *Minzu* was borrowed from Japanese and has come to mean "ethnic group."

Ethnic minorities are literally *shaoshuminzu*, but used alone the term *minzu* almost always refers to minorities. Some of these are fairly well known, like the Tibetans—the seventh largest group, about 4 million. Some are so few in number that only specialists are familiar with them, like the Hezhe, of whom there are only 1,500.

The current classification scheme arose immediately after the founding of the People's Republic of China (PRC) in 1949 and has roots in three types of conceptual soil:

1. Qing dynasty (1644–1911) administration of border areas, in which there was a government bureau designated to handle Mongolian and Tibetan affairs.
2. Soviet-style nationality policy, especially the anti-nationality policies of Stalin, claiming a role as an interpreter of Marx.
3. Late-nineteenth- and early-twentieth-century considerations of nationalism as a desirable force. The goal of transforming a dynastic empire into a modern nation-state was shared by many countries in this century; ethnic groups were seen as the building blocks of nations, with a single majority group seen as central to the nation.[2] Chinese intellectuals looked at Japan, Germany, the Soviet Union, and the United States to see how such nations had been constituted and what the appropriate relations were between constituents. The Kuomintang (KMT or GMD), the Nationalist party that claimed authority from the fall of the last Chinese dynasty in 1911 until the Communist victory in 1949, was ruthless from the beginning; ethnic groups were expected to assimilate to the majority. The government saw its role as "encouraging" such assimilation through fairly intolerant repression of difference.

The nationalities policies of the PRC are built upon contradictory premises (that nations are desired in a society's modernization process and at the same time that they create undesirable divisions) and hence many of the implementations of the policies have vacillated. Nationality/ethnic differences were considered inevitable in the present, but in a distant utopian future, with the accomplishment of Communism these differences were expected to wither and die, just like the nation itself. Meanwhile, differences among groups were acceptable; at more tolerant moments, they were encouraged, while at more repressive moments they were punished. A swing between repression and tolerance of ethnic difference has followed that of political openness or closure.

In order to determine what the constituents were of this new jigsaw puzzle, using a new classificatory logic, Chinese social scientists were enlisted, to differentiate "genuine" and "spurious" cultural groups. Borrowing a notion from the Soviet Union, scholars evaluated each applicant group on the basis of four criteria: common territory, common language, common economic life, common psychological (cultural) life.[3] Notice that "race" is not among them. The classificatory schema as it stands does not focus on descent or biology but rather on contemporary practices, though it is usually assumed that the contemporary practices are similar because of shared history. People often claim that they can identify ethnic minorities by looking, but their judgment is based on a *gestalt* of clothing, gait, cleanliness, hair style, and many other items. It is common for individuals to change ethnic identity, either becoming Han through assimilation of Han civilization or becoming minority through marriage or migration to minority areas.

The use of appearance for racial/ethnic identification seems obvious to people in the United States but is not the primary concern in Chinese ethnic identification. Anthropologists have been demonstrating for quite some time that the physical appearance of members of given *populations* is not a reliable indicator of genetic relationship. There are *no* physical features that can uniquely specify any so-called race; all "races" contain virtually all physical features, though in varying proportions. There is much more overlap among groups than distinctions between them. Skin color is most salient for North Americans (this is what pops into our minds as an obvious index of identity), but all "races" contain a continuum of skin colors. It is as if one were to say "men are taller than women"—true in many cases and true on average, but there are certainly cases where one could find women who are taller than men. Anthropologists have avoided the term "race" as a biological (as opposed to cultural) category for many decades, because superficial physical appearance does not predict what other genetic traits a person possesses. In terms of classifying populations, biological anthropologists tend to use frequencies of genetic features much more than those of appearance (a difference between genotype and phenotype).[4] In the case of China, there may be physical features that tend to occur more often in some groups (Tibetans and Yi, for example, are often tall) but this does not provide a definitive means of classifying, and this is *not* what the Chinese use for classification.

With 400–500 applications, recognition has to date been granted to only fifty-five groups, resulting in the schema we now use. It was determined that some groups shared enough traits with other groups to be merged with them, often because linguists determined their dialects to be mutually intelligible. Other groups were concluded to be authentically distinctive, even though they had believed themselves to be part of another group (see table 3.1).

New names were proposed for many groups. In the past, Han often referred to minorities, either by terms for the "barbarians" of the four directions (*Man Yi Rong Di*) or by other pejorative terms, such as "Lolo" for groups now called Yi, where Lolo was the Chinese version of a word meaning a basket said to hold the soul of a person upon death—an allusion to apparently "superstitious" beliefs. Respect for minority wishes was to be signaled by renaming them with desirable terms.

Of the fifty-five minority groups recognized by China, nearly all these groups live on China's borders. The territory inhabited largely by minority groups constitutes 50–60 percent of the area now claimed by China. Tom Grunfeld explains the state's deep concern over this fairly small fraction of its population as stemming from three sources: (1) this area buffers strategic international borders, (2) there are critical natural resources in this territory, and (3) China's population needs area into which to expand.[5] While ordinary people living in China's central areas may have little direct experience with minorities and may pay little attention to them, the government has devoted an enormous amount of effort to minority policies, support of minority areas, or repression of minority activities. In areas where there are sizable numbers of minorities, majorities are quite aware of them, often bemoaning the fact that there are some benefits associated with minority status—including exemption from the one-child policy (in some areas only). Han often told me that individuals asked for classification as minorities—for example, if they had one Han parent and one minority parent—to gain such benefits.[6]

The government promotes harmony and unity among nationalities, but in fact this is not always borne out. Many people of ethnic minority status told me of instances of hostility, disdain, or prejudice. A dear friend, who is Yi, came from the countryside to Kunming. At first she was quite reluctant to venture out in her native dress, fearing ridicule or worse. In time, she appeared less and less obviously *minzu* and grew more bold. Yet I have observed Han prejudice directed at her and other minority friends in a combination of ethnic and socioeconomic hauteur, mitigated only slightly by my presence as a foreign observer. Most ethnic minorities, especially in southwest China, live in rural areas where the levels of education and

Table 3.1 Ethnic Minorities

Ethnic Group	Population (1990 census)	World Religion	Principal Location
Han	1,042,482,187	Buddhism, Daoism	
Zhuang	15,489,630		Guangxi, Yunnan, Guangdong, Guizhou, Hunan
Manchus	9,821,180		Liaoning, Heilongjiang, Hebei, Gansu, Shandong, Inner Mongolia, Xin jang, Ningxia; Beijing, Chengdu, Xi'an, Guangzhou, and other cities
Hui	8,602,978	Islam	Ningxia, Xinjiang, Gansu, Qinghai, Henan, Hebei, Shandong, Yunnan
Miao	7,398,035	Christianity (some)	Guizhou, Yunnan, Hunan, Sichuan, Guangxi, Hainan, Hubei
Uighur, Weiwu'er	7,214,431	Islam	Xinjiang
Yi	6,572,173	Christianity (some)	Sichuan, Yunnan, Guizhou, Guangxi
Tujia	5,704,223		Hunan, Hubei
Mongols	4,806,849	Buddhism (Lamaism)	Inner Mongolia, Liaoning, Jilin, Heilongjiang, Xinjiang, Qinghai, Gansu, Ningxia, Hebei, Henan, Sichuan, Yunnan, Beijing
Tibetans	4,593,330	Buddhism (Lamaism)	Tibet, Qinghai, Gansu, Sichuan, Yunnan
Bouyei	2,545,059		Guizhou
Dong	2,514,014		Hunan, Guizhou, Guangxi
Yao	2,134,013		Guangxi, Hunan, Yunnan, Guangdong, Guizhou, Jiangxi
Koreans	1,920,597	Christianity	Jilin, Heilongjiang, Liaoning
Bai	1,594,827	Buddhism (Theravada)	Yunnan, Sichuan, Guizhou

Table 3.1 Ethnic Minorities (*continued*)

Ethnic Group	Population (1990 census)	World Religion	Principal Location
Hani	1,253,952		Yunnan
Kazaks	1,111,718	Islam	Xinjiang, Qinghai, Gansu
Li	1,110,900		Hainan
Dai	1,025,128	Buddhism (Theravada)	Yunnan
She	630,378		Zhejiang, Jiangxi, Anhui, Guangdong
Lisu	574,856	Christianity (some)	Yunnan, Sichuan
Gelao, Gelo	437,997		Guizhou, Yunnan, Guangxi
Lahu	411,476	Buddhism	Yunnan
Dongxiang	373,872	Islam	Gansu, Xinjiang
Va, Wa	351,974	Buddhism (Theravada) (some)	Yunnan
Shui	345,993		Guizhou, Guangxi
Naxi	278,009		Yunnan, Sichuan, Tibet
Qiang	198,252		Sichuan
Tu	191,624	Buddhism (Lamaism)	Qinghai, Gansu
Xibe	172,847		Xinjiang
Mulam	159,328		Guangxi
Kirgiz	141,549	Islam	Xinjiang, Heilongjiang
Daur	121,357		Inner Mongolia, Heilongjiang
Jingpo	119,209	Buddhism (Theravada)	Yunnan
Salar	87,697	Islam	Qinghai, Gansu, Xinjiang
Blang, Bulang	82,280	Buddhism (Theravada)	Yunnan
Maonan	71,968		Guangxi
Tajiks	33,538	Islam	Xinjiang
Primi, Pumi	29,657		Yunnan, Sichuan
Achang	27,708	Buddhism (Theravada)	Yunnan
Nu	27,123		Yunnan

(*continued*)

Table 3.1 Ethnic Minorities (*continued*)

Ethnic Group	Population (1990 census)	World Religion	Principal Location
Ewenkis	26,315	Christianity (Eastern Orthodox)	Inner Mongolia, Heilongjiang
Gin, Jing	18,915		Guangxi
Jino, Jinuo	18,021		Yunnan
Benglong, De'ang	15,462	Buddhism (Theravada)	Yunnan
Uzbeks	14,502	Islam	Xinjiang
Russians	13,504	Christianity (Eastern Orthodox)	Xinjiang, Inner Mongolia
Yugurs	12,297	Buddhism (Lamaism)	Gansu
Bonan	12,212	Islam	Gansu
Monba, Moinba	7,475		Tibet
Oroqen	6,965		Northeast China
Derung, Drung	5,816		Yunnan
Tatars	4,873	Islam	Xinjiang
Hezhe, Hezhen	4,245		Heilongjiang
Gaoshan	2,909		Taiwan, Shanghai, Beijing, Wuhan, Fujian
Lhoba	2,312		Tibet
Others not identified	49,341		
TOTAL	1,133,682,501		

(Sources: Mackerras 1994: 238–240, 1990 Census, Ma 1989)

income are quite low (see Oakes, this volume). When they interact with urban Han, they are assumed to be poor, ignorant, and sometimes generally "backward." A kernel of truth lies within this prejudice; poverty and illiteracy are much higher in rural areas, and the majority of ethnic minorities are found in these areas.

One of the most significant policies at the political level concerns the establishment of five "autonomous regions" (*zizhiqu*). These are provincial-sized administrative areas in which minorities were traditionally a majority and were supposed to have substantial political power (see table 3.2). In fact, minority cadres have often occupied positions of secondary power, sometimes little more than ornamentation. A real challenge has been the fact that before 1949, most minorities were not educated in the Chinese system and were not appropriate for positions of power. Some traditional "feudal" leaders were placed into leadership positions, while younger people began to be educated in newer ways of practicing politics—and were Sinified. In many ways the classification of minorities in China is similar to the project of ethnic identification among Native Americans; a fascinating comparison could be drawn between the reservation system in the United States and Canada and the system of autonomous areas in China. The reservations in the United States were largely begun as a way of containing Native Americans in remote areas, following the violent wars with the Anglo populations. They were meant to provide subsistence, often with the support of outside resources, since they often involved relocating tribes into areas that were not their traditional homelands and combining groups that had little historical connection. Poverty and ill health often characterize life on the reservations. These are also true of areas with dominant minority populations in China. In China the penetration of the central government is quite significant; policies set by the government may be vetted by local, native officials, but this is at the pleasure of the nonminority authorities. Autonomous areas exist at all three levels of administrative division: 5 province-level autonomous regions (*zizhiqu*), 31 autonomous prefectures (*zizhizhou*), and 96 autonomous counties and banners (*zizhixian*). They are not intended to be independent, but different rules may apply in them than in the country as a whole. Some, for instance, are multilingual, in recognition of the fact that they contain several different groups in substantial numbers. There are many areas of minority life in which the state has intervened, differing with the different groups. Some receive special subsidies in recognition of the fact that their income is significantly below the

Table 3.2   Autonomous Regions

Autonomous Regions	Significant Ethnic Groups	Date Established
Inner Mongolia Autonomous Region	Mongolian, Hui, Korean, Manchu, Daur, Oroqen, Xibe, Russian	1947
Xinjiang Uighur Autonomous Region	Uighur, Kazak, Hui, Kirgiz, Uzbek, Mongolian, Daur, Xibe, Tajik, Tatar, Russian, Manchu	1955
Ningxia Hui Autonomous Region	Hui, Dongxiang, Bonan, Salar, Tu, Manchu	1958
Guangxi Zhuang Autonomous Region	Zhuang, Yao, Miao, Dong, Mulam, Maonan, Hui, Yi, Shui, Jing, Gelo	1958
Tibet Autonomous Region	Tibetan, Hui, Moinba, Lhoba	1965

(Source: Ma 1989: 434–448)

average in nearby areas. Some are exempt from the one- or two-child policy. Some have bilingual schools.

In the remainder of this section, I will introduce a few of the fifty-five groups and some points of significance of each (see figure 3.3).

The largest is the Zhuang, with 15.5 million, related to people across the border in Vietnam. The Zhuang were largely assimilated, Sinified, when the PRC admonished them to pay more attention to their own cultural characteristics.[7] Though this seems counterintuitive, because of the principles of nationality differences and classification, the Zhuang were encouraged to differentiate themselves from Han culture. Some regard the Guangxi Zhuang Autonomous Region as a trial before the government tackled its most difficult case, that of Tibet, the fifth, and last, autonomous region to be established, in 1965.

Ten of the fifty-five recognized *minzu* are Muslim (Hui, Uighur, Kazak, Tatar, Tajik, Uzbek, Kirgiz, Dongxiang, Salar, Bonan). They speak a wide range of languages, from Indo-European (spoken by Tajiks, who speak a kind of Iranian) to Turkic/Altaic (spoken by Kazakhs, Kirghiz, Tatars, Uzbeks, and Uighurs, Yugurs, Salars—seven Turkic minorities)[8] to Chi-

Fig. 3.3. Distribution of China's ethnic minorities

nese (Hui). They total about 17 million, and two of China's five "autonomous regions" are dominated by Muslims: the Xinjiang Uighur Autonomous Region (formerly called Chinese Turkestan) and the Ningxia Hui Autonomous Region. Uighurs—the fifth largest minority ethnic group in China—number about 7 million. Uighur separatists in Xinjiang, in northwest China, have been creating violent incidents in the name of pan-Turkism, wishing to unite with other Turkic-speaking Muslims across the border in Kazakhstan, Kirghizstan, and Tajikstan (see Dautcher, this volume). Scholars who focus on these groups are often puzzled at the Western media neglect of these groups and their cause, seeing their struggles as quite analogous to the Tibetans' struggles for independence, albeit without a charismatic leader such as the Dalai Lama. There have been Muslim rebellions in China for at least a century, and some, notably the Ili Rebellion in Xinjiang (1944–49), have created a great challenge to the authority of the Chinese nation-state.

The Hui ethnic group—third largest minority in China, at about 8.6 million—live everywhere in China, mostly in cities. They are not usually concentrated in particular areas but live throughout China, hence are probably the most widely known by inhabitants of central China. Chinese-speaking Muslims, they probably have some central Asian ancestry dating from the seventh to the fourteenth century,[9] followed by frequent inter-marriage with Han. Devout Hui chant the Koran five times a day in Persian, observe Ramadan, and refuse to eat pork. At least a thousand go to Mecca each year. Han often clash with Hui, and there is no shortage of stories of Han–Hui conflict. Some Hui have begun cultivating ties with the greater Islamic world outside China, which supports China's foreign policy interests in some ways (political alliance, economic cooperation) while also threatening them in other ways (fostering religion and allegiance to sacred rather than secular authority).

The Hui are a fairly visible group in Kunming. The city has five mosques, though the most visible and well attended was torn down in 1997 (perhaps to be rebuilt). Hui are often mentioned for their "independence" and lack of cooperation, including the possession of weapons and being fearless, "unafraid to die" (*bu pa si*), making them a formidable challenge to the authority of the central government.

Other groups with secessionist tendencies include Mongols. The province-sized autonomous region of Inner Mongolia acknowledges the traditional dominance of Mongols in this region, though Mongols have not been the majority for quite some time. The people of this autonomous region share many features with the Mongolians who live in the independent country just to their north. Some rely on pastoralism as a subsistence system, and some speak the Mongolian language as their native tongue. Chinese government policies have reflected disdain for traditional Mongolian herding practices for centuries; in this century the efforts to transform such practices have been quite effective, often with disastrous consequences.

Not all minority groups have secessionist tendencies, yet they often have many features that set them apart from the other groups surrounding them. For instance, in Yunnan province in southwest China, where twenty-five minority *minzu* have been recognized, there are groups (Wa) who are reported to have practiced headhunting as recently as the 1950s. These people are often seen as extremely "primitive" and in need of guidance by the more developed Han people, who are the majority group. Many ethnic groups have their own system of religious beliefs, usually called "animist," speak their own non-Chinese language, wear different clothing, practice different marriage customs, and have their own forms of musical, verbal, and visual arts.

The Dai ethnic group in Yunnan are kin to the Thai people of Thailand: they speak the same non-Chinese language (Thai), practice the same brand of Buddhism (Theravada, in contrast to the Jingtu, Pure Land, Buddhism practiced by most Chinese Buddhists), wear the same clothes, and eat the same food. There are just over a million Dai in China. They are often mentioned in conversation as being gentle, clean, and picturesque; their pavilion at minority villages is usually the most elaborate, and their representation is found in virtually all complimentary contexts, such as tourist brochures or murals.

Other ethnic groups include 1.9 million Koreans in northeast China, some 13,500 Russians, and 9.8 million Manchus. Some groups are nomadic pastoralists, raising livestock and living in grasslands. Some are fishers, living on boats. Some eke out a living in fairly barren mountain regions, like the various Yi of Sichuan and Yunnan (about 6.6 million, the sixth most numerous minority ethnic group). Some eat corn as their staple food, some potatoes, some rice. Historically acute readers will recall that corn and potatoes are so-called New World crops, introduced from the Americas by Portuguese missionaries via the Philippines in the fifteenth century. Recent in Chinese terms, these are considered "traditional" foods for these groups by most analysts.

Most Chinese know of ethnic minorities as quaint relics of humanity's more "primitive" past, seeing their images on China's paper money and in song-and-dance performances that portray each ethnic group in succession—often by performers of different ethnic groups. Those who travel may visit "minority villages," ethnic theme parks where young people represent their "typical" rural brothers and sisters (see Lam, this volume). These exist in many areas in China, with a famous one on the outskirts of Kunming. It is expensive to enter, and only some of the more dramatic minorities are represented. One of my most memorable sights is of the "primitive" village, portraying four ethnic groups categorized as "primitive." Their religion is "animism," they practiced headhunting and totemism, produced fertility symbols, and constructed longhouses where unmarried youth could meet.

Ethnic minorities are often misunderstood, stereotyped, and scapegoated. Yet the enduring presence and increase of ethnic minorities suggests that they are important for an understanding of China, beyond the small percentage of the population that they represent.

This brief introduction of minority groups and some of their characteristics should alert the reader to some of the complexities China faces—considerations of how to combine a tolerance for cultural diversity with goals of national integration and modernization. China has vacillated between policies of tolerance for pluralism and policies that urge assimilation or prohibit traditional practices. It is currently in a period of relative tolerance, yet there are clear limits to how much minority practices may diverge from those of the majority. Tibet and increasingly Xinjiang are places where the state feels its political and cultural authority to be greatly challenged. Its response is generally repression.

CULTURAL AND REGIONAL DIVERSITY

Another complicating factor in China, even disregarding the 96 million non-Han, is cultural diversity among Han Chinese. Here I will use "culture" to mean lifeways in general, foodways, and language; my main contrast will be between North and South China. For most of China's history, these areas were not equally part of something we might now term "China proper." South China was incorporated into "China" only in the latter half of the Song dynasty (960–1279)—a thousand years ago, it is true, but still nothing like the virtual eternity that many speak of when talking about China. (In fact, the Song is often considered the beginning of "modern" China, for a variety of economic and social reasons.) At the time, the people living in what is now south China were "barbarians," believed to eat all sorts of repugnant things—snakes, rats, and frogs. In time, these people were Sinified, and many would argue that the cultural and economic centers of China have been southern ever since. The north is the land of government and politics but is otherwise far from being the gravitational center of the polity. The south is the land of rice, water buffalo, dramatic landscapes, richly developed cuisine, and revolution. The north is the land of noodles, steamed bread, garlic, cabbage, and yellow dust.

It is possible to argue that regional identification in China exceeds national identification (though these are hard to assess). People hold very strong stereotypical beliefs about regions other than their own—usually negative: Sichuanese are sly and tricky, Hunanese are quick-tempered, Guangdong people are only interested in business, Shandong people are bumpkins. It is true that the rich in China hop on planes and travel for business and pleasure. For instance, in January 1997 I flew from Kunming to Beijing; my seatmate was a former teacher who is now a stock investor from Shandong. She was returning from a stock-buying trip in Yunnan, where a hot stock market had just opened—people had to buy in person. Similarly, the desperate poor wander the land in search of employment or, failing that, some other way to survive. But still the majority of people in

China scarcely leave their home towns. China's growing middle class *is* traveling for pleasure, but we should be cautious about drawing an analogy from the United States where nearly everyone claims middle-class status. In China most people may still live their entire lives without leaving their own provinces.

In the 1980s and 1990s, the city of Canton, in southern China near Hong Kong, as well as other economically strong regions, refused to pay the full amount of taxes demanded by Beijing. Why should they? They saw themselves as the productive members of the country, contributing to programs that did not benefit their own region at all. (Tension about the issue of taxation is certainly a common feature in China and the United States. Many people dislike paying for things that do not directly benefit them, though one could argue that a common good in a nation benefits all citizens.) The central authority was insufficient to combat regional strength.

There are also differences in physical type between north and south China. In China's southward march, Chinese civilization was adapted by people who encountered it, but the overall population was not annihilated. In general, northerners are taller and have "higher" noses, while "typical" southerners are shorter and have "flatter" faces. Even in matters of kinship there are differences. In south China, lineages—extended families on the male line—often constitute the backbone of villages, with lineage halls supported by a large kinship network. In north China, such clans are not as a rule the core of villages, though people may keep track of their kin relations as well.

Another important aspect of regional diversity involves language. It is a commonplace that there are many dialects of Chinese (see figure 3.4). The official national language, Mandarin (or *Putonghua* or *guoyu*), is the native tongue of only 70 percent of the people of China. That leaves 360 million— one and a half times the population of the United States—who speak some other dialect at home. These "dialects" cannot be understood by speakers of other dialects without long contact and vary as much as European languages such as English and Dutch. The decision whether to call these "dialects" or "languages" has political ramifications, as "languages" are often considered properly to belong to different countries. Victor Mair has attempted to bypass this dilemma by translating the Chinese term *fangyan* as "topolect." This issue is long-standing; Uriel Weinreich, a famous sociolinguist, claimed that "A language is a dialect with an army and a navy"—pointing out the arbitrary division between the two. (This quip is also attributed to George Bernard Shaw.) The standard definition is that

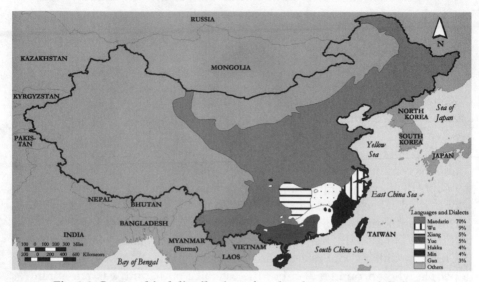

Fig. 3.4. Geographical distribution of spoken languages and dialects

dialects are mutually intelligible, but, of course, there is a continuum rather than a clean boundary between them. Think of Cockney English, or certain varieties of African-American Vernacular English, or French and Italian.

The southern dialects, such as Cantonese and Hokkien, spoken in Taiwan and the province of Fujian, are *gaining* in strength and power as the regions where they are spoken increase their economic power. Literature and films in those languages are flourishing. Even Hakka, the language of a sub-Han ethnic group, often stigmatized and very poor, has risen in status. Deng Xiaoping, the leader of China during its post-Mao transformation, was whispered to be a Hakka (Erbaugh, 1992). Some people have claimed that his 1992 visit to Shenzhen, the first and most spectacular special economic zone near Hong Kong, though usually understood as giving his blessing to economic development, was actually a gesture of support for the Hakkas.[10]

China's policies regarding linguistic pluralism have been much more realistic than most of its early economic policies. Most leaders came from the south. Recordings of Mao Zedong, Sun Yatsen, and Chiang Kai-shek all reveal speakers with nonstandard accents. Such accents are not stigmatized, since they are so common. Many speakers are multilingual, having knowledge of a local and regional variety along with some familiarity with the national language. All education is officially supposed to be conducted in *Putonghua* but in fact in most local schools only the Chinese courses (like American "English"—writing and literature—courses) are actually conducted regularly in *Putonghua*. Complex material is usually presented in local varieties.

The intersection of ethnicity and language produces a complex situation; in most autonomous areas some official status is granted to the dominant minority languages. Many minorities (including most of the Muslim minorities) speak non-Chinese languages; some represent their language in scripts that are not Chinese and not roman—usually inspired by either Sanskrit or Arabic. In the Dehong Dai Jingpo Autonomous Prefecture, on Yunnan's west border, both Dai and Jingpo are "official languages." In practice, this means that government buildings have plaques in three languages (Han Chinese is always included), that in bookstores some works are available in Dai and Jingpo, that radio broadcasts may be done in Dai and Jingpo, and that in some cases elementary school instruction is conducted in the minority languages.

Fig. 3.5. A building in western Yunnan bears its name in three different scripts. (Photo by Susan Blum)

Regional and local diversity has been one of China's greatest challenges and great strengths, at least when acknowledged. Any nationally uniform policies have been accepted differently in different regions, and even with a veneer of uniformity, enormous variations in wealth, style, strength, and social relations lie brewing just beneath the surface.

DIVERSITY OF RELIGIOUS EXPRESSION

Finally, I will address briefly the diversity of religious expression in China, something that casual observers may miss if not seeking to notice it. Officially an atheist state, with a belief in "historical materialism," yet tolerating diversity of religious belief, China nevertheless is host to a great variety of religions, some permitted and others forbidden. China has been tolerating institutional, world religions for several decades now, especially when support has come from foreign "brothers" across national borders. These include Buddhism, Islam, and Christianity. When people from Thailand wanted to build a Theravada-Buddhist temple in Yunnan, the Chinese government permitted it. Muslim investment in religious architecture in northwest China is, sometimes, tolerated (see table 3.3).

Buddhism, whether the popular Tiantai or Jingtu sort commonly practiced, or variants such as Tibetan Buddhism or Theravada Buddhism in southwest China, is flourishing. Some estimate more than 100 million Buddhists—but the figure is misleading since Buddhism is not an exclusive religion, which is to say one can be both Buddhist and the follower of another religion, such as Daoism. Daoist temples, especially in Fujian province, across the Taiwan Straits from Taiwan, are bustling with life and activity. When the economic reforms began in 1978 and 1979, Fujianese first invested in refurbishing their temples, even before they repaired their own homes.[11]

Table 3.3   Religion in China

Religion	Number of Adherents (estimated)
Buddhism	100,000,000
Daoism (Taoism)	?
Protestantism	12,000,000 to 20,000,000
Islam	17,000,000
Catholicism	4,000,000 to 12,000,000

China is a place where religion, commerce, and politics have coexisted for thousands of years,[12] and despite Western inclinations to keep these domains separate, they interact and intersect significantly in contemporary China. It may be the god of wealth who is restored first as people become prosperous, or it may be that religion functions as just another form of insurance. But however explained, religious expression is a significant feature of Chinese life today (see figure 3.6).

Christian missionaries first entered China in the fifteenth century. These were Jesuits (belonging to a scholarly branch of Catholic monks), and their success in China was fairly modest. Their greatest impact may have been back in Europe, where they introduced Chinese thought to curious Europeans. Protestant missionaries, especially of the nineteenth century, had much more success establishing converts in China. Chinese distinguish between "Christians" (i.e., Protestants), *Jidujiaotu*, and "Catholics," *Tianzhujiaotu*, as these entered China in distinct ways and have quite different profiles. Associated with foreign imperialism, missionizing activity was made illegal in 1949, and much policy toward religion has been extremely restrictive in this century.

Missionaries are still illegal, though as every long-term visitor to China

Fig. 3.6. *Caishen* (wealth god) ensconced in a make-do shrine on the northern periphery of Kunming. (Photo by Susan Blum)

knows, there are great numbers of them, well entrenched in a variety of activities—some religious, many economic. The state permits Christian worship but with great restrictions. Chinese Catholics are not allowed to accept the doctrine of papal infallibility, because that would make the Pope higher than the Communist Party, and no human can surpass that august body. But the Catholic Church insists on this doctrine, so if Chinese Catholics want to follow the Vatican's teachings, they do so at their peril. Bishops have been jailed for refusing to renounce their loyalty to the Church. Rather than belonging to world Catholicism, Chinese Catholics must belong to the Chinese Catholic Patriotic Association. In cities throughout China, Christian services are well attended, often overflowing with worshipers. Informers from the state attend as well, so foreign Christians are careful not to associate too much with Chinese Christians, lest a crackdown on religious activities endanger their friends. The very numbers of believers are contested, China claiming 4 million Catholics and the Vatican as many as 12 million.[13]

Protestants also continue to increase in number, much through surreptitious conversion. Many people I have known in China are foreign Protestants sent either by conscience and calling or by an organization to carry out a combination of good works and missionizing. Those who convert then function as liaisons to other Chinese. Protestantism is especially successful among minority groups in Yunnan. Some of these converts explained that Christianity celebrates qualities that they themselves value, such as honesty and humility, while Han Chinese are known to outwit the minorities by being wily and proud.

In stark contrast to the technical tolerance for "religious belief," the official attitude toward less institutionalized practices is of intolerance. "Superstition" is strictly forbidden, as this is believed to threaten people's livelihood and even lives, in extreme cases. This may include spirit possession and other contact with spiritual entities—practices increasingly common, especially in the countryside where the majority of people in China live. These practices, along with more institutionalized religion, were severely punished during the 1950s, 1960s, and 1970s, as stemming from "feudal" ideas. All of these practices, and others, have experienced a resurgence in the past decade, especially in the south. Outside Buddhist temples one can find a treasure-house of fortune-tellers, using a variety of techniques, and at every large market one can buy the religious paraphernalia needed for an assortment of traditional ways of carrying out matters of the spirit.

The traditional practices known in the West as "ancestor worship" (an unfortunate translation) have been revived throughout China in recent years, and paper money and goods burned for the use of ancestors in the afterworld are easily found on city streets, at least in the south. (My favorite paper goods are computers, cell phones, and credit cards, burned so that ancestors can acquire anything they might need. In the past the paper goods consisted more typically of everyday objects such as food and clothing.) Nearly every restaurant now has a family shrine. Beyond the familial aspects of household worship, there are a vast number of other forms of belief—many of which can coexist quite well with worldly success and so-called modernity. The venerable practice of *fengshui*, or the science of optimal placement according to geomantic principles, is maintained in Hong Kong alongside some of the world's most sophisticated engineering.

Akin to some ancient Daoist practices, *qigong* is a collection of exercises having to do with regulation of *qi*, often translated as "vital energy." This includes most martial arts, *taijiquan* exercises, and some more mystical practices involving lifting heavy objects through concentration and curing at a distance. Enormous numbers of people practice various forms of *qigong*, often forming voluntary associations to study, usually under a master. *Qigong* research institutes investigate its efficacy using "scientific" methods.

In the spring of 1999 a group called Falun Dafa (Great Method of the Wheel of Law) and also known as Falun Gong (Skills of the Wheel of Law) became prominent in the West because of a peaceful demonstration organized spontaneously in front of Zhongnanhai, the Beijing residential compound of China's political leaders. Ten thousand followers of this New Age faith meditated silently at dawn. They were forcibly removed and the "sect," which claims a great number of Communist Party members as followers, was outlawed. Their leader, Li Hongzhi, had been in exile in the United States since before that time. At the time that this book went to press in late 1999, the increasing international celebrity of Falun Dafa (it has a popular Web site at www.falundafa.org) and the stridency of its followers in China have prompted the Chinese government to seek Li's extradition and to make new laws forbidding cults and imprisoning cult followers.

Falun Dafa uses most of the *qigong* methods for health, becoming wealthy and powerful, and so forth. Their name is Buddhist, but most of their methods are more traditional; the form of the organization resembles that of a "secret society" in which information is carefully concealed. Their membership internationally is estimated at 3 to 100 million! In past centuries, such secret societies have proven critical to the overturning of dynasties; the government is quite wary of them. The mixture of religion and politics and information is both precedented and ever-changing. Thus, the few types of religious expression I've mentioned here should give us pause as we try to generalize about what China is like and where it is going. It is certainly not returning wholesale to some late-imperial form of society, nor is it plunging ahead to a purely scientific, rational, monolithic economic and political "player" on the stage of world affairs. The local aspects of China are unfolding in complex and often unique ways that can't be grasped entirely from watching the news deemed of global significance.

CONCLUSION

I have catalogued a few of the lesser known aspects of China to remind us that, as Conrad Schirokauer points out in his popular textbook, for most of China's history "the web of government rested only lightly on society and . . . the world of officialdom was remote from most people's lives."[14] Though this formulation must be reversed in the twentieth century, in some ways China may be seen as returning to an earlier structure, wherein the government and politics operate at one level and people operate their lives at another. Cynics might observe that politicians are counting on that separation, permitting economic development to placate people while at other levels of politics, repression is the watchword.

There are challenges, struggles, and holes in any sense of China as a unified monolithic nation, and potential challenges to authority are well understood by the authorities to come from China's plural nature. In traditional China, threats to ruling houses often came from charismatic cult-like leaders who would now be classified as practitioners of "superstition," or they came from non-Han, non-Chinese "barbarians," often pastoralists, living north of China proper. China's leaders are increasingly concerned about south China's strength, though no public acknowledgment of the possibility of secession or rebellion is heard.

Challenges as well as possible sources of creativity and diversity may both be seen to lie within China. Future developments in that vast country will be determined at least in part by the paths taken by all those groups, not only by China's foreign policy and economic development. The character of nations lies in the unique configurations of those who speak to the outside world *and* of those who speak only to their neighbors. In trying to comprehend China's position in the world, it behooves us to remember that China is a place of many faces, even if they don't all have an equal voice. When they speak, they may speak in a cacophony of tongues about quite diverse topics.

The final image I would like to suggest as a supplement to the other big three is that of Multilingual, Multicultural, Local, Religious China. This one can't be as easily visualized, since its essence is variety. It may look like a national minority worshiping a local spirit in a non-Chinese language. Or it may look like a southern business person speaking a local dialect, talking about the *fengshui* results and how to incorporate them into the building of a new university. The moral is: Beware of pat generalizations! They can almost all be challenged.

Is there an advantage to multiculturalism? In the United States, in Europe, Africa, and China—to name just a few places—debates about how to think of cultural differences abound. Some places celebrate differences, some deplore them and seek ways to eradicate differences. In some places coexistence between divergent groups is possible; in other places there is nothing but tension and schism. One could argue that there are multiple ways of thinking of multiple cultures. Just as plant diversification endures because of its benefits to the plant kingdom, in the realm of humankind we see a profusion of cultural forms, even within the artificial political boundaries that we call nations. I would argue that a nation's strength may be viewed in its tolerance of pluralism, but that permitting such pluralism may be one of its greatest challenges. In this chapter I have demonstrated some of the ways China has struggled and continues to struggle with the question of multiplicity of cultural forms. My point is not to judge it as good or evil but to show that like other nations, its path must be forged anew. Unlike other nations its scale is enormous, and even tiny minorities number in the millions. Keep your eyes on this complex kaleidoscope, recalling that any image you see at any moment is only one of the many possible images of Multilingual, Multicultural, Local, Religious China.

NOTES

This is a revised version of a paper delivered at the symposium "China after Deng: Considerations on Politics, Society, and Culture," held at the University of Colorado, Boulder, Colorado, on November 14, 1997. Thanks to Timothy Weston and Lionel Jensen for invitations to participate in this symposium, and to my fellow participants for extremely stimulating conversations about the current situations in China. Tim Weston also made very helpful suggestions about the article, though remaining shortcomings and flaws are my responsibility. Some of the material in this article derives from field research sponsored by the Committee on Scholarly Communication with the People's Republic of China and by the American Philosophical Society; the generous support of both organizations has been invaluable.

1. Alan Dundes, "The Number Three in American Culture," in *Interpreting Folklore* (Bloomington: Indiana University Press, 1980).

2. Benedict Anderson, *Imagined Communities: Reflections on the Origin and Spread of Nationalism*, rev. ed. (London: Verso, 1991).

3. Fei Xiaotong [Fei Hsiao-tung], "Ethnic Identification in China," trans. Wang Huimin and Wu Zenfang, *Social Sciences in China*, no. 1 (March 1980): 94–107.

4. Alan R. Templeton, "Human Races: A Genetic and Evolutionary Perspective," *American Anthropologist*, vol. 100, no. 3 (September 1998): 632–650; Matt Cartmill, "The Status of the Race Concept in Physical Anthropology," *American Anthropologist*, vol. 100, no. 3 (September 1998): 651–660; Faye V. Harrison, "Introduction: Expanding the Discourse on 'Race,'" *American Anthropologist*, vol. 100, no. 3 (September 1998): 609–631.

5. A. Tom Grunfeld, "In Search of Equality: Relations between China's Ethnic Minorities and the Majority Han," *Bulletin of Concerned Asian Scholars*, vol. 17, no. 1 (1985): 54–67.

6. Herold J. Wiens, *China's March toward the Tropics* (Hamden: Shoe String Press, 1954); June Teufel Dreyer, *China's Forty Millions: Minority Nationalities and National Integration in the People's Republic of China* (Cambridge, Mass.: Harvard University Press, 1976); Fei, "Ethnic Identification in China," 94–107; Dru C. Gladney, *Muslim Chinese: Ethnic Nationalism in the People's Republic* (Cambridge, Mass.: Council on East Asian Studies, Harvard University, 1991); *Cultural Encounters on China's Ethnic Frontiers*, Stevan Harrell, ed. (Seattle: University of Washington Press, 1995); Colin Mackerras, *China's Minority Cultures: Identities and Integration since 1912* (Melbourne, Australia: Longman, 1995); Susan D. Blum, *Portraits of "Primitives": Human Kinds in the Chinese Nation* (Lanham, Md.: Rowman & Littlefield, 2000).

7. Dreyer, *China's Forty Millions* (1976), 127, 149, 158.

8. S. Robert Ramsey, *The Languages of China* (Princeton: Princeton University Press, 1987), 180, 182.

9. Gladney, *Muslim Chinese* (1991), 37.

10. Mary S. Erbaugh, "Southern Chinese Dialects As a Medium for Reconciliation within Greater China," *Language in Society*, no. 24 (1995): 79–94, esp. 90. See also her "The Secret History of the Hakkas: The Chinese Revolution As a Hakka Enterprise," *China Quarterly*, no. 132 (December 1992): 937–968.

11. Kenneth Dean, *Taoist Ritual and Popular Cults of Southeast China* (Princeton: Princeton University Press, 1993), 4–5.

12. Emily Martin Ahern, *Chinese Ritual and Politics* (Cambridge: Cambridge University Press, 1981); Hill Gates, *China's Motor: A Thousand Years of Petty Capitalism* (Ithaca, N.Y.: Cornell University Press, 1996).

13. Richard Madsen, *China's Catholics: Tragedy and Hope in an Emerging Civil Society* (Berkeley: University of California Press, 1998).

14. Conrad Schirokauer, *A Brief History of Chinese Civilization* (San Diego: Harcourt Brace Gap College Publishers, 1996), 134.

SUGGESTED READINGS

Susan D. Blum, *Portraits of "Primitives": Human Kinds in the Chinese Nation* (Lanham, Md.: Rowman & Littlefield, 2000).

Michael Dillon, *China's Muslims* (Hong Kong: Oxford University Press, 1995).

June Teufel Dreyer, *China's Forty Millions: Minority Nationalities and National Integration in the People's Republic of China* (Cambridge, Mass.: Harvard University Press, 1976).

Dru C. Gladney, *Muslim Chinese: Ethnic Nationalism in the People's Republic* (Cambridge, Mass.: Council on East Asian Studies, Harvard University, 1991).

A. Tom Grunfeld, "In Search of Equality: Relations between China's Ethnic Minorities and the Majority Han," *Bulletin of Concerned Asian Scholars,* vol. 17, no. 1 (1985): 54–67.

Stevan Harrell, ed., *Cultural Encounters on China's Ethnic Frontiers* (Seattle: University of Washington Press, 1995).

Thomas Heberer, *China and Its National Minorities: Autonomy or Assimilation?,* trans. Michel Vale (Armonk, N.Y.: M. E. Sharpe, 1989).

Ma Yin, ed., *China's Minority Nationalities* (Beijing: Foreign Languages Press, 1989).

Colin Mackerras, *China's Minorities: Integration and Modernization in the Twentieth Century* (Hong Kong: Oxford University Press, 1994).

Richard Madsen, *China's Catholics: Tragedy and Hope in an Emerging Civil Society* (Berkeley and Los Angeles: University of California Press, 1998).

S. Robert Ramsey, *The Languages of China* (Princeton: Princeton University Press, 1987).

4

Promoting Human Rights in China:

An Activist's Perspective

Xiao Qiang

If someone takes away your bread, he suppresses your freedom at the same time. But if someone takes away your freedom, you may be sure that your bread is threatened, for it depends no longer on you and your struggle but on the whim of a master.

—Albert Camus, 1953

In this paper I will focus on China's gradual political liberalization and how to promote human rights in that context. Before beginning, though, I want to make clear in what capacity I am writing. I have been the executive director of Human Rights in China (HRIC) since 1991.[1] HRIC's mission is to assure that the human rights of Chinese citizens in China are respected and protected. We approach this goal by, first, directly supporting victims of human rights abuses and human rights activists in China; second, raising awareness about Chinese human rights cases both inside and outside China; and third, encouraging international scrutiny of China's human rights policy and practice.

Human Rights in China was founded in the United States by Chinese students and scholars in March 1989. At that time I was a graduate student at Notre Dame University in Indiana, having come to the United States in 1986 to work toward a Ph.D. in astrophysics. Before coming to the United States I graduated from the University of Science and Technology of China (USTC), where Professor Fang Lizhi, one of China's most outstanding scientists and human rights fighters, taught. In 1989, in the wake of the June 4th Massacre in Beijing, I gave up my academic work to become a full-time human rights activist. I have no regrets about that decision, though I am sorry I never finished my projects in astrophysics, a subject I studied passionately for ten years during my youth. I still dream that someday the various parts of my life will unite, that I will be able to connect my work on human rights with a feeling of being in touch with the cosmos, but for now those things seem disconnected in my hectic daily life.

I am still a Chinese citizen, but because of my human rights activities I cannot return to China without fear of being turned away at the border or, worse, imprisoned. The last time I was in China was from June to August 1989. I have only seen one member of my family since then, though I am in regular phone- or e-mail-contact with my loved ones in China. By now my Chinese passport has expired, but I have no plans to give up my Chinese citizenship because I want to be a Chinese and I don't believe any government has the right to deprive me of that right. Also, as director of Human Rights in China, whose mission is to work for human rights in China from a Chinese perspective, I need to remain a Chinese citizen.

However, I have been living outside China for more than a decade now, so my daily work and personal life are, of course, quite different from that of any Chinese living in China. In my work I deal with China, with Chinese people, and with people who have just come back from China, and I think about Chinese issues and analyze information coming out of China on a daily basis. I am in contact with people in China and read Chinese publications on the Internet every day. But I also have to function in this society, from taking the subway to my office in midtown Manhattan to doing fundraising and advocacy work among high-ranking officials in Washington, D.C., and elsewhere. After twelve years of living in the United States and marrying an American woman, I do not feel that the United States is a foreign country but instead my second home. I have love for both countries. HRIC's mission is to establish an office in Beijing one day and this fits with my personal hopes as well. But years of human rights work at the international level have expanded my field of concerns beyond any single country's borders. Therefore, while I sincerely hope the day comes soon when HRIC can open an office in Beijing overlooking Tian'anmen Square, I fully intend to develop my work so that it takes on a global scope.

THE HUMAN RIGHTS CHALLENGE IN A REFORMING CHINA

Human Rights in China's definition of human rights is based on the Universal Declaration of Human Rights, passed in 1948 by the United Nations, and on subsequent UN treaties and covenants, such as the International Covenant on Economic, Social, and Cultural Rights (ICESCR) and the International Covenant on Civil and Political Rights (ICCPR). Those two covenants uphold not only traditional political freedoms—speech, association, and religious belief—but also social and economic rights such as the right to work and to an education. In other words, HRIC conceives of human rights in broad terms that include but also move beyond the conventional concern with political torture and political freedoms to address the negative consequences for Chinese citizens of China's free market–style economic reforms. This is essential because today's development in China, in addition to taking place within a repressive and rigid political system that deprives the Chinese people of political rights, involves rapid and dramatic transformations in economic and social life that are causing massive and wide-ranging problems that impact the economic and social rights of millions and millions of people. Many of these negative consequences are addressed in detail in the other essays in this volume.

When the tanks rolled into Tian'anmen Square in June 1989, the destruction of a popular movement that had captured the aspirations for freedom of millions of Chinese people appeared complete and the future of China's reform movement was drawn into question. Since then, however, China has gone through rapid social and economic changes and Chinese Communism has evolved into state capitalism under the rigid control of the Communist Party elite. With Deng Xiaoping's market-oriented economic reforms, living standards have risen; economic freedom has expanded dramatically; and the ability of the Communist Party to control people's lives has been sharply eroded. Today, information is getting into China via e-mail, the Internet, satellite TV, radio, and other mediums at unprecedented rates. Consequently, many Chinese people today do enjoy greater freedoms—although these are not institutionally protected—than they did in the 1970s under Mao Zedong's rule or in the 1980s under the aegis of Deng Xiaoping.

However, there is no sign that increased prosperity has increased the Chinese government's commitment to human rights. Despite some positive signs, the current leadership has no intention of liberalizing its political system and no vision to lead the country in the direction of greater protection of human rights. The broadly democratic goals expressed during the popular movement of 1989 remain unfulfilled. Economic development is essentially a project aimed at enhancing the power of the state rather than promoting the enjoyment of rights—political, economic, or social—

by the Chinese people. An increase in the gross national product (GNP) has not led directly to equal benefits for individual Chinese citizens or the protection of the society's weakest elements. An inherent contradiction remains between the authoritarianism of the one-party system and the protection of human rights. Because of the lack of accountability on the part of authorities at a time of rapid economic growth, the basic rights to an education and health care, safe working conditions, independent worker's unions, equal employment opportunities for both sexes, and a clean, safe environment are being sacrificed.

Today tens of millions of laborers who have migrated to urban areas are working under unprotected conditions in the joint ventures of special economic zones and on construction sites in expanding urban areas. These workers have neither medical insurance nor benefits. By law they cannot form unions. When they are fired, injured, or poisoned by chemicals at work, they are not able to seek compensation or file grievances. Another striking example of deteriorating quality of life is found in education: although China's growth rate has reached into double digits for the last six years, educational opportunities for many have decreased as a result of new government policies that do not give adequate emphasis to the funding of education, despite rhetoric that would suggest otherwise. China now has 220 million illiterate adults. In 1992, more than 450,000 teachers quit their jobs to make a living elsewhere. In 1993, 7.4 million children under age sixteen had not gone to school or had dropped out. The National Statistics Bureau found that only 75 percent of elementary school graduates went on to middle school, and only 30 percent of those progressed to high school. Most of the students who are dropping out of school are female, especially in rural areas where parents tend to choose education for their sons over their daughters if they feel the need to make a choice. Where are all the female students going? One-third of the 50,000 country girls working as housekeepers and nannies in Beijing are under fifteen. One quarter of the country's 14 million migrant construction workers are child laborers, some of them as young as ten. While there are now a number of interest groups working on these issues, the government itself has no policies that can adequately address the severity of these problems.

Rather than working aggressively to solve these and other grave social problems, the Chinese government has increasingly turned to the law as a weapon for the suppression of public dissent. For example, the Detailed Implementation Regulations for the State Security Law, signed into force by former Premier Li Peng on June 4, 1994, the fifth anniversary of the Beijing Massacre, were clearly aimed at dissidents. In an oblique attack on recent attempts by dissidents to use legal means to appeal unfair detainment and arrests, a *Legal Daily* commentary on the regulations stated: "We should be vigilant against these hostile organizations and hostile elements at home and abroad who try a thousand and one ways to find gaps in the present laws, in an attempt to use so-called legal forms to cover their illegal activities." The regulations defined writings or speeches deemed "harmful to state security" (a term left completely undefined) as "sabotage" and outlawed cooperation between activists in China and "hostile" nongovernmental organizations (NGOs) outside the country.

In the last several years the Chinese government has trumpeted the slogan "ruling the country by law" (*yifa zhiguo*) and has proudly pointed out that the category "revolutionary crime" no longer exists. But now the government makes use of the equally vague and open-ended crime of "endangering state security." Clearly, rule *by* law is not the same thing as rule *of* law. True rule of law is a system whereby the people of a nation have a voice in formulating and enforcing the laws that govern them. What Chinese authorities mean by rule by law is the imposition on citizens of laws promulgated, enforced, and arbitrarily interpreted to suit the interests of the ruling elite. Unlike in democratic countries with well-established rules of law, in China people do not generally consider the law to be for their protection, nor do they have any role in the legislative process. In a system in which the judiciary is accountable to the ruling party and not to the people, rule by law is nothing more than a cleverly veiled phrase for dictatorship.

The Chinese authorities often argue that by crushing voices calling for human rights, the government is ensuring stability and unity. Yet it is precisely the lack of respect for human rights and a legal system protective of individual rights that puts China in danger and threatens stability. In my opinion, the rapid economic and social transition China is currently undergoing will be extremely difficult and violent unless fundamental political and civil liberties are made available to the Chinese people so they can participate in the decisions that affect their lives. Over the last two years the serious problems of unemployment, appalling factory work conditions, and corruption have led thousands of workers in dozens of Chinese industrial cities to take to the streets in protest. Without independent trade unions, a free press, and other autonomous channels for voicing dissatisfaction, many of these protests have escalated into violent confrontations between demonstrators and the police, resulting in hundreds of arrests.

But suppression cannot make the core problems go away. Without peaceful means for people to address their grievances and seek redress, the dislocations born of the reform process will eventually undermine China's economic development.

CHINA'S GROWING HUMAN RIGHTS MOVEMENT

Although the term *human rights* (*renquan*) itself is not yet widely used among the Chinese people, government violations of the basic citizens' rights are commonly condemned by people from all walks of Chinese society and I do believe it is possible to point to a fledgling Chinese "human rights movement." Common people may not use the term *rights* and they may not understand its larger theoretical underpinnings, but they do know, for example, that the freedom to form an independent trade union is essential to protect their own interests as workers, especially now that the state has become the guarantor of low wages. It is only because of the repressive policies of the government that most people do not dare to express these requests openly. Nevertheless, consciousness about human rights has increased dramatically since 1989. Before that time the subject was taboo, but after the massacre, owing to trenchant and sustained international criticism, human rights became a subject increasingly discussed within Chinese society. Whereas the government once refused to even broach the topic, it now regularly does so, even if its main purpose is to defend China's human rights record or to argue that the Chinese situation is different from that in developed countries.

In another development, in October 1997, the Chinese government signed the International Covenant on Economic, Social, and Cultural Rights (ICESCR) and in 1998 it signed the International Covenant on Civil and Political Rights (ICCPR)—goals HRIC had been actively working toward for some time. While China's signing of the two international covenants has not resulted in immediate, dramatic changes in human rights practices, I believe it is very important because it enables Chinese activists as well as reformers within the Chinese government to point to the covenants as standards the government is committed to upholding. As Tim Weston discusses (in this volume), activists calling for independent trade unions have already begun to base their claims on the terms of the ICESCR. Also, foreign governments and human rights groups can now use the terms of the ICESCR as a baseline; indeed, HRIC is currently gathering information so that it can issue a report comparing China's stated commitments to its actions. In the short term the Chinese government's signing of the ICESCR and ICCPR may appear to be more show than substance, but in the long run I believe it will prove to be as significant as the Soviet Union's signing of the Helsinki Accords in 1975. With the terms of those accords in place, Soviet dissidents were able to set up Helsinki Watch committees to call attention to the Soviet government's violations of civil liberties it had sworn to uphold. In China there are already many government-sanctioned initiatives that promote rights protections in Chinese society in areas such as law, journalism, education, and social services. These efforts do not go nearly far enough, in HRIC's opinion, but they are still highly significant and need to be recognized, because they reflect an elemental government sensitivity toward the growing Chinese popular consciousness of rights.

What China's signing of the two international rights covenants means is that the Communist Party has now at least rhetorically accepted human rights as a legitimate topic, thereby making it harder for the government to suppress others for raising the subject. This empowers the human rights movement in China. After twenty years of social and economic change, during which the Communist Party's micro-control over people's lives has steadily declined, ordinary Chinese citizens today do feel freer than ever before to express their desire for greater freedom in private or semiprivate settings. There are many Internet chat groups where rights-related issues are discussed and more and more journalists and editors working for government-run newspapers and magazines are skillfully inserting discussion about corruption and other once-forbidden topics into their writing. I have participated in many radio and television programs that receive live calls from China and can attest that questions from ordinary listeners demonstrate an increasingly sophisticated understanding of human rights and how they relate to Chinese reality. These callers are ordinary citizens, not high-profile intellectuals, which shows the extent to which change has and continues to take place in China with regard to the human rights discourse.

China's growing human rights movement is being led by grassroots activists, who are often labeled "dissidents" in the Western media. As these are the only independent individuals publicly advocating human rights and democracy by name, they constitute the front line of the Chinese struggle for expanded rights. Because they present such a challenge, they are naturally subject to the greatest persecution from the government.

In the following passages, I will briefly describe the activities of a few such people.

Even before the troops withdrew from the streets of Beijing in 1989, Professor Ding Zilin, the mother of a seventeen-year-old high school student who was shot and killed by the troops that stormed the city on June 3, 1989, began going door to door to collect the names of the dead and wounded. In June 1999, she and one hundred fifty-nine other family members of the victims of the June 4th Massacre filed a lawsuit against former Premier Li Peng for his role in the massacre and asked the National People's Congress to investigate the deaths of their children and husbands and to reverse the Party's verdict that the students, workers, and ordinary citizens who massed at Tian'anmen Square in 1989 were engaging in a "counterrevolutionary act."

Lin Mu, a former high-ranking Party official in the northwestern city of Xi'an who spent eight years in a labor camp during the Cultural Revolution (1966–76), has written a series of articles rebutting the government's argument that China has "different standards" of human rights, that it is somehow an exception to standards and norms agreed upon as universal by human rights experts. The censorship exercised by the Party makes it impossible for him to publish such writings in China, but the articles continue to circulate widely among rights activists there. Lin was an initiator of numerous petition letters, including one signed by forty-five prominent scientists and intellectuals calling for China to mark the UN's International Year of Tolerance in 1995 by releasing political prisoners.

One of the others who signed this document was Wang Dan. Wang, a student leader in 1989, emerged unbowed from a three-and-a-half-year jail term he received as a consequence of his involvement in and leadership of that movement. In May 1995, after continuing to speak out about China's legal and political problems upon his release from prison, Wang was secretly arrested for the second time. He was given a show trial the following year and sentenced to eleven years for conspiring to overthrow the Chinese government. Following two years of imprisonment, he was released on the condition that he leave China. Wang Dan is currently studying at Harvard University and is the organizer of an international network of dissidents called "Tian'anmen Generation," which is actively seeking to get the Chinese Communist Party to reverse its verdict on the events of 1989. The government's verdict that the democracy movement was a "counterrevolutionary riot" is a key obstacle in the way of political liberalization to this day. The Party is afraid to reverse its position, since a reversal of the verdict would naturally lead to demands that political prisoners be freed, that families of victims be compensated, that exiles be allowed to return to China, and that the press be allowed to discuss what happened in 1989 in an open and free way.

In 1998 Wang Youcai—another student leader who was on the Party's 21 Most Wanted List in 1989—and his dissident colleagues made a groundbreaking move when they attempted to register the Zhejiang Province branch of a new political party called China Democracy Party. Within several months, inspired by Wang Youcai's actions, dissidents applied to register party branches in twenty-one other provinces. Following that development, in November 1998, the government initiated a harsh crackdown against the Party organizers. Nationwide, hundreds of arrests took place, and three top China Democracy Party organizers—Wang Youcai (Zhejiang), Qin Yongmin (Wuhan), and Xu Wenli (Beijing)—were sentenced to eleven, twelve, and thirteen years in prison, respectively. Despite the harsh crackdown, activists continue to try to establish a China Democracy Party, though at present they still have not been successful.

Ding Zilin, Lin Mu, Wang Dan, and Wang Youcai represent a kind of human rights activism that is spreading across China. Many of the activists were affected in some way by the 1989 protest movement or were directly involved in it. Their activism often began with a need to defend their own rights and then moved on to defending the rights of others. Despite the constant risk of arrest and imprisonment and a daily routine of surveillance, harassment, and intimidation, hundreds of brave individuals in loosely connected networks have carried out human rights investigations throughout China. These perilous investigations have included interviewing a woman who was kidnapped and sold, collecting details of the charges against all the political prisoners held in a particular labor camp, sending such information to international organizations and the United Nations, and raising aid for former political prisoners and the families of those in jail.

A general consensus exists among dissidents in China that human rights work must be conducted publicly rather than through clandestine groups, that human rights activists must be committed to nonviolence and must abide by the law, seeking redress for rights violations through the courts. Rights activists consistently demand that the government allow the supervision of officials by citizens through the implementation of a free media and the establishment of truly independent nongovernmental organizations.

In today's China, these activists constitute a very small portion of the

Chinese population. Yet they are a minority only in the sense that the government persists in isolating them from the rest of society through means such as imprisonment and press censorship. However, in my opinion, their ideas have an increasing resonance and are gaining a larger constituency within all levels of Chinese society and in fact represent the hopes of the majority—that is, all the powerless people in China. For example, Wang Dan, along with twenty-two other "dissidents," wrote an open letter to the Chinese National People's Congress. The letter urged this legislative body to abolish one of the most severe systems of arbitrary detention in China: "Reeducation through Labor." Every year, there are up to a million Chinese citizens sentenced to labor camps without trial (only a small percentage of these people are political prisoners) through this form of administrative punishment. Small groups of "dissidents" have risked their own personal safety to speak out against such injustices, even though they are merely exercising the freedom of speech constitutionally guaranteed to them as Chinese citizens. They are speaking out for the protection of human rights for all of the Chinese people and are widely respected and supported for this.

Clearly, China's human rights activists believe that the Chinese people desire and deserve the same human rights that people across the world desire and deserve. Unlike conservative forces within the Chinese government and other authoritarian governments in Asia, therefore, they generally oppose the notion of special "Asian Values"—such as an emphasis on the group over the individual or a desire for harmony and a disdain for conflict—that can be used to justify the withholding of human rights to Chinese citizens. I, too, believe the so-called "Asian Values Debate" is a false one, that human rights are universally applicable and need to be respected in every society. The fact that the discourse of human rights originated in "the West" in no way means that it is therefore irrelevant to China. Communism and market economics originated in the West as well, but that has not prevented them from being adopted in China. If we look at who is supporting the idea of "Asian Values," we see that it is being played up by authoritarian leaders and their apologists to defend their human rights abuses.[2]

Moreover, these same people will often point to the fact that the United States has all sorts of serious social problems and that, therefore, it has no business criticizing China. I believe this, too, is a faulty argument. While I would be the first to agree that the United States is far from perfect and that many people should be working to solve the problems in this society,

I don't think the human rights problems in this country are equivalent to the institutionalized, systematic, and extensive violations in China. It is important that a country as powerful as the United States, with such a strong tradition of concern for human rights, speak out on human rights problems in China and elsewhere. I would also add that there is no reason one has to be perfect oneself in order to earn the right to criticize another. For example, despite the fact that China has serious human rights problems, that did not prevent it from criticizing the terrible abuses committed against ethnic Chinese during the riots that led to the fall of the Suharto regime in Indonesia in 1998.

This is not to say that cultural and historical sensitivity is not called for between countries such as the United States and China. I absolutely do believe that the United States needs to approach China thoughtfully instead of arrogantly and that it has to offer partnership along with criticism. For effective human rights policies there needs to be a dimension of reciprocal oversight and criticism. In my opinion, President Clinton's admission that the United States has many serious problems, with race and other issues, during his talk at Beijing University in summer 1998 was both appropriate and helpful. At a time when the Chinese government is intentionally making use of and fanning the flames of nationalist sentiment among its people (see Lam, this volume) as a political resource to secure its much-eroded legitimacy in the wake of the massacre in 1989, it is critically important that those who wish to help the Chinese people understand how to get their message across.

Owing to restrictions on foreign journalists in China and the U.S. media's market-driven focus on issues in China that are of interest to U.S. citizens, the coverage of China available to average people in the United States is sometimes very incomplete. On the other hand, many subjects that receive a lot of attention in the U.S. media are not necessarily well known in China. For example, the issue of Tibet. Most Han Chinese are uninformed about the repression there because of press censorship, and most—"liberal intellectuals" included—tend to have racist and chauvinistic attitudes about Tibetans and agree with their government that Tibet is and should be part of China. Few Chinese have been to Tibet, desire to go there, or have a deep understanding of the problems there. To them, Tibet feels like a minor and peripheral issue. The stories about Tibet that appear in the official Chinese media generally tout the bravery and foresight of the Communist Party's liberation of these people from slavery and feudal labor conditions. So, while certain issues preoccupy and upset U.S. citizens, they tend to get little play in China. Like ordinary people every-where, ordinary Chinese are most concerned about issues that adversely affect them in their daily lives, like corruption and unemployment. But these issues largely center on ideas about social and economic rights that do not as easily capture the imagination of U.S. citizens and that people in the United States are less likely to view as human rights matters.

INTERNATIONAL STRATEGY RECOMMENDATIONS

In the last two years the Chinese government has released from prison China's two most famous dissidents—Wei Jingsheng and Wang Dan. Human Rights in China applauds their release and believes this demonstrates that international pressure does exert an influence on the Chinese government. However, HRIC is under no illusions that the release of Wei and Wang marks the beginning of a fundamentally new policy in Beijing. After all, the government never admitted that Wei and Wang were improperly imprisoned in the first place (it ostensibly released them because they were in poor health) and it only released the two dissidents after they agreed to leave China. They are in the United States now and are not able to go back to China. What the Chinese government has learned, cynically, is that it can gain favorable world opinion by freeing its political prisoners while at the same time making them far less effective by sending them abroad where they are not known and can no longer serve as a symbol of China's human rights problems.

As I have tried to make clear, while the situation in China is gradually improving in many ways, the Communist Party has not indicated that it is willing to fundamentally alter its human rights approach. The economic reforms are opening China to new possibilities and eroding old boundaries within society (at the same time they are also creating a legion of new problems), but they are a means for the government to maintain its power, not a sign of dawning political freedom. It is therefore very important that we continue to apply pressure on the Chinese government so that it will improve its record with regard to human rights.

I recommend a multifaceted approach to promote a general respect for human rights in China. First of all, governments and human rights organizations must continue to monitor and critique China's human rights practices and insist upon the Chinese government's observance of international human rights norms. At the same time, the international community, especially at the nongovernmental level, can also play a role of engaging China in order to expand its awareness of human rights. The international community should seek China's enhanced participation in the institutions of the international human rights regime. This includes pressing China to ratify and implement the two international rights covenants (ICE-SCR and ICCPR) and encouraging China to extend invitations to the United Nations thematic mechanisms, such as the special rapporteur on torture, freedom of expression, independence of the judiciary, violence against women, and religious intolerance.

I do not oppose economic engagement with China. But a policy of economic engagement is neither an alternative to, nor a substitute for, a human rights policy. For a large country such as China the progress of any human rights movement depends on both internal initiative and external pressure. The former is essential but the latter is also indispensable. To be effective, international pressure must be consistent, persistent, and push in the same direction as internal reform forces. Internal grassroots activists have often been aided when foreign criticism has brought rights issues to the attention of domestic specialists or motivated policy makers to seek expert opinion on them.

With regard to these matters, I would give President Clinton's 1998 trip to China high marks. In general, he said the right things at the right times at the right places. But immediately after Clinton left China, the group of dissidents in Zhejiang Province (led by Wang Youcai) that is seeking to establish the China Democracy Party was arrested. It is therefore important that the administration not congratulate itself too much for the trip or lose its focus on human rights problems in China. This is especially true because Clinton's trip to China helped legitimize the Jiang Zemin government.

Furthermore, U.S. businesses also bear a responsibility since they are playing an important role in the Chinese economic reforms and have tremendous influence in both China and the United States. Human rights cannot be separated from business activities; environmental impact and labor conditions in China are directly related to the behavior of multinational corporations. U.S. corporations are not the worst abusers of workers and the environment in China (that distinction belongs to smaller South Korean, Hong Kong, and Taiwanese businesses), but they need to work more actively to serve as a model for those conducting business in that country. Moreover, U.S. consumers can also play a role by forcing U.S. companies to stop subcontracting with abusive South Korean, Hong Kong, and Taiwanese investors responsible for the exploitation of Chinese workers in sweatshops.

Some of the reforms currently being advocated for China by both external and internal constituencies include: amending state security law to end the abusive use of the term "endangering state security," which is broadly interpreted and used against political dissidents; establishing a presumption of innocence; providing earlier access to defense lawyers for criminal defendants; shortening police detention of suspects; and abolishing the Four Cardinal Principles—which stipulate that all Chinese must adhere to the socialist path, the leadership of the Communist Party, Marxism-Leninism-Mao Zedong Thought, and the people's democratic dictatorship. If the Cardinal Principles can be abolished, the rest of the Chinese constitution contains an admirable list of rights and promises; what the government needs to do is observe its own laws. The internal debates on human rights in China and the gradual changes taking place indicate that a strong constituency of Chinese lawyers, scholars, journalists, and party liberals accept the universality of human rights, the legally binding status of the international law of human rights, and the political wisdom of China bringing its domestic practices into line with international human rights norms.

The best illustration of the effectiveness of international pressure in combination with the efforts of internal reformers is the revision of the criminal procedure law. This legislation was first drafted and passed by the National People's Congress (NPC) in July 1979. It lacked any protection of the rights of the accused and often contradicted international human rights norms. During the entire 1980s, the NPC passed only two amendments, which actually further enhanced the power of the police since the government's major concern was to curb the rising crime rate in the wake of economic reforms. Only the international outrage that followed the 1989 massacre produced significant enough pressure on the Chinese government to facilitate the reform process of this legislation already being advocated by domestic legal scholars and some officials. In March 1996, the NPC finally passed a new version of the Criminal Procedure Law. In this revision, significant progress in human rights protections is evident, including enacting the presumption of innocence into law, a measure legal scholars and human rights groups have long advocated.

CONCLUSION

Today, human rights is an international concept, not a code word for Westernization, much as Wei Jingsheng points out in the following chapter. It is human nature to want to live with freedom and dignity. In today's more and more interdependent world, development needs to be measured not just in economic terms but also in human terms—that is, according to the extent to which human rights, citizen participation, education, the equitable distribution of wealth, the protection of vulnerable groups within society, respect for the environment, and serious concern about the preservation of cultural integrity are prioritized and championed. The rapid, profound changes Chinese society has undergone during the last twenty years are proof that the Chinese people desire more meaningful and productive lives. Political repression only creates potential instability for society and jeopardizes the gains in economic development the country has achieved.

The promotion of human rights in China requires a concerted effort on the part of citizens and their leaders in all international and domestic communities. Ultimately, while I believe the struggle for the realization of human rights in China can only be won by the Chinese people themselves, strong international support is crucial for bolstering and legitimizing the efforts of the many individuals, both those working inside of the system and those participating in independent grassroots organizations, who are bravely sacrificing so much to advance the rights of one-fifth of humankind.

NOTES

For their invaluable assistance with this article, I thank Timothy Weston and Kristina Torgeson.

1. Human Rights in China is a nonprofit organization based in New York City. In addition to the main office, HRIC has a research office in Hong Kong and an extensive network of informants in China.

2. For critiques of the "Asian Values" argument, see Randall Peerenboom, "Confucian Harmony and Freedom of Thought," in *Confucianism and Human Rights*, Wm. Theodore de Bary and Tu Wei-ming, eds. (New York: Columbia University Press, 1998), 234–260, and Lionel M. Jensen, "Human Rights, Chinese Rites, and the Limits of History," *The Historian* 62, no. 1 (February 2000).

SUGGESTED READINGS

Amnesty International has information on China's human rights situation, with a special section on the death penalty: http://www.amnesty.org

China Rights Forum. This magazine is published by Human Rights in China.

Michael C. Davis, ed., *Human Rights and Chinese Values: Legal, Philosophical, and Political Perspectives* (New York: Oxford University Press, 1995).

Wm. Theodore de Bary and Tu Wei-ming, eds., *Confucianism and Human Rights* (New York: Columbia University Press, 1998).

Fang Lizhi, *Bringing Down the Great Wall: Writings on Science, Culture, and Democracy in China* (New York: W. W. Norton, 1992).

Human Rights in China's Web site has many articles about human rights problems and political prisoners in China, as well as a list of publications you can order on special topics: http://www.hrichina.org

Human Rights Watch/Asia also has information and publications on China on their Web page: http://www.hrw.org

International Campaign for Tibet can lead you to information on the situation in Tibet: http://www.ict.org

Ann Kent, *China and Human Rights* (New York: Oxford University Press, 1992).

Andrew Nathan, *Chinese Democracy* (Berkeley: University of California Press, 1985).

Orville Schell, *Mandate of Heaven: The Legacy of Tiananmen Square and the Next Generation of China's Leaders* (New York: Simon & Schuster, 1994).

Wei Jingsheng, *The Courage to Stand Alone* (New York: Viking Press, 1997).

5

China's Road to a Democratic Society:

Perils and Prospects

Wei Jingsheng

The following essay was written by one of the most celebrated and best known of China's twentieth-century revolutionary figures, who first came to international attention in December 1978 with the posting of a manifesto on a wall across the street from the municipal bus station in an area of Beijing known as Xidan. This hand-lettered poster, "The Fifth Modernization," plainly asserted that China's national campaign to modernize agriculture, industry, science and technology, and national defense by the year 2000 (The Four Modernizations) could never be realized without the establishment of democracy—the Fifth Modernization. By this he meant, "the holding of power by the laboring masses themselves" so that they "have the power to replace their representatives any time." For this mani- festo, and for amplifications published the following month in his journal Explo- ration, *Wei was arrested near the end of March 1979. His crime, like that of many of his Democracy Movement cohorts, was "impairing the state system with the aid of foreigners." Yet he was also charged with treason for allegedly leaking infor- mation to a reporter for the* New York Times *on China's war with Vietnam, a violation that merited the penalty of execution. International pressure on the Chi- nese government helped spare him execution; nonetheless, he was tried in Octo- ber 1979, found guilty of crimes against the state, and sentenced to fifteen years in prison for opposing, rather than merely criticizing, Marxism-Leninism-Mao Zedong Thought. Enduring torture, dietary sabotage, sleep deprivation, and a host of other intentional violations for fourteen years, Wei was released Septem- ber 14, 1993, while the International Olympic Committee entered its final delib- erations for selection of the site (Beijing or Sydney) for the 2000 Olympics. But in April 1994, after Sydney had been selected as the Olympic site, he was mysteri-*

ously detained by the Public Security Forces in Beijing and in December 1995 for-
mally arrested and charged with engaging in "illegal activities under the cloak of
legality." In late November 1997 he was released again, this time for "medical rea-
sons," and flown to Detroit for treatment at the Henry Ford Hospital. Wei's
release was contingent, as was that of many other dissidents, on the admission that
he would not remain in China. Since his exile, Wei has traveled exhaustively to
conferences and symposia and met with a great number of the world's leaders. He
remains for many the conscience of China and, quite fittingly for this book, he is
an interloper, someone who has moved in and out of the headlines of the last two
decades of the complex intertwinings of China and the West. His essay, "China's
Road to a Democratic Society: Perils and Prospects," counters the common asser-
tion by some Chinese reformers and a great number of China watchers in the West
that autocracy is the only political system appropriate to China, there having been
no previous history of democratic institutions. Wei's reflection offers instead a
broad historical outline of the Chinese struggle for democracy and speculates on
the contemporary prospects for its attainment while providing new perspectives
on the most recent events in the politics of China and the West.   [L.M.J.]

> When spiders' webs mercilessly sealed up my stove,
> When the ashes of my last cigarette sighed with the sorrow of poverty,
> I stubbornly still sowed the ashes of lost hope,
> With beautiful snowflakes I wrote: Trust the Future . . .
> The eyes of the people who trust in the future
> Make me firmly believe in the future myself—
> Their eyelashes bat off the dust of history,
> Their pupils pierce the years of writings.
>   —Shi Zhi, "Trust the Future," 1970/1978

Since antiquity, China has sought a social system that best sustains the existence of the individual. In this sense, China is exactly like other excellent nations. During the past one hundred years, more and more Chinese have come to realize that democracy is the most reasonable political system to ensure this individual sustenance. Thousands of people with lofty ideas have devoted their lifetime to this goal—democracy.

However, in this past century, we Chinese have gone through quite many tortuous roads, very few of them leading to democracy. There are different reasons for this: some are inevitable, while others are contingent. Regardless, the blame may be spread among the rulers, the revolutionaries, and even each individual.

For instance, the Westernization Movement of the late Qing Dynasty (1644–1911) promoted political reform during the reign of Emperor Guangxu (1875–1908), particularly in the Hundred Days Reform of June to September of 1898. That movement's failure caused China to lose an opportunity to realize democracy and thus join advanced countries. Nevertheless, it was the first time that China attempted to change the autocratic political system, which has been carried on for two thousand years, through peaceful evolution. It also clearly affirmed the idea that political reform is the only means to save China, in other words, political reform is the prerequisite for reforms in other areas. Later ideas such as "science saving the nation" or "education saving the nation" cannot be compared to the idea of political reform because it is the most foresighted and possessing. There are many reasons for the failure of the Westernization Movement, the major ones being that the ruling class was unwise and the people were indifferent. This indifference of people toward their own fate and future still existed even during the Revolution of 1911, and so the ruling class consequently steadfastly *"insists on the same old basic principles."* In the end, people accepted Sun Yat-sen's revolutionary theory and abandoned their hope for peaceful evolution. Chinese history from that time to the present day has been one of China rapidly falling behind, changing from a weak but rich country during the Qing to one of the poorest countries in the world today.

After two great revolutions (the Republican Revolution of 1911 and the Communist Revolution of 1949), the reality that Chinese face today is autocracy masked by "democracy." This has brought them an even worse disaster. Not only have Chinese lost the opportunity to become relatively developed in economy and culture, they have also lost their originally limited, pre-revolutionary freedom. This limited freedom is what Chinese were used to in the previous two hundred years. So when the new autocratic system of single-Party rule was begun, it was widely opposed by Chinese people. During the first thirty years, popular opposition to it was accompanied by the inner struggle of the ruling class. They tangled together, rose one after another, but never stopped. Although such struggle could be very intense, as in the Cultural Revolution, its basic form was to solve problems through mending the autocratic system. Sometimes this form did help to solve some imminent problems. But, because it could not reach the fundamental problems of the system, the result of its application could only be "cutting out one piece of its flesh to cure a boil." In doing that, basic problems were left unresolved, thereby causing endless future troubles. After thirty years of tempering, the theory of "patching the sky" (tinkering with the preexistent state structure) received the favor of the ruling class during the Deng era (1978–1995). It advanced from theory to practice and to the height of its effectiveness. In a short time of ten years, it brought about great changes as well big problems for China, which led to the 1989 Democracy Movement.

While the theory of "patching the sky" reached its effective limit, the idea of "changing the sky" emerged in the minds of Chinese young people. Exactly when and in whose mind it appeared is an unanswerable question. But what we can say is that it made its first appearance between November 1978 and May 1979—the Democracy Wall Era. It was at this time that ordinary working people became familiar with this idea. From that time, democracy, a new concept different from political reform, started to enter people's minds. More than an ideological trend, democracy also became a movement and it even forced the political reformers (those who "patch the sky") to assume the garb of democracy. These young Chinese, after going round and round in their thinking, found a truth that had been neglected by their forerunners. The truth is, "Without democracy, there is no modernization to China." This conclusion is not only a result of theoretical deduction but also represents the summation of more than a century of revolution. Chinese had experienced and experimented with all kinds of autocratic systems, systems that had brought about similar negative results in Chinese society with respect to the freedom of the people. Given this experience, Chinese people today naturally ask for new ways and are especially open to following the roads that have proven practical by others' efforts.

Before the practice of the "patching the sky" school (one that only reforms the economy but keeps the autocratic system) fully demonstrated its absurdity and corruption, people found it hard to accept the theory brought forth by the "changing the sky" school. Yet it only took ten years for the great 1989 movement to break out. Though that massive groundswell of the Chinese people did not negate the demand for reform, it pronounced its claim: to substitute the communist system with its own democratic system. At the time, the young people on the square had already planned to march toward Zhongnanhai (the privileged lifestyle enclave of the highest ranking members of the Communist Party). People on the street echoed this claim. This phenomenon explained the essence of the movement: people wanted democracy and were not satisfied with reform; they wanted to change the sky instead of only patching it. From that time until the present, the target of changing the sky and demanding democracy have developed from being accepted by many Chinese to being accepted by most Chinese. Thus, the challenge that China now faces is no longer a problem of reform or democracy but a problem of how to realize democracy.

I spent many years in prison because I called for democracy. While in prison I became an internationally recognized symbol of opposition to the Chinese Communist Party. In late November 1997, the Communist Party decided to make use of my symbolic status by freeing me from prison on the condition that I leave China. In this way, they hoped to gain credit in Western countries for having done the right thing. However, they would not allow me to stay in China because they feared that I would join with others who are seeking to bring about political change. They took away my passport to make sure I could not return. They thought that by sending me to a foreign country whose language and culture I do not know and where I did not know many people, they would be able to make me disappear from view. But they did not understand that there are many people in the West who care about me and want to help me achieve my goals for China.

At this time I have no plans to return to China, though I hope to do so in the future so that I can help build democracy there. It's hard for me to say when that time will come. Maybe I will never be able to return. However, I can make a substantial contribution outside China as well by working through diplomatic channels. Because of my special status, I regularly meet with the political leaders of Western countries and with other kinds of leaders to advise them about the situation in China and how to put pressure on the Chinese Communist Party. I am also able to support and assist the democratic movement within China from abroad and, consequently, I am able to help build bridges between the people working for democracy within China and those of us working for the same goal outside.

Though my basic ideas about the political situations in China and the West haven't changed dramatically since I was released from prison and expelled from China, I have learned some things as a result of my constant interactions with politicians on the outside. I believe Chinese politicians who live in the West and who are working for democracy in China put too much emphasis on agreement among themselves. I believe it is natural that members of the same movement will have different views and opinions about things. We (democracy and human rights activists) have very little money and still lack people. We face a very strong opponent in the Chinese Communist Party, so we must not be divided. As the recent nuclear spying case makes clear, the Chinese Communist Party has many connections in the United States and is very resourceful. We need to remember who our main opponent is.

I have also learned about the political system in the West. This democratic system is not without its own weaknesses. I find that most Western politicians do not really have a very good understanding of politics. They are so busy trying to get elected and reelected all the time that they have no time to think about serious political ideas. I have not yet had much time to do any serious thinking about U.S. society, but I do have the feeling that people in the United States are overly reliant on the law. They think the law can solve even moral problems, which it cannot. In China the problem is just the opposite. There is a long tradition in China of relying on morality to bring order. But in today's China, with so many serious problems, morality is not enough. What China needs is more law.

Even politicians in Western countries who are serious and intelligent are forced by political considerations to think only in short-term ways. They have to raise money and win votes and therefore they cannot think deeply. I'm impressed when I meet a politician who has a perspective that goes beyond one year in the future and have met almost none who think about time in ten-year increments. The citizens in Western countries are very intelligent, but the politicians are not as intelligent.

The citizens are more intelligent than the politicians in China as well. The demonstrations in May 1999, after NATO's destruction of China's Belgrade embassy, made this clear. The Chinese government was not as unhappy about the bombing as people think. This was a case of hard-liners in the Chinese government trying to gain the political advantage over the more moderate leaders by playing the nationalism card through criticism of the United States. The Chinese people were at first very upset about the bombing. They had limited access to information and were unsure what to think. But their mood calmed down after a few weeks and serious people started to question what was happening within the Chinese government. These citizens aren't philosophers, but they are naturally skeptical. They began to put one and one together and came to the conclusion that the government that took so many innocent Chinese lives at Tian'anmen Square in 1989 could not be sincerely upset about the loss of three Chinese lives in the Belgrade embassy. They began to understand that if the hard-liners succeeded in gaining the political advantage as a result of the tragedy in Belgrade, then not only would politicians like Jiang

Zemin and Zhu Rongji lose out, but all the people of China and the United States would lose out as well.

So what can be done for China? I am neither entirely optimistic nor entirely pessimistic. There are opportunities for positive change in China, but to succeed the right people need to seize them. There is a fight for China's future between the Chinese Democratic Party and the Chinese Communist Party. Western politicians knowing of this fight need to think in the long term. As I see it, there are but three ways for China to get to democracy.

The simplest and most reliable way is to have democracy forced upon it by foreign invasion, as was the case with Japan, Germany, and Hong Kong. It will only happen in a certain time and environment. Also, it will arouse the opposition of a majority of people and thus cause future troubles in Chinese social psychology and with the democratic system. This is not the ideal way or a way that people can select.

The best way is the way of peaceful evolution. Taiwan, South Africa, the Soviet Union, and East European countries are examples of this case. Though such evolution takes a long time and encounters a lot of difficulties and many unpredictable factors, it is very reliable. It requires three basic conditions. First, a strong opposition force that will become the core of the people's democratic movement serves as the organizing and leading power. Second, the power of a group of enlightened people within the ruling class who can work in concert with the democrats in order to subdue the opposing power and achieve reconciliation with it. This will prevent intense confrontation from escalating into violent confrontation. A third condition is through the powerful pressure of the international community. Without this pressure, the previous two forces will be weakened greatly. The result will only be fruitless. At present, the situation that Chinese people face is very difficult. On the one hand, the opposition power of the Chinese Communist Party is very weak and the enlightened group in the Party is not forceful, and the help that the international community provides the Party is much greater than the pressure it exerts against it. On the other hand, economic and social crises are rapidly accelerating. More and more people are ready to wage a war in exchange for a living, since they have lower and lower expectations for a peaceful evolution toward democracy.

If this most reliable means with the least loss, peaceful evolution, is not to succeed, then various domestic problems, including an increase in the number of people starving, will finally cause a third possibility violent revolution or intra-military conflict. We hope this situation can be delayed or avoided; but history has its own rule and it will not change according to our wish. Our responsibility is to make something develop in a favorable direction by using all possible conditions, but we cannot create history according to our own design. Consequently, we should get prepared beforehand for all possibilities.

NOTES

A significant amount of this essay was originally translated by Wang Ping and edited by Lionel Jensen. Some portions are based on an interview with Wei Jingsheng conducted by Timothy Weston and were inserted into the essay with Wei's permission.

SUGGESTED READINGS

Geremie Barmé and John Minford, eds., *Seeds of Fire: Chinese Voices of Conscience* (New York: Noonday Press, Farrar, Strauss & Giroux, 1989).

Gregor Benton and Alan Hunter, ed., *Wild Lily, Prairie Fire: China's Road to Democracy, Yan'an to Tian'anmen, 1942–1989* (Princeton: Princeton University Press, 1995).

China Rights Forum

Michael C. Davis, ed., *Human Rights and Chinese Values: Legal, Philosophical, and Political Perspectives* (New York: Oxford University Press, 1995).

R. Randle Edwards, Louis Henkin, and Andrew J. Nathan, eds., *Human Rights in Contemporary China* (New York: Columbia University Press, 1986).

Merle Goldman, *Sowing the Seeds of Democracy: Political Reform in the Deng Xiaoping Era* (Cambridge, Mass.: Harvard University Press, 1994).

David S. G. Goodman, ed., *Beijing Street Voices: The Poetry and Politics of China's Democracy Movement* (Boston: Marion Boyars, 1981).

Maurice Meisner, *The Deng Xiaoping Era: An Inquiry into the Fate of Chinese Socialism 1978–1994* (New York: Hill and Wang, 1996).

Andrew J. Nathan, *Chinese Democracy* (Berkeley: University of California Press, 1985).

Andrew J. Nathan and Robert S. Ross, *The Great Wall and the Empty Fortress: China's Search for Security* (New York: W. W. Norton & Co., 1997).

Orville Schell and David Shambaugh, eds., *The China Reader: The Reform Era* (New York: Vintage Books, 1999).

Wei Jingsheng, *The Courage to Stand Alone: Letters from Prison and Other Writings* (New York: Viking, 1997).

6

Beyond Exceptionalism:

China's Intellectuals from Tragic Heroes to U.S. Allies

Timothy Cheek

In getting to know Ah Q, those Western readers for whom China is most alien will discover a valuable fact that remains obdurately hidden both from the Yellow Peril theorists and from the apostles of Red China: this fact is that the Chinese too are human, or to put it another way, *we are all Chinese.*

—Simon Leys, "Is Ah Q Alive and Well?,"
in *Broken Images: Essays on Chinese Culture and Politics,* 1980

China's intellectuals appear in the U.S. media mostly as heroic victims. We see them suffer the abuses of an authoritarian state, trying to be like us and being oppressed. U.S. citizens, on the other hand, appear in the Chinese media as bullies or bosses. For all our differences, Chinese and U.S. citizens share one thing, at least: a sense of exceptionalism. We in the United States are the world's good guys who have the best way of life and are willing to help—or cheer along—the Chinese in their efforts to be like us; the Chinese often see themselves as the unappreciated new world power and victim of efforts by the United States to keep China down. This common exceptionalism extends to intellectuals who lead public discussion in China and the United States. This exceptionalism bedevils U.S.–China relations because it denies our common humanity and clouds our cultural and value differences. There's a Chinese saying for this: "Same bed, different dreams" (*tongzhuang yimeng*). We need to wake up to our shared problems and concerns in the twenty-first century and get over dreams that no longer help either side.

In this chapter we will see that China's intellectuals, as always, have been *agents* rather than passive victims, that our media and government focus on dissidents tells us more about the United States than China, and that it would be more useful for us and for them if we conversed with China's intellectuals rather than used them as a screen upon which to project our hopes and fears. Instead of heroes and victims, such as Fang Lizhi (the astrophysicist who was attacked for his democracy advocacy in 1989) or Harry Wu (labor camp survivor and democracy advocate), we need to look for Chinese intellectuals on a more human scale. For this purpose the anti-hero of Lu Xun's short story, the despicable Ah Q, pricks our pretensions and reminds us of our common humanity. As Simon Leys describes Ah Q, he appears to be the Chinese ancestor of U.S. television's Homer Simpson: ". . . a blend of wiliness and stupidity, arrogance and cowardice, self-importance and servility, cynicism and naïveté, obscurantism and wisdom, abjection and pride—in a word, a formula for humanity."[1]

This follows a key theme of this volume: that to understand China more accurately, we must figure in a self-conscious appraisal of ourselves (see particularly Henry Rosemont's chapter).[2] It is not Postmodern Chic to reflect upon our assumptions and basic hopes and fears; it is critical thinking. The failure to do that in the past has been disastrous for U.S. foreign policy. Take, for example, the twenty-year postmortem on Vietnam by one of the leading U.S. officials in that war, former secretary of state Robert McNamara:

> We viewed the people and leaders of South Vietnam in terms of our own experience. We saw in them a thirst for—and a determination to fight for—freedom and democracy. We totally misjudged the political forces within the country.[3]

The United States is not alone in its misjudgments of the other. Much rubbish has been written in China, as well, about the West and the United States and our evil plans to control, delimit, and generally not give China "her due." If China plays the victim that we can feel good about helping, then the United States plays the bogeyman that allows Chinese to feel blameless for everything not being quite right yet. It is the job of thinking people on both sides to overcome those easy stereotypes and work toward real conversation.

Why? It would be nice to think we might be intellectually and morally improved by an authentic engagement with China's articulate scholars and writers and that they might benefit from unfettered conversation with us. But the compelling reality is that we have more pressing problems in economic development, environmental sustainability, and regional security that cannot afford the fantasy life of U.S. smugness and Chinese finger-pointing (as is evident from several of the essays in this collection). When we accept China's intellectuals as agents in their own right, they will no longer fulfill our ideal stereotype, they will disappoint our hopes, they may not love all our cherished ideals, but they will be powerful allies with us in confronting the perils of the twenty-first century. And as Simon Leys suggests, the Chinese are great allies for the human condition.

HENRY HIGGINS'S COMPLAINT

Who are we talking about when we say "Chinese intellectuals"? The *New York Times*, for example, announced in July 1998 that a "wave of crack-downs" (netting nine dissidents) had swept over China in the weeks since President Clinton's visit and echoed assessments that this demonstrated the "failure" of Clinton's visit to China.[4] Are these representative Chinese intellectuals? We need to distinguish between at least three actors: intellectuals, dissidents, and students. Some of the famous student leaders of the Tian'anmen demonstrations in 1989 were all three, but in normal life the three are distinct. "Intellectuals" (*zhishifenzi*), are by official designation any persons with a high-school education or higher. "Students" (*xuesheng*) are current high-school and college students, as in the West.[5] "Dissidents" (*yijian butong zhe*) are often intellectuals and sometimes students, but the most famous, Wei Jingsheng, was an electrician at the Beijing Zoo. If we want to understand Chinese intellectuals, the first step is to realize that 99 percent of them are *not* dissidents. They are professionals, technicians, artists, and teachers. Their engagement with the state ranges from official spokesmen to public critics; there are Chinese versions of our Henry Kissinger, Noam Chomsky, and Bill Moyers. Many care deeply about China's problems and speak up about them, but they do not speak in the political language common to U.S. citizens and so the U.S. press misses them, for the most part.

How *do* we talk about China and China's intellectuals? Key issues about China thread from U.S. government policy, to intellectual debate in the

public arena, to local conceptions through metaphors that all recognize but
that mean different things to a politician, a newspaper editor, or a farmer.
For example, why do Kansas farmers care passionately about "gulag
labor" in China but not about sweatshop labor in Los Angeles; or want to
free Tibet but not Chechnya, not to mention Chiapas? Why do so many
average Chinese view the United States as the land of gold and its people
as all rich and too stingy to help a Chinese friend? Why are we stuck on
U.S. slights or Chinese improprieties—Yankee Imperialism or Chinese
human rights violations—instead of working to secure clean sources of
energy for our children, an international security apparatus that works, or
joint efforts to extend decent living to humans everywhere?

Chinese intellectuals have been interesting to us, so far, mostly in terms
of these preoccupations—what we will see later in this chapter as manifest
destiny. In all the cases involving Chinese intellectuals the main line of academic and media attention has been on how Chinese intellectuals may be
like us.[6] From the Communist Party critic Wang Shiwei playing David to
Mao Zedong's Goliath in the 1940s (in this case, Goliath won), to non-Party
critics in the 1957 Hundred Flowers campaign, to scholarly critics in the
early 1960s, to youthful dissidents in the late Cultural Revolution, and, of
course, the 1979 Democracy Wall and 1989 Tian'anmen demonstration,
U.S. attention to China's intellectuals has focused on the exceptional (and
often truly courageous) cases rather than on the range of intellectual activity in the People's Republic of China (PRC). We have used that information mostly to decode how we should feel about the PRC at various times,
from praising Deng Xiaoping for "opening" in 1979 to denouncing him for
"closing" in 1989. Recent scholarship on Chinese intellectuals, in fact, has
been mixed in its approaches—some scholars maintain the search for Chinese refuseniks, sprouts of democracy, and indigenous traditions of freedom and civil association. Others seek to explain why Chinese intellectuals do not conform to our ideals in their search for the good society.[7]

Still, little of recent U.S. scholarship has made an impact on popular
views and government policy.[8] Why? Why do we view China's intellectuals as we do? Perhaps it is because we hold ourselves to be Henry Higgins
and China's intellectuals to be Eliza Dolittle. Most of us can imagine Rex
Harrison as the pompous educator of elocution in *My Fair Lady*, the film
version of George Bernard Shaw's *Pygmalion*. Higgins bellows, "Why can't
a woman be more like a man?" We blanche at his privileged presumption
and grin at what we know will be his comeuppance at the hands of Eliza
Dolittle. Henry Higgins, that self-satisfied do-gooder, is a good metaphor

for us, including U.S. scholars working on contemporary China. Like Higgins, we want to save the Elizas among China from their terribly incorrect articulation of domestic and international politics. We presume to be China's teacher. Yet we are perplexed when China's Elizas won't speak our way. Why do we do this?

Students of Chinese intellectual life, as well as U.S. China watchers in general, are not alone in reading from Henry Higgins's script. We reflect a general attitude in U.S. public life. Seymour Martin Lipset most recently has investigated this attitude in *American Exceptionalism: A Double-Edged Sword*. "Americans," says Lipset, "are utopian moralists who press hard to institutionalize virtue, to destroy evil people, and eliminate wicked institutions and practices." He cites parallel views from other scholars and commentators—Robert Bellah, Samuel Huntington, and George M. Keenan—in support of this assessment. Lipset puts this down to the "American Creed"—a package of five core values: liberty, egalitarianism, individualism, populism, and laissez-faire. He traces the creed to the Protestant sectarian tradition in the United States in contrast to the state-supported churches in Europe. It affects all aspects of U.S. political life, Lipset contends, and ". . . it has determined the American style in foreign relations generally." Most central to our concerns, Lipset concludes: "The emphasis on Americanism as a political ideology has led to a utopian ori-entalism among American liberals and conservatives. Both seek to extend the good society."[9] This is one of the best explanations of the odd joining of forces in Congress and the media today between human rights leftists and anti-abortion rightists on the topic of China. The profound costs of American exceptionalism thus cross left–right, Republican–Democrat divides in U.S. politics. Both the Protestant right and the labor left get to feel good about themselves by bashing China. The only problem is, their efforts do not help anyone in China, but they do make bilateral relations tense and waste time on symbols rather than organizing efforts to address problems the United States and China share in environment, regional security, and human welfare under the current international order.[10]

For example, look at the popularity of the moral alarmism in Richard Bernstein and Ross Munro's *The Coming Conflict with China*. It fits the moral expectations and anxieties that animate the "Americanism" of our popular culture:

> The People's Republic of China, the world's most populous country, and the United States, its most powerful, have become global rivals, countries whose

relations are tense, whose interests are in conflict, and who face tougher, more dangerous times ahead.[11]

The attentive reader can note the carefully defined terms here and the focus on "more dangerous times ahead," and the book seeks to offer some advice on how to navigate them. But the tone here and in most pages of the book is one of outraged Henry Higginsism. Given the ubiquity of "Americanism" outlined by Lipset, this book simply pats us on the exceptionalist back as we dream; it does not challenge us to find new ways to engage China and China's intellectuals.

By contrast, the cautious counsel of the papers in Ezra Vogel's *Living with China: U.S.–China Relations in the Twenty-First Century* are less emotionally satisfying. The practical political advice that fills the pages of essays by Michel Oksenberg, David M. Lampton, Harry Harding, and Kenneth Lieberthal in comparison just looks like hard work—not morally challenging; not exciting. Vogel begins *Living with China* this way:

> When clear national purposes collapsed in the United States at the end of the cold war, no consensus remained to counterbalance either the appeals of special interest groups or the images projected by the media, both of which gained greater prominence in the ensuing policy vacuum.[12]

Clearly, "global rivals" with "interests in conflict" are a more compelling story than "ensuing policy vacuum" and talk of *our* problems with special interests and the media. The real task before us is precisely to create a new consensus by *really* talking with China's many and diverse intellectuals.

What makes such real conversations tougher still is that we are often not really talking about each other anyway. Richard Madsen, in his thoughtful book *China and the American Dream*, nicely deconstructs popular debates in the United States on China and shows that they are often a metaphor for the nature of freedom and the meaning of being a U.S. citizen. That is, when farmers, pundits, and politicians go on and on about Most Favored Nation (MFN) trading status, dissidents, or forced abortion, the facts of China are really only the "secondary issue" that enlivens the debate. Threatening China's MFN trading status with the United States is so stunningly stupid as a practical policy, no other analysis explains why the U.S. Congress keeps bringing it up: it is a ritual reaffirmation of national values projected on something big, scary, and not well understood—China. The primary issue is the United States. In a similar fashion—as we shall see further on, with China's misinterpretation of the coherence and thus intent of U.S. policy—Chinese analysts misconstrue U.S. actions and really are addressing a domestic need: pride, the need for recognition of China's achievements over the past fifteen years. Much like Japan after the Russo-Japanese War of 1905, China feels like it has played by the international rules of the game but is being denied its rightful benefits: the Olympics, World Trade Organization (WTO) membership, pre-eminence in Asia. Blaming the United States is a way of talking about this resentment inside China, as is painfully evident from the volatile Chinese protests against the NATO bombing of their embassy in Belgrade.

Madsen introduces a troubling new master narrative—three, actually—that destabilizes the U.S. fantasy of "making them be good guys, like us." Madsen brings to bear the insights of a considerable body of sociological research on the international system and how it affects China and the United States. The internationalization of capital, the professionalization of management, and a trend toward particularism—Madsen's three themes—are social facts on a global scale that expose our professional concern for Chinese dissidents as a noble but woefully incomplete understanding of the world that China and the United States share. The case of Nike shoe factories in south China is a good example. Labor abuses in China are now more the result of "free market" forces of international capitalism, with a strong U.S. component—and fall disproportionately on young women workers—than they are a product of China's communist state.[13] If we reflect explicitly on our circumstances when thinking about China's intellectuals, we become mindful of the complex reality that shapes us and to which we each respond with our different cultural tools. In the troubling global context Madsen paints for us, the "search for freedom" in America and China is no longer the overweening topic of concern. Rather, it is "the search for human dignity and social survival" in the face of these new global forces. From this perspective the whole topic of China's intellectuals changes from helping them be like us to helping each other.

MANIFEST DESTINY

What obscures these global realities and our shared predicament is the sense of exceptionalism in each country. U.S. citizens have a faith in their *manifest destiny* to save the world by making others be like them, and the

Chinese hold *qiangguomeng*—literally, "the dream to make China rich and strong" in a hostile world. The desire to export the "American Creed" to the world rests on a basic philosophical presumption, one held instinctively by most Western scholars. Roger Ames and David Hall, for instance, characterize this presumption as the *transcendental pretense* that assumes that the categories and logic of ancient Greece, as developed in Islamic and Early Modern European intellectual history, adequately describe the experiences of other cultures in all particulars.[14]

In fact, this transcendental pretense distorts our perception of how China works. Recent scholarship has detailed how local societies (and thus national society) in China today work to blend old and new cultural resources—from Confucian family values to business contract law to use of the Internet—to regulate their community lives. We, however, tend to focus upon those bits of cultural DNA—social autonomy, market mechanisms, democratic elections—that *we* value not only as our own, but that we presume transcend culture and apply everywhere for the good of all. In the process of this active perceptual filtering, we distort the picture of social life in various parts of China like a drooping Dali watch or a twisted Cubist painting.[15] The current Western scholarly debate over "civil society" in China (on the model of Jurgen Habermas)—and our hopes that market reform will make the PRC "just like us"—suffers from exactly this sort of "transcendental pretense."[16] This perceptual error causes us no end of consternation, miscalculation, bitter disappointments, and misplaced anger.

Our root problem, as Semour Martin Lipset points out, is *manifest destiny*—our belief that it is our job to save other people by making them like us. Yet manifest destiny is not some "politically incorrect" habit we can just throw away; it is our multicultural definition of the U.S. self.[17] When Chinese commentators interpret our manifest destiny as some evil imperialism they, in turn, misunderstand the central role that ideal plays in our *domestic* society as one thing all people of the United States can share. We cannot move beyond manifest destiny until we create some better vision that also serves to provide U.S. citizens with a similar sense of shared purpose.

DREAMS OF A STRONG CHINA

Chinese public debate, and much Chinese scholarship in the PRC press, fares little better in its attempts to deal with the "Beautiful Imperialists" (*meidi*, the shorthand for *meiguo diguozhuyi*—"American imperialism"). Chinese attempts to find an authentic blend of cultural tools to call their own cannot be separated from dealing with *meidi*. The unalterable fact is that China has been forced to deal with the "new world order" since Commissioner Lin Zexu discovered in 1840 that the rectitude of Confucian ritual administration was no match for European military technology powered by commercial hunger and religious zeal under the nation-state system. When a small British naval contingent sank the Chinese navy in the Opium War (1839–42), China could no longer ignore an intrusive international system. We can tell the story of the attempts by Chinese elites and governments to cope with imperialism, global capitalism, and the Westphalian nation-state system in many ways, but the point remains that Chinese people in all parts of society have been forced, and continue to be forced, to adjust and adapt to this evolving world system. (We used to call it the "Western system," but the transnational capitalist genie is out of the bottle and Washington and London can no more direct this genie than can Beijing or Tokyo.) However, while the contemporary world economic system defines the rules to which the United States and China are both subject, the fact remains that these rules grew out of and are congenial to Western social and philosophical experience and are not so for China.

It is thus no surprise that the United States can play the role of "Evil Empire" for Chinese nationalists. Suisheng Zhao (a PRC native who earned his Ph.D. in political science in the University of California system and now teaches at Colby College) offers a trenchant analysis of resurgent nationalist thought among Chinese intellectuals today.[18] He traces a continuous history through the twentieth century of "the intellectual quest for national greatness and modernization," which Zhao calls *qiangguomeng*.[19] If manifest destiny has been the foundation of U.S. thought about its role in the world, then *qiangguomeng*, "the dream to make China rich and strong," has been the foundation of reformist and revolutionary thought alike in China for more than a century. Zhao sees this quest turning into some very angry and xenophobic nationalism in the 1990s, as in the case of *The China That Can Say No* (*Zhongguo keyi shuo bu*) and *Behind the Demonization of China* (*Zai yaomohua Zhongguo de beihou*).[20] (See Tong Lam's chapter on the new Chinese essentialism—also an Asian-American phenomenon.) As Ezra Vogel notes, because China's political system is less responsive to democratic process and more concerned with coherent long-range strategies, China's analysts tend to believe that other countries' policies also have a similar cohesiveness. The Chinese find it hard to believe that the Congress and the press can really be in any significant way out of line with executive policies or intents. Thus, Chinese think-tank researchers have concluded that the United States *does* have a coherent policy and that policy is to destabilize and slow down the growth of its major rival—China.[21] They see U.S. emphasis on human rights as a transparent ploy (given U.S. tolerance of similar abuses elsewhere) to weaken its rising rival in the international arena, and so forth, and so on.

Zhao's point is more basic, for he acknowledges that not all—or even most—Chinese subscribe to such ultra-nationalist sentiments. He writes:

> While some scholars have criticized the nationalistic viewpoint, they have never challenged its quest for a resurgence of national pride and for a new greatness towards the end of the 20th century. They also share its inspiration of making China as strong as, if not stronger than, Western powers.[22]

Finally, in a telling parallel to the critique offered in this chapter, Zhao concludes that "Chinese intellectuals have yet to find their way to forms of cross-cultural dialogue in which Chinese and Westerners may more critically understand themselves in light of each other."[23]

The root of the problem for much of Chinese discourse about global and local problems, as well as when dealing with the United States, is the unresolved search for identity—expressed in the current nationalist writings as "pride"—that dates back 150 years. Since 1840 the Chinese have seen Manchu conservatism, wild Taiping visions, the muscular Confucianism of Zeng Guofan, racial nationalism of Zou Rong and later Sun Yat-sen and the Guomindang (Kuomintang, KMT—the Nationalist Party), utopian Confucianism of Kang Youwei, and numerous attempts to splice foreign political branches onto the Chinese social trunk—classical liberalism (Liang Qichao), anarchism, state socialism of the Chinese Communist Party (CCP) and the KMT, American liberalism (Hu Shi), Stalinism (Mao Zedong), utopian socialism (Mao Zedong), and market socialism (Deng Xiaoping).

This is all very complicated, and Chinese nationalist writings obscure what is going on in Chinese society as much as U.S. idealism.[24] Yet there are clear outlines that we can see from a distance: local community, family, and government in China have been homologous—they share reconfirming values and practices. People are defined by their relationships (especially family roles), society is hierarchical, and state and society work together like an organism. We can see similar patterns in "actually existing Confucian society" from at least as early as the fifteenth century. They continue to be reproduced socially today with remarkable strength despite what Samuel Huntington calls the corrosive effects of market (and industrialization).[25] These patterns continue not because China is "changeless," but (we must conclude) because they work. Chinese civilization continues to reproduce itself on the level of the family—particularly, a child's education to care about the whole family—and the local community where individual rights do not transcend reasonable needs of the community. These authority patterns do not look like those found in the United States. But they are not despotic. Chinese argue *all the time* about what is fair and what to do, but they do it with their own terms, their own social expectations, and their own language. This is the world for Chinese intellectuals that is as alien to most U.S. citizens as Oz.

WHAT DO CHINESE INTELLECTUALS WANT?

These historical and social realities shape the memories and opportunities open to the *zhishifenzi*—China's intellectuals. It is easy to equate them with writers for the *New Yorker* or television analysts or university professors in the United States. But as we can see, their world is very different. And their place in Chinese society is at once more august (unlike the United States, the government actually pays attention to them) and more perilous (the Chinese government therefore tries to control intellectuals) than that of intellectuals in the United States (who generally feel both ignored and free). In the decade since our great hope and dismay around the popular protests in Tian'anmen and the brutal crackdown, the majority of China's intellectuals have not acted in accord with the "American Creed."[26] They have not tried to form independent political parties based on a public constituency in the Western fashion. Why? The root causes for intellectuals' continuing focus on the state rather than independent association are a lack of faith in intellectual autonomy and weak social support for autonomous activities. In short, most Chinese intellectuals maintain a value orientation that seeks to negotiate with and improve the state, in the end to serve or be part of the state, rather than to improve governance by challenging the state in some adversarial role.[27] There are positive reasons for this, as well, in the cultural tools handed down to Chinese intellectuals from historical experience. Propaganda on behalf of the ideals of the state is an honorable vocation in Chinese culture, as well an explicit expectation of the current Party-state.

Chinese intellectuals' attitudes about their relationship to political power further reinforce the cooptive and "conversational" cooperation of government party and public associations (most often business associations these days) and do not fit the adversarial model of public debate we are used to in the United States and Europe (i.e., the *publicum* in Habermas's model of civil society). These build on the bases of local community mentioned previously. As well, PRC intellectuals' attitudes toward that state have been characterized by a fierce *patriotism;* their behavior with superiors, peers, and subordinates reflects an acceptance of vertical *patronage;* and, their self-expressions reflect a profound elitism and sense of *paternalism* (which we see echoed in the habits of Chinese entrepreneurs).[28] These are not the values and habits of republicanism, as we know it.

These values have supported an unwritten deal between the CCP and intellectuals in the PRC: in return for obedient service to the Party, establishment intellectuals are promised the opportunity to serve China and to engage in intellectual pursuits at a reasonable standard of living. It is clear from the activities and writings of a number of the founding generation of establishment intellectuals between the 1930s and the Cultural Revolution that they found this deal to be a desirable revision of the old "contract" between the educated elite and the state, which had collapsed with the fall of the Chinese empire. Under this arrangement with the CCP, the educated elite gave up claims to the wealth and political power of their scholar-gentry ancestors to serve what they felt was a more egalitarian and socially just government. They rejected the status of landlord and scholar-elite (*shenshi*) and accepted that of intellectual (*zhishifenzi*) and cadre (*ganbu*). They honored the common people as never before in history and gave of their talents to raise the cultural and economic level of every Chinese—by serving in the Party-state.[29] This is the world in which China's senior intellectuals—such as Fang Lizhi and Yan Jiaqi (political scientist and now exiled democracy proponent)—grew up.

This model has changed with the repercussions of the post-Mao reforms. There have been periods when sharp criticism, not to mention sullen silence, from intellectuals has been tolerated by the CCP. Yet, down to the present, the CCP has continually reasserted its prerogative to silence and punish any critics.[30] We can certainly see examples of intellectuals who tried, valiantly, to extend the realm of intellectual autonomy, to find a fulcrum outside Party dogma on which to leverage the Party in the direction they felt best. However, all who were at all influential were interested in improving the Party. Even Fang Lizhi, the famous astrophysicist turned gadfly, spent his time trying to work with the Party, until it tossed him out of the country.[31] There are certainly Chinese intellectuals, particularly now among the post-Tian'anmen exiles, who seek liberal democratic institutions for China, and there is a lively and growing "postmodern" (*houxin shiqi*) pop culture that calls youth further from Party and state. But I do not see much of them in China, and I do not see their influence among most Chinese intellectuals. The discourse of positive rights, limited government, and antagonistic public contention remain alien to Chinese intellectuals in general.[32] Intelligent maneuvering, tactful negotiating, and a pragmatic sense of finding the best dollar for one's skills, however, are more common among Chinese intellectuals.

High-level intellectuals are thus unlikely to act as a major force for democratization. However, they can easily fit into the institutions of governing party and public associations in a way that will promote *liberalization*. Opportunities for intellectuals in the 1990s are greater by *xiahai*, "jumping into the sea of commerce." In joint-venture businesses or as consultants they will likely contribute to the official–private negotiations that will determine some limits on state rule.[33] Literary intellectuals have turned to the international cultural marketplace, especially film, to make their statements—from attacks on Confucian tradition in the films of Chen Kaige to explorations of what constitutes the "roots" of Chinese culture in the films of Zhang Yimo.[34] All of this brings Chinese intellectuals into the same international economic system that Richard Madsen has pointed out; it behooves us therefore to notice that they are next to us on this express train to who-knows-where and to listen to them as fellow passengers.

APPROACHING CHINESE INTELLECTUALS AS ALLIES

In light of the context offered previously, treating Chinese intellectuals as heroic victims trying "to be like us" is neither accurate nor very helpful. What, then, would be a better approach? There is a simple answer: listen, and listen for a variety of Chinese voices on topics of mutual concern with U.S. citizens. As Richard Madsen shows in *China and the American Dream*, the "liberal myth" of China that sought out these heroic victims served the United States pretty well as a way to talk about our domestic debates over the creation of a free and just society during the Cold War. But in the context of new global forces and the end of the Cold War with the collapse of Soviet power, there are new problems the old "myth" cannot address: the need for "new integrative visions that can help people reconcile and balance the ambiguities unleashed by the market, the necessities recognized by the social science professions, and the yearnings activated in the quest for community." Madsen names our current task: "What is required is not so much for the United States to teach China about democracy as for people in both societies to help each other search for democracy amid the confusing contradictions of the modern world."[35] Jeffrey Wasserstrom suggests we do this work by "listening more closely to the diversity of Chinese opinion on where the PRC is headed."[36] The key here is not only listening but *diversity*. There is no more a single voice for China and China's intellectuals than there is for the United States. This calls us to listen to and engage with Chinese intellectuals not only in the PRC proper but in Hong Kong, Taiwan, Singapore, and the wide diaspora from Kuala Lumpur to Sydney to Vancouver, and most especially the Chinese who make up a large part of the Asian-American community.

How might we listen to build more effective encounters? We return to the image of Ah Q. Madsen raises the ideal of humility in U.S.–China relations. He means it in the sense used by theologian Reinhold Niebuhr, as an attitude that seeks high ideals while acknowledging the "vanity in all human ambitions and achievements." "This is no excuse," writes Madsen, "for ignoring human rights violations in the name of cultural relativism. It is motive for continuing to pursue the cause of basic human decency around the world while realizing that this can never be accomplished unless one also reforms oneself."[37]

We are likely to find three specific places of encounter as we approach Chinese intellectuals as allies: *texts, concepts,* and *projects.* There have long been Chinese who are trained specialists in classical and contemporary Western thought and society, and today there are even more; there are U.S. scholars similarly trained in ancient and modern China. We will discover different readings of some common texts—from Plato to Confucius to Hobbes to Mao.[38] We may well discover that we have different meanings attached to key concepts—such as "individual" or "civil society." And we will no doubt come to see that we have different, but not necessarily incompatible, projects—philosophical and political goals we hope to achieve through our studies. A few examples will suggest the promise of moving our understanding of Chinese intellectuals from heroes to allies. Li Zehou is an example of what different readings can bring to our shared project of making sense of the troubling new world order we share. Shih Yuan-kang and Zhang Rulun remind us of how common terms such as "individual" or "civil society" can have challengingly different meanings. And, Yanqi Tong and Xiao-huang Yin suggest the contributions Chinese in the United States can make to our understanding not only of China but of the United States.

AESTHETICS AND MORAL AGENCY

Li Zehou is one of China's most prominent, and controversial, contemporary philosophers. A researcher in the department of philosophy in the Chinese Academy of Social Sciences, Beijing, he has largely been working and teaching in the United States since 1989 because the Beijing authorities suspect him of supporting the student demonstrations in Tian'anmen. What Li offers, however, are not ideas on democracy but on aesthetics—theories of beauty. And, his core reading is not just in Chinese classics but especially in Immanuel Kant and German philosophy. He takes a Western text (Kant) and offers a refreshing counterpoint from which to reconsider European aesthetics. His aesthetics is not arcane; it is pragmatic. Li Zehou represents the core of his project in the word *subjectality* (which he coins in English for the term *zhutixing*), the active and experientially defined moral agent. His goal is to help Chinese to find their way out of the social and cultural vacuum in post-Mao China through the cultivation of aesthetic experience that reveals humans as themselves magnificent living works of art, able to break through their "cultural-psychological formations" to develop humanity. He shows how the experience of the beautiful provides a way for humans to create a civilized society.[39] Most of Li Zehou's essays are in Chinese or in dense academic journals, but his history of Chinese aesthetics, *The Path of Beauty*, is easily available in paperback.[40] Li Zehou offers a path toward celebrating and extending human dignity that fits the broader conversation Richard Madsen and others seek. And Li Zehou is but an example. Tu Wei-ming at Harvard, Liu Shu-hsien at the Chinese University of Hong Kong, and Roger Ames at the University of Hawaii each seriously take up, though in different and even contradictory ways, the moral vision and current practical uses of ideas from Chinese culture for addressing current global problems.[41]

EXPANDING OUR HORIZONS

Real conversation over common challenges of the new world order brings some real surprises. Some basic assumptions about what our ideas mean—and which therefore shape and limit what we can consider by way of solutions—are challenged by serious Chinese intellectuals who study Western thought. Shih Yuan-kang at the Chinese University of Hong Kong deconstructs what we mean by "individual." He does this, in part, on the basis of a Confucian sense of the social construction of self (i.e., as a certain person's son or daughter, partner, parent, neighbor, etc.—all concrete and carrying mutual obligations in order to preserve civility) but also in part from a reading of Canadian philosopher Charles Taylor.[42] As with Li Zehou, Shih roots his conversation in a shared problem—how do we create equitable and civil communities today rather than cultural or ethnic particularism. Like Roger Ames, by applying Chinese assumptions to key terms of U.S. discourse, Shih expands our horizons. For example, perhaps we need to think about what constitutes an "individual" and her or his rights and needs in new ways. Similarly, Zhang Rulun at Fudan University, Shanghai, calls into question assumptions most of us have about "civil society." "Civil society" is generally seen by Western writers as a key mechanism by which free markets promote liberal democracy through strengthening society over the state. Zhang, as a specialist in European philosophy, challenges that assumption and depicts "civil society" as a parasite living off the organization and social order provided by the state. Zhang mostly uses *Western* thinkers—from Plato to Nietzsche—to make this criticism.[43] Zhang challenges us to consider more carefully—and in the context of changing global economics—whether or not market economic relations alone promote the good things we associate with democracy.

Zhang Rulun can also serve as an example of the great number of active Chinese intellectuals who are not picked up on the *New York Times*'s radar. He is an established professional (associate professor of philosophy) with Ph.D. training and international research experience. He is not a dissident. Yet his work on Chinese issues, especially on Chinese intellectuals, reflects a profound moral commitment. With what I would call a post-Marxist analysis reminiscent of Li Zehou's, Zhang concludes his study of "Intelligentsia and Modernization" by asserting: "Humanity not only needs material prosperity, it also needs spiritual (*jingshen*) prosperity. The intelligentsia may not participate directly in the creation of material wealth, but it ought to give humanity spiritual wisdom."[44] This may not be U.S. democracy, but it is a voice from which we may learn something of value. Again, these intellectuals are but examples. Unfortunately, these kinds of writings are not easily available, though a little effort at your public library can get you a selection of their writings.

NEW VOICES ON OLD TOPICS

Finally, if we look more widely for voices of Chinese intellectuals, we come full circle back to the United States. Chinese immigrants include a good number of intellectuals, especially since 1989 when the U.S. government allowed PRC students in the United States to obtain residency after the Tian'anmen crackdown. We have seen the fresh perspective on Chinese intellectuals that Suisheng Zhao provides (see earlier in this chapter). Yanqi Tong, a PRC native with graduate training in the United States, is a professor at the University of Utah. She uses current academic political science to analyze one of the key questions that concern Chinese intellectuals: What's happening in China's post-Mao reforms? Instead of finding heroes and villains (per the "American liberal myth"), Tong compares China and Hungary as examples of late-Stalinist economies that chose market reform to address problems in their societies. Hungary went democratic; China did not. Why? She finds that a coalition of moderates in the regime and in the opposition succeeded in making the democratic transition for Hungary in 1990, while hard-line conservatives confronted hard-line democrats in China to produce the confrontations and repression associated with Tian'anmen in 1989. Tong offers a horizon-expanding conclusion: a decade later Hungary has become an impotent state, unable to deliver the promises of market reform and democratization to the average (and aggrieved) citizen, while undemocratic China has become a fairly successful "developmental state." Her purpose is not to support authoritarian regimes; rather, it is to confront us with outcomes that shake our assumptions and suggest alternatives.[45]

Xiao-huang Yin, a professor of American studies at Occidental College, brings his PRC background and Harvard training to a fresh understanding of China and Asian Americans. As his appointment indicates, his primary focus is on the United States. This is the final step in listening: hearing what Chinese intellectuals have to say about us. While polemical works from Beijing like *The China That Can Say No* catch our attention with their paranoid fantasies, what serious scholars such as Yin have to say about Asian-American life is not easy to hear, even for Asian Americans. For example, he highlights not only the role Chinese should have as Asian Americans in the public debates about China (and he is a frequent contributor to newspapers) but also exposes the economic gulf between "uptown" professional Asian Americans and "downtown" working poor and often recently arrived Asian Americans.[46] With this dual perspective, Yin raises another horizon-expanding question: What are the human rights consequences of economic reform in China? Instead of our happy assumption that markets lead to the good life, Yin reminds us that there are currently over 157 million laborers in China who have lost jobs in the reform and are struggling in poverty. "China's economic reform," Yin concludes, "has been sustained by encroaching on the rights of the unprivileged workers and peasants."[47]

Xiao-huang Yin's questioning of market reform in China, or at least raising the human rights costs of rapid privatization, is just the sort of challenging and productive question the old "liberal myth" avoids. It is also a critical holding of the PRC to international norms that U.S. citizens and their government should continue (as Xiao Qiang rightly raises in another chapter in this volume), but it keeps us honest by connecting such criticism to a frank appraisal of ourselves and our social order. In this way the United States and China can work as allies pursuing shared dreams.

CONCLUSION

We began this chapter with Ah Q but should end with Eliza Dolittle. We have seen that neither are China's intellectuals like us nor, in general, do they intend to be. Our focus on saving dissidents too often prolongs our dreams of manifest destiny and Henry Higginsism, which do not fit the realities of the post–Cold War international order. Instead, our didactic democratic dreams only arouse the anxieties about *qiangguomeng* and inflame nationalist exceptionalism among Chinese intellectuals. Moving away from the old teacher–student relationship between the United States and China, we find that Chinese intellectuals have much to offer us by way of fresh perspectives on philosophy—Western, as well as Chinese—by challenging our assumptions about what we mean by "individual" and "civil society" and by bringing new angles on comparative studies and international links—in the case of labor problems—that tie China and the United States together.

Ah Q can serve as a cure for false pride on both sides, but we do not need to embrace him, other than ironically. More useful to our lives is to turn on the presumptions of Henry Higginsism. Better to acknowledge that we— Chinese and U.S. citizens—are as energetic and as clueless of the new world we must deal with as the promising flower girl. Henry Higgins cannot learn, but Eliza Dolittle can and does. Chinese intellectuals become a valuable part of our lives, and we can be for them, when we remember: we are *all* Elizas. And there is hope.

NOTES

I would like to thank my colleagues at the November 1997 symposium, "China after Deng: Considerations on Politics, Society, and Culture" (especially Richard Bernstein), for their critical comments and convey my gratitude to Lionel Jensen and Tim Weston for their careful editorial work.

1. Leys, "Is Ah Q Alive and Well?," 33. This outrageous loser was fictionally generated at a point of tense cultural conflict in the early twentieth century when Chinese intellectuals adapted some elements from Western culture to reconstruct the failed Imperial Confucian order. His image reminds us also of the long and troubled history of U.S.–China relations.

2. For a challenging philosophical reflection that in many ways serves as a model for engaging China as an ally in the face of shared problems, see Henry Rosemont, Jr., *A Chinese Mirror: Moral Reflections on Political Economy and Society* (La Salle, Ill.: Open Court, 1991).

3. *In Retrospect: The Tragedy and Lessons of Vietnam* (New York: Times Books, 1995), 332. Quoted in David Kelly, "Freedom—A Eurasian Mosaic," in *Asian Freedoms: The Idea of Freedom in East and Southeast Asia*, David Kelly and Anthony Reid, eds. (Cambridge: Cambridge University Press, 1998).

4. "China Detains 9 Dissidents Who Sought to Form a Party," *New York Times*, Sunday, July 12, 1998, 3.

5. For an excellent overview and sound sociological picture of the role of intellectuals in post-Mao China, see Lynn T. White, III, "Thought Workers in Deng's Time," in *China's Intellectuals and the State: In Search of a New Relationship*, Merle Goldman, Timothy Cheek, and Carol Lee Hamrin, eds. (Cambridge, Mass.: Harvard Council on East Asian Studies, 1987), 253–274.

6. I see this reflected in almost all U.S. scholarship, save those among the "difference finders" (see note 7). Notable and influential studies include: Roderick

MacFarquhar, *The Hundred Flowers Campaign and Chinese Intellectuals* (New York: Praeger, 1960); Merle Goldman, *Literary Dissent in Communist China* (Cambridge, Mass.: Harvard University Press, 1967), and *China's Intellectuals: Advise and Dissent* (Cambridge, Mass.: Harvard University Press, 1981); Peter R. Moody, *Opposition and Dissent in Contemporary China* (Stanford: Hoover Institution Press, 1977); and the general picture given in the PRC volumes of the *Cambridge History of China*.

7. Good scholarship acknowledges the complexities of intellectual life in China. Still, we can distinguish those who seek expressions of democratic organization and liberal ideals and those who suspect Chinese construction of the public arena and social goods will likely be significantly different from ours. Among the identity seekers: Merle Goldman, *Sowing the Seeds of Democracy in China: Political Reform in the Deng Xiaoping Era* (Cambridge, Mass.: Harvard University Press, 1994); Bill Brugger and David Kelly, *Chinese Marxism in the Post-Mao Era* (Stanford: Stanford University Press, 1990); Kelly and Reid, *Asian Freedoms*; Timothy Brook, "Auto-Organization in Chinese Society," in *Civil Society in China*, Timothy Brook and B. Michael Frolic, eds. (Armonk, N.Y.: M. E. Sharpe, 1997), 19–45. Among the difference finders: *China's Establishment Intellectuals*, Carol Hamrin and Timothy Cheek, eds. (Armonk, N.Y.: M. E. Sharpe, 1986); *China's Intellectuals and the State: In Search of a New Relationship*, Merle Goldman, Timothy Cheek, and Carol Hamrin, eds. (Cambridge, Mass.: Harvard Council on East Asian Studies, 1987); *Popular Protest and Political Culture in China*, Jeffrey Wasserstrom and Elizabeth Perry, eds. (Boulder, Colo.: Westview Press, 1992/1994); Yanqi Tong, *Transitions from State Socialism: Economic and Political Change in Hungary and China* (Lanham, Md.: Rowman & Littlefield Publishers, 1997); B. Michael Frolic, "State-Led Civil Society," in *Civil Society in China*, Brook and Frolic, eds., 46–67.; and *Market Economics and Political Change: Comparing China and Mexico*, Juan T. Lindau and Timothy Cheek, eds. (Lanham, Md.: Rowman & Littlefield Publishers, 1998).

8. An excellent account of U.S. media coverage of China in the form of a considered conversation among journalists, government advisers, and Chinese journalists is available in *U.S. Media Coverage of China*, Conference Report by Teresa J. Lawson, National Committee on U.S.–China Relations, Policy Series, no. 14 (New York, June 1998). This conference maintains a Web site that tracks and accepts further conversation and commentary: http://chinamedia.soc.american.edu.

9. Semour Martin Lipset, *American Exceptionalism: A Double-Edged Sword* (New York: W. W. Norton & Co., 1997), quotations in order from pages 63, 17, 20, and 63.

10. And the costs of this alliance are nicely analyzed in Jeffrey N. Wasserstrom, "Distortions in the China Debate," *Dissent* (Summer 1997): 17–23.

11. Richard Bernstein and Ross Munro, *The Coming Conflict with China* (New York: Knopf, 1997), 1.

12. Ezra Vogel, ed., *Living with China: U.S.–China Relations in the Twenty-First Century* (New York: W. W. Norton & Co., 1997), 17.

13. See Li Xiaojiang, "Economic Reform and the Awakening of Chinese

Women's Collective Consciousness," in *Engendering China: Women, Culture, and the State,* Christina K. Gilmartin, Gail Hershatter, Lisa Rofel, and Tyrene White, eds. (Cambridge, Mass.: Harvard Council on East Asian Studies, 1994).

14. David Hall and Roger Ames, *Anticipating China: Thinking through the Narratives of Chinese and Western Culture* (Albany, N.Y.: State University Press of New York, 1994). Hall and Ames use the very different cosmology of Han Dynasty Confucianism to confront the logic of Greco-Roman philosophy with the relational ethics of the Confucian-Taoist-Yin/Yang synthesis of Han philosophy.

15. See the other chapters in this volume, especially Tim Oakes's on rural life and Tim Weston's on labor. These issues are explored in the chapters of Lindau and Cheek, *Market Economics and Political Change,* esp. Cheek, "Gaps in the Civil Society Model," and Pitman Potter, "Market Reform and Legal Culture in Shanghai." Both chapters review several recent studies that try to figure out how China *is* working, rather than how we hope it might be working.

16. Civil society in China has been the topic of hot debate among scholars outside China in the aftermath of the Tian'anmen crackdown, replacing previous emphases on revolution and modernization. The debate has revolved around the search for sprouts of liberal democracy in China and hopes that market economics will promote their growth. See Brook and Frolic, *Civil Society in China,* and Cheek, "Gaps in the Civil Society Model."

17. A brief accounting of this history is given in Anders Stephanson, *Manifest Destiny: American Expansionism and the Empire of Right* (New York: Hill and Wang, 1995).

18. Suisheng Zhao, "Chinese Intellectuals' Quest for National Greatness and Nationalistic Writings in the 1990s," *China Quarterly,* no. 152 (1997): 725–745.

19. Zhao, "Chinese Intellectuals' Quest for National Greatness and Nationalistic Writings in the 1990s," 743.

20. Zhao, "Chinese Intellectuals' Quest for National Greatness and Nationalistic Writings in the 1990s," 731.

21. Vogel, *Living with China,* introduction.

22. Zhao, "Chinese Intellectuals' Quest for National Greatness and Nationalistic Writings in the 1990s," 745.

23. Zhao, "Chinese Intellectuals' Quest for National Greatness and Nationalistic Writings in the 1990s," 744.

24. For thoughtful critiques of Chinese modern analyses of their own history, see Prasenjit Duara, *Rescuing History from the Nation: Questioning Narratives of Modern China* (Chicago: University of Chicago Press, 1995), and Ann Anagnost, *National Past-Times: Narrative Representation, and Power in Modern China* (Durham, N.C.: Duke University Press, 1997).

25. Samuel Huntington, "Will More Countries Become Democratic?," *Political Science Quarterly,* vol. 99, no. 2 (Summer 1984): 193–218, esp. 204. For thoughtful essays on this question, see *Culture and State in Chinese History: Conventions, Accom-*

modations, and Critiques, Theodore Huters, R. Bin Wong, and Pauline Yu, eds. (Stanford: Stanford University Press, 1997).

26. Indeed, the Wasserstrom and Perry volume argued that even the students in Tian'anmen were not clearly pursuing democracy and instead reproduced older models of intellectual leadership.

27. Timothy Cheek, *Propaganda and Culture in Mao's China: Deng Tuo and the Intelligentsia* (Oxford: Oxford University Press, 1997). Some of this work and the concept of "establishment intellectuals" in the PRC are presented in Hamrin and Cheek, *China's Establishment Intellectuals,* especially our introduction. See also, Philip Kuhn, "Ideas behind China's Modern State," *Harvard Journal of Asiatic Studies,* vol. 55, no. 2 (December 1995): 295–337. Kuhn's analysis is all the more challenging as his key examples are the late-nineteenth-century reformers Wei Yuan and Feng Guifen, who have been admired by Western scholars as forward-thinking.

28. For details, see Cheek,"Gaps in the Civil Society Model." Margaret Pearson describes the role of business associations (*xiehui*) in her book *China's New Business Elite: The Political Consequences of Economic Reform* (Berkeley: University of California Press, 1997). Studies of lower-level institutions, or factories, suggest similar understandings (about expressions of patriotism, or loyalty to the Party, and patronage) extend to the working classes. See Andrew G. Walder, *Communist Neo-Traditionalism: Work and Authority in Chinese Industry* (Berkeley: University of California Press, 1986).

29. See the examples in Hamrin and Cheek, *China's Establishment Intellectuals.* An example among the so-called democratic parties of China is given for the case of the historian Wu Han in Mary Mazur, "The United Front Redefined for the Party-State: A Case Study of Transition and Legitimation," in *New Perspectives on State Socialism in China,* Timothy Cheek and Tony Saich, eds. (Armonk, N.Y.: M. E. Sharpe, 1997), 51–75.

30. For recent examples, see Elizabeth J. Perry, "China in 1992: An Experiment in Neo-Authoritarianism," *Asian Survey,* vol. 33, no. 1 (January 1993): 14, and John Bryan Starr, "China in 1995: Mounting Problems; Waning Capacity," *Asian Survey,* vol. 36, no. 1 (January 1996): 21. A vivid account of recent battles between China's "counter elite" and the post-Mao state is given in Goldman, *Sowing the Seeds of Democracy in China,* and participant analysis by Chinese who left after 1989 in Carol Hamrin and Suisheng Zhao, *Decision-Making in Deng's China: Perspectives from Insiders* (Armonk, N.Y.: M. E. Sharpe, 1995).

31. James H. Williams, "The Expanding Universe of Fang Lizhi," *The China Quarterly,* no. 123 (1990): 458–483.

32. For the contrary view, which sees more hope for precisely these democratic values among contemporary Chinese intellectuals inside the PRC, see Barrett McCormack and David Kelly, "The Limits of Anti-Liberalism," *Journal of Asian Studies,* vol. 53, no. 3 (1994): 804–837. See also Zha Jianying, *China Pop: How Soap*

Operas, Tabloids, and Bestsellers Are Transforming a Culture (New York: The New Press, 1995), and Geremie R. Barmé, *In the Red: On Contemporary Chinese Culture* (New York: Columbia University Press, 1999).

33. See the examples in Pearson, *China's New Business Elite.*

34. Both literary and cinematic developments are intelligently covered in Zhang Xudong's *Chinese Modernism in the Era of Reforms: Cultural Fever, Avant-Garde Fiction, and the New Chinese Cinema* (Durham, N.C.: Duke University Press, 1997).

35. Richard Madsen, *China and the American Dream: A Moral Inquiry* (Berkeley: University of California Press, 1995), 227.

36. Wasserstrom, "Distortions in the China Debate," 22.

37. Madsen, *China and the American Dream*, 227.

38. This is precisely what a dozen Chinese scholars from Fudan University and the Chinese University of Hong Kong and American counterparts discovered at a recent symposium, "Visions of the World in the 21st Century: A Chinese-American Dialogue," at Colorado College in May 1998. While the reflections given at the symposium are not for publication, the review of recent Chinese scholarship in the final sections of the present essay is informed by the encounters provided by this symposium.

39. See the set of essays by Li Zehou, Woei Lien Chong, and Jane Cauvel, in the special section "Subjectality: Li Zehou and His Critical Analysis of Chinese Thought," *Philosophy East & West*, vol. 19, no. 2 (Summer, 1999).

40. Zehou Li [Tse-hou Li], *The Path of Beauty: A Study of Chinese Aesthetics* (Meidi licheng), Gong Lizeng, trans. (New York: Oxford University Press, 1994).

41. See Tu Wei-ming, *Way, Learning, and Politics: Essays on the Confucian Intellectual* (Albany, N.Y.: State University of New York Press, 1993), and *Confucian Traditions in East Asian Modernity*, Tu Wei-ming, ed. (Cambridge, Mass.: Harvard University Press, 1996). Shu-Hsien Liu, "A Critique of Paul Tillich's Doctrine of God and Christology from an Oriental Perspective," in *Religious Issues and Interreligious Dialogues*, Charles Wei-hsun Fu and Gerhard E. Spiegler, eds. (New York: Greenwood Press, 1989), 511–532, and Liu Shu-hsien, "Confucian Ideals and the Real World: A Critical Review of Contemporary Neo-Confucian Thought," in *Confucian Traditions*, Tu, ed., 92–111. Liu has most recently been working on Hans Küng's UNESCO Universal Ethics Project. Hall and Ames, *Anticipating China*. Hall and Ames are also editors of the valuable series on Chinese Philosophy and Culture at the State University of New York Press, which includes Tu Wei-ming's volume.

42. Yuan-kang Shih, *Cong Zhongguo wenhua dao xiandaixing: Dianfan zhuanyi?* (From Chinese Culture to Modernity: A Paradigm Shift?) (Taibei: Dongda tushu gongsi, 1998). Shih's approach is echoed in a thoughtful comparative essay by Henry Rosemont, Jr., "Classical Confucian and Contemporary Feminist Perspectives on the Self: Some Parallels and Their Implications," in *Culture and Self: Philosophical and Religious Perspectives East and West*, Douglas Allen, ed. (Boulder, Colo.: Westview Press, 1997), 63–82.

43. Zhang Rulun, "The Myth of Civil Society," Colloquy on Civil Society, Fudan University, August 1996.

44. Readers should note that "spiritual" is only a rough translation of the Chinese term *jingshen*. Its meaning is closer to ethical spirit or morality. See Zhang Rulun, "Renwen zhishifenzi yu xiandaihua" (Literary Intellectuals and Modernization), *Yuandao*, no. 2 (1995): 101–125, quotation from 125.

45. Happily, this study is available in paperback. Yanqi Tong, *Transitions from State Socialism: Economic and Political Change in Hungary and China* (Lanham, Md.: Rowman & Littlefield Publishers, 1997).

46. Xiao-huang Yin, "Immigration and the Asian-American Experience," *The World and I* (February 1998): 331–337.

47. Xiao-huang Yin, "US Needs a Broader View of Human Rights in China," *The Boston Globe*, Saturday, June 14, 1997, A15.

SUGGESTED READINGS

Geremie R. Barmé, *In the Red: On Contemporary Chinese Culture* (New York: Columbia University Press, 1999).

Geremie Barmé and John Minford, eds., *Seeds of Fire: Chinese Voices of Conscience* (New York: Hill and Wang, 1988).

Timothy Brook and B. Michael Frolic, eds., *Civil Society in China* (Armonk, N.Y: M. E. Sharpe, 1997).

Merle Goldman, *Sowing the Seeds of Democracy in China: Political Reform in the Deng Xiaoping Era* (Cambridge, Mass.: Harvard University Press, 1994).

David L. Hall and Roger T. Ames, *Anticipating China: Thinking through the Narratives of Chinese and Western Culture* (Albany: State University of New York Press, 1995).

———. *Democracy of the Dead: Dewey, Confucius, and the Hope for Democracy in China* (LaSalle, Ill.: Open Court, 1999).

David Kelly and Anthony Reid, eds., *Asian Freedoms: The Idea of Freedom in East and Southeast Asia* (Cambridge: Cambridge University Press, 1998).

Simon Leys, *Broken Images: Essays in Chinese Culture and Politics* (New York: St. Martin's Press, 1980).

Juan D. Lindau and Timothy Cheek, eds., *Market Economics and Political Change: Comparing China and Mexico* (Lanham, Md.: Rowman & Littlefield Publishers, 1998).

Richard Madsen, *China and the American Dream: A Moral Inquiry* (Berkeley: University of California Press, 1995).

Margaret Pearson, *China's New Business Elite: The Political Consequences of Economic Reform* (Berkeley: University of California Press, 1997).

Henry Rosemont, Jr., *A Chinese Mirror: Moral Reflections on Political Economy and Society* (LaSalle, Ill.: Open Court, 1991).

Jeffrey Wasserstrom and Elizabeth Perry, eds., *Popular Protest and Political Culture in China*, 2d ed. (Boulder, Colo.: Westview Press, 1994).

Zha Jianying, *China Pop: How Soap Operas, Tabloids, and Bestsellers Are Transforming a Culture* (New York: The New Press, 1995).

Zhang Xudong, *Chinese Modernism in the Era of Reforms: Cultural Fever, Avant-Garde Fiction, and the New Chinese Cinema* (Durham, N.C.: Duke University Press, 1997).

7

Identity and Diversity:

The Complexities and Contradictions of Chinese Nationalism

Tong Lam

The sense of loss and resentment at this overwhelming Western influence in the Third World is a breeding ground for a growing, anti-Western postcolonialism. As a consequence, saying no to America will become more and more common in the world, particularly in Asia.
—Zhang Xiaobo and Song Qiang, *China Can Still Say No*, 1996

Only after we left our society and arrived at a different one, would we then realize the limitations of our minds.
—Qian Ning, *Studying in the U.S.A.*, 1996

When in early May 1999, shortly after NATO's bombing of the Chinese Embassy in Belgrade, Chinese student protesters raised posters and chanted slogans like "Kill any American in China that dares come outdoors!" and "Bomb the White House!" and stoned the U.S. Embassy in Beijing, China's newly unleashed forces of nationalistic and anti-American sentiment radiated far beyond the embassy compound and were felt thousands of miles away in the United States. A *Newsweek* poll of mid-May reported that virtually all Chinese believed that the bombing was masterminded by the United States, while the majority of U.S. citizens considered China to be unfriendly. An article in the *New York Times* warned that the United States had become China's "international archenemy." A CNBC evening program of May 11 characterized the Chinese student demonstrations as the product of "anti-American feelings run red hot in Red

China." This hostile and ominous image of China was strangely neutralized, however, by a subsequent comment made by one of the co-anchors, who, not without a sense of irony, noted that the starving U.S. officials who were held hostage by the angry crowd outside of the embassy in Beijing were "rescued" by Pizza Hut.[1]

The irony of this comment reminds us that Chinese society today is no longer secluded by an inscrutable "bamboo curtain" as it was during the height of the Cold War, nor is it simply made up of a xenophobic mob as it was commonly portrayed during the anti-Western Boxer Uprising a century ago and again during the protests of the NATO bombing. Indeed, when I arrived in Beijing four months after the anti-American protests, I was not struck by the still visible traces of the damage inflicted on the U.S. embassy. More startling to my eye was the prosperity of hundreds of street stalls displaying fake American brand-name garments and pirated videos of Hollywood movies in an alley just outside one of the embassy buildings, as well as the success and popularity of U.S. cultural icons such as McDonald's, Pizza Hut, and even Starbucks that have practically penetrated into every neighborhood of the city.

Nevertheless, these overwhelming signs of U.S. commercial influence cannot conceal Chinese resentment of what they have referred to as the "global hegemony of U.S. imperialism." Any visitor to the People's Republic of China today would be struck by the sheer number of newspaper articles, television programs, books, and magazines that discuss U.S. military power and China's global political, military, and economic strategies vis-à-vis the United States. Most people with whom I spoke were still deeply enraged by the United States' "intentional" bombing of the Chinese embassy in Belgrade, although they were always much more interested in learning more about life in the United States, as well as the procedures of getting a U.S. visa.

This strange coexistence of hate and love for what the United States does and what it represents has in effect been a prominent feature of the Chinese cultural landscape throughout the 1990s. Our mainstream media's treatments of Chinese nationalism, unfortunately, have often disproportionately emphasized its antagonistic and intimidating character while overlooking its complexities and contradictions. But ever since China has become a key player in the rapidly transforming global political economy and has frequently collided with the United States over certain political and economic issues (i.e., human rights, ecological adversity, Taiwan, international copyright, and China's admission into the World Trade

Organization), it has become clear that a more accurate depiction and understanding of the emerging sense of Chinese national pride is urgently needed.

TWO IMAGES OF CHINESE NATIONALISM

The critical discrepancy between the domestic meanings and international perceptions of Chinese nationalism was clearly manifested in the ways in which the significance of Hong Kong's return to China in 1997 was interpreted by the Chinese government and the outside world respectively. Just a few days before China's recovery of Hong Kong in the summer of 1997, an enthusiastic crowd gathered in an open space in the southern Chinese town of Humen. They were surrounded by burning flames ignited by government officials in a re-enactment of the opium burning that had provoked the Opium War of 1839 and led a few short years later to the concession of Hong Kong to Britain. Along with a newly released television series, a CD-ROM computer game, as well as the most expensive movie ever made in China, called *The Opium War,* the re-enactment was part of the Chinese government's attempt to arouse public interest in the history of the Opium War and Western imperialism amid the nationwide celebration of Hong Kong's return to China. Meanwhile, near the burning field, busloads of excited students jammed the Opium War Museum, where they could learn the official narrative of the Sino–British conflict and fire rubber balls from cannons at pictures of nineteenth-century British ships.[2] All over China, the government was anxious to seize this precious moment to deliver its message to the people that more than a century of "disgrace and humiliation" had finally come to an end and China was ready to reclaim its rightful place in the world.

For the outside world, China's absorption of Hong Kong has created a very different image; it represents a bolster to the Chinese ego in the theater of world political economy that has consequently heightened regional and global tensions. At the heart of this anxiety is the image of a burgeoning Chinese nationalism that has been portrayed as a revival of the ancient notion of the Middle Kingdom, where China conceived itself as the "center of the world" surrounded by "barbarians." In fact, many Southeast Asian nations have come to worry that the South China Sea will eventually become a Chinese lake; Taiwan has certainly realized that it is China's next and final target of national unification.[3] As for the United States, many believe that cultural differences as well as potential political and military confrontations will eventually make it China's number one enemy. Similar arguments routinely appear in American public discourse, and recent books like *The Clash of Civilizations and the Remaking of World Order* and *The Coming Conflict with China* are cases in point.[4]

Take, for instance, Richard Bernstein and Ross Munro's *The Coming Conflict with China*, a closer look at which would reveal that their argument is, in part, a reaction to the recent upsurge of anti-American sentiments in China, especially as expressed in the notorious 1996 Chinese bestseller *China Can Say No—Political and Emotional Choices in the Post Cold War Era*.[5] With chapter titles like "We Don't Want MFN and We Will Never Give You One" and "I Won't Get on a Boeing 777," the Chinese bestseller has captured the attention of the U.S. media. And its contention that the American century will soon be replaced by a Chinese century has triggered a sense of discomfort among many American politicians and China observers. It reminds many Americans of the controversial, onetime Japanese and American bestseller, *The Japan That Can Say No*.[6] This latter work, written by a leading Japanese nationalist, Shintaro Ishihara, provided the inspiration for the authors of *China Can Say No*. Meanwhile, Bernstein and Munro's work reminds us of another book, *The Coming War with Japan*, that came out in the United States the same year that Ishihara's book was translated into English.[7]

Do these resonances indicate that the United States will inevitably engage in conflict with China or other emerging Asian powers? Or do they simply represent unnecessary panic due to mutual misunderstanding? To answer these questions, I suggest that we should try to unpack the meanings of Chinese nationalism through examining its complex nature, rather than viewing it as an overarching notion shared by the state and the entire population. I propose we rethink Chinese nationalism in terms of the tensions within Chinese society itself rather than the tensions between China and the West. This line of analysis requires us to conceive of nationalism not simply as political postures or xenophobic rhetoric but also as a form of cultural practice. The complexity of Chinese nationalism, in other words, is manifested in the state's attempt to forge a sense of nationhood through the management of cultural symbols and memory that are sometimes collaborated with, as well as contested by, other forms of domestic interests and cultural expressions. In the same fashion, if Chinese nationalism is to be comprehended in terms of its internal dynamism, an examination of Chinese nationalism equally offers us an invaluable opportunity to reflect upon not only the differences but, even more important, the similarities between China and the United States.

More specifically, in the following, I will first begin with an introduction to the most conspicuous aspect of contemporary Chinese nationalism, as represented by popular publications such as *China Can Say No*, which have inflamed much of the mutual distrust and hostility on both sides of the Pacific. Especially worth mentioning here is the striking similarity in their journalistic accounts of the other side as an evil empire. Next, I will discuss the complexity of the problem by presenting some counter-examples to those nationalistic publications. I will then further demonstrate that the so-called "Chinese nationalism" or "ultra-nationalism" is not a totalizing ideology but an agglomeration of political concerns, commercial interests, and consumer desires that may or may not be consonant with each other. Similarly, I will suggest that the impetus behind Chinese ultra-nationalism, paradoxically enough, is China's ever deepening global connection rather than its isolation. Finally, I argue that the real problem of Chinese nationalism is not its threat to the external world but its repressive nature within China proper. As a form of cultural imagination, I further argue, the ongoing cultural debates surrounding China's national identity are conceptually very limited and one-dimensional after all.

RISING ANTI-AMERICANISM

The primary intention of *China Can Say No* is U.S.-bashing and, to a lesser extent, Japan-bashing. The book is written from the viewpoint of a group of young Chinese intellectuals who are disillusioned with the United States. According to the authors, despite the fact that the Cold War has ended, the United States still maintains a Cold War mentality toward China. They assert that the United States has conspired to suppress the rise of China in international competition by invoking issues such as human rights, nuclear proliferation, intellectual property, and environmental protection. Also, China has been receiving unequal treatment in trade as well as in international politics, and the so-called Most Favored Nation (MFN) status, conceived by the United States, is nothing but a way to hinder China's economic development. It is China, they say, that has been treating the United States with favorable terms. They advise the government that China does not need MFN status and urge it to cease offering favorable treatment to U.S. businesses. In addition, a great deal of their discussion is devoted to pointing out the social and political problems in the United States, the inconsistency of U.S. foreign policies, and the "defection" of Japan from Asia in its pro-American stance.

The authors proclaim that the younger generation of Chinese, who had uncritically absorbed Western—particularly U.S.—values, has now awakened to the growing economic and political power of their own country as well as their own cultural and historical legacy. China should not compromise its national dignity by following Japan's path to imitate the West blindly or even to submit to the West. They warn that if the United States continues to be nostalgic about the Cold War and to pursue its current "confrontational" policy, China will not be afraid to stand up against U.S. imperialism, even to the extent of using military force— for example, to "defend" Taiwan (an area of concern that has intensified since Taiwan's president, Lee Teng-hui, announced that the relations between his country and China should be understood as those of "state to state").

Despite a considerable amount of evidence that was taken out of context or distorted, the sensationalist style of *China Can Say No* assured its commercial success. In the months following the book's publication, newspapers and magazines were flooded with reactions to it, so much so that public debates in China became overwhelmingly shaped by the "China versus the U.S." dichotomy. Even in overseas Chinese communities where reactions were less sympathetic to the authors' position, discussions were dominated by questions like "Can China say no?," "Why does China want to say no?," and "How does China say no?" Meanwhile, the jingoistic overtones of the book also attracted widespread criticism from the United States, Japan, Taiwan, and countries of Southeast Asia. And a sequel entitled *China Can Still Say No* by the same group of authors was published a few months later to rebut their critics who had challenged their original contentions. The sequel, which became another instant bestseller, carries similar provocative chapter titles such as "Confrontation Is Also an Important Form of Human Communication" and "Suppressing Japan."[8]

While the entire "China Can Say No" enterprise (which is still flourishing today) could be dismissed simply as a conjunction of a naïve understanding of international politics, official propaganda, and commercial interests, it is essential to point out that similar nationalistic sentiments are shared by a considerable segment of the Chinese population from a variety of backgrounds, even including, for example, many educated elites who have had extensive experience in the West. In another popular Chinese book titled *Behind the Scene of Demonizing China*, a group of mainland Chinese scholars, journalists, and lawyers who live and work or had lived in the United States contend that constant attempts by the U.S. media to portray China in a negative light were the result of a widespread conspiracy. According to them, the U.S. media is anti-Communist because it works to protect narrowly defined capitalist interests. In addition, they maintain that the U.S. media has been using "the Western Christian human rights concept to oppose the Oriental Confucianist human rights values" and this racist prejudice can be traced back as early as the Western representation of the Taiping Rebellion in the mid-nineteenth century.[9]

What is particularly striking here is that the very notion of human rights that has often been used to reproach the Chinese authoritarian regime by the West is now being deployed by educated Chinese to criticize the United States. Likewise, expressions like "parochial" and "xenophobic," which are usually used to characterize China's new ultra-nationalism, are being used to portray the anti-China ideological bias of the U.S. media.[10] Therefore, all differences aside, the political logic behind each side's perception of the other is indeed much more similar than many of us are willing to admit. For the ordinary U.S. citizen, the accusations that the U.S. media is racist and ideologically biased may obviously provoke a reflexive irritation. Nevertheless, even though the book's conspiratorial claim of the U.S. media's defamation of China is obviously too simplistic and hard to sustain, some of the cited examples of what the authors called "demonizing China" are not entirely inaccurate.[11] As a U.S. journalist recently admitted, China is a formidable and difficult country to report on and many of the misrepresentations of it in the press are often the result of insufficient background knowledge and, in some cases, even personal prejudices.[12]

In sum, while the many contrasting political differences should caution us that a vast cultural and political gap still exists between China and the United States, and the numbers of McDonald's and Kentucky Fried Chicken establishments are not the best measures of the two countries' affinity, their shared political reasoning and critical attitudes toward each other should also remind us that the two societies have much in common. Thus, the popular sentiments of U.S.-bashing in China and China-bashing in the United States, as represented by publications like *China Can Say No* and *The Coming Conflict with China*, respectively, are merely examples of mutual fears and suspicions.

COMPLEXITY AND COUNTER-EXAMPLES

Having acknowledged both the enduring cultural and political differences as well as the emerging common ground between China and the United States, it is wise counsel to approach China from different vantage points. In fact, tendentiously emphasizing the anti-Americanism would not render justice to the complexity of contemporary Chinese society. Years of economic reform have transformed China into a far more diverse and dynamic society than it was twenty years ago. Even in the midst of a growing popular nationalism, for instance, opposite ideas are equally appealing to the public. Shen Jiru's *China Will Not Be Mr. No* is an obvious example. In this new bestseller, Shen, a social scientist at a prestigious research institute, argues that China need not adopt a confrontational stance toward the United States and even praises the achievement of capitalism and suggests that the West has reached the standards avowed in Marx and Engels's *Communist Manifesto*.[13]

Qian Ning's *Studying in the U.S.A.* is another voice that is completely at odds with the nation's currents of anti-Americanism. Published just shortly after *China Can Say No* and quickly climbing to the bestseller list, Qian's book is culled from his personal impressions of the United States when he stayed there as a student. Like many books about the United States that were published in China, *Studying in the U.S.A.* is not really about the United States, per se, but is a self-conscious comparison of the two countries. Indeed, to a large degree, Qian's book reads like an encomium or even a fantasy of the United States. He depicts, for instance, the United States as a land of great opportunity and deliciously free, in contrast to China where lives have been endlessly preoccupied with ideological struggles.[14] While Qian is not the first or the only one who has presented a positive image of the United States, the weight of his voice surpasses many others' because of his unique position. Qian is not a blind worshiper of the West; he chose to go back to China to work after his graduation. Nor is he a political dissident who would seize every opportunity to criticize the government and the Party. Indeed, he is the son of China's foreign minister, Qian Qichen, and such a status has earned him more credibility than those promoters of sensational anti-Americanism.

Another common misrepresentation of Chinese nationalism is to identify popular anti-U.S. sentiments as state-sponsored ultra-nationalism. To be sure, official political rhetoric and public sentiments often resemble one another and hence are difficult to separate. To illustrate, a high-ranking

Chinese official, when confronted by the media, characterized the recent allegations of China's industrial espionage as contrived by the "Cold War mentality" of some conservative U.S. politicians.[15] Expressions such as this, obviously, can easily be mistaken as echoes of those emotionally charged popular publications such as *China Can Say No*. Yet this instrumental appropriation of popular expressions and ideas is not the same as a singular political view shared by both the state and the society. In the case of *China Can Say No*, the book was hailed by the official press, upon its publication, as "fully reflecting popular opinion." However, a few months later when the government was anxious to repair its relationship with Washington and to secure further loans from Japan, the book was criticized by authorities as "irresponsible" and causing "ideological confusion," both inside and outside China, and was subsequently banned.[16]

The conflation of popular sentiment and official foreign policy narratives denies the complexity of the contemporary scene of Chinese nationalism by failing to acknowledge the real tensions between the society and the state. Moreover, it often results in a discomforting belief that China is a hostile nation with 1.2 billion people. Granted that much of the current xenophobic sentiment among Chinese is, by and large, cultivated or reinforced by the state, it is still essential to note that Chinese nationalism has many faces and consists of multiple intentions that may not be consistent with each other. And even as anti-U.S. sentiment has seemingly gained a broad support, oppositional voices are no less popular. Therefore, rather than see nationalism as an uncontested and homogeneous expression of the Chinese nation, it is better to regard it as a coalescence of diverse interests and concerns.

NATIONALISM AND POLITICAL LEGITIMACY

The most powerful engine that propels China's renewed nationalism, perhaps, is the Party-state's desire for political stability and legitimacy. After decades of revolution, political turmoil, and isolation, Chinese people's faith in the Communist Party and the government has been significantly shaken. In the 1980s, as the government began to introduce pragmatic economic policies it hoped would replace the dated revolutionary struggles, it also sought to produce a national culture that would fill the ideological vacuum left behind by unfulfilled revolutionary promises. Thus, nationalism, along with controlled economic liberalization, has become the most important technique employed by the government to retain the people's confidence and to reassert its authority. This is especially true since the 1989 Tian'anmen Uprising, when the legitimacy of the government was further called into question, particularly among the educated and younger segments of the population, who are more likely to be influenced by the outside world.

In this respect, then, the impetus for Chinese nationalism is not so much one of the expansive desire of militarism. Rather, it is a desperate attempt by the government to maintain political and social stability at a moment of rapid transformation. Chinese nationalism, especially, has replaced the outdated official doctrine, that is, Marxist-Leninist-Maoist thought, with the idea of a national self that is built upon a common past and a shared destiny. Examples abound: Beijing's bid for the Olympics 2000 in 1993, the military exercises in the Taiwan Strait in 1996, and the recovery of Hong Kong and Macao in 1997 and 1999, respectively, all demonstrate how the government carefully orchestrated or utilized historical events and opportunities to underscore the collective past and future of the Chinese nation.

For instance, the government has portrayed the recovery of Hong Kong and Macao as the symbol of the end of European colonization and the end of "a century of shame" in modern Chinese history. The handover of Macao was even strategically set in the last month of the millennium to indicate the end of an era as well as the beginning of a new one. Likewise, during the Olympic bid, the government repeatedly emphasized the twenty-first century as the Chinese century (in contrast to the twentieth century as the "American century"), and therefore China deserved to be the host of the first Olympics in the new millennium. So much emotional and symbolic significance had been invested in the Olympics 2000 that when the bid failed, it became a catastrophic blow to the Chinese national psyche.[17] Similarly, the military exercises near Taiwan acted as a reminder not just to the Taiwanese but, more important, to the mainland Chinese that only a completely unified China could bring about the rejuvenation of the Chinese nation.

COMMERCIAL INTERESTS AND NATIONALISM

While these high-profile events captured international headlines and have often been regarded as examples of growing nationalist sentiments in

China, they are but a single aspect of Chinese nationalism. Oftentimes, nationalism is appropriated by other social forces, such as commercial interests, and this is particularly true as consumerism has emerged as an indispensable feature of contemporary Chinese society. An obvious example is the use of nationalistic rhetoric in the ever-increasing commercial advertisements that have become an integral part of China's urban life. One Chinese fast-food restaurant in Beijing used the slogan "Chinese should dine with chopsticks" to compete with its neighboring McDonald's; a shampoo commercial appealed to the patriotic consumers by saying, "People with black hair should use native goods."[18]

Commercial interests do not always coincide with the state's attempt to build a cohesive national culture, however. The same shampoo product that claims to be designed for Chinese people, for instance, is indeed named "Aoni," a character compound that has no particular meaning in Chinese but carries certain foreign and feminine connotations. This marketing strategy of presenting the product as "made in China" while choosing a name with foreign connotations testifies to the ambiguous meaning of contemporary Chinese nationalism, as well as to the divergent interests between the state and the commercial sector. Since the economic reforms began, more and more consumers have come to associate high quality with goods and services bearing foreign names. The influx of foreign words has even prompted the government to struggle against the "pollution of Western words" and to maintain the "purity" of the Chinese language. The State Language Commission has recently warned that foreign words are threatening to dilute China's national identity, and it has reportedly advised the government to introduce new laws to protect the Chinese language from the invasion of foreign words.[19] A government newspaper cited in particular an entertainment center in Wuhan of Hubei province named "Formosa"—a name given to Taiwan by the Portuguese in the seventeenth century—as an example that was "insulting to national dignity."[20]

In short, nationalism and economic development have entered into a highly ambivalent and ambiguous relationship in China's modernization drive. Obviously, rapid economic growth has led to the restoration of a sense of national pride among the people, in turn fostering the legitimacy of the regime. The rise of consumerism also provides opportunities for the state to produce and disseminate a national culture. Meanwhile, state-sponsored commercial entertainment such as movies and museums is being mobilized to indoctrinate people with the state's version of Chinese nationhood. Moreover, in countless incidents, commercial establishments of the rapidly expanding private sector have proven themselves equally adept at utilizing nationalistic rhetoric to advance their interests. But the frequent intertwining of the political rhetoric of the state with that of the commercial sector does not mean that the two are accomplices in the production of a monolithic national ideology. In fact, economic prosperity could also undermine the official definition of Chineseness, and nationalistic expressions that are commercially driven are never quite fully identical to the interests of the state. Most recently, for example, many Chinese analysts have expressed their fears that China's entry to the World Trade Organization (WTO), albeit economically desirable, would expose the political leadership and ideology of the government to the "spiritual pollution" and other uninvited influences of the West. And just on the eve of the country's fiftieth anniversary in 1999, the government issued an order to remove all major commercial billboards near Tian'anmen Square in order to preserve the solemnity of this spiritual heart of China.[21] Together with the banning of *China Can Say No* mentioned earlier, this endless cultural disquiet surrounding the purity of language and accession to the WTO demonstrates that Chinese nationalism, whether it is the official or the popular version, is constantly being contested by commercial interests and pragmatic concerns.

COMMERCIALISM, CULTURAL AUTHENTICITY, AND NATIONHOOD

In addition to the Party-state and the commercial sector, another active agent in the production of contemporary Chinese nationalism is the emerging Chinese middle class. Not unlike members of the U.S. middle class, who are often conscious about their own lifestyles and attempt to adopt a set of cultural values that is represented as homogeneous and unique, middle-class Chinese are ready to accept the state's calling to produce wealth and assist China's transformation into a middle-class society while also preserving their native cultural identity. Consequently, to become a member of the burgeoning Chinese middle class is not just to ascend the economic ladder, it also means to uphold the state's post-revolutionary political ideal and participate in the patriotic cause of making China a modern nation-state. To put it another way, the Chinese middle class is caught up in a dilemma between choosing to join the global trend of capitalism and consumerism, on the one hand, and to celebrate Chinese exceptionalism and national pride, on the other. The rise of consumerism and materialistic pursuit among many educated middle-class Chinese, specifically, has created a moment of cultural flux in which the very meaning of Chineseness is being called into question. And this cultural anxiety, in turn, has also engendered a mighty desire to search and redefine the meaning of being Chinese.

But the solution to the tension between consumerism and nationalism, ironically, is the very act of consumption itself. As China's market reform accelerates and deepens, so does the pace and scale of its commercialization. Increasingly, middle-class Chinese have become collaborators of Chinese nationalism through the marketplace. So, instead of losing their Chinese identity, middle-class Chinese seek to retain and even reinvent their "unique" culture and tradition through their consumption of commoditized cultural products and values. One excellent example of how Chineseness is being articulated through consumerism is the theme park named "Splendid China," located in Shenzhen, the affluent industrial city and Special Economic Zone just north of Hong Kong. Built in the late 1980s, Splendid China showcases miniature versions of China's famous historic landmarks, live entertainment performed by dancers and actors in minority costumes, and Chinese artifacts and foods.

The juxtaposition of various notable landmarks that are associated with different historical times and cultural spaces in the exhibition is particularly revealing. For instance, along with the replicas of the Great Wall and the Forbidden City, the theme park displays the miniatures of the Potala Palace in Tibet and the Mausoleum of Genghis Khan in Inner Mongolia. As a result, despite the contested legitimacy of China's claim of possessing these territories, the exhibition nevertheless naturalizes them as fixed features of the Chinese nation-space. Similarly, by including Genghis Khan in its exhibition, the theme park implicitly reinforces the notion that the Mongol domination of China (1279–1368) prior to the Ming dynasty (1368–1644) was part of China's continuous civilization rather than an interruption of it.

Although Splendid China is not directly controlled by the government, its representation of China is eminently consistent with the official vision of Chinese nationhood; it espouses a particular version of geographical and historical knowledge that is sanctioned by the state. And more important, Splendid China is not just a new form of mass entertainment in China but a conscious construction of an image of an "authentic" China that aims to satisfy the cultural desire of China's middle-class consumers.

Above all, it commodifies the meaning of Chineseness through its depiction of space, history, and people, and encourages visitors to experience and participate directly but nonreflectively in the imagination of Chinese nationhood.[22]

In fact, it is precisely the consumerist orientation of this theme park culture that reminds us of the striking similarity, rather than the difference, between Chinese and U.S. society. In 1993, just a few years after the establishment of Splendid China in Shenzhen, Florida Splendid China, a near duplication of the former, opened for business in Orlando. Consequently, together with its neighboring Walt Disney World, Universal Studios, and Sea World, Splendid China has joined the mainstream of cultural entertainment in the United States. In its promotional materials, Florida Splendid China promises that the visitor will experience "5,000 years of authentic Chinese history and culture," as well as "the mysterious kingdoms of the Orient."[23] So, much like the domestication of Tibetan and Mongolian culture and history in the exhibit of Splendid China itself, Florida Splendid China represents the U.S. domestication of an exotic and foreign culture. Accordingly, on the one hand, it helps to invigorate the idea of a coherent and unique Chinese culture and thus foster the notion of Chinese exceptionalism. And on the other hand, it strengthens the very belief that U.S. culture is an exceptionally and uniquely multicultural one. The final irony, of course, is that neither China nor the United States is unique or exceptional, but the two are increasingly linked in their rapid commercialization of values.

In other words, in a fast-changing world in which we sense the uneasiness of the displacement of culture and tradition, both Chinese and U.S. citizens alike are aspiring to preserve and reinvent what is believed to be vanishing. Hence, remarkably, the definition of Chineseness is no longer authored solely by the Chinese themselves but increasingly is produced by a global commercial culture. And despite much of the exceptionalist claim of Chineseness, the national particularity that the Chinese middle class is embracing today is merely a part of a cosmopolitan culture after all. And in this sense, the so-called Chinese ultra-nationalism as currently instigated by many educated Chinese elites, both inside China and abroad, is better comprehended as a defensive cultural mechanism.

While my attempt to dissect the meaning of Chinese nationalism and the suggestion to view it as a coalescence of political concerns, commercial interests, and consumer desires may be at odds with the more dominant view that portrays Chinese nationalism as a formidable and totalizing ideology, I certainly do not mean to suggest that Chinese nationalism is a healthy domestic phenomenon. Far from it. In the remainder of this essay, I will discuss the repressive nature of nationalism in China and argue that we should pay more attention to the threat and danger it poses in the domestic realm. I will also point out that despite its apparent diverse manifestations, Chinese nationalism, as a form of cultural imagination, nonetheless remains confined in a one-dimensional cultural milieu.

NATIONALISM AND INTERNAL REPRESSION

Perhaps because a society as complex and diverse as China's inevitably encompasses a great variety of interests, political and cultural differences within the society are often regarded by the state as subversive and hence intolerable. Consequently, in the names of the nation and patriotism, voices of political dissidents, women, and minorities are frequently neglected or suppressed. In what follows, I shall use the problem of minority nationalities as an example to show how national interest is given priority over other domestic concerns.

China is a multiracial, or multinational, society and the government generally does not deny this; in fact, it promotes a myth of racial harmony, joining culturally advanced Han with their less advanced minority brothers. Foreign visitors, for instance, are frequently hosted by staged minority cultural shows performed by China's national minorities or, more often than not, Han Chinese dressed as minorities. While the official view tends to present China as a nation in which the Han majority lives harmoniously with other minority groups, racial tensions are reported in Western media from time to time and have even been captured by Hollywood, most notably in Jean-Jacques Annaud's *Seven Years in Tibet*. In fact, the recently reported violent incidents attributed to racial conflict, though representing only the tip of the iceberg, suggest that anti-Beijing sentiments are escalating in some of the peripheral provinces such as Tibet, Xinjiang (see Dautcher, this volume), and Inner Mongolia.[24] Faced with the threat of growing separatism, the government has routinely used nationalist rhetoric such as "defending of the integrity of the nation" as the legitimate cause to suppress, often violently, these dissenting activities.

And along with these serious and violent incidents, another kind of minority repression has gone undetected by the Chinese and foreign media. In recent years, some studies have pointed out the widespread problems of internal exploitation of the non-Han nationalities, especially non-Han women. In China today, it is not difficult to discover that representatives of the officially designated minority groups are routinely displayed in major cultural events such as the nationally televised New Year celebration produced by the central government each year.[25] Typically, these shows feature ethnic dances and songs that are performed by minority nationalities who are in their colorful costumes. The significance of these shows, as many scholars have mentioned, is not simply commercial exploitation as such. Deeply embedded in this form of mass entertainment is an image that China's minorities are colorful, exotic, primitive, and therefore they represent the "Others" vis-à-vis the Han majority. The emphasis on multiple ethnicity, in other words, works to essentialize a uniform cultural identity for the Han majority, which is indeed an extremely diverse group. Alongside commercial exploitation is a political exploitation by the government, which attempts to define the social status, political rights, and cultural lives of the national minorities.[26]

A few years ago, I personally witnessed this dual exploitative phenomenon when I traveled in the southwest province of Yunnan. At the provincial border between Yunnan and Sichuan, there is a place called Lugu Lake, where the local Moso society has been copiously documented, owing to the contention in some popular Chinese literature that it is China's last matriarchal society. The place was very remote, requiring two days' bus journey from the nearby county seat, and because of the hazardous road conditions, explicitly non-Chinese foreigners are not allowed to visit without official permission. Westerners, in particular, were routinely turned back by police at various roadside checkpoints.

I was surprised to find out that despite its impoverished and isolated conditions, the local community was constantly visited by mainland Chinese tourists. These modern-day independent travelers were predominately Han Chinese males who came from all over China, especially from the wealthier coastal provinces. Once a week, half a dozen to a dozen visitors would gather enough money to pay the village head to arrange a dance party where the local native women, clad in their festive costumes, would dance and sing around the campfire. During one of these evening events, a middle-aged man who identified himself as a schoolteacher from north China told me he was so glad that "we" Han Chinese could witness this culture at its last moment of existence. He said that although the local people were backward and primitive, Han Chinese had the obligation to educate and civilize them. When I quickly voiced my disagreement and revealed as well that I was quite unconcerned about being Han Chinese—and indeed, legally speaking at least, was not even a Chinese—he became really upset, even furious. I was accused of being unpatriotic and influenced by colonialism. He said that people like me would jeopardize the interests of the nation.

Later, I learned more about the meaning of bringing civilization to the Moso from the local Party secretary, another Han Chinese. He told me that although many of the local customs such as dances and songs had great value (especially for the development of tourism) and needed to be preserved, matriarchy was regarded by the state as an archaic and barbaric cultural practice. Its persistence hindered the "progress of the nation" and therefore had to be abolished. In fact, Moso matriarchal practice had gradually been replaced; young men from the village were now sent to schools at the county seat and were expected to come back to assist this transformation by actively participating in village affairs. And the government's effort seemed to be working. A young Moso man who was studying at the county seat told me that he appreciated the opportunity of receiving a formal education and believed that the local Moso would be transformed into a more "normal" society soon. Yet, ironically, instead of longing to come back to make his contribution, he wished he could work in the more prosperous coastal provinces. He admitted, nevertheless, that it was very unlikely that he could pursue such a dream since the government expected him to return to Lugu Lake and to help to reform the local community.

My experience at Lugu Lake suggests that minority nationalities are exposed to a double—commercial and political—exploitation in contemporary China. Minority cultures and even minority peoples themselves are increasingly being treated as commodities for domestic consumption. Moreover, they are denied many basic social and political rights such as the choice of occupation and freedom of movement, which are increasingly enjoyed by Han Chinese in this era of economic reform and market liberalization. In short, economic structure and the political interests of the nation have defined the political rights, gender relations, social mobility, employment opportunities, cultural practices, and many other aspects of the daily life of the minorities.[27] Even more telling in regard to this particular incident is that if the Moso minority was victimized by the modernization project of the nation-state, I too, was placed in the larger framework of the Chinese nation. Being defined as part of the Han majority, I was expected to participate in this internal colonization by behaving like a good "compatriot" from Hong Kong and Macao. But whereas the cultural differences between the Han majority and the Moso indicated the cultural backwardness of the latter, my disagreement with the schoolteacher was regarded as ideologically subversive and had to be corrected.

CONCLUSION: THE LIMITS OF CULTURAL IMAGINATION

In recent years, many scholars of nationalism have forcefully pointed out that a nation-state is not a natural entity but is always inventive and imaginary in nature, and the control of the representation of the imagined community is often crucial to the stability and cohesiveness of the nation-state.[28] In China, similarly, public memory, geographical knowledge, linguistic idioms, and other forms of cultural medium are prevalent instruments used to nourish a sense of Chineseness as well as a sense of communal unity. The state, especially, has utilized various cultural techniques to foster the notion of China as being culturally and politically cohesive. But as we have seen, while the official version of nationhood and nationalism is sometimes in consonance with the public sentiments and commercial interests, they are never fully identical to each other.

In this regard, Chinese nationalism should not be seen as a totalizing ideology but as an agglomeration of interests, ideas, and practices that are appropriated by the state, business corporations, intellectuals, and the middle class for different purposes. Yet despite the tension and incongruity between the official and popular forms of Chinese nationalism, the content underneath is strikingly homogeneous and monolithic. Expressions of Chinese nationalism, regardless whether they are spontaneous, state-sponsored, or commercially driven, are all articulated in terms of the simple East–West or China–U.S. binary opposition. Furthermore, the singularity and simplicity of this worldview tends to systematically overlook internal differences—for example, suppressing dissenting political voices and ignoring the rights of minorities and women, the interests of Tibet, the independent status of Taiwan, and the autonomy of Hong Kong.

Even among intellectuals who are highly critical of the government, the use of categories East and West to locate China's cultural position in the world is very prevalent. And similarly, Chinese intellectuals are often reluctant to examine or question the imaginary and constructed nature of China as a cultural and political unity. In a recent interview, for example, Wang Dan, a leading Chinese intellectual in exile in the United States and one of the student leaders of the 1989 Tian'anmen demonstrations, suggested that the future of China should be a "multicultural" state that would "take up a position between East and West—inheriting some things from the East and adopting others from the West."

His ideas of a multicultural China, while commendable, were certainly poorly articulated and narrowly confined in a dichotomous view that has limited Chinese intellectuals' cultural imagination for more than a century. And his commitment to a multicultural China was further undermined when he—a key figure within an already precious circle of critical Chinese intellectuals—later explicitly refused to comment on the sensitive issues of Taiwanese independence and the Sino–Vietnam War of 1979. Indeed, he even advocated that China should formulate its foreign policies according to its "national interests."[29]

This refusal, in our era of a "new world order," to renegotiate China's identity in favor of its numerous and diverse cultural and political currents indicates that even disaffected Chinese intellectuals, who are constantly celebrated by the U.S. media as champions of democracy and human rights, are indeed victims of a very confined and monolithic worldview.

It has been my intention in this essay to urge readers not only to acknowledge the diverse and complex nature of so-called Chinese ultra-nationalism but also to reflect upon the one-dimensional nature of the ongoing cultural debates in contemporary China. The success of China's economic reform has enabled the nation to redefine its cultural boundaries continuously for two decades. For many Chinese, economic success and global competitiveness represent the rejuvenation of their nation. Others optimistically believe that China will soon become more like the West. And yet there are those who warn that influences coming from the West will pollute China's "spiritual civilization." The unsettled nature of these contending views reveals, if anything at all, the state of intellectual diversity and cultural flux in late-twentieth-century China. And for the first time in more than half a century, Chinese people are permitted to engage in rather lively, albeit still very limited, cultural debates.

For a society that had long been suffocated by an extremely confined worldview, these debates and contentions should certainly be seen as encouraging developments. But the present cultural flux and political restlessness has yet to yield a truly diverse cultural milieu in which meaningful intellectual dialogues can be carried out and cultural and political alternatives can be explored. Beneath the current form of diversity is merely a singular or one-dimensional vision of the world, in which Chinese self-understanding is bound by an East–West dichotomous view. In other words, rather than seizing the current moment of cultural disquiet to interrogate the often taken-for-granted cultural and political unity of China, many educated Chinese have instead committed themselves to celebrate, often in jingoistic tones, their national pride and cultural difference.

Paradoxically, as I have demonstrated throughout the chapter, it is the cultural displacement caused by China's increasing integration into global society, rather than China's cultural and political isolation, that invigorates the current wave of Chinese nationalism. Thus, not surprisingly, those who have championed nationalism in the strongest voices are precisely those who have experienced the rapidly transforming economic and political landscapes firsthand. Nationalistic publications that made it to the bestseller list were written by educated elites and intellectuals who live either in urban China or in the United States. Yet regardless of their exceptionalist overtones, the pride-imbued notion of a "Chinese century" is simply a resonance of the idea of an "American century"; and, more important, the cultural and political logic behind these mutual claims of difference is strikingly alike. Likewise, much like the intellectuals and educated elites, the obsession of the Chinese middle class with the meaning of Chineseness, as expressed in their consumption of commodified culture and values, is regulated by the forces of global capitalism, and the "unique" and "authentic" Chinese culture they embrace is only a fragment of the increasingly globalized public culture.

In this sense, if representations of China in the U.S. media are incomplete or misleading due to the rise of anti-U.S. sentiments and the potential tensions between the two countries, the tide of anti-U.S. feeling equally distorts the Chinese understanding of the West as well as of itself. By focusing on a question such as whether China should say no to the United States, Chinese intellectuals—those belonging to the anti-U.S. camp as well as their opponents—are confining themselves to a very narrow scope of cultural imagination.

Perhaps, there is nothing new about using the West to understand and define China's own position in the world. For more than a century and a half since China first encountered the powerful industrial culture, the West—especially the United States—has captured the Chinese imagination. And just as there are numerous U.S. views of China, Chinese impressions of the United States have been diverse and constantly changing; they range from seeing it as an exotic land to a land of opportunities, from a friendly ally to a threat, and from a model to an underworld.[30]

Thus, the recent Chinese bestsellers, whether it is *China Can Say No, Studying in the U.S.A.*, or *China Will Not Be Mr. No*, are only latecomers in a long history of the evolution of the Chinese cultural imagination.

As China has increasingly emerged as a global economic and political superpower and has become more self-conscious about its rising influence in international politics, many Chinese, who are eminently self-conscious about their own culture and tradition, have come to believe that it is the time for their nation to restore its pride and to reclaim a rightful place in the world in the new millennium. But the current tide of anti-U.S. sentiment indicates that China has yet to recover from the shock of its contact with the West. Perhaps only when the Chinese cultural imagination is able to move beyond the enduring East–West dichotomy, will China be able to deal successfully with its domestic problems, as well as play a more constructive role in the international community.

NOTES

I would like to thank Lionel Jensen for his support of this essay and suggestions for revising it.

1. These are samples of the mainstream U.S. media's reactions to the anti-U.S. demonstrations that occurred all over China after the bombing. See Ted Plafker, "Demonstrations in China Subside," *Boston Globe*, May 12, 1999, A24; PR Newswire, *Newsweek* Poll (electronic version), in Lexus-Nexus, May 16, 1999; Robert Kagan, "China's No.1 Enemy," *New York Times*, May 11, 1999, A23; Geraldo Rivera and Diane Dimond, "Upfront Tonight," CNBC News Transcripts (electronic version), in Lexus-Nexus, May 11, 1999.

2. See Liz Sly, "Reliving the Opium War: Handover Restores Land, Former Glory," *Chicago Tribune*, June 26, 1997, 1.

3. See Richard Halloran, "Back to China: Hong Kong Handover Bathes Asia in National Pride," *Houston Chronicle*, June 29, 1997, A28.

4. Samuel P. Huntington, *The Clash of Civilizations and the Remaking of World Order* (New York: Simon & Schuster, 1996); Richard Bernstein and Ross H. Munro, *The Coming Conflict with China* (New York: Alfred A. Knopf, 1997).

5. Song Qiang, Zhang Zangzang, Qian Bian, et al., *Zhongguo keyi shuo bu: Lengzhan hou shidai de zhengzhi yu qinggan jueze* (China Can Say No: Political and Emotional Choices, in the Post–Cold War Era) (Beijing: Zhonghua gongshang lianhe chubanshe, 1996).

6. Shintaro Ishihara, *The Japan That Can Say No: Why Japan Will Be First among Equals*, Frank Baldwin, trans., with a foreword by Ezra Vogel (New York: Simon & Schuster, 1991).

7. George Friedman and Meredith Lebard, *The Coming War with Japan* (New York: St. Martin's Press, 1991).

8. See Song Qiang, Zhang Zangzang, Qian Bian, Tang Zhengyu, Gu Qiansheng, *Zhongguo haishi neng shuobu: Guoji guanxi bianshu yu women de xianshi yingfu* (China Can Still Say No: The Variables in International Relations and Our Realistic Handling) (Beijing: Zhongguo wenlian chuban gongsi, 1996).

9. See Li Xiguang and Liu Kang et al., *Yaomohua Zhongguo di beihou* (Behind the Scene of Demonizing China) (Beijing: Zhongguo shehui kexueyuan chubanshe, 1996), 26. For an English digest of this book, see Dai Xiaohua, "China behind the Scene of Demonizing China," *Beijing Review*, August 4, 1997, 8–11.

10. Li Xiguang and Liu Kang et al., *Yaomohua Zhongguo di beihou,* 16.

11. A notable case of such instinctual demonization of China by the mainstream media occurred during the opening ceremonies of the 1996 Summer Olympic Games in Atlanta. NBC sports announcer Bob Costas ranged beyond color commentary to deliver opinions about China's human rights problems and the illegal use of performance-enhancing drugs by China's athletes. Eventually, following a sharp protest by the Chinese government, NBC adopted an apologetic posture. While Costas's remarks reflected only his personal knowledge about two very widely reported Chinese political issues, the incident has been cited repeatedly by Chinese nationalists as an example of the U.S. media's conspiratorial effort to slander China.

12. See John Byron, "Reading between the Lines," *Washington Post*, March 9, 1997, X4.

13. See George Wehrfritz and Michael Laris, "Beijing Spring," *Newsweek* (April 13, 1998): 38–41.

14. Qian Ning, *Liu xue Meiguo—yige shidai de gushi* (Studying in the U.S.A.: A Story of an Era) (Nanjing: Jiangsu wenyi chubanshe, 1996), 101–102.

15. Federal News Service, "Press Conference with Minister-Counselor He Yafei of the Embassy of the People's Republic of China" (electronic version), in Lexus-Nexus, March 18, 1999.

16. Francois Godement, "Weighing Up the Conflict Factor between China and Japan," *Asia Times,* June 10, 1997, 8; British Broadcasting Corporation (BBC), "Authorities Change Attitude towards Book 'China Can Say No' " (electronic version), in Lexus-Nexus, December 13, 1996.

17. The Chinese government and many Chinese have held the United States government responsible for the failure in 1993 of China's bid to host the 2000 Olympics. Today, anti-U.S. publications like *China Can Say No* and *China Can Still Say No* continue to refer to this incident as an example of the United States' anti-China policy.

18. See Dai Jinhua, "Quanqiu jingguan yu minzu biaoxiang beihou (Behind Global Spectacle and National Image-Making)," paper presented at "Mapping the 'Popular' in Post-Socialist China," Duke University, Durham, N.C., May 8–9, 1998, 1.

19. See Reuter News Services, "Chinese Language Polluted by Rush to Be Western" (electronic version), in Lexus-Nexus, November 5, 1995. The Chinese obsession with foreign, and especially American, products and services is best illustrated in the reception of McDonald's in Beijing. See Yunxiang Yan, "McDonald's in Beijing: The Localization of Americana," in *Golden Arches East: McDonald's in East Asia*, James L. Watson, ed. (Stanford: Stanford University Press, 1997), 39–76, esp. 44–45.

20. See Reuter News Services, "China Declares War on Feudal, Foreign Names" (electronic version), in Lexus-Nexus, November 21, 1996.

21. China News Digest (CND), "China Suffers by Not Joining WTO," <http://www.cnd.org>, April 13, 1999. See also Edward Cody, "Beijing Campaigns for a 'Spiritual Civilization,'" *International Herald Tribune*, January 3, 1997, 4. For the removal of billboards, see Val Wang, "The Great Clean-Up," *City Edition*, January 21-February 3, 1999, 6–7.

22. For a deeper discussion of this theme park, see Ann Anagnost, *National Past-Times: Narrative, Representation, and Power in Modern China* (Durham, N.C.: Duke University Press, 1997), 161–175.

23. See *Splendid China*, <http://www.floridasplendidchina.com>, April 10, 1999.

24. In recent years, violence attributed to racial unrest is no longer confined only to Tibet, Xinjiang, and other peripheral provinces. Since the beginning of 1997, several deadly explosions had reportedly occurred in public places in major cities such as Beijing and Wuhan. For examples, see reports by *China News Digest* on January 1, 1997; February 28, 1997; March 3, 1997; February 18, 1998; and March 16, 1998.

25. Dru C. Gladney, "Representing Nationality in China: Refiguring Majority/Minority Identities," *The Journal of Asian Studies* 53 (February 1994): 92–123; Louisa Schein, "Gender and Internal Orientalism in China," *Modern China*, no. 23 (January 1997): 69–98.

26. On the politics of ethnicity and its commoditization in China, see Susan D. Blum, *Portraits of "Primitives": Human Kinds in the Chinese Nation* (Lanham, Md.: Rowman & Littlefield, 2000).

27. While I have emphasized the constraint imposed by the economic and political structure of the nation-state, it is essential to point out that minority nationalities are never passive actors in the existing social order. Oftentimes, they are able to use their minority status as prescribed by the state to pursue their own interests, such as celebrating their own cultures and traditions to defy or mock the dominant Han culture. See Schein, "Gender and Internal Orientalism," 86.

28. The uses of historical and geographical knowledge in the construction of a nation-state are discussed in recent books by Prasenjit Duara, *Rescuing History from the Nation: Questioning Narratives of Modern China* (Chicago: University of Chicago Press, 1995), and Thongchai Winichakul, *Siam Mapped: A History of Geo-Body of a Nation* (Honolulu: University of Hawaii Press, 1994), respectively. A more general

discussion of the constructiveness of nationhood can be found in Benedict Anderson, *Imagined Communities: Reflections on the Origin and Spread of Nationalism*, rev. ed. (New York: Verso, 1991).

29. See "A Dialogue on the Future of China," *New Left Review* 235 (May/June 1999): 62–106, esp. 89, 98–100.

30. See R. David Arkush and Leo O. Lee, eds., *Land without Ghosts: Chinese Impressions of America from the Mid-Nineteenth Century to the Present* (Berkeley: University of California Press, 1989).

SUGGESTED READINGS

Ann Anagnost, *National Past-Times: Narrative, Representation, and Power in Modern China* (Durham, N.C.: Duke University Press, 1997).

R. David Arkush and Leo O. Lee, eds., *Land without Ghosts: Chinese Impressions of America from the Mid-Nineteenth Century to the Present* (Berkeley: University of California Press, 1989).

Dru C. Gladney, "Representing Nationality in China: Refiguring Majority/Minority Identities," *Journal of Asian Studies*, vol. 53, no. 1 (February 1994): 92–123.

Louisa Schein, "Gender and Internal Orientalism in China," *Modern China*, vol. 23, no. 1 (January 1997): 69–98.

Ben Xu, "From Modernity to Chineseness: The Rise of Nativist Cultural Theory in Post-1989 China," *positions: east asia cultures critique*, vol. 6, no. 3 (Spring 1998): 203–237.

Yunxiang Yan, "McDonald's in Beijing: The Localization of Americana," in *Golden Arches East: McDonald's in East Asia*, James L. Watson, ed. (Stanford: Stanford University Press, 1997), 39–76.

8

China's New Economic Reforms:

Replacing Iron Rice Bowls with Plastic Cups

Henry Rosemont, Jr.

In governing, the first task is to make sure the people are fed.
—Kongzi ("Confucius")

PERSONAL PROLOGUE

The bloom is off the rose. After more than a decade of reporting China's "economic miracle" in euphoric terms once it initiated free market capitalist reforms, the U.S. media has begun to note the darker side of life in contemporary China. But the injustice, suffering, and environmental devastation currently being visited on the great majority of Chinese peoples is being attributed more or less to the continuing legacy of the Maoist era (1949–1976) and the maintenance of a party dictatorship; what is needed, these reports imply, is more capitalism, which should not only solve the country's economic problems but must also lead eventually to political democracy, Western-style.

Without in any way condoning the horrors of the Maoist regime or ignoring the present government's corruption and violations of basic human rights, it can nevertheless be argued that further capitalist "reforms" cannot alleviate humanely the misery in China, because they are in significant measure the cause of it. In order to advance this position it is necessary to focus on what U.S. media accounts of the Chinese obscure, namely, the moral issues that underlie and constrain the possible options open to Chinese policy makers in dealing with the country's problems. In

171

the real world there are no solely economic solutions for alleviating poverty; all options have moral dimensions.

Being a philosopher by trade, it is these moral issues that I will focus on in this essay. Philosophizing about China solely in the abstract, however, would be vacuous, and hence much of what follows is indeed economic, sociological, and/or political in nature—but always with an eye to the moral conflicts that China's (and Southeast Asia's) problems magnify. At the same time, I do not believe these moral problems are unique to Asia, and consequently I will juxtapose analogues to them in the United States. Not being a relativist, these analogies are intended to suggest that my own country, no less than China, needs to confront directly a number of basic moral issues that have been ignored or overlooked for too long.

Thus this essay must be read as a partisan account, which I readily acknowledge; I can't imagine anyone being neutral about the issues considered herein.

THE COMPLEX UNDERSIDE OF THE CHINESE "MIRACLE"

Beginning in July 1997, the economies of Southeast Asia, Japan, and South Korea went into a tailspin. Currencies, stock prices, real estate values, growth rates, and job security all declined precipitously. In less than a year the problems had become so acute in one country (Indonesia), that a regime in power for almost a third of a century was brought down by massive demonstrations, riots, and strikes. To be sure, the Suharto government deserved its fate, yet it was not corruption or repression but basic economic pain that led to its demise.[1]

This steep economic decline throughout most of East and Southeast Asia led to a number of media pronouncements that the "Asian Miracle" of development had run its course.[2] As is usual in such matters, business journals were more astute, noting—albeit obliquely—that the economies of Southeast Asian countries were and are fundamentally healthy in terms of their real economies, that is, in terms of actual goods produced, services provided, and how these are bought, sold, and traded both domestically and abroad. The *Far Eastern Economic Review* made the point clearly:

Indeed, the hard work, entrepreneurship, high savings, low taxation, family values, and flexible labor markets that helped the region grow at 7%–8% a year for more than a decade are still in place. So too the highways, factories and office towers these countries built at breakneck speed.[3]

In a similar, if more predatory, vein *Business Week* reported:

> For American companies, the opportunities are breathtaking. Asia's crisis gives them a chance to grab strategic ground—on their own terms—in economies still expected to be among the world's biggest growth markets in the 21st century. "The whole area is going to expand in the next decades," says Ford Motor Co. Chairman Alexander J. Trotman. "We plan to be part of that."[4]

But if the business media itself insists that these economies were fundamentally healthy, how are the sharp downturns to be explained? Virtually all of the analyses place the blame on the countries themselves: "corruption," "crony capitalism," and "Asian authoritarianism" supposedly characterize the way business was conducted there,[5] and the situation cannot improve, according to the media, until and unless far more "free market" reforms enforced by the International Monetary Fund (IMF), World Bank, and U.S. government are firmly in place.

China is supposedly the exception to Asia's troubled economies. While growth rates have slowed from highs of 11–13 percent in the early 1990s, they remain a respectable 8 percent, and a *Business Week* article deemed it "The last great hope of the region."[6] But such comments make the explanation for the woes of the other countries suspect, because, as these same business journals are quick to note, China has no shortage of "corruption," "crony capitalism," and "Asian authoritarianism."

There is a fairly simple and straightforward explanation of why China has not suffered the mischief inflicted on its neighbors, which simultaneously reveals a basic source of that mischief: China's currency (the *renminbi*, literally, "people's money") is not fully convertible, and its stock markets are not fully open to foreign investment. Hence, neither are readily available in international markets for speculation and manipulation by high-rolling currency traders and deep-pocket speculative investors, whose activities brought the other countries virtually to their knees, with incalculable suffering by millions of people in the region who were and are altogether blameless for their plight.

Contrary to the *Business Week* expression of optimism, the Chinese economy is in serious difficulties, and the most rational and nonpropagandistic (i.e., noneconomic) analysis must be that the situation there will probably worsen. Former economic "czar," now premier, Zhu Rongji, has reined in an overheated economy and reduced inflation to the vanishing point (significantly due to growing un- and underemployment); he is endeavoring to curb the influence of the corrupt "princeling faction" and is moving to radically restructure both the large state-owned industries and the banking system.[7]

But these are arguably Band-Aid measures. China's problems run much deeper, from the massive under- and unemployment that Timothy Weston discusses in this volume, to increasingly starker income inequalities; from grain production shortfalls to greater minority dissent in border regions; from environmental degradation that grows more nightmarish with every passing day to the somewhat more whimsical continuing spell of an ages-old cultural concern with placating ghosts and spirits.

All of these and related issues will be taken up in this chapter. These introductory remarks on the Southeast Asian economies are proffered to emphasize that Chinese governments—corrupt, cronyist, authoritarian, or altogether decent and moral—are not fully free to deal with their problems strictly in and of themselves. Their options, despite the size and importance of the country in world affairs, are significantly constrained by those same multibillionaire high-rolling currency traders, deep-pocket stock investors, and profit-seeking transnational corporations that have wrought so much havoc in the rest of Asia, but whose machinations have been, and continue to be, obscured by the main U.S. media (themselves transnational in scope and power), which are by no means disinterested in matters of currency fluctuations, world stock prices, and profits.

Those machinations are designed to pressure China and other Asian governments to abandon the protectionist economic measures they earlier adopted so that their populations would not have to endure the horrors visited on the great majority of the working people of Western Europe and the United States during the nineteenth and early decades of the twentieth centuries under laissez-faire capitalism. Moreover, the protectionist policies employed by these East and Southeast Asian countries are almost precisely the same as those promulgated by each and every one of the Western industrialized (and later imperialist) countries themselves during that time and maintained until their own industries were believed to be competitive in the world market. No Western industrial democracy ever advocated a "level playing field" or "free trade" for economic games it did not believe it had a high probability of winning.[8]

Hong Kong further illustrates this argument. In the first six months of

1997, leading up to its reversion to China on July 1st, the U.S. media devoted a great many column inches, airspace, and time to speculating on the colony's economic and political future, almost all of it worriedly.

One reason for all the noise was to make clear to China that it shouldn't begin to see Hong Kong as a source of revenue after the reversion. It has long since ceased being a major exporter of toys, clothing, Christmas ornaments, and small appliances; these manufactures have moved north to Guangdong and Guizhou provinces. Hong Kong still engages in production, but it is mostly high-tech, high value-added manufacturing. The bulk of the economy has shifted to services, especially multifaceted financial services. The former colony is now a major player in the arena in which the high-rolling currency speculators, investors, and transnational corporations hold their games, and these groups don't want any changes in the rules of the games that might restrict their search for profits. Hence, the Chinese government must be disabused of any idea that some of the fruits of the Hong Kong economy might be taxed to provide social services for the 1.2 billion-plus—and growing—Chinese peoples.[9]

Media worries about the future of democracy in Hong Kong were also highly misleading in a number of ways. First, little note was made of the fact that for 151 of the 156 years that Great Britain governed the colony, its citizens had no meaningful voice in government whatsoever; the first election that could even roughly be described as representative wasn't held until 1992.

Second, the "democracy" that developed after 1992 was (and is) a democracy very much like that of the United States: a hollow democracy, dominated by money and manipulated by those who have it or serving those who do. The great majority of Hong Kong proponents of democracy—Tung Chee-hwa, Joseph Yam, Anson Chan, even Martin Lee—are well-to-do members of the Hong Kong elite and do not espouse any populist ideas. They appear to have learned a lesson from places like Singapore—a lesson their Beijing brethren have not mastered—namely, that money-managed representative rule by an elite can be at least as effective in controlling an economy and a population as any nonelected one-party dictatorship. And under such rule the elite can simultaneously claim moral as well as political legitimacy for themselves.

U.S. media propagandistic worries about Hong Kong coming under the thumb of Beijing also serve to keep alive the racist fear of a "Red Menace" China bent on expansion. Such fears continue to justify a bloated U.S. defense budget and are easily manipulated to justify a "get tough" foreign policy whenever it suits business interests to do so. Such fears currently run higher among Americans, thanks to the media, than at any time since the 1950s, when the "blue ants" replaced the "Yellow Peril" and Fu Manchu's successors began training the Manchurian Candidate.

The press gave much less attention to the fact that elections in Hong Kong for the Legislative Council went forward in May 1998 just as they were scheduled and that the "pro-democracy"—but staunchly capitalist—party of Martin Lee did very well at the polls. Similarly, in his trip to China the following month, President Clinton was able to do what no foreign leader has ever done when visiting the United States, namely, publicly criticize the host county and government for its policies—while in the country and face-to-face with its head of state.

Turning now to China proper, the basic job, housing, food, and clothing allowances that have been guaranteed by the government since shortly after Liberation in 1949 (the "iron rice bowl") are being eliminated, replaced by the insecurities that also face an increasing number of American workers (the "plastic cups"). Instead of merely reading U.S. media headlines, we can glean a more realistic picture of China's present circumstances and near-future prospects by attending to the statements and policies put forward at the Fifteenth Party Congress in September 1997 and affirmed when Zhu Rongji assumed the premiership at the National People's Congress in March 1998. Such a reading will reveal not that hard-line communist ideology might overwhelm Hong Kong, but rather that Hong Kong laissez-faire capitalist ideology is overwhelming Beijing and will almost surely not be conducive to the well-being of the great majority of the Chinese peoples.

This ideological shift—which began in 1992 with Deng Xiaoping's Southern tour—will remove any vestiges of political legitimacy the Party could claim for itself. Its moral legitimacy has gradually disappeared over the years, beginning with the later horrors of the Cultural Revolution, through the Beijing Massacre of June 4, 1989, and the wholesale corruption of many high (and not so high) Party officials and their families.

But the recent Congresses have now undermined the Party's political *raison d'être* as well; the Vanguard of the Proletariat claimed at its Fifteenth Congress (1997) that upward of 35 million proletarians were redundant and, in order to "deepen the reforms," needed to be laid off. These workers may soon be living in the streets as well, for as Zhu Rongji announced at a press conference, "We will stop all the allocation of welfare housing and all housing will be commercialized."[10]

The Party is not only abandoning the Chinese workers in whose name it ostensibly rules, it is expressing contempt for them. Ren Menghui, a central governmental health-care official—trained at Harvard—explained why heavily subsidized health care would have to cease: he said of the workers that "If the money is not their own, they will not care."[11] Marx's (and classical Confucian) views on human nature have given way to Milton Friedman's.

Worse, the Party and its state and local organs are increasingly squeezing the workers financially, as the need to raise money grows more acute. Premier Zhu can't keep printing *renminbi* notes forever, and China does not yet have anything remotely resembling an efficient tax collection system; thus, as he endeavors to overhaul the banking system and stop the issuance of nonrepayable loans, more and more governmental units are turning to decidedly nonsocialist scams to generate revenue.

Migrant workers in major cities, for example, are not eligible for any of the few remaining social services provided for their citizens, because they do not hold residency cards in those cities. They can, however, be bought by the migrants, for approximately six months' wages. (This is not a particularly high price: migrant workers are wretchedly paid throughout China.)[12]

Another scam being used by production units is requiring workers to buy the jobs many of them have held for years. The going rate in Shanghai is approximately the worker's annual salary, amortized over a multiyear period. Technically, these workers are not buying their jobs but merely becoming "shareholders" in the corporation; but they are no more likely to have any voice in corporate affairs than before, especially in being able to evaluate the performance of their supervisors, in other words, the very persons largely responsible for the miserable way most of those corporations have been run.[13]

Even soldiers and sailors are not exempt from having their pocketbooks emptied by the state. The People's Liberation Army—the largest corporate conglomerate in China—is strongly pressuring its recruits to take out life, health, accident and other forms of insurance; guess who owns the insurance companies and pockets the premiums?[14]

These and related forms of extortion are especially cruel for workers to bear now, coming as they do after almost all other benefits have already been taken away through "reforms." Free day care has long since disappeared in most areas, and many of their private successors charge two weeks' wages of one worker in a family to care for one child per month. Higher education is no longer free in China, and this will lead to increasing socioeconomic stratification. According to knowledgeable faculty and administrators at one distinguished university, the imposition of tuition and fees has resulted in the student demographics changing from approximately 20 percent coming from worker and peasant backgrounds fifteen years ago to .1 percent in 1997.[15]

Another means by which state-owned firms are being obliged to stem the flow of red ink is by demolishing the older, Stalin-style concrete apartment buildings that workers used to rent for pennies a month and replacing them with new complexes that the workers (or anyone else) may purchase—for the equivalent of several years' wages.[16] Such tactics are making some workers desperate, especially those who have been furloughed, and pensioners, both groups of which, in a number of work units throughout the country, have not been paid for six months or more.

The government and the Party are not unaware of the potential volatility of the workers as their general situation continues to worsen. Shortly after Liberation in 1949 a labor arbitration committee was established, but it was abolished in 1956 because it had no work to do; supposedly, there could be no genuine conflicts between workers and their governmental representatives in the Workers' State. The committee was re-established with the new Constitution of 1983 but was seen as a purely formal fillip toward democratic procedures. Now, however, the committee has work to do: in 1994 over a thousand cases were brought before it, and more than double that number in 1995; in 1996 (the last year for which records are available) the committee took up 9,737 cases.[17]

Workers have also begun taking to the streets: increasingly, as Timothy Weston discusses, there are reports of wildcat strikes, demonstrations, and riots (often including peasants) over failure to pay wages or for crops, and attacks on local party headquarters for the corruption or incompetence, or both, of Party cadres. In early April 1998, for example, retirees in Shenyang blocked traffic all one morning, protesting not having received any pension payments since the prior August.[18]

Thus far, the government has not resorted to violence in quelling these strikes and demonstrations, despite its ongoing refusal to acknowledge its culpability for the Beijing Massacre; it is hard to portray hungry old pensioners as counterrevolutionary "black hands." But physical repression of such protests may begin at any time, because a concern for stability is 3,000 years old in China, and there is currently no clear way for the government to meet the legitimate demands of the great majority of its peoples, even if it was totally committed to doing so. Nearly every choice open to the Party places it between a rock and a hard place. Some illustrations:

1. Thanks to the machinations of currency traders mentioned earlier, virtually all of Southeast Asia's currencies have been sharply devalued, perversely making their exports highly competitive with

China's. Unlike those countries, China does not have a large mountain of currently due debt in U.S. dollars, so it could conceivably devalue the *renminbi* to become competitive again. But notwithstanding its much-publicized trade surplus with the United States, over 60 percent of China's exports goes to its neighbors, who would have to curb imports sharply if the *renminbi* was devalued, and who would thereafter look with greater suspicion at the efforts of their large neighbor to forge closer regional political and economic ties.

2. A seeming alternative would be for China to stimulate domestic demand for its manufactured goods, and it could do so by further reducing interest paid on savings. But if savings are reduced significantly, the only other source of capital needed for increased development would be foreign investors, who would apply increased pressure on the government to weaken its ability to regulate how, when, where, and why those investments were made, and to guarantee them, pressures Southeast Asian governments are already feeling, as discussed earlier.

3. Domestic demand might also be stimulated if the government eased up on the imposition and attempted collection of taxes. But it has nowhere near enough money on its own to run the country, which is one major reason for its units resorting to the several scams described earlier. Without taxes, and ceasing to squeeze workers, the only way for the government to obtain money would be to print it around the clock (which would sharply curtail any forms of investment).

4. The government may have the power to stem the economic and political corruption that is endemic in China, a major hindrance to development, equitable or otherwise. Much of this corruption grows out of the system of personal relations (*guanxi*) that stem from family and community roots and are deeply ingrained in Chinese culture. But at the same time, China remains a very large and very poor country, sufficiently so that neither the present nor future governments will ever have the power and resources to provide adequate social services to a billion and a half people who will never enjoy the standard of living of (a shrinking number of) their U.S. counterparts, and families and communities are just about the only possible alternative institutions capable of providing such services.[19] (And see the "one-child" policy, below.)

5. China wishes to join the World Trade Organization, because without the Most Favored Nation status that is guaranteed by membership its

exports would cease to be competitive. But to be eligible for membership it must enforce, among other things, intellectual property rights not only in tapes and CDs but in such areas of biotechnology dealing with seed strains, cloned livestock, and pharmaceuticals, in which it knows it probably never will be competitive, and the fruits of which—foods and medicines necessary for life—will surely remain far beyond the means of most of its peoples, if protected by "rights" that the government must enforce.[20]

6. Sweatshops are another evil confronting the government. Workers are producing goods for the likes of Nike, Adidas, K-Mart, Wal-Mart, JCPenney, and others, some of them working seventy hours a week, living ten to a room, subsisting on a few vegetables and rice gruel, and receiving less than U.S. $4.00 a month for their efforts.[21] Spokespersons for these exploitative firms claim "clean hands" (because the work is subcontracted out) and decry these conditions. But their laments are not confined to speaking of "worker abuses" but include "worker and human rights abuses,"[22] suggesting that the Chinese government is complicit in this systematic degradation of the human body, mind, and spirit on a wide scale. The government, however, is not the villain in these pieces: the overwhelming majority of the sweatshops are owned by Taiwan, Hong Kong, and Thai businessmen, over which the central government has relatively little control.

But surely Zhu Rongji could put a stop to such horrors? Perhaps, but return again to the number of workers estimated at the Fifteenth Party Congress to be redundant: 35 million. Now add the 72 million new jobseekers projected to come on the market over the next five years (overwhelming the number of projected retirees), and then add the 40-plus million migrant workers whose labor is predicted to become unneeded during the same period. If these projections and predictions—made by the government itself[23]—are even roughly accurate, they mean Zhu Rongji will have to generate more new jobs during his first term of office than there are existing jobs in the United States. It is thus not morally obvious that he must immediately crack down on the Taiwan, Hong Kong, and Thai businessmen, who would just as immediately move their operations to Vietnam or Myanmar, increasing Chinese unemployment still further; the "race to the bottom" in wages is already well underway worldwide, thanks to "globalizing," transnational corporations. Africa awaits, when and if Asian workers should get "uppity" enough to demand a living wage.

As acute and as painful as such choices are to contemplate, however, they are overshadowed by the specter of the collapse of the Chinese natural environments (as explained by Vaclav Smil's essay in this volume). Beijing's water table has been falling at such a rate for the past three decades that unless it is reversed—not merely checked—it is predicted that the city will be uninhabitable by the year 2015. Seven of the world's ten most air-polluted cites are in China. (Shanghai is not among them, its concentration of particulate matter being only fourteen times greater than that of New York.) Arable land (only 10 percent of the country) is being lost through erosion, construction of homes, factories, highways, and so on, twice as rapidly as new land can be brought under cultivation. Less than 20 percent of chemical wastes from factories, and human sewage from dwellings, receives any treatment before being directly deposited in China's rivers. (Except for four- and five-star hotels, which have their own filtration systems, water cannot be drunk safely from a tap anywhere in China.) Less than 3 percent of the lands remain forested.[24]

But what is to be done to improve the situation requires yet another Odyssean effort to steer between Scylla and Charybdis without charts. Lacking a relatively inexpensive source of energy, there will be little demand for such household amenities as refrigerators, TVs, and air conditioners; nor can the producers of these and other appliances manufacture them competitively for export. The only cheap source of energy currently available in China is a low-grade coal that poisons the atmosphere when burned and that becomes even cheaper when worker safety equipment is not utilized in its extraction (which is why coal miners are the most at-risk workers in all of China, averaging over 1,000 deaths every year).[25]

The air infected by burning this coal destroys vegetation in surrounding areas, dirties and etches away at buildings and roads, and produces chronic respiratory ailments in significant numbers—up to one-quarter of the population in long-industrialized urban areas. But enhancing worker safety, increasing their wages, and moving to nonpolluting sources of energy would eventuate in the loss of the price differential between a T-shirt made in China and one made in the United States; how many Americans would thereafter buy the former? Or, come from the other way: how many Chinese could then afford their own manufactures?

These environmental horrors are well known to many Chinese themselves, who now have a commonplace but by no means inaccurate response to them, stated in various temporal terms that can be generalized: "We know that if we do not stop destroying our air, water, and soil, we may no longer be able to survive in three decades; but if we do not, we may well not survive for three years."[26] (This statement sounds similar to those made by U.S. developers in arguing against environmentalists. But whereas such statements are patently false for the United States, they unfortunately are very near the mark in China.)

There are also a number of cultural factors that collectively suggest not that China's problems are intractable but that the odds of their being over-come are unpredictable. The "one child, one family" policy in effect for almost two decades now flies in the face of the Chinese celebration of large families since time immemorial. Unless its population is stabilized—nay, reduced—there is little hope for China's future no matter what economic policies its government pursues.

For a number of years the "one-child" policy was fairly successful, at least in urban areas, because the government had benefits it could confer, and penalties to impose, on families that did, and did not, adopt the policy. Throughout the 1980s, mothers giving first birth received up to a year's maternity leave at 80 percent or more of their salary, a milk allowance, free pediatric check-ups, access to free day-care services when leave was up, and more. A second child was denied these benefits, and they were taken away from the first. Mother was given only six weeks leave at 40 percent of pay, milk was no longer free, and day-care costs were imposed, as were other economic sanctions.[27]

But, as outlined earlier, many work units no longer provide such benefits to mothers and families, and, consequently, the costs for any births can only be met by those who have profited by the turn to laissez-faire capitalism. In the countryside—where the government could provide little or no social services or benefits—the policy was largely ignored, except as individual local cadres enjoyed sufficient popular support to enforce it.

Today, however, nearly everyone—urban and rural dwellers alike—is rightfully skeptical that their government can or will provide for them in the future and hence must invest in the equivalent of nursing homes, social security, medicare, and medicaid in the only way open to them: producing filial children. (See *guanxi*, earlier in this chapter.)

During the early decades of Party rule the status of women was enhanced measurably, but the trend is now being reversed. Newspaper editorials regularly note that if women returned to being homemakers, there would be less need for day care and services for the elderly and, most important, there would then supposedly be enough jobs for men. In rural areas, only a few women have any but the following options: (1) Leave home to work in one of the sweatshops described previously. (2) Leave home to sell their bodies in a large city. (3) Stay at home and sell a child to work either at (1) or (2). (4) Stay at home and sell a part of their body (kidneys are currently in high demand).

These are not truly human options but could be seen to be such against the stark realities of most rural women's lives. These hard-pressed women must not only care for their homes, their children, the aged, and the infirm, they must also do the great bulk of the farming—with hardly any machinery—by themselves, because so many of the village men have gone off to become migrant workers.

Against this background, statistics recently compiled in a study by the World Health Organization become less surprising, if not less gruesome to contemplate: with only 21 percent of the world's female population, Chinese women account for almost 57 percent of all suicides worldwide—as many as a quarter of a million each year.[28] Michael Phillips, a Canadian psychiatrist who has worked in China for a dozen years, recently said: "The rate of rural suicide is threefold the urban rate, and many more women commit suicide than men. In fact, China is the only country in the world where more females commit suicide than men."[29]

Other problems facing the government are far more difficult to evaluate, because they are closely intertwined with cultural factors by means of which people measure the worth of their lives but differ significantly from economic assumptions about people being purely rational "profit maximizers." At milestone events, for example, conspicuous consumption is traditionally obligatory: At the New Year, at the birth of a child, at the opening of a business, when moving to a new dwelling, and at weddings, funerals, and other occasions, firecrackers set off by the hundreds are mandatory. (They are now technically illegal in several cities, to zero effect.) Marriages are made "official" at banquets for which the marrying families are expected to provide enough food for thrice the number of invited guests to consume, and at which much clothing and decorations are on display that will never be seen or used again. Thousands of dollars are spent each day in rural areas, either to exorcise demons or hungry ghosts plaguing the area or to attract nearby deities to protect it; an equal amount for the purchase of incense, other offertories, and spirit money, to ensure the well-being of the departed.

These practices have social, moral, and spiritual dimensions that must be given great weight, for they are the means whereby people measure the worth in their lives, and they also even contribute minimally to the economy; but they do not conduce to the economic development of a people whose average per capita income is still less than U.S. $500 a year, even after a decade and a half of double-digit growth of the Gross Domestic Product.

Moreover, these cultural "superstitions"—if such they be—are not confined to remote rural areas, exacerbating the problem of defining "rationality" in purely economic terms. In Shanghai's Pudong district—whose development is supposed to make Shanghai the most economically important city in all of Asia—one luxury four-building apartment complex has only a 15 percent occupancy rate three years after completion.

Overbuilding is not the problem at this particular site, even though it has reached a crisis point elsewhere in the city; "Space for rent" signs are now more ubiquitous than those portraying the Marlboro Man.[30] In this case, however, ghosts are the problem, and two successive squads of guards hired to protect the buildings have quit after claiming to have seen them. These ghosts are inhabiting apartments designed to sell for over U.S. $1,000 per square meter and are definitely believed to be there, not only because they have been seen by a number of people, but—here the proof is conclusive—they occupy building number 4, the word for which, in Chinese, is homophonous with the word for "death," or "to die" (no one in China wishes to get married on the fourth day of any month or fourth month of any given lunar year).

Taken together, all of these considerations argue that even if Zhu Rongji is a highly moral minister dedicated to the well-being of the Chinese peoples, his task is exceedingly difficult. On the one hand, he knows that if he steers an idealist tack in keeping the welfare of the majority of the Chinese peoples uppermost in decision-making, the U.S. government, the IMF, currency traders, speculative investors, and multinational corporations will visit him with the same or similar penalties earlier directed at Mossadegh, Arbenz, Castro, Allende, the Sandinistas, and other idealists, and, more recently, directed against the Southeast Asian countries. On the other hand, caving in to international capitalist demands requires forsaking the well-being of the majority of the Chinese peoples, again, as the governments of Southeast Asian countries are currently realizing. And all the while he contemplates his options, the natural environment continues to deteriorate.

This point about foreign capitalist investment requires comment, because what supposedly keeps investors excited about China is the potential of 1.3 billion-plus customers, who must come to have the financial wherewithal to increase their "standard of living" by becoming proper consumers. Thus, the "trickle down" phenomena, beloved by academic economists, must ensure a bright future for all. But this view is mischievous. Three-quarters of the Chinese peoples could remain living in the most abject poverty, and the remaining relatively affluent one-quarter— 300+ million people—would still provide the world's largest consumer market, significantly larger than that of the world's current largest, the United States. Neither Daimler-Chrysler, nor American Express, nor Microsoft needs a billion-plus Chinese customers; a quarter of them will do nicely, thank you.

Issues of democracy must also be viewed differently against the background of China's problems. Given China's history of meritocratic, rather than representative, form of government, if Zhu Rongji allowed full and free elections tomorrow morning, who would run for office, and on what kinds of platform would they run? To ask these questions is not to demean the democratic ideal that everyone should have a voice in matters that directly concern them (an ideal far from realization in the United States), nor is it intended to diminish the joy felt at the release of pro-democracy dissidents such as Wei Jingsheng in November 1997 and Wang Dan in April 1998, despite the continued incarceration of a great many of their peers.

On the contrary, these questions raise issues that have also been raised by arch-conservatives such as Llewellyn Rockwell, Jr., president of the Ludwig von Mises Institute, who argued:

What is the right to vote compared with the right to start a business, draw wages . . . keep the fruits of our labor . . . Save for the future? These are all components of capitalism, which the Chinese people are discovering is the only system compatible with the first and most important of human rights: The right to own and control what is yours.[31]

These musings—given a full page in the *Far Eastern Economic Review*— generate a painful question for people of goodwill to contemplate: How important is it for people to vote? Ultimately, the answer must be that it is very important indeed. But arriving at this answer must take into account other issues implied by Rockwell, but which he didn't (couldn't) address: What good is the right to start a business if you don't even have enough money for food and housing? What good is the right to draw wages if there are no jobs? What good is the right to control what you own when you don't own anything? What good are any "rights" when your sisters are swallowing pesticides all around you to end their misery?

Sensitivity to these questions suggests that it is still important for people to vote, but that the voting can only be meaningful if the people have an opportunity to elect a government that will see to their own basic needs rather than to the "needs" of foreign (and domestic) currency traders, large investors, transnational corporations, and domestic elites. This gives the final lie to concerns about "democracy" among U.S. business and political groups, as a *Business Week* editorial made clear when it instructed U.S.— not Chinese—politicians to realize that in a global "free market" economy, every government must adapt a noninterventionist approach to trade and investment;[32] only the naive—Jefferson, Franklin, Hamilton, Madison, and so forth—could believe that one of the primary functions of a national government is to regulate commerce within its own borders for the well-being of its citizens.

In this twisted sense of "democracy," another *Far Eastern Economic Review* editorial expressed optimism for its future in China, citing as evidence the fact that there are now three hundred brands of toothpaste for sale in Beijing, after which it went on to say: "Is it really tenable to maintain that a Chinese people who have learned to be this discriminating about what they expect from their toothpaste will forever be passive when it comes to what they expect from their leaders?"[33]

Compared to this lunatic line of thinking a belief in ghosts becomes paradigmatically rational, even when real estate values are depressed thereby. By these lights the people of Beijing are already far more "free" and discriminating than their American brethren who, even in the largest of supermarkets, have at most a dozen brands of toothpaste to choose from.

All of these considerations suggest that China faces a number of socioeconomic, political, and environmental problems of great magnitude, and that these problems will only be exacerbated by complying with the demands for a "free market" economy made by the U.S. government and the IMF at the behest of the super rich. The nations of Southeast Asia and South Korea are already feeling the economic injustice and social pain that accompanies these demands, but neither individually nor collectively can those demands be resisted in Asia unless China joins the resistance.

Michael Camdessus, head of the IMF, and former U.S. Treasury Secretary Robert Rubin offered to lend great sums of money to Asia—money taken in the way of taxes from the working people of the United States and Western Europe—if the Asian countries would agree to "structural adjustment" policies, an Orwellian expression that means cutting wages, eliminating job security, ceasing to subsidize the necessities of life, opening their countries fully to foreign exploitation, and raising interest rates so that domestic banks will be able to guarantee loans to foreign billionaires. The great majority of the peoples in each of these countries will endure great suffering, of course, but their burden must be borne in the name of "free markets."

William Grieder has summed up this issue well: "[T]his new round of bailouts exposes the enduring hypocrisy of the free-market crowd: People must submit to the dictates of market forces, but capital need not. Bankers and major investors want a free run on the upside—that is, no controls whatever—and they expect to be rescued from their own big mistakes on the downside."[34]

What will happen to the Chinese and Southeast Asian peoples if capital is allowed its own way should be clear to the American peoples, who are already beginning to have similar experiences, owing to their government representing not them but capital. Some examples:

1. British Petroleum (BP) recently closed a factory in Lima, Ohio, not because it was losing money, but because it was not considered profitable enough. BP was the town's main employer and its decision was devastating for the entire local community. Corporate Vice-President David Arron acknowledged the pain the community would suffer because of the closing but defended the decision by saying that its "first responsibility was to our stockholders." (At the time he said this, the largest stockholder in BP was the government of Kuwait, which shortly thereafter sold a number of its shares at a great profit.)[35]

2. More recently, the Reuters news agency extracted a $1.1-million-a-year tax break from the city of New York—to run for twenty-three consecutive years—by threatening to move to New Jersey if it didn't get the break. Reuters insisted, of course, that the city maintain the infrastructure for the corporation as well, which means raising someone's taxes—in other words, those of the city's working people, not Reuters.[36]

3. In these ostensibly equalitarian United States, the wealthiest sixty of

its citizens have assets totaling $311 billion, according to a recent
United Nations study—more than the combined wealth of the poorest 25 percent of the world's peoples.[37]

4. The courts are beginning to feel the pressure of big business flexing
    its muscles, too, in the social as well as the economic sphere. Having
    lost a sexual harassment suit, Burlington Industries petitioned the
    Supreme Court for review, and its brief contained the following
    thinly veiled threat:

> Increasing employers' liability for sexual harassment entails significant
> monetary costs. Diligent employers already incur substantial costs in
> attempting to create a harassment-free workplace. . . . Further extend-
> ing employer liability would make this economic burden overwhelm-
> ing. . . . These burdens which employment discrimination laws place on
> employers influence employer's decisions to automate production, to
> outsource duties, and to locate operations in foreign countries.[38]

Confronting these realities of unadulterated corporate greed is painful
and can easily give rise to the wish that whatever calls attention to that
greed—in this case, China—would simply go away. But it will not. Muslim minorities in the West will continue to nip at its Western borders,
Tibetans yearn to be Tibetans, and many Mongols wish to reunite with
their former Soviet brethren. Even if all of these separatist dreams come
true, however (and reasons can be given why they should), almost a billion Han Chinese would continue to carry and transmit the world's oldest
continuous culture within the boundaries of an enormous land mass.

Most of them will remain poor by "developed" world standards, and
this poverty, when coupled with sheer numbers and a fair degree of perceived cultural cohesiveness, can easily cause a historically and culturally
ungrounded fear of expansionist tendencies. But expansionism is not a
genuine option for China. Its army will ably defend it in all probability, but
it altogether lacks the resources and ability to cross the great deserts to its
north and west, the mountain ranges to its southwest, the jungles of the
south, and the seas of the southeast and east; it has no "blue ocean" navy
and cannot afford one, any more than it can afford an air force that could
genuinely threaten even Taiwan, let alone any Western nation's command
of the skies.

No, China is not an enemy threat, real or potential, in military terms. It
is a threat to the laissez-faire, "free-market" capitalist ideology that is

used to defend U.S. policy toward China, to mask the real causes of the eco-nomic downturn in Southeast Asia, and to explain away as inevitable the collapse of the "American dream" for many of those who have dreamed it. The social, political, economic, environmental—and hence spiritual—ills that currently confront the Chinese peoples will confront all of us, sooner or later; they differ only in degree of immediacy and desperation, not in kind.

Seen in this light, U.S. media–manipulated views of China as basically corrupt, authoritarian, and a threat prevent the American peoples from not only having accurate perceptions of China but accurate perceptions of their own circumstances as well. Only when a U.S. government can be elected that will cease aiding and abetting those who view the human race solely as six billion potential consumers can truly "global" dialogue take place on the issues of human rights, democracy, social justice, and the quality of human life.

China has been, is, and will continue to be a mirror reflecting the mani-fold possibilities and limits of human being, and therefore it behooves all human beings to look closely into the mirror.[39] The great English meta-physical poet and cleric John Donne said it best:

> Therefore do not send to know for whom the
> Bell tolls; it tolls for thee.

NOTES

This is a revised and expanded version (with references), of an article that orig-inally appeared in *Z Magazine*, June 1998. Great care must be taken in evaluating virtually all statistics, a problem particularly acute with respect to China, where there are almost as many estimates of everything from population growth to grain production to untreated sewage as there are estimators thereof. In general, I have chosen the more conservative figures relating to a problem, except in those cases where the figures cited by the government itself are used to justify policy state-ments. For assistance in preparing this manuscript for publication, I am deeply indebted to Linda Vallandingham and Mary Bloomer, and to Lionel Jensen for many helpful suggestions for improving it.

1. A number of good pieces in *The Nation* (June 15–22, 1998) describe and ana-lyze Suharto's fall, preceded by one in the March 30, 1998, issue describing the sit-uation prior to the overthrow. None of these, however, notes a salient fact that explains much: so long as Suharto stood in defiance of the International Monetary

Fund's (IMF) demands for restructuring the Indonesian economy, the country remained fairly quiet. Only when he began to implement the cruel IMF strictures did the people take their protests to the streets in large numbers. For details, see my "Waging a New War in Southeast Asia," in *Z Magazine* (May 1998).

2. See, for example, *Washington Post*, October 24, 1997.

3. *Far Eastern Economic Review* (February 12, 1998): 49.

4. *Business Week* (March 2, 1998): 37.

5. *Far Eastern Economic Review* (February 12, 1998): 46, is but one example. President Clinton has also used these terms, even after his June 1998 trip to China. *New York Times*, July 5, 1995.

6. *Business Week* (November 10, 1997): 50.

7. Some of these issues are described in the *Far Eastern Economic Review* (March 5, 1998): 10–14.

8. This point has been clearly made—and thoroughly documented—in many of the political writings of Noam Chomsky. See Noam Chomsky, *Year 501: The Conquest Continues* (Boston: South End Press, 1994), which is particularly perceptive.

9. The material in this and the succeeding five paragraphs is taken from my "Hong Kong and China: What's News?," *The Raven* (November 1997).

10. *Washington Post*, March 20, 1998, A30. This article also describes the policy statements emanating from the Fifteenth Congress, as does another *Post* article of October 16, 1997.

11. *Washington Post*, March 20, 1998, A30.

12. See the excellent article in this volume by Tim Oakes, "China's Market Reforms: Whose Human Rights Problem?"

13. Taken from several personal discussions in Shanghai, Hangzhou, and Beijing, June and December 1997.

14. *Far Eastern Economic Review* (January 8, 1998): 19.

15. Personal conversations, December 1997. For a similar situation in Shandong, see n. 13.

16. This is happening in almost all urban areas. One example—in Shanghai—is described in the *Baltimore Sun*, April 4, 1998.

17. *Washington Post*, March 20, 1998, A30.

18. *Washington Post*, March 20, 1998, A30. The problem is by no means restricted to Shenyang. In Shanghai, probably a million workers are *xia gang*, i.e., furloughed. *Asian Wall Street Journal*, December 16, 1997, 27.

19. This issue is taken up in my "China & U.S. Morality," *Z Magazine* (December 1995).

20. Rosemont, "China & U.S. Morality."

21. Gruesome but necessary reading on this issue is *Behind the Label: "Made in China,"* by Charles Kernaghan, Collingdale: DIANE Publishing Company (1998).

22. From the spokesperson for Liz Clairborne, Inc., *Washington Post*, March 19, 1998, 14.

23. See n. 11. Some other estimates are that China already has over 130 million under- or unemployed workers. *Far Eastern Economic Review* (June 11, 1998): 48.

24. For reports on these statistics, see Henry Rosemont, Jr., "Why the Chinese Economic Miracle Isn't One," *Z Magazine* (October 1995). A much more thorough analysis was made by Vaclav Smil, in *Environmental Problems in China: Estimates of Economic, Costs,* East–West Center Special Reports, Honolulu, no. 5 (April 1996).

25. For a good general survey of this issue, see Mark Hertsgaard, "Our Real China Problem," *Atlantic Monthly* (November 1997).

26. A uniform response made by virtually everyone in China with whom I have discussed environmental issues over the past seventeen years.

27. See Rosemont, "Why the Chinese Economic Miracle Isn't One."

28. *New York Times*, January 24, 1999.

29. *New York Times*, January 24, 1999.

30. Not merely my own observation. See, for example, the *Washington Post,* November 29, 1997.

31. *Far Eastern Economic Review* (February 12, 1998): 29.

32. *Business Week* (February 9, 1998): 138.

33. *Far Eastern Economic Review* (February 5, 1998): 5.

34. "Saving the Global Economy," *The Nation* (December 15, 1997): 15.

35. Marc Cooper, "A Town Betrayed," *The Nation* (June 14, 1997): 13.

36. *New York Times*, April 16, 1998.

37. Quoted in the *New York Times*, September 27, 1998.

38. Quoted by James J. Kilpatrick in the *Tampa Tribune*, February 14, 1998.

39. To the reader of these notes, it may seem highly hypocritical to have castigated the U.S. media in these pages, given the number of citations to that media herein. Of course, the "news" can be obtained from these sources, but only well-paid academic and other professionals have the luxury of being able to read carefully through a wide variety of sources over an extended period of time in order to differentiate rhetoric and reality.

SUGGESTED READINGS

Frank Ackerman, et al., eds., *Human Well-Being and Economic Goals* (Washington, D.C.: Island Press, 1997).

Catherine Caulfield, *Masters of Illusion: The World Bank and the Poverty of Nations* (New York: Henry Holt, 1996).

Noam Chomsky, *Year 501: The Conquest Continues* (Boston: South End Press, 1994).

David L. Hall and Roger T. Ames, *The Democracy of the Dead: Dewey, Confucius, and the Hope for Democracy in China* (LaSalle, Ill.: Open Court, 1999).

He Bochuan, *China on the Edge* (San Francisco: China Books and Periodicals, 1991).

William Hinton, *The Great Reversal: The Privatization of China, 1978–1989* (New York: Monthly Review Press, 1990).

Henry Rosemont, Jr., *A Chinese Mirror: Moral Reflections on Political Economy and Society* (LaSalle, Ill.: Open Court, 1991).

Saskia Sassen, *Globalization & Its Discontents* (New York: The New Press, 1998).

Vaclav Smil, *China's Environmental Crisis: An Inquiry into the Limits of National Development* (Armonk, N.Y.: M. E. Sharpe, 1993).

Part Two:

Below the Fold

The West is suffering under three serious misconceptions about events in China. The first misconception is the view that post-Mao China has remained a strictly Communist state and has been able to resist the pressure of political reform despite, or because of, tremendous progress in economic reform. This situation, according to some experts, is unlikely to change in the near future. The second misconception is the conventional view that the continuation of China's economic reform is inevitable, because this reform has brought about one of the greatest developments of human welfare in Chinese history. And the third misconception is the prediction that China is on the way to becoming an economic giant and therefore a threat to the West, particularly the United States.

—Cheng Li,
Rediscovering China: Dynamics and Dilemmas of
Reform, 1997

9

Development and Destruction:

The Dimensions of China's Environmental Challenge

Vaclav Smil

It is well established and widely known that China has the world's largest population as well as its fastest growing economy. These commonplaces underwrite the developed world's interest in China's future and investment in its present while ensuring an obsessive media representation of them in the West. For the capitalists of Western nations such as the United States, prospective rates of return are too great to ignore and the presence of more than a billion consumers so tantalizing that China does not lack markets for its manufactured goods. Although China has demonstrated unparalleled economic development sufficient to have brought more than 180 million out of absolute poverty since 1980, its people are growing anxious over the real, environmental consequences of the nation's aspirations to affluence.

Now, amid a widening Asian economic crisis, it is ecology, and not markets or currencies, that poses the greatest threat to China's survival. But in stating this, I also point up a dilemma no less common in the developed world and even the United States, that of a persistent disregard for sustainable growth. In this respect alone China and the United States are more alike than we might be inclined to recognize; however, they are also the global leaders in the production of greenhouse gases and in energy consumption, as well as in resistance to international efforts to reduce pollution. Considering this uncanny commonness of our status as environmental pariahs, a better understanding of the ecological adversity bred by the Chinese can prove illustrative for us.

The environmental challenges facing China today are immense (indeed, far more so than the task of modernizing the country) and are visible in five key areas: (1) water pollution, (2) air pollution, (3) deforestation, (4) farmland losses, and (5) generation of greenhouse gases. Water availability in North China, home to 500 million people, is already less than a third of the national average of India, a country with a population more than 400 million fewer than that of China. About 50 million people in northern Chinese provinces do not even have a reliable supply of drinking water. Recurrent northern water shortages have led to massive overuse of groundwater and to extensive surface sinking. Quality of surface water has been steadily declining: new water-treatment facilities have helped in some large cities, but the overall volume of untreated waste water has increased, especially with the explosive growth of small rural and township industries. Even according to the official, and certainly overly optimistic, figures, less than 15 percent of China's waste water is treated to meet the state discharge standards.

The water crisis brought by China's rapid economic growth is mirrored by a rapidly increasing air pollution that is likely to get worse. Because of its limited oil and gas resources, China will have to burn even more coal to energize its economic expansion. The country is already the worlds' largest producer of coal and hence the largest emitter of particulate matter and sulfur dioxide (SO_2). Concentrations of soot and sulfur dioxide in northern Chinese cities, especially in winter, are commonly five to ten times higher than the Western hygienic limits. Moreover, acid deposition generated by this combustion is already causing concern downwind, in South Korea and Japan. But even if efficient controls would remove nearly all dust and SO_2, China's high consumption of fossil fuels will become an even more prominent source of carbon dioxide, the leading greenhouse gas.

China will also become the world's largest emitter of greenhouse gases during the coming generation. Should global warming become a matter of a high international priority, then China's economic and population growth would have enormous effects on the Earth's climate—and yet there would be no obvious technical fixes for this unprecedented challenge.

Although China has more farmland than is officially claimed, it has been losing some of its best arable land at obviously unsustainable rates. And even if these losses could be made up by reclamation of new land (such opportunities are increasingly scarce), population growth alone has reduced per capita farmland availability by more than 10 percent during the 1990s and perhaps by another 15 percent before the year 2025. From this cultivated area the Chinese will have to produce not only more food grain for more than 300 million additional people but also much more feed grain to satisfy a huge demand for more meat. Further intensification of already very intensified cropping is thus inevitable—but this route has its obvious physical limits. China is the world's largest producer of fertilizers and presently irrigates half of its farmland. Moreover, higher fertilizer applications produce lower yield increments, and water is simply not available where it is needed most.

The recent steady decline in arable land has been further exacerbated by increasing soil erosion due, in part, to deforestation and unsuccessful afforestation (replanting). The principal reasons for China's higher soil erosion are deforestation, improper agronomic methods, and, in northwestern provinces such as Xinjiang, spreading desertification. Traditionally extensive deforestation has not been reversed by massive post-1960 afforestation campaigns: only about a third of all plantings have survived, while overcutting, including illegal tree harvesting for fuel, has severely reduced China's stands of natural forests. Deforestation has reduced forest cover in a number of southern provinces by between 20 to 40 percent since the late 1950s. In per capita terms China's wood reserves are now the lowest of any other populous nation.

Some people in the top Chinese leadership are clearly aware of the threat posed by environmental degradation to the country's long-term socioeconomic well-being. My conservative calculations indicate that the abuse of China's environment costs the country annually an equivalent of at least 10 and possibly 15 percent of its GDP—but practical steps, remedial or preventive, remain wholly inadequate. Many new environmental laws enacted since the early 1980s have not noticeably changed the pace of degradation. Cleaner fuels and better waste water treatment in some major cities, large-scale distribution of more efficient stoves in rural areas, better protection of farmland in some highly productive agricultural regions, and the setting up of new natural reserves have been perhaps the most successful changes.

Even a democratic China could do little to change radically either the country's absolute population growth or its long-term environmental prospects, especially because the nation's quest for affluence transcends politics. Ultimately, all economies are just subsystems of the biosphere; therefore, when China behaves as if there were no limits to its prosperity, it inflicts irreparable damage on its environment as well as on that of the rest of the world.

China's quest for affluence is understandable—but the recent Western admiration of double-digit percent growth rates is naive and misguided. Foreign observers make a fundamental categorical error by ignoring the effects of scale: the size of China's population and the stresses it puts on the environment prevent any simplistic contemplation of China ever emulating Japan or duplicating fully the achievements of smaller dragons of the region. Countries can overcome national resource constraints or bypass environmental limits with imports—but there is a clear biospheric limit to such strategies.

The Chinese can never import 98 percent of their fossil fuels as do Japanese or 75 percent of their food and feed grains as do South Koreans: the world market simply does not have this much fuel and food. Thus, China must rely overwhelmingly on its own resources. In terms of food production this reliance would dictate the most assiduous maintenance of viable agroecosystems, ranging from strict conservation of farmland, to prevention of erosion and replenishment of soil's organic matter. In terms of energy consumption this would mean vigorous fuel and electricity conservation, use of the most energy-efficient industrial processes, and careful development of China's huge hydroenergy potential. In what follows, I will detail the magnitude of existing problems and outline possible trends, as well as the sobering prospects, by concentrating on the five key areas I have sketched out previously—water pollution, air pollution, deforestation, farmland losses, and the generation of greenhouse gases.

WATER SUPPLY AND POLLUTION

Strong seasonality of precipitation, recurrent fluctuations between droughts and floods, and highly uneven spatial distribution of both annual and seasonal moisture are the key constants of China's water supply concerns—and water pollution tops the list of worries among China's informed respondents questioned about the priorities of environmental management.

The government's official data confirm the worsening trends for both the overall and regional water supply, as well as for water pollution. Areas of cropland affected by drought show an upward trend since the late 1980s. The situation in the north has been particularly difficult. This region, covering about one-third of China's territory, now has about two-fifths of China's population and identical shares of agricultural and industrial output—but it receives only about one-fourth of the country's precipitation, and its high summer evapotranspiration means that it has access to less than one-tenth of stream runoff. This combination of socioeconomic and geophysical realities is not amenable to any quick technical fix.

The Yellow River (Huang He), the region's principal water source, has had its flows drastically reduced during the past fifteen years. In 1981 the river's flow into Bohai Bay was 48.5 billion cubic meters, in virtual agreement with its long-term average. However, after 1985 the runoff dropped repeatedly to less than 30 billion cubic meters and even just below 20 billion cubic meters, or less than two-fifths of the mean. During the 1990s, the river's normally very low early summer flow downstream from Jinan, Shandong, had ceased altogether, sometimes for more than a month.

A decline in Yellow River flow of this magnitude necessitates a high degree of reliance on underground water reserves. Water supply is particularly tight in large northern cities. Beijing's situation has been one of a chronic water deficit. In the 1950s the water table was just five meters below the surface in places, but today the city's more than 40,000 wells draw water from depths around fifty meters, and during the 1980s the annual drop in the water table during the driest years surpassed two

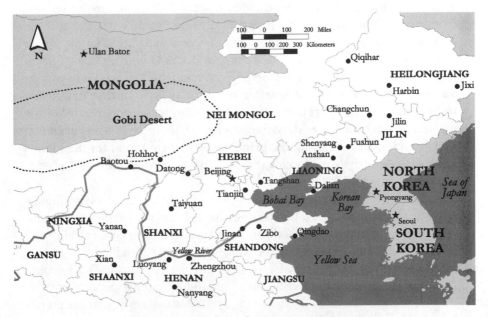

Fig. 9.1. North and northeast China

meters. The city's total water deficit is forecast to be at least 1.3 billion cubic meters by the year 2000, an equivalent of about half of the desirable supply. Not surprisingly, these worsening water shortages have become a matter of anxious debate among scientists and public officials, some of whom have questioned the city's viability as a future capital of China.

To be sure, Beijing is no exception. By the mid-1990s more than two hundred Chinese cities were short of water, and in fifty of them—including Beijing, Tianjin, Taiyuan, and Xi'an—these shortages were serious enough to limit their economic development. The average daily water deficit in these cities rose to about 15 cubic meters by 1990, and some of its estimates for the year 2000 are as high as 88 megatonnes.

Urban water shortages tend to attract a disproportionate share of attention but, as in any other populous Asian country, China's water use is heavily dominated by irrigation requirements. And to make matters worse, current Chinese operations do not reflect scarcity value of irrigation water. This leads, in one important respect, to the continuation of unsustainable and wasteful irrigation that could be greatly curtailed with the introduction of realistic water fees. Problems such as these are especially salient in the North China Plain.

The combination of strained supplies of irrigation, urban, and industrial water now affects an area extending over some 585,000 square kilometers from eastern Shandong through northern Henan and Hebei, to southern and central Liaoning and includes the cities of Beijing and Tianjin. Water use rates on the North China Plain also have a most undesirable effect on the region's principal water source. Diversion of Yellow River water, amounting to more than a quarter of its total flow during dry years, reduces the silt transport to the Bohai Bay: as much as one-quarter of the high sediment load is now deposited each year on the river's bed in Henan and Shandong, aggravating the principal long-term threat for the Plain's habitation—the inexorable elevation of the river's bed above the surrounding countryside.

And there is an important and inimical qualitative dimension to China's irrigation prospects: irrigation waters have been increasingly contaminated by industrial wastes in addition to carrying higher concentrations of leached fertilizers and insecticides. Rural water pollution has been greatly increased by the huge expansion of local industrial enterprises absorbing the surplus peasant labor during the 1980s and operating without any pollution controls. The official nationwide total of waste water discharges has been going up despite substantial recent investment in water treatment facilities in large cities, so much so that annual economic loss attributable to water pollution was at least 30 billion Chinese dollars (*renminbi*) in the early 1990s.

The opposite water problem has also been on the rise: after a period of relatively limited flooding during the 1970s, the average area disastrously affected by floods increased to about 5.5 million hectares a year during the 1980s (nearly a 2.5-fold increase). This trend has continued throughout the 1990s but never as disastrously as in the summer of 1998, when both southern and northern regions were inundated. Altogether about one-tenth of China's territory, inhabited by nearly two-thirds of the population and producing roughly 70 percent of all agricultural and industrial output, is below the flood level of major rivers.

In spite of the absence of flooding for nearly half a century, potentially the most dangerous situation is along the lower course of the Yellow River in Henan and Shandong, where there has been no extensive dredging, particularly between Zhengzhou in Henan and the estuary, where the river remains confined between about 1,400 kilometers of dikes that are anywhere from three to fifteen meters above the surrounding countryside, perilously protecting roughly 250,000 square kilometers of the North China Plain.

With higher erosion on the Loess Plateau the river's silt load has increased at least 25 percent since the early 1950s, the annual riverbed build-up has amounted to about 400 megatonnes, and the average river bed rise has been one meter a decade. The latest Chinese estimates are that a breach of the Yellow River south of Jinan (in the most vulnerable area) would flood up to 33,000 square kilometers, affecting 18 million people and cutting all north-south transportation.

AIR POLLUTION

China is now the world's largest producer and consumer of bituminous coal: both its nationwide output and domestic consumption have been above one billion metric tons since 1989, and by 1995 it surpassed 1.3 billion metric tons. Particulate emissions now total almost 15 million metric tons, and SO_2 releases exceed 20 million metric tons, the highest national totals worldwide. In general, Chinese coals are of reasonably good quality and the country's average gross air pollution emission factors are not unusually high—but the ways in which most of this coal is burned are increasing both the outdoor and indoor concentrations and creating some of the world's highest exposures to particulate matter, SO_2, and benzo(a)pyrene.

More than three-fourths of China's coal is burned without any preparation, and about half of it fuels either small, outdated, and hence highly inefficient boilers or even less efficient household stoves (typically, less than 30 percent efficient) and, most wastefully, steam locomotives (with an efficiency of less than 10 percent). Consequently, Chinese emission factors per unit of delivered useful energy are extraordinarily high. High density of Chinese cities, common commingling of residential and industrial areas, releases of uncontrolled emissions from low chimneys, residential crowding, improperly vented household stoves, and use of smoky biomass fuels in rural areas are the most important additional variables responsible for extremely high short-term concentrations of both outdoor and indoor air pollutants and for their harmfully high long-term levels (see figure 9.2).

Typical Chinese air pollution exposures are so high that annual means are surpassing recommended daily maxima. Every major northern city, and many southern urban areas, have been exposed to excessive concentrations of particulates and SO_2. The capital's mean annual dust levels are

Fig. 9.2. **Approximate densities of SO_2 emissions by province (1990) (Adapted from Vaclav Smil,** *China's Environmental Crisis*)

typically between four and five hundred micrograms per cubic meter (400–500 mg/m³). The World Health Organization's (WHO) daily particulate maximum of 230 micrograms per cubic meter (230 mg/m³) is not to be exceeded during more than 2 percent of the days in a year, but Beijing's peak concentrations have repeatedly surpassed 1,000 mg/m³. And the capital is hardly an exceptionally polluted place. All major northern cities have similar annual particulate means, and the worst-off cities have recorded annual total suspended particulate (TSP) means above 600 mg/m³.

For SO_2, these WHO guidelines—with all values in micrograms per cubic meter (mg/m³)—specify means of no more than 500 for ten minutes, 350 for one hour, 100 to 150 for twenty-four hours and 40 to 60 for one year. Annual averages of SO_2 concentrations have been above these levels in every northern Chinese city and, in many areas south of the Yangzi River, largely because of the high sulfur content of many southern coals. Beijing's annual mean concentrations of sulfur dioxide have run between 80 mg/m³ in the cleanest suburbs and twice that in the most polluted locations. These levels are low compared to the annual mean concentrations of more than 400 mg/m³ in Taiyuan and Lanzhou, and more than 300 mg/m³ in Linfeng, Chongqing (Sichuan), and Guiyang (Guizhou).

We do not have any detailed breakdowns of population totals exposed to different levels of particulates and SO_2, but on the basis of available urban measurements and the latest census figures I estimate that at least 200 million Chinese are exposed to annual dust concentrations of above 300 mg/m³, and at least 20 million are exposed to twice that level. These are extraordinarily high exposures, currently comparable only to some Indian, Russian, and Central European levels, and resembling the prevailing West European and North American urban values of two to three generations ago.

Extending these estimates to the rural population is much more problematic. While typical outdoor air pollution levels in the Chinese countryside may be fairly, or frequently even very, low, the recent rapid expansion of cooperative and private industries into these areas has introduced numerous uncontrolled sources of air pollution, causing locally high pollution levels. More important, rural inhabitants are repeatedly exposed to very high levels of indoor air pollution, but we have no representative studies breaking down time spent outdoors and indoors in various provinces or for different population groups.

The heavy toll taken by China's air pollution on human health is readily seen by a very high incidence of chronic obstructive pulmonary diseases now accounting for just over 25 percent of all deaths, resulting in a standardized rate of more than 160 deaths per 100,000, or about five times the U.S. average. Obviously, not all of this effect can be attributed to outdoor air pollution. Cigarette smoking, given its great prevalence and the intensity of the habit among Chinese, contributes much, of course, to the growth of respiratory illness in China. Nevertheless, tens of millions of urban, and hundreds of millions of rural, Chinese are also exposed to undesirable levels of indoor air pollution from improperly vented coal-burning stoves, so much so in fact that it prompts one to conclude that the heating and cooking necessities of daily life are a more significant cause of their pulmonary disease than cigarette smoke. And this irony is most pronounced when one reviews illness statistics for women.

These noxious effects of indoor pollution are particularly dramatic among Chinese females, for they are far less likely to be smokers than are males and are the most likely to prepare family meals. The country's ratio of female/male lung cancers is about 2:1, much lower than the ratio of smoking incidence, and an epidemiological survey in Guangdong revealed that smoking alone cannot explain the high incidence of glandular cancer in women. In households cooking with raw coal, or with poor quality briquettes burned in simple stoves, indoor concentrations of SO_2, dust, and benzo(a)-pyrene are frequently much higher than the outdoor levels of these pollutants, and their peak concentrations significantly correlate with cooking hours.

If one assumes that: (1) about 500 million Chinese are exposed to particulate levels of sulfur dioxide above 200 mg/m³ (with actual exposures mostly between 300–500 mg/m³); (2) the remaining 700 million residents are exposed to no more than 200 mg/m³; and (3) there is approximately a 1 percent increase in mortality for every 20 mg/m³ of exposure, then less than 10 to 15 percent of chronic obstructive pulmonary diseases could be attributed to air pollution. A conservative attribution of lung cancer to air pollution—necessary in view of high rates of Chinese smoking—would be no higher than 15 to 20 percent of all cases, or roughly 15,000 to 25,000 deaths a year. In light of the this, at least 5 percent of all cardiovascular deaths (total of 45,000 cases) should be attributed to air pollution. Owing to the many probable and overlapping causes, the matter of pulmonary disease in China is very a complex one. Moreover, the long-practiced reliance on unwashed coal for fuel and the increased amount of time women spend in the domicile cooking have conspired to produce a disproportionate incidence of respiratory illness among women—a troubling consequence of China's new sexual economy.

LOSS OF FARMLAND

Chinese official figures imply substantial decline in average per capita availability of farmland, from about 0.18 hectares in 1949 to just below 0.08 hectares in 1995. Per capita rates are now below one *mu* (that is less than 667 square meters) in one-third of all provinces. If true, this would put China in the same class as Bangladesh, and the only other populous nations with less arable land would be Egypt, Japan, and Korea.

Fortunately, there is no doubt that official figures underestimate the actual extent of China's crop cultivation. The first generalized mapping of China's land use yielded a total nearly 40 percent higher than that year's official figure. Estimates as high as 150 million hectares were offered on the basis of satellite images. While the official figures certainly underestimate the farmland total, satellite surveys tend to overestimate it. So far the best indication of the real extent of China's arable land comes from detailed country-wide sample surveys begun during the late 1980s. These studies came up with the most likely range of 133 to 140 million hectares. Provincial differences are considerable, with the poorest areas reporting less than a third of actually farmed land! The most likely nationwide total is about 139 million hectares, about 45 percent above the official total. This would prorate to 0.115 hectares per capita, more than twice the rates for South Korea and Taiwan and three times as high as the Japanese mean (see figure 9.3).

Whatever the country's real farmland total, Chinese experts feel that the degree of inaccuracy in reporting the area of cultivated land has not changed significantly in the last thirty years, and hence there can be no doubt about substantial, and continuing, losses of cropland. This is why I believe that the best possible assessment of these losses is much more profitable than trying to pinpoint the total of China's farmland.

As in any other large country, there are a variety of reasons for China's continuing farmland decline. Principal causes stem from a combination of population growth and economic modernization (industrial, urban, and residential expansion; extension of transportation links; construction of irrigation and power generation reservoirs) and degradative processes (heavy erosion, desertification, salinization, alkalization) frequently initiated or accelerated by improper land management.

Fig. 9.3. Average grain availability per capita by province (1989) (Adapted from Vaclav Smil, *China's Environmental Crisis*)

Many cumulative arable land totals have been published in China since 1978, all generally confirming a staggering gross loss of almost 30 million hectares between 1957 and 1977. Since 1978, farmland losses have been dominated by the demands of economic modernization, but during the initial years of the reforms (1979–1984) a substantial portion of the loss also resulted from the restoration of wetlands, grasslands, or slopelands converted into farmland during the two decades of Maoist campaigns.

Official totals published by the State Land Management Bureau put the average annual farmland loss at 492,000 hectares between 1980 and 1985. In 1985, the peak loss of one million hectares was reached—a staggering total reflecting, above all, the frenzied pace of rural house building by newly private farmers. Two years later, the State Land Management Bureau introduced new regulations for the use of farmland for nonagricultural construction, permitting nationwide conversion of no more than 200,000 hectares for all construction projects, including just over 60,000 hectares for peasant housing. Steady declines in nationwide farmland loss followed afterward.

By 1989 the Bureau felt that the situation was again under control, as the annual loss was reduced to just 198,000 hectares and as the cultivated area actually increased in six provinces. But then the increased pace of economic expansion, especially the virtually uncontrolled multiplication of rural industries and the establishment of special industrial and processing zones, led to a renewed round of substantial farmland losses. The annual mean for the first half of the 1990s was about 500,000 hectares. Predictably, this brought a new wave of official comments and decrees aimed, once again, at reversing this worrisome trend (see figure 9.4).

Unfortunately—given the continuing pressures of increasing population, rapid industrialization, and extension of transportation links—no radical long-term changes in China's rate of farmland decline seem to be likely. Many of these losses will inevitably include some of the best-yielding land: for example, in the past decade thousands of newly established manufacturing zones have taken more than 80 percent of their land from intensively cultivated fields near towns and cities. Staying below the State Management Bureau's target of about 200,000 hectares a year would have removed nearly 2 million hectares of farmland during the 1990s—but my disaggregated estimates show that actual losses could be at least 300,000 hectares a year and possibly up to twice as high. Besides representative annual rates we should have at least a rough breakdown of losses by

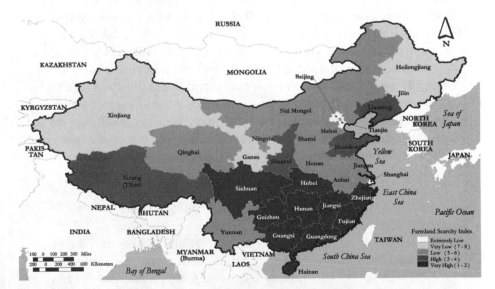

Fig. 9.4. Farmland scarcity index for the 1990s by province (Adapted from Vaclav Smil, *China's Environmental Crisis***)**

region and/or soil quality in order to apply more specific values of lost production. But even our less precise calculations of arable loss suggest a disturbing trend for such a populous nation.

The human dimensions of China's declining farmland area are best illustrated by translating these losses into annual food production equivalents or comparing them with some farmland totals from other developing countries. The cumulative loss of about 40 million hectares since the late 1950s represents an equivalent loss in food production capacity sufficient to feed at least 350 million people! The mean annual loss of over 400,000 hectares during the 1980s was equivalent to losing the food production base for about 5 million people every year. Losing a total of 40 million hectares of farmland equals an area slightly larger than all the cultivated fields in Argentina, and even if such losses could be kept to 200,000 to 250,000 hectares a year in just a decade, they would still add up to all the arable land in Egypt.

Regardless of the prevailing rate of future losses, by the year 2000 Bangladesh and Egypt will be the only two populous nations with less arable land per capita than China. In order to offset the substantial decline in farmland area, Chinese farming has had to become even more intensive, and the country has emerged as the world's largest producer and consumer of synthetic fertilizers. Even so, there are many questions about the nation's future capacity to feed itself. This is because Chinese agriculture is facing not only the challenge of decreasing farmland availability but also one of declining soil quality. The two most important reasons for these stark challenges are the spread and intensification of soil erosion and an unusually rapid decline in both the extent and the intensity of traditional organic recycling. The first phenomenon is an unfortunate worsening of a degrading process, the impacts of which have been regionally severe for centuries—but the second one represents a relatively abrupt change in one of the key defining practices of Chinese agriculture.

DEFORESTATION AND AFFORESTATION

In 1979 reports of extensive deforestation were among the first revelations concerning China's worrisome environmental degradation. Subsequently, three growth surges had rapidly increased China's demand for timber: record economic growth rates, unprecedented pace of housing construction, and rapid expansion of coal mining. Afforestation campaigns restored tree cover on 28 to 30 million hectares of land during the years 1949–1979, or on less than 30 percent of the area claimed by the past official planting statistics.

In the 1980s the quality of afforestation improved significantly in most of the newly permitted private fuelwood lots, but average success rates in state-sponsored plantings remained relatively low. And even properly planted trees have had a great difficulty surviving the combined impacts of prolonged droughts (both their duration and frequency increased in most of northern China during the 1980s), pest infestation, and fires. Another serious threat to China's tree plantings has been the inadequate prevention of forest fires and poor fire-fighting capabilities. The best nationwide estimate is that about a third of successfully established new plantings were eventually damaged by fires.

In December 1990 the Ministry of Forestry decided that although the total forested area had increased rather substantially, wood consumption continued to surpass the growth rate and, in order to remedy this imbalance, timber harvests should be limited during the next five years to a maximum of 243.6 million cubic meters per year. Wood shortages already forced China to prohibit many uses of wood and to become a major timber importer. Widely disregarded prohibitions forbid the use of wood for, among other things, floors, stairs, windowsills, railway sleepers, cremation, and coffins. With the exception of 1985, the country had spent more than one billion U.S. dollars a year every year since 1984, mainly for shipments from Canada and the United States.

Such realities are not reversed in a year or two, but by 1992 the Chinese media were claiming that afforestation had generated a surplus of timber. And in December 1993 it was announced that the total annual growth surpassed 400 million m^3, while consumption declined further to 320 million m^3. These figures represent a fundamental reversal in a single decade.

If true, China's 1993 wood harvest/growth ratio would have stood at 0.8, just marginally worse than the ratios of such prodigious, and heavily forested, producers of wood as the United States or Finland, which were, respectively, 0.75 and 0.73 in 1990. This comparison alone should alert us to the fact that the Chinese figures are not really what they seem to be. But even if we were to assume that most, or even all of the 45 percent gain was real, its practical import appears in a different light once one realizes the changing composition of China's forest biomass.

Because of the rising share of new plantings in the total coverage, 82 percent of China's timberland in 1990 were young or middle-aged stands.

Timber reserves available for commercial harvesting declined by 2.308 billion cubic meters during the 1980s, with mature stands contracting by 170 million m³ annually, and the growing stock ready for harvesting in mature forests amounted to less than 1.5 billion m³, a total that could be cut in just seven to eight years. Reserves approaching maturity will decline from about 2.6 billion cubic meters in the late 1980s to just 1.25 billion cubic meters by the year 2000.

Many new plantings—be they relatively large southern pine plantations or small private lots of fast-growing fuelwood species—may be doing well, and their growth will be reflected by the rising volume of the standing stock, but the state record in replanting principal commercial logging areas has been poor. This neglect is creating a major resource crisis: of the 131 state forestry bureaus in the most important timber production zones 25 had basically exhausted their reserves by 1990, 40 can harvest up to the year 2000—and by that time almost 70 percent of China's state forestry bureaus will be without trees to fell.

From a large-scale ecosystemic point of view, it makes a great difference if trees are disappearing in steeply sloping upper basins of major rivers and are newly planted on oddland in alluvial farming areas. Reports by the Ministry of Water Resources admitted that the deforestation in the upper Yangzi basin has already done more damage than soil erosion control can restore. Prospects are made even more worrisome by the very low productivity of new plantings. The official figure for the average growing stock in forest plantings—about 20 cubic meters per hectare—makes it quite clear that the new extensive plantings, whose growing stock may be now yielding a statistical nationwide wood surplus, offer little hope for replacing the felled mature forests for many decades. Growing stock in these forests should be four or five times higher! The inevitable conclusion is that even if real, the recent quantitative growth of Chinese forests hides a major qualitative decline.

When valued in terms of the lost sustained supply of timber, China's recent overcutting would cost between 13 and 26 billion Chinese dollars a year. The long-term impact of timber-loss on ecosystemic services includes diminished water storage capacity, reduced protection against both wind and water erosion (its rates are likely to increase by two orders of magnitude), and—effects that are most difficult to quantify—changes to local and regional climate, contributions to changes in the biospheric carbon cycle and possible planetary warming, and consequences for national and global biodiversity.

GREENHOUSE GASES

China is already the world's second largest producer of greenhouse gases, emitting about 14 percent of the global total, compared to the United States' 22 percent. This ranking will change during the coming generation as China overtakes the United States. In addition to the large increases in CO_2 emissions from the continuing expansion of coal use, large increases in the other important greenhouse gases are expected as well (the much promoted "clean coal" techniques could actually increase specific CO_2 emissions per unit of useful energy). As China develops its natural gas reserves, more methane losses are expected to result from recovery activities. In the agricultural sector, more rice will mean more methane from bacteria in paddies, and higher fertilizer use will mean more nitrous oxide (N_2O). N_2O is about 200 times more effective at absorbing the outgoing radiation than CO_2, and China is already responsible for more than 20 percent of the world's N_2O emissions from nitrogenous fertilizers. In terms of chlorofluorocarbons (CFCs), a group of greenhouse gases with even higher radiative forcing capacity per molecule, China is now the world's largest refrigerator producer, with the goal of providing a refrigerator for every Chinese family. Its adherence to the London Protocol controlling CFC emissions is tied to Western payments for replacement refrigerants; however, such compensatory disbursement has lagged behind specified commitments. With inevitable increases in CO_2, CH_4, and N_2O emissions, and with (almost certainly) delayed elimination of CFCs, China will become the world's largest producer of greenhouse gases sometime between 2010 and 2020.

By that time rich industrialized countries, which are now responsible for most of the greenhouse gas emissions, will contribute less than one half of the total global flux. If there is no clear indication of substantial global warming, this shift will make little difference. But should we sense an unmistakably strong warming signal sometime during the next generation, then China's emergence as the world's largest producer of greenhouse gases may greatly complicate any serious control efforts.

The China-inspired Beijing Declaration of 1991 states the developing world's position that the rich countries are responsible for the rise in greenhouse gases, both in terms of current emissions and in a cumulative sense. It says essentially that the developing countries will not do anything to limit their emissions until they reach the developed world's level of per capita emissions, as well as its historical cumulative emissions. This means they should not be expected to do anything for decades to come! If any-thing is wanted of them, not only does the rich world have to pay, but it has to give very substantial sums over long periods of time.

This position will change under international pressure, but it would be naive to expect that China would assent to any massive greenhouse gas emission cuts as long as its per capita energy consumption will be an order of magnitude behind the U.S. mean. Undoubtedly, in terms of global cli-mate change China is the biggest wild card, and few of its recent steps indi-cate any long-term quest for maximized efficiency of energy use. Indeed, official policies seem to be informed by the delusion that there are no lim-its to the country's development. Instead of copying Japan with its exten-sive subways and efficient inter-city trains, the Chinese are building six-lane highways through rice fields and Beijing bureaucrats want to provide private cars to 270 million families within ten years (there are now about 300 million families in China and 660 million cars worldwide).

LOOKING AHEAD

I have deliberately focused on embedded trends, on realities that are either beyond anybody's control or can be substantially changed only over a course of decades rather than years. While I do not share the view of some catastrophically inclined Western analysts that the deterioration of China's environment could be a critical factor in the coming unraveling of the cen-tralized state, I am concerned that a concatenation of negative trends could usher in a period of worrisome instability.

The most pessimistic of such realistic appraisals offers very little hope for an early reversal of these degradative trends. Even a costly and con-certed effort could only slow down the rate of pollution and ecosystemic deterioration during the next generation. The addition of more than 150 million people during the 1990s (an equivalent of Brazil's total population in 1990) could not but result in elevated environmental stresses arising from the necessity of feeding, housing, educating, and employing this enormous increment. And even the most optimistic demographic scenario must reckon with another 150 million added by the year 2020. Given the continuing quest for higher living standards, the environmental impact of these increments will almost certainly exceed the horrific damage done to China's waters, soils, and forests during the 1980s.

The confluence of unbridled economic expansion and advancing environmental catastrophe analyzed here casts in relief the Sisyphean quality of China's modernization drive under an increasingly weakened State capitalism—the Party's survival depends largely upon its ability to deliver a wide, and increasing, array of benefits to a growing number of consumers. Yet its survival is also constantly threatened by the deepening ecological disaster wrought from its necessary economic expansion. It is this devil's bargain aspect of the environmental crisis—faced by individual Chinese, as well as the Party—that is perhaps the most definitive feature of China's mounting contemporary crisis and it is one that should give us pause as we continue to applaud the nation's "embrace of capitalism."

In this respect, we might consider again China's aspirations for affluence and its troubling claims for second-generation rights to modernize made against the fully modernized, first-generation rights West, claims that have attained such stridency that many Chinese believe the United States conspired to prevent the Chinese from hosting the 2000 Summer Olympic Games (see the essays by Rosemont and Lam in this volume). Even for dissidents like Wang Dan, democracy of the sort found in the United States is understood in terms of profit and so China's economic growth represents one path to a more democratic polity. Affluence, many Chinese believe, will breed a greater range of civil and political rights; this, of course, cannot be attained without further development, the destructive ecological consequences of which are already legion.

Thus, we can best understand China's particular environmental nightmare as an epiphenomenon of the larger developed world's Faustian calculus of progress, for one must not forget that leading Western nations have so far failed to implement integrated, systematic environmental management truly compatible with long-term sustainability of an advanced, global civilization. China's national environmental fate is increasingly an international one in a global ecosystem such as we have always lived but are only now beginning to realize. A proper, nuanced understanding of China's enormous challenge in this respect can be achieved only through a proper Western self-consciousness.

The greatest hope for our global commonwealth lies in a growing recognition of biospheric realities throughout the world. Chinese scientists have provided a solid base for appreciation of the country's environmental degradation and they have made the political leadership clearly aware of the link between environmental protection and the country's economic well-being. And there is a broad, informed consensus about the necessity of stabilizing China's population at the earliest possible date. These two realizations harbor the promise of an eventual turnaround. Yet such a reverse developmental trajectory, one governed by a greater concern for the planetary costs of growth, is unlikely to bite deep enough into the flesh of China's desperate gamble to generate sufficient profit to avoid political revolt, largely because the nation it most emulates in this regard is the United States. Avoiding further environmental degradation can only result from a consensus favoring global salvation over economic accumulation reached by both China and the United States. Furthermore, if the latter can recognize the political links Chinese citizens have forged between human rights and ecological adversity, then there may be even more incentive to scale down U.S. national aspirations for growth in the face of biospheric necessity.

My best ecological forecast, in light of the emerging domestic awareness of China's Hobson's choice, is for a mixture of further environmental deterioration and important sectoral and local improvements into the first years of the twenty-first century, paired with substantially increased investment in environmental protection, and a possibility (though far from inevitable) of broader, but hardly universal, gains leading to the stabilizing of per capita adverse impacts after the year 2010. This China will most likely accomplish on its own, but for the planet to escape its dark impending fate, Western industrialized nations, most notably the United States, must forsake the blandishments of affluence and embrace sustainable growth. Only then will China's government recognize environmental quality as a human right and understand that its true challenge, its singular responsibility, is, like that of the United States, to ensure a workable planetary future.

SUGGESTED READINGS

B. R. Allenby, *Environmental Threats and National Security* (Cambridge, Mass.: M.I.T. Press, 1998).

China's Environment, special issue of the *China Quarterly* (December 1998).

R. L. Edmonds, *Patterns of China's Lost Harmony* (London: Routledge, 1994).

Mark Elvin and Li Tsui-jung, eds., *Sediments of Time: Environment and Society in Chinese History* (Cambridge: Cambridge University Press, 1998).

Qu Geping and Li Jinchang, *Population and the Environment in China* (Boulder, Colo.: Lynne Reiner Publishers, 1994).

Vaclav Smil, *The Bad Earth: Environmental Degradation in China* (Armonk, N.Y.: M. E. Sharpe, 1984).

————, *China's Environmental Crisis: An Inquiry into the Limits of National Development* (Armonk, N.Y.: M. E. Sharpe, 1993).

————, *Environmental Problems in China: Estimates of Economic Costs* (Honolulu: East–West Center, 1996).

————, *Cycles of Life: Civilization and the Biosphere* (New York: Scientific American Library, 1997).

————, "China Shoulders the Cost of Environmental Change," *Environment*, vol. 39, no. 6 (1997).

————, *Energies: An Illustrated Guide to the Biosphere and Civilization* (Cambridge, Mass.: M.I.T. Press, 1999).

E. B. Vermeer, "An Inventory of Losses due to Environmental Pollution," *China Information*, vol. 10, no. 1 (1995): 19–50.

10

Marketing Femininity:

Images of the Modern Chinese Woman

Harriet Evans

The prevalence of women in advertising corresponds with [women's] aesthetic characteristics and with human nature; it also corresponds with the current social situation.
                    —*Zhongguo funü bao* (Women of China) (April 3, 1992)

All women hope to be beautiful, but there are many misunderstandings about what beauty means.
                    —*Hunyin yu jiating* (Marriage and Family) 6 (1998)

Images of women are a prominent feature of public spaces in China's towns and cities. From street billboards and shop windows, erotic and prosperous young beauties look out invitingly at their spectators. Image after image of the fashionable urbanite directs her languorous gaze at passers-by, promising romantic fulfillment. She shows off fine jewelry, silks, and sunglasses, and lounges in luxuriously upholstered sofas, basking in wealth and glamour. She glides through fields of flowers in soft-flowing dresses and pastel colors. She also proudly shows off her modern domestic appliances. The beautiful young woman is a composite of the flirtatious coquette, the satisfied sexual partner, the desirous romantic, and the contented homemaker. Feminine beauty, romance, and consumer capacity are visually enmeshed in public display of desire.

By contrast, between the 1950s and the late 1970s—the early decades after the Communist Revolution—the official ideology of gender equality demanded almost complete removal from the public eye of conventional signs of femininity and female eroticism. Women appeared as steelworkers, parachutists, and cotton-workers, or militant Red Guards, often in contexts where production for the good of society was the dominant theme. With shining eyes gazing into the distance, strong hands, and robust bodies, they symbolized energy, hard work, and passionate commitment to a revolutionary ideal. "External beauty" became a metaphor for sexual licentiousness and ideological impurity. "Internal beauty" illuminated the frugal appearance of the true revolutionary. That clothing should be gender-neutral in the drab grays, greens, and blues of the Mao suit became an automatic corollary of the rhetoric of gender equality. It also effectively obscured the female body from public perusal. Appearance was banished as a publicly accepted standard of women's social value; sexuality and eroticism were excluded from the vocabulary of revolutionary gender relations.

Practice has also changed, though not to the same extent. With designer-label clothes, expensive accessories, and foreign cosmetics, the young people of China's large cities move today in a world of bodily desire that their parents' generation was educated to believe was ideologically beyond the pale. Young men and women as fashionably clad as those of Tokyo or Paris parade the streets of downtown Shanghai. Impeccably dressed young women flock to the glossy department stores in central Beijing, to window shop—to observe and absorb—as well as to buy. By contrast with earlier generations, it is now possible to identify a person's age, her social and economic status, and even certain aspects of her cultural outlook from her clothes alone.

It is difficult to imagine that only two decades ago young women rarely wore even simple skirts in public. Though a range of costume clues, such as the fabric of a jacket or the number of pockets it had, formerly functioned as markers of political and social status, clothes revealed a much less diverse range of meanings and hierarchies. Letting a flowery, patterned collar peep out from under the high-necked Mao jacket was a sign of extreme daring. Female hairstyles ranged between the short bob, short pigtails, and braids—no ribbons allowed. As Rae Yang put it in her autobiographical account of growing up during the Cultural Revolution, "Anything that made girls look like girls was bourgeois. We covered up our bodies so completely that we almost forgot we were boys and girls. We were Red Guards, and that was it."[1]

The refeminization of images of the female body at the end of the Mao era did not explode into public overnight. Soft-focus images of Mao's second wife, Yang Kaihui, started appearing in public just as the Gang of Four were being denounced. Though the resuscitation of her image was, of course, an intentional attack on Mao's last wife, Jiang Qing, then under arrest for her "counter-revolutionary" crimes, it also signified a departure from the dominant gender representations of the former decade. By 1979, urban street walls displayed large posters of the smiling young mother sweetly cradling her single child. The front covers of the re-launched *Zhongguo funü* (*Women of China*, the official journal of the All China Women's Federation) increasingly depicted young women in flowing skirts or encased in body-hugging "traditional" *qipao*.

However, it was following the establishment of the first Special Economic Zones in southern China and the gradual go-ahead to capitalist-style privatization of the local market after 1984 that the feminization of public images really mushroomed. The beginnings of domestic and international advertising, the establishment of joint ventures in China, increased social mobility, including travel to the West, and the massive increase in popular publications and film all heralded the "explosion" of media images of femininity. Boosted by the Party's ideological shift—taking place at the same time—from emphasis on the public to the private sphere, the publication of women's fashion magazines made it clear that women's desire to wear high heels, for example, or to use cosmetics, was no longer the expression of a bourgeois outlook. The first women's fashion magazine, *Xiandai fuzhuang* (*Contemporary Fashion*), started publication in 1980. By the mid-1980s, young urban women, in domestic and occasionally professional contexts, replete with their tailored jackets, fashionable sportswear, and fancy dresses, were *de rigeur* on the front pages of popular magazines. Looking pretty, women were now told, was an important way to a man's heart. Love and romance were restored to their status as matters of the individual's personal life. The family was released from its obligations to the collective and emerged as a private "haven from a harsh world." Family harmony and consumer capacity now went hand in hand, both dependent on the married couple's ability to exploit the new opportunities of the reform program. By the early 1990s, with increasing urban unemployment (see Weston, this volume), the reassertion of the "private" sphere as women's domain—both in its domestic and its "personal" associations—was even deployed to legitimize arguments that "women should return home" and assist economic modernization by withdrawing from the public labor force.[2]

The romantic and erotic images of the mass media and advertising have been— and continue to be—a crucial component of this process. A persua-

Fig. 10.1. A typical magazine cover from the early 1990s.

sive emblem of the reintegration of "affairs of the heart" into the private sphere, romantic love now appears as an ideal, holding out the promise of ultimate happiness and fulfillment in return for subscription to the commercial opportunities of the reform project. As a metaphor for individual possibilities, it also appears as a parallel to the commercial, professional, and social opportunities claimed for the individual in market relations.

The contrasts between the view of Chinese women that emerges from these images and texts and the lives of ordinary women in China are enormous. Though increasing per capita incomes and social mobility now make the lifestyles and consumer goods represented by these images much more accessible to ordinary women than even ten years ago, the opportunities and experiences they describe are far removed from the horizons of aspiration of most women. Alongside the fashionable youth in Beijing's clothing stores and nightclubs, there are also vast numbers of women whose clothes, gestures, and demeanor indicate experiences totally removed from those suggested by the images I have described here.

Yet not only are these images extremely prominent in the media. They have also exploded into public life within a very short space of time, in effect since the mid-1980s. They are important not only as powerful aspects of the social and cultural environment in which women and men acquire a sense of themselves as "having a gender"—as being women or men. They are also important as indicators of the ways in which state and market, often indistinguishable in the way they operate, make use of—and exclude—women's bodies for commercial and political purposes. Together, they are the most obvious and omnipresent form of the commercialization of women's bodies.

Accounts of the processes through which women are subordinated, in China as elsewhere, tend to give priority to socioeconomic forces in explaining the perpetuation of gender inequalities. This essay does not take such an approach. Instead, it looks at particular aspects of the commercialization of women's bodies as a social and cultural site, or zone, where gender inequalities are constantly reproduced. In particular, it looks at dominant media representations of women—media and advertising images, in women's magazines, TV soaps, and so on—as significant components of what one might call a "discourse of gender" contributing to ordinary women's and men's understandings of gender.

Images matter; the gendered meanings (of femininity and masculinity) inscribed in them are an important, though often overlooked, arena where assumptions and beliefs about who and what women and men are are sus-

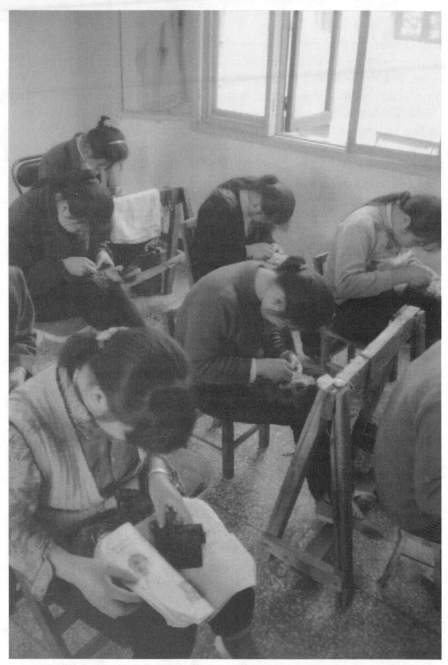

Fig. 10.2. These women, stitching ethnic textiles onto fashionable products for foreign export, like most Chinese women, cannot afford to mimic the lifestyle of the beautiful woman copiously displayed in the commercial media. (Photo by Tim Oakes)

tained and challenged. In an era in which nearly everyone has some kind of access to television, in which virtual travel on the Internet has expanded enormously the terrain across which images travel, and in which public images are an essential and dominant aspect of a market culture, the media image has immense power to influence attitudes and behaviors. Regardless of how their audiences respond to them, the dominant images of the media form a constant presence in the visual, physical—and arguably psychic—spaces of daily life. They do not determine how women behave, any more than they offer any uniform or unitary set of meanings. However, as aspects of a dominant and widely disseminated media, they are extremely influential in shaping how ordinary people think about gender. They can be understood as essential aspects of the process in which dominant (hegemonic) meanings and values come to shape day-to-day interpretations and practices.

In a social and cultural context in which brutal uses of women's bodies are far from uncommon and are frequently treated as an "effect" of China's feudal legacy, an examination of the meanings of gender prevalent in public media becomes even more important. I do not argue that the meanings of femininity embedded in dominant public images of women are responsible for or determine the more violent forms of commoditization of women's bodies. I do, however, suggest that the reproduction of hierarchical assumptions about gender and sexual relations in public images of women helps sustain similar assumptions about women in other areas of society. A recent comment made to me by a professional woman from Beijing crucially brought home the significance of this. In a lengthy conversation about marriage and domestic violence, including her own experience, she said that as long as dominant images of women continue to suggest women's dependence on and inferiority to men, and as long as they do not challenge men's as well as women's understanding of gender hierarchy, men will continue to assume that their wives' main responsibility in life is to service them. She also noted that in a context in which it is mainly women, and not men, who are targeted as the audience of discussions about changing gender roles and relations, there is little reason for men to think critically about their own approaches to gender.[3]

This essay, then, examines some of the dominant meanings associated with womanhood and femininity that come through contemporary media images. What kinds of gender values are represented in the images that cover the pages of women's magazines? What kinds of values and experiences do they exclude? In answering these questions, this essay also considers how images of femininity are interpreted differently by different Chinese women. It looks at their function in the context of the market interests responsible for producing them. Most important, it seeks to explore links between the meanings of gender inscribed in these images and those embedded in other commercial practices involving women's bodies.

WOMEN FOR SALE: THE MARKET CONTEXT

The tide of economic reform that has swept over China since the 1980s has been widely greeted as "creating advantageous conditions for women's development." Policy programs oriented to women have emphasized the importance of education, professionalism, technical skills, and scientific knowledge, as well as profitability and consumer demands and interests. In the early years of the modernization program, the government frequently referred to women as "half of heaven," indispensable to the success of the reform program as a whole. Yet throughout the late 1980s and early 1990s, increasing numbers of scholars and women's activists have argued that reform was not bringing to women in China the improvements they might have been led to expect. Tan Shen, for example, has argued that while on the one hand, economic reform has diversified employment opportunities and choices for women, it has simultaneously exacerbated gender differences in power, income, and status.[4] Through a process often referred to as the feminization of agriculture—the process through which agricultural activities are increasingly taken over by women as men engage in off-farm employment—it has also accentuated gender differences in access to wealth and, by implication, education.[5] As Elisabeth Croll has put it, "day-to-day reality" has been increasingly and openly characterized by discriminatory actions against women and by increasingly explicit recognition of all forms of female discrimination, including female infanticide.[6] Alongside these developments, the marketization of the economy has also commoditized women's bodies for a range of productive, sexual, and reproductive purposes.

One of the most appalling consequences of market reforms has been the commercialization of women for sale—and often violent abuse—on the open market. The commercialization of women for their sexual value has many different facets, from the banal use of pretty women to advertise fashions and domestic appliances to the violation of women's basic rights to bodily integrity. "Feudal practices"—the common Chinese term widely used to label the resurgence of venal marriage practices, including the abduction and sale of young women as wives—have been reported in every province of China.

In conditions of extreme poverty, where marriage is virtually universal, and where marriage is virilocal (on marriage, women usually move to their husband's village), the sale of a daughter into marriage may represent a means to finance a son's marriage as well as a last-resort response to desperate economic need. Furthermore, when a combination of demographic factors, lack of employment opportunities, and female out-migration result in a scarcity of women of marriageable age, the poor and isolated may have few options but to seek a wife through the market. Some reports also note that in such conditions the men who become the husbands of "bought wives" not infrequently have some physical and mental disability that would make it difficult for them to find a wife if simply left to their own devices. Anthropological reports also suggest that some young women accept sale into women as an economic necessity; "marry a man, and you have clothes to wear and food to eat" (*jia han, jia han, chuan yi chi fan*).[7] The purchase of women can thus appear as a mutual convenience for prospective husband and wife alike. National newspapers, however, have published horrifying accounts of brutality against young women sold, sometimes by auction, into marriage thousands of miles away from their birthplace. There are frequent media reports about police roundups and punishment of traffickers operating nationwide networks for the abduction and sale of women and children. A 1995 legal report claimed that between 1991 and 1994, nearly 70,000 cases of abduction of women and children were uncovered, leading to the arrest of more than 100,000 criminals.[8]

Prostitution is another commercial practice that has been given renewed vigor by the marketization of the economy. After thirty years during which prostitution had officially been "eradicated," prostitution once again, and with increasing frequency, came to the attention of the authorities in the 1980s.[9] According to official figures, between 1986 and 1990 the numbers engaged in prostitution increased fourfold over the previous five years, despite repeated crackdowns and police raids.[10] Sixty-two detention centers were reportedly set up for prostitutes between January 1986 and the end of 1987 alone. In early 1994, the national government announced that 1993 arrests of prostitutes alone totaled 250,000.[11]

However, official commitment to eradicating the sex trade seems to have borne little fruit, since despite repeated campaigns to eliminate it, sex work has continued to flourish in a variety of forms in urban areas. Red-light districts are well-established features of large cities, as are private services in hotels, bars, and even university campuses.[12] No longer is prostitution only the response of impoverished and uneducated young women at the bottom of the urban and rural social hierarchy to the problems of making a livelihood. Educated and socially desirable young women are reportedly joining the sex trade since it offers more lucrative prospects than the relatively meager incomes afforded by many other professions. The big joint-venture hotels and expensive restaurants of the large cities are now major work locations for professional sex workers whose trade involves foreigners and wealthy Chinese businessmen.

A third area in which marketization has encouraged the commercialization of women's bodies is in the production and consumption of pornographic (yellow) materials, a loose category that may include anything from erotic art and international award-winning films to violent pornographic movies. Immediately after its violent suppression of the June 4 democracy movement, the government launched a nationwide campaign against the "six evils," one objective of which was to "sweep away the yellow" (*saohuang*) and rid society of pornographic materials. The circulation of pornographic materials in China was explicitly linked with the "bourgeois" potential in Chinese society—represented particularly by the young supporters of the democracy movement—and the commercial infiltration of salacious influences from abroad.

Since late 1989, considerable publicity has also been given to the legal penalties, including capital punishment, that producers and distributors of pornographic materials face. In 1994, for example, a Beijing court sentenced to death Gu Jieshu, head of the capital's largest pornographic network, which was reportedly responsible for printing 833,000 illegal books and magazines.[13] Not so long ago, the Chinese Customs vowed to intensify its efforts to halt the influx of "moral toxin" being smuggled into China.[14] The increasing incidence of rape and other sexual crimes against women is also widely associated with the impact on social and sexual behavior of the commercialization of sex. A legal text published in 1990, for example, claimed that some 80 percent of the defendants in rape cases heard in the court of one small town became rapists after seeing or reading pornographic materials.[15]

Many writers, journalists, and women's activists are deeply concerned about the climate of violence in which so many women live. Volunteers have set up telephone hotlines to advise and counsel women in distress.

Other organizations, often described as the newly emerging NGOs (non-governmental organizations) are appearing to represent the demands of hitherto marginalized or silenced groups. The serious women's press, most notably what was until recently the monthly journal *Women's Studies* (*Nüxing yanjiu*), published by the Beijing Women's Federation, has carried a number of articles about the violent abuse of women's rights in the forms briefly described here.

However, various friends and informants in Beijing have commented that public debate about such issues is woefully inadequate. One woman suggested that given what she considered to be the widespread incidence of domestic violence across the social strata, including among professionals and intellectuals, the divide between debate and "reality" in itself constituted a form of abuse. Many commentators characterize the commercialization of women's bodies and sex as manifestations of a "social disease" (*shehui bingtai*) accompanying the open door policy and the reappearance of private ownership in China. Media analyses also tend to emphasize other socioeconomic factors, such as rural poverty, lack of education, and urban unemployment. Some adopt a more moralistic stance in condemning prostitution, for example, as a form of base corruption. Little space, however, is given to looking at the gender assumptions and attitudes sustaining these commercial uses of women's bodies and lives. Furthermore, the public opportunities for examining such issues, for example, in the pages of *Nüxing yanjiu*, have recently diminished. With its re-naming and glossy re-styling, *Women's Monthly* (*Nüxing yuekan*), as it is now called, devotes more attention to the proper response of a daughter-in-law to her mother-in-law than to the delicate and difficult issues of marital rape and domestic abuse.

By contrast with the more brutal forms in which women's bodies are used for commercial ends, the use made of female images in the media and advertising is in many ways unremarkable and banal. However, a closer analysis of the meanings of femininity and femaleness that are inscribed in dominant visual images suggests that they are important in the ways in which they position women as objects, rather than as subjects of economic and social processes. First, the urban beauty appears as an effect of economic reform, a recipient (or victim) of goods (or evils) created by others. Second, popular media images assume a view of womanhood that is enmeshed in economic structures largely of others' making, in which she is dependent for her health and happiness on others' (husband, boyfriend, enterprise, state) initiative. Rarely does she appear as an independent or autonomous person, able to make decisions and act without the mediating influence of the male. Third, her image reinforces the oppositional hierarchies made between the rural (backward/victim/suffering) and the urban (modernized/fulfilled/successful) apparent in many discussions about gender and social transformation. In none of these guises does the beautiful media image seem to offer any challenge to the dominant climate of gender attitudes in which the more extreme forms of commercial use of women take place. Rather, she represents another means of affirming her own subordinate status—whether as beneficiary or victim—in the reform process as a whole.

LOCAL AND GLOBAL FEMININITY

To many observers, both in China and the West, the post-Mao explosion of the sexy feminine image is explained as part of an inexorable process of "Westernization." Liberal supporters of the approach to "modernization," exemplified by the Dengist reform program, see this as synonymous with diversity, plurality, and new opportunities. On the other hand, "Westernization" has also frequently been used as a term to denigrate the individualistic, self-seeking, and ultimately immoral interests of the self-interested consumer. It was, for example, commonly used in association with the campaign against the "six evils" launched in August 1989 against pornography, prostitution, gambling, drugs, abduction and selling of women and children, and profiteering from superstition. According to this view, the explosion of sex in public spaces is inseparable from the "importation" and sometimes "imposition" of Western values on Chinese culture as an unwanted aspect of the "open door" policy.

By contrast with these views, the sexy images of the female body that are so common in China's mass media may also be seen as prominent among the forms of cultural expression that have emerged out of the complex and uneven flow of interests and ideas between the local (China) and the global (the world). Even though contemporary Chinese culture has been shaped in large part by modern forces associated with colonialism and its aftermath, China's transformation over the past century has produced a new version of capitalism that cannot be defined as either Eastern or Western. Rather, China's transformation is being shaped by forces within and between the movements of global capital and the interests, needs, and desires of people and societies at the local level.[16] Within this intersection between the global and the local, the cultural formations that emerge are influenced by a shifting series of mutual influences and effects. They belong neither to the "West" nor to "China," in any discernible form. In the context of the present discussion, one notable aspect of this has been the proliferation of images circulating between the local and the global through which different possibilities of Chinese identity (including gender identity) are explored.

Thus, though apparently very similar to those found in U.S. or European advertising, the images now current in the Chinese mass media display a range of meanings that differ substantially from those in the West. For a start, they have emerged in a radically different historical and socioeconomic context, following a particular experience of a nationalist and state ideology that—under the Communist Party's authority—linked the individual body, female and male, to the state. Many Chinese women affirm the liberating appeal of these images. Particularly for young women who associate their understanding of gender with the cultural and social environment of the post-Mao period, they represent new possibilities of femininity after the suppressed eroticism of the Maoist years.[17] From this perspective, the erotic appeal of contemporary images of the female body is a result of the renewed possibilities of "private" pleasure and desire that were denied by the public-oriented, gender-neutral discourse of the Cultural Revolution.

The mere possibility of exploring romance and desire opens up channels to self-discovery that necessitate a radical rethinking of past assumptions about gender and sexual relationships, as Zhang Jie's famous short story called "Love Must Not Be Forgotten," published in the early 1980s, suggested many years ago.[18] Younger women, born and brought up in contexts in which such images are commonplace, may not even stop to question their meaning. For them, these images are taken for granted as a natural expression of femininity. That women want to look beautiful through applying (and buying) cosmetics and keeping the body in good shape is an unquestioned fact of nature. In the words of a recent article in a woman's magazine for sale on any street newsstand in Beijing or Shanghai, "all women want to look beautiful."[19] Alternatively, young women may use the possibilities of adornment now available as a form of rebellion against their parents, in much the same ways as their sisters in the West might indulge in body-piercing or tattooing as a physically evident form of distancing themselves from their parents' generation.

Young women in the nightclubs and bars of Beijing represent the range

Fig. 10.3. Magazine advertisement for a breast-enhancing device (1996).

of these possibilities, from the feminine beauty, rigged out in fashionably cut dresses, to the grunge look of shabby jeans and greased hair. Between these different possibilities, many women now celebrate the female body as a source of pleasure that legitimates their private, erotic feelings. Without this approach to the female body, the reflections of contemporary women writers such as Chen Ran, who describe a kind of fragmented, free-floating female sexuality, unattached to object or context, would be unthinkable. As Wendy Larson argues, the erotic appeal of contemporary visual images of women is a central component of a post-revolutionary (post-Mao) discourse of desire.[20]

On the other hand, the dominance enjoyed by public images of the eroticized female body has also created a nostalgic longing—for the freedom not to be identified first and foremost as "having a gender," the freedom to be approached and seen as a person with the same cultural and social possibilities as any other, and the freedom to participate anonymously in the same activities as men. The inundation of the market by the image of the sexy modern woman makes it difficult to believe that the "Maoist image" of the socialist androgyne was, in effect, the only one available for nearly three decades.[21] Women who are now in their forties and fifties grew up in surroundings in which "positive" images of women as workers and soldiers were the only ones publicly available, regardless of the stories their mothers and grandmothers might have told them. Many women of the Mao generations also grew up valuing the possibilities for rethinking their identities as women that these images represented.[22]

In personal conversations, various women who were brought up to regard gender neutrality in dress as a sign of emancipation have commented to me that they feel antagonized by the images of the sexy and flirtatious female. They interpret them as demeaning to women, since they define women by their bodies and their looks. Corresponding with this view, the All-China Women's Federation, the official body responsible for women's affairs in China, continues to oppose women's beauty contests on the grounds that they "misguide" young women by encouraging an erroneous emphasis on "external beauty." Many articles in the women's press published in the early 1990s suggested that commercial images of women were totally biased, in that they limited women's range of skills to biological and reproductive factors. By contrast, images of women during the Cultural Revolution demonstrated the extent of what women could—and can—do, without "destroying femininity" (*cuican nüxing*).[23]

There is a frequent disjuncture in women's magazines between visual and written versions of femininity. The visual image of the romantic beauty (the agent of desire) often contrasts sharply with the normative standards of feminine conduct that appear in written form. Standard articles published in popular women's magazines are invariably more sober in the attributes and aspirations they associate with appropriate femininity than are the visual images that accompany them. Indeed, depending on the specific topic under discussion, articles may describe behavior that departs, sometimes radically, from the suggestions communicated by the visual images. Representations of the "ideal wife" in women's journals and TV soaps provide a good example. Since the mid-1980s, women's magazines have published numerous debates about the characteristics of the ideal wife or advice about how a wife should behave in order to patch up domestic quarrels or to liven up a dull marriage. Surveys conducted among students and professionals have repeatedly indicated that men want a "gentle and soft" (*wenrou*) wife who will put her interests after their own. The argument that men "really do have more responsibilities than women" is quite commonly used in one form or another to legitimize expectations of wifely support for her husband.

Male response to a recent popular television drama series indicates the same kind of preference. A *Beijing Native in New York,* made by the Beijing Television Production Center, was shown in China in October 1993.[24] In it a Chinese cello player and his wife go to New York City where they find themselves at the bottom of the social scale, working as a dishwasher and a seamstress. Eventually, the wife, Guo Yan, goes off with the cellist's employer, McCarthy, while the husband joins up with his employer, A Chun, an astute and single-minded businesswoman from Taiwan. In Mayfair Yang's analysis, the male film discussants all admired A Chun for her knowledge of the market and Western culture, but they preferred the "eastern beauty and virtue" (*dongfang meide*) represented in the character of Guo Yan. They also noted that though a woman like A Chun was good for the economy, she was not what they looked for in a wife.

These kinds of images idealize the conjugal relationship as a harmonious complementarity between the caring, responsive female and the protective, work-oriented, and sexually active male. Though they do not exclude erotic female desire, they offer a version of female sexuality that is more passive and undemanding—and bound by monogamous marriage—than the overtly flirtatious and provocative images of the front covers of women's magazines often suggest. The fashionable and consumer-oriented image may ultimately serve to reinforce conservative assumptions about femininity and masculinity. Young readers of these magazines may thus turn to their pages as a source of pleasure and fantasy as well as of comforting information. An eighteen-year-old young woman working in Beijing recently told me that she loved looking at the images of women's magazines because they were so modern. More important, though, she really liked reading the articles of one magazine—*Zhi xin*—in particular, because it gave her ideas about matters she found it difficult to talk about with workmates.

The tensions between written and visual representations and interpretations of them by Chinese women and men thus emerge as a particular arena of a public discussion where different meanings of the category "woman" are being contested. In this sense, the female body has become a symbolic figure where different voices, identities, and experiences are explored that both affirm and challenge dominant themes of the reform policies. However, all these readings of contemporary femininity assume a rupture between the Maoist and post-Maoist discourses. They imply that the failure of Maoist politics heralded a kind of fundamental break in the understanding of gender and in so doing denied the many ways in which contemporary China's forms of cultural expression—concerning gender as much as anything else—interact with what came before. However, this view of the contrast between the Maoist and the reform eras overlooks the many continuities in assumptions about gender and sexuality, crossing the Maoist and post-Maoist periods, that continue to characterize contemporary discussions. It also ignores the question of how and why, after more than three decades of erasure from public life, the contemporary image of the desiring and desired feminine woman so quickly and easily reappeared as the "natural" accompaniment of post-Mao femininity.

Issues of sexuality were a regular, though still minor, component of public (official) discussions in the 1950s and the 1970s. Within these discussions, women were far from appearing as "sexless" or "degendered," even though they were not depicted in suggestive clothing and jewelry. The understanding of female sexuality that emerged in these discussions suggested an essential biological link between women's reproductive functions and other responsibilities and attributes. The biological foundation to women's sexual structure and attributes, moreover, established "natural" boundaries to sexual activity, between the more passive and hesitant female, on the one hand, and the eager, dominant male on the other. Though current Chinese representations of femininity and female sexuality seem to indicate a radical departure from those of the earlier period, a similarly "biologistic" approach continues to mold debates about women's appropriate functions and modes of gendered relationships, as articles in women's magazines so prevalently suggest. Far from disrupting former assumptions about gender and sexuality, the "explosion" of sex into public life that has taken place since the early 1980s has utilized, built on, and even reinforced some earlier assumptions about natural femininity and masculinity.[25]

Crucially, however, approaching these images as either liberating or discriminatory within the local Chinese context ignores two factors that are vital to any discussion about women and gender in China today. First, it overlooks the ways in which the apparently radical shifts in public representation of the female function to reinforce the value of certain understandings of womanhood and femininity at the cost of others. It also disregards the use of the feminine image to reproduce gender hierarchies in the service of publicizing China's position in the contemporary world. The female body is thus ignored as marker of difference (between different categories of women) and exclusion (of certain experiences and aspirations of womanhood)—in the hierarchical social structures reinforced by the intersections of local and global capitalism.

THE FEMININE EMBLEM OF REFORM

While it is undoubtedly the case that many women experience contemporary images of women as emancipatory, liberation, as the historian/philosopher Michel Foucault reminded us with reference to the early twentieth-century sexual discourse, also introduces new structures of power and exclusion.[26] The erotic female image has emerged as one of the key metaphors of market-oriented interests. It is widely associated with the material values that, in part at least, explain the success of China's market policies. Romanticizing and eroticizing the female body has become a clear symbol of social and economic success. The youth, health and beauty, fashionability and prosperity of the modern woman all denote the individualized—and urban-based—opportunities and practices offered by the reform strategy.

The rewards held out to women for identifying with the visual images in women's magazines are the material and emotional emblems of commercial success; romantic engagement with wealthy young entrepreneurs, good looks, and exciting social and travel opportunities. The romantic

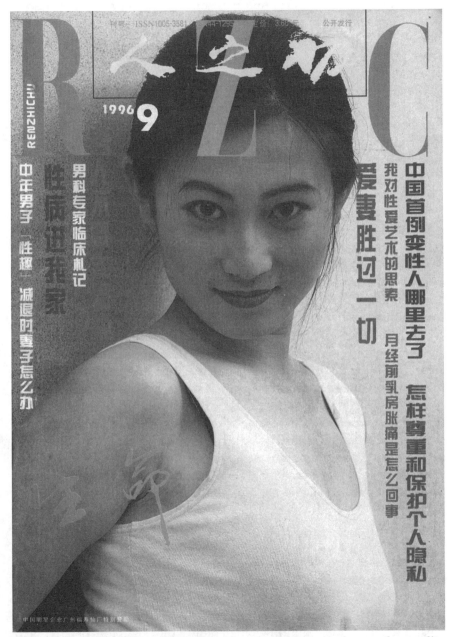

Fig. 10.4. Suggestive cover of a magazine devoted to marriage and sexuality (1996).

appeal of these images thus reinforces some of the key principles associated with the reform program at the same time as it gives pleasure to the viewer. Their importance is also evident in consumer practice. Young urban people spend considerable proportions of their personal budget on fashionable clothes, expensive cosmetics, and foreign appliances. On weekends, elegantly turned out young couples flock to the doors of Beijing's fashionable shopping centers. Young women who decide to undergo cosmetic surgery, typically in the form of eye enlargement, reportedly often model their desired self-image on photographs of Caucasian fashion models.[27]

The image of the beautiful Chinese woman also clearly invokes the global consumerism within which the Chinese market is situated. Her Pierre Cardin clothes, Japanese makeup, domestic appliances, and even cosmetically enlarged eyes denote access to a transnational, worldly, public culture as a further sign of her own success. Even when she appears as the "traditional oriental beauty" in international beauty contests, or in the form of Gong Li, the beautiful actress of *Red Sorghum, Judou,* and *Farewell My Concubine,* her features correspond with a view of the "oriental woman" that is, in the opinion of a number of Chinese observers, more Western than Chinese.[28] The Chinese woman in these images is no longer mainly identified with local Chinese concepts of Chinese identity, whether these invoke the past or Chinese patriarchy. Indeed, displayed on Western screens, the "oriental beauty" is given the status of an erotic and exotic symbol that corresponds more closely with Western fantasies and stereotypes than with native Chinese notions of womanhood, femininity, and beauty. The feminine beauty becomes a central icon of China's desire for recognition as a leader on the world stage. She symbolizes China's economic success on the international stage, China's dominant position in the rise of the Asian economies, and by extension China's emergent status as a great Asian-Pacific power.

This icon, however, is denied the power given to the male spectator. As the homemaker, she consumes the commodities her husband creates. As the beautiful and gentle companion, she awaits the guidance and protection of her husband. Her completion as a woman depends upon the implied presence of the male. She affirms Chinese masculinity as the creator of China's economic success. Furthermore, the eternal youth and urban identity of the beautiful woman denies the possibility of success to those women—the vast majority of Chinese women—whose images are never seen in the same privileged places: the old women, the peasant women, the young female migrants working sixteen hours a day in the factories of Shenzhen, those who have had the benefit neither of foreign travel nor of education and whose socioeconomic position prevents them from gaining access to her pleasures. She affirms the superiority of the urban/modern/educated over the rural/backward/ignorant through the total exclusion of all those who do not subscribe to her terms. Her dominance of the visual spaces of the media condemns those marginalized by her image to obscurity and silence.

The dominant female ideal of the Maoist decades represented the transformation of the Chinese woman subjected to patriarchal and colonial oppression into a woman recognized as a full and equal person. This image arguably offered a universal message of transformation to all Chinese women. By contrast, the beautiful Chinese woman does not stand for a universal notion of womanhood applicable to all Chinese women. She now stands for a global production of femininity that reinforces hierarchies of difference, between herself and the male spectator, and between herself and the women excluded from access to her image. She thus represents a double subordination; she appears either as the dependent consumer of male creativity, or she is excluded from access to the opportunities that creativity offers. Overall, she is denied the possibility of real power in the processes of social change.

The current plethora of feminized images in China has emerged in a socioeconomic context in which women potentially enjoy a greater diversity of experiences and possibilities than ever before in China's modern history. The wide range of journals, visual media, literature, film, music, and fashion now available in China's urban culture hold out to women unprecedented outlets for articulating new understandings of themselves and the world around them. However, the extension of the private market has created not only new opportunities in employment, education, and travel; it has also produced new marginalizations and exclusions, as well as bringing back—in new forms—hierarchical gender practices only thinly disguised by the rhetoric of the Mao decades. Globalization is frequently glossed over as a kind of relativistic meeting and interchange between equal entities. This view of globalism obscures the ways in which new, and apparently liberating, cultural forms reinforce differentials of power between those who have access to its benefits and those excluded from them.

From this perspective, the images of women that now dominate public visual spaces do not simply, or even predominantly, invite Chinese women to explore new meanings in their day-to-day lives. They cannot simply be read as signs of emancipation from former constraints. (This is not to say, of course, that there are no other discourses—in women's literature and art, for example—where meanings of female agency and autonomy are explored.) As part of a dominant public discourse of gender, such images promote desire, aspiration, and fantasy within boundaries that reinforce relations of subordination and exclusion, most notably of the rural, uneducated, and poor. The supposedly private sphere of beauty, desire, and romance emerges as an arena in which "woman" is constructed by the commercial interests of the state/market in its bid to occupy center stage in the "Pacific Century."

CONCLUSIONS

Of course, none of this is to suggest that women who wear makeup are willfully subordinating themselves. Nor does it suggest that women should or do deny themselves the pleasures represented by the glossy feminine image. What it does suggest is that women's status as active agents of change in China's reform program is no more acknowledged in these images than in those of earlier decades or in contemporary representations of women as victims and perpetrators of marital conflict. Recent suggestions put forward to reform the 1980 Marriage Law contribute to the same conclusion. Proposals to punish legally the "third party" in divorce cases have been treated with robust criticism by feminists in China, who argue that such punishment is neither feasible nor desirable, and that it simply does not address the fundamental issues of women's vulnerability in divorce settlements.[29]

Romantic images give pleasure because they promise a future of completion, fulfillment, and bliss. Inasmuch as they are associated not only with the female as an object of desire, but with the female's need and longing for the male, they also contribute to sustaining a series of values premised on the active power of the male. In this sense, they support the gender values on which patriarchal interests—in the state and market—rest. By extension, they also support the gender values embedded in the other forms of commercialization of women's bodies currently common in China.

I have not, in this essay, discussed the ways in which many different women in China, in various forms, both organizational and individual, are challenging the values and norms sustained by the kinds of images I have described here. Discussions about divorce, about domestic and sexual violence against women, about violations of women's rights through abduction and sale, about discrimination against women who choose not to marry, and about homosexuality give expression to voices that do not conform to the representations I have analyzed previously. However, many of these discussions are not immediately accessible to ordinary women or men in their daily lives. They are not nearly as prominent in mainstream publications and broadcasts, either in quantity or in their printed place and layout, as the representations I have discussed here.

Moreover, conventionally hierarchical assumptions about the proper boundaries of femininity continue to shape much of the organizational work currently being conducted among and for women. For example, the singles bar in Beijing still favors the registration of those who are actively looking for a marriage partner. While evidence suggests that extramarital sexual relationships are on the increase,[30] choosing neither to marry nor to have a male lover is still widely considered a sign of some "abnormality," or "odd" difference. Alternatives can be found but have to be sought out from the massive amounts of sugary and dependent femininity that saturate popular and official publications. While these more marginal debates indicate that women are empowered, for the first time in the history of the People's Republic, to examine their own gender and sexual identity in contexts that are not automatically mediated by state or masculine interests, they constitute a still minor aspect of public debates. Despite the clear construction of new spaces in Chinese society, removed from direct control by the state, the emergent signs in the media of an autonomous women's voice are too vulnerable to both commercial and political pressures to be able to identify the range of new positions they open up to women. Expressed to the consumer through images deeply embedded in global forces of capitalism, femaleness—being a woman—still denies women the possibility of defining their own desires and aspirations in the process of change, whatever they might be.

NOTES

I would like to thank Tim Weston and Lionel Jensen for giving me the opportunity to explore the issues contained in this essay. I would also like to thank Susan Brownell for her inspiring ideas as I was writing the first draft of this essay.

1. Rae Yang, *Spider Eaters: A Memoir* (Berkeley: University of California Press, 1997), 213.

2. Zheng Yefu, "Nannü pingdeng de shehuixue sikao" (Sociological Reflections on Male and Female Equality), *Shehuixue yanjiu* (Sociological Research), no. 2 (1994): 108–113. When the rising star sociologist of China's Academy of Social Sciences, Zheng Yefu, announced that gender equality in employment was incompatible with the requirements of economic efficiency, his arguments were roundly condemned by feminist scholars, one of whom simply suggested that if anyone was going to call for women's withdrawal from the labor force, it should be women themselves. For a feminist criticism of his views, see Lin Chun, "Guojia yu shichang dui funü de shuangzhong zuoyong" (State and Market: Dual Impact on Women), in *Zhongguo funü yu nüxingzhuyi sixiang* (Chinese Women and Feminist Thought), Qiu Renzong et al., eds. (Beijing: Zhongguo shehuikexue chubanshe, 1998), 27–37. Zheng Yefu's arguments, however, have clearly—explicitly and implicitly—received widespread support in view of the massive layoffs of women from the urban labor force in recent years. Margaret Woo has furthermore suggested that the net effect of recent laws to protect women's labor conditions and rights has been to reinforce inequitable practices in employment policies. See Margaret Y. K. Woo, "Chinese Women Workers: The Delicate Balance between Protection and Equality," in *Engendering China: Women, Culture and the State,* Christina K. Gilmartin et al., eds. (Cambridge, Mass.: Harvard University Press, 1994), 279–295.

3. This conversation took place during a recent trip I made to Beijing. My friend's comments also resonate with arguments set out in my recent book, in which I note on a number of occasions the significance of the failure to include men as major agents in the references and audiences of public discussions about gender. See Harriet Evans, *Women and Sexuality in China: Dominant Discourses of Female Sexuality and Gender since 1949* (Cambridge: Polity Press, 1997).

4. Tan Shen, "Biange zhong funü de liangge zhongda wenti" (Two Major Issues Facing Chinese Women in the Reform Period), in *Zhongguo funü yu nüxingzhuyi sixiang* (Chinese Women and Feminist Thought), Qiu Renzong et al., eds. (Beijing: Zhongguo shehuikexue chubanshe, 1998), 3–12.

5. Tamara Jacka notes that one report claimed that by the mid-1990s, 60 percent of all agricultural labor was performed by women. Though the total percentage of the labor force engaged in agriculture is declining, agriculture has increasingly become the responsibility of women, especially married women, in areas where off-farm employment is dominantly male. Women are often able to supplement their incomes from agriculture with earnings generated through nonagricultural production in domestic sidelines, and in some parts of southern China, in particular, earnings from agriculture may be similar to, or even higher than, those earned in local industry. However, the average income from agriculture is commonly considerably lower than industrial wages. Reports suggest that where

women are under considerable family pressure to take on a heavy workload in agriculture and domestic work, they may sometimes attempt to manage by transferring a portion of their domestic work onto their daughters' shoulders, "even if this means withdrawing them from school at an early age." Tamara Jacka, *Women's Work in Rural China: Change and Continuity in an Era of Reform* (Cambridge: Cambridge University Press, 1997), 128–139.

6. Elisabeth Croll, *Changing Identities of Chinese Women: Rhetoric, Experience and Self-Perception in Twentieth-Century China* (London and New Jersey: Hong Kong University Press and Zed Books, 1995), 111.

7. Guo Yuhua, "Yuan dao er lai de xifumen" (Daughters-in-Law from Distant Parts), Beijing, unpublished draft, 1993.

8. Evans, *Women and Sexuality in China*, 168–171.

9. Even though, as Gail Hershatter points out, "prostitution's disappearance under Mao was apparently less than complete," a series of government campaigns to eradicate it in the 1950s vastly diminished its scope and visibility. For more on these campaigns, see Gail Hershatter, *Dangerous Pleasures: Prostitution and Modernity in Twentieth-Century Shanghai* (Berkeley: University of California Press, 1997), 304–333.

10. Quanguo renda changweihui fazhi gongzuo weiyuanhui xingfa shi (The Criminal Law Office of the Legal Work Committee of the Standing Committee of the National People's Congress), "Guanyu yan jin maiyin piaochang de jueding, guanyu yan cheng guaimai bangjia funü ertong de fanzui fenzi de jueding" (Decisions on strictly prohibiting prostitution and decisions on strictly punishing criminals who abduct and kidnap women and children) (Bejing: Zhongguo jiancha chubanshe, 1991), 12, quoted in Evans, *Women and Sexuality in China*, 175.

11. Hershatter, *Dangerous Pleasures: Prostitution and Modernity in Twentieth-Century Shanghai*, 334.

12. This is based on an "eyewitness" account from a friend and colleague who works in one of Beijing's universities.

13. China News Service, *The Guardian* (September 19, 1994).

14. *China News Digest* (January 8, 1996).

15. Wang Ranji, Zhang Zhiyou, Cui Jin, and Wan Chun, *Qiangjian zui de rending yu fangzhi* (Defining and Preventing the Crime of Rape) (Beijing: Zhongguo huaqiao chubanshe, 1990), 119, quoted in Evans, *Women and Sexuality in China*, 181.

16. Allen Chun, "Discourses of Identity in the Changing Spaces of Public Culture in Taiwan, Hong Kong and Taiwan," *Theory, Culture and Society*, vol. 13, no. 1 (1996): 51–75.

17. Susan Brownell, *Training the Body for China: Sports in the Moral Order of the People's Republic* (Chicago: University of Chicago Press, 1996), 236–237.

18. Zhang Jie's "Love Must Not Be Forgotten" was one of the first stories of the post–Cultural Revolution "wounded," or "scar," literature to challenge the stan-

dard approaches to love and marriage of the "Maoist period." The narrator of the story describes the tragedy of her mother and the man she loves, both of whom entered into loveless marriages, and of her own decision to break off her own engagement rather than be bound to a man out of duty. When it was first published, the story made Zhang Jie a celebrity for its exposure of the failures of "socialist" approaches to marriage. For a useful introduction to writers and literature of the post-Mao period, see Bonnie S. McDougall and Kam Louie, *The Literature of China in the Twentieth Century* (London: Hurst & Company, 1997).

19. *Hunyin yu jiating* (Marriage and Family), no. 6 (1998): 24–26.

20. Wendy Larson, "Women and the Discourse of Desire in Postrevolutionary China: The Awkward Postmodernism of Chen Ran" *boundary 2*, 24, no. 3 (1997): 201–223.

21. "Socialist androgyny" was the term used by Marilyn Young, "Chicken Little in China: Some Reflections on Women," in *Marxism and the Chinese Experience*, Arif Dirlik and Maurice Meisner, eds. (Armonk, N.Y.: M. E. Sharpe, 1989), 253–268.

22. Gail Hershatter, "Gender and Rural Work in the 1950s," in *Re-Drawing Boundaries: Work, Households, and Gender in China*, Barbara Entwisle and Gail Henderson, eds. (Berkeley: University of California Press [2000]).

23. Some such articles are found in successive issues of *Zhongguo funü bao* between 1992 and 1993.

24. Mayfair Mei-hui Yang, "Mass Media and Transnational Subjectivity in Shanghai: Notes on (Re)Cosmopolitanism in a Chinese Metropolis," in *Ungrounded Empires: The Cultural Politics of Modern Chinese Transnationalism*, Aihwa Ong and Donald Nonini, eds. (London: Routledge, 1997), 287–319.

25. *Women and Sexuality in China* offers detailed evidence for this argument. However, in putting it forward, I do not wish to overlook the ways in which meanings of gender and sexuality are also being contested and debated. Contemporary representations signify multiple movements of meaning, reinforcing biologistic assumptions about gender and sexual hierarchies at the same time as they open up a discursive space for exploring new possibilities.

26. Michel Foucault, *The History of Sexuality, Volume 1: An Introduction* (Harmondsworth: Penguin, 1984).

27. I would like to thank Susan Brownell for her ideas about the body, appearance, and gendered identities, derived from her recent fieldwork in the clinic of a cosmetic surgeon in Beijing.

28. In a recent article entitled "The Body and the Beautiful in Chinese Nationalism: Sportswomen and Fashion Models in the Reform Era," *China Information* (vol. xiii, no.2/3 [Autumn/Winter 1998]: 36–58), Susan Brownell described the selection criteria and procedures of a supermodel contest held in Beijing in 1991. The selection panel, which consisted of Chinese, Japanese, and one Western member, decided that the "traditional oriental beauty" was high on their list of criteria, and yet when the final-

ists were chosen, they were taller than the "traditional oriental beauty" and had wider eyes. Susan Brownell noted that the women sitting at her side watching the contest were perplexed at the panel's choice of finalists on the grounds that they did not correspond with their own understanding of "oriental beauty." Rather, it seemed to be a kind of orientalist take of the Chinese/East Asian view of Western ideas of oriental beauty.

29. For a critical article about these proposals, see Li Yinhe, "Peiou quan: hunwai xing guanxi yu falü" (Partners' Power: Extra-Marital Sexual Relations and Law), *Du shu* (Reading), no. 1 (1999): 3–18. In this article, Li Yinhe analyzes the historical and contemporary factors contributing to women's vulnerability in divorce cases, and argues that in the current period, "both in economic terms and in access to jobs and facilities, women are in a position of relative disadvantage, and [because of this] their economic dependence on men may perforce increase" (18). She also writes that "in a significant category of divorce cases, particularly those in which the intervention of a 'third party' is involved, invariably the party that seeks divorce (the majority of whom are middle-aged men) is wealthy, successful and has a certain social status" (14). In her view, therefore, the new proposals do nothing to address the material problems faced by the divorcée. Added to the continuing disdain frequently shown to female 'third parties' as well as divorcées, her argument further implies that any attempt to punish the 'third party' would reinforce women's vulnerability and victimization, rather than seriously address its causes. Li Yinhe is a feminist sociologist working in the Institute of Sociology, Chinese Academy of Social Sciences. Her recent publications on homosexuality, female sexuality, and sado-masochism have provoked widespread critical comment in the Chinese media.

30. Li, "Peiou quan: hunwai xing guanxi yu falü."

SUGGESTED READINGS

Susan Brownell, *Training the Body for China: Sports in the Moral Order of the People's Republic* (Chicago and London: University of Chicago Press, 1996).

Allen Chun, "Discourses of Identity in the Changing Spaces of Public Culture in Taiwan, Hong Kong and Taiwan," *Theory, Culture and Society*, vol. 13, no. 1 (1996): 51–75.

Elisabeth Croll, *Changing Identities of Chinese Women: Rhetoric, Experience and Self-Perception in Twentieth-Century China* (London and New Jersey: Hong Kong University Press and Zed Books, 1995).

Harriet Evans, *Women and Sexuality in China: Dominant Discourses of Female Sexuality and Gender since 1949* (Cambridge: Polity Press, 1997).

Michel Foucault, *The History of Sexuality, Volume 1: An Introduction* (Harmondsworth: Penguin, 1984).

Gail Hershatter, *Dangerous Pleasures: Prostitution and Modernity in Twentieth-Century Shanghai* (Berkeley: University of California Press, 1997).

Tamara Jacka, *Women's Work in Rural China: Change and Continuity in an Era of Reform* (Cambridge: Cambridge University Press, 1998).

Margaret Woo, "Chinese Women Workers: The Delicate Balance between Protection and Equality," in Christina K. Gilmartin, Gail Hershatter, Lisa Rofel, and Tyrene White, eds., *Engendering China: Women, Culture and the State* (Cambridge, Mass.: Harvard University Press, 1994), 279–295.

Mayfair Mei-hui Yang, "Mass Media and Transnational Subjectivity in Shanghai: Notes on (Re)Cosmopolitanism in a Chinese Metropolis," in Aihwa Ong and Donald Nonini, eds., *Ungrounded Empires: The Cultural Politics of Modern Chinese Transnationalism* (London: Routledge, 1997), 287–319.

Rae Yang, *Spider Eaters: A Memoir* (Berkeley: University of California Press, 1997).

11

China's Labor Woes:

Will the Workers Crash the Party?

Timothy B. Weston

Nobody's patience is limitless and Chinese workers are no exception. We believe that if the NPC [National People's Congress] continues to ignore the problems confronting it, then the law will no longer be law and if the patience of the people finally runs out, then even the state itself will cease to exist.
—Labor union organizer, Han Dongfang to
Qiao Shi, the Chairperson of the National People's
Congress, January 21, 1998

Casual watchers of the news are likely to have the sense that Chinese economic might is growing fast. Much attention has been paid to the point that the U.S. trade deficit with China has surpassed that with Japan and to the fact that China's economy has been among the fastest growing in the world over the last twenty years—since 1978 it has averaged 9.5 percent a year. Today the Chinese economy is the world's second largest in terms of gross domestic product measured in purchasing-power parity, and sometime early in the next century it is projected to become the largest in absolute terms. China's economic takeoff during the last twenty years has been phenomenal. In the nineteenth century it took the United States nearly fifty years to double its per capita income; China has doubled its national income not once but twice since the start of the post-Mao reforms in 1978. The number of people lifted out of poverty since that year, some 150 to 200 million—equivalent to half the population of Western Europe— may have set an all-time record. China's per capita income is extremely low by U.S. standards but is rising quickly; since 1978 it has grown about 6 percent a year, more than that of any Asian country except South Korea.

By 2000 it is expected to reach U.S. $800, and by 2010 optimistic Communist Party officials estimate the figure will reach U.S. $1,500.[1]

These statistics suggest an "economic miracle" brought about by China's movement toward the free market. What they mask, however, are the Chinese economy's many deeply embedded structural problems (see Rosemont's essay in this collection), as well as the tremendous human suffering that attempts to fix them are causing. In the countryside, where some 60 percent of the Chinese people live, tens of millions of people are either unemployed or underemployed, and China's cities are experiencing a devastating unemployment crisis. It is on the plight of China's urban workers that I will concentrate in the rest of this essay. Before now, my research has been focused on modern intellectuals and political change. Today, as in 1989, Chinese intellectuals have serious grievances against their increasingly market-driven society and against their government, which many of them accuse of being both corrupt and undemocratic. Might such grievances lead to renewed activism on Chinese campuses? It's likely they eventually will, and there's no doubt that the Communist leadership is carefully monitoring the situation. But the authorities are far less worried about intellectuals agitating for better conditions for themselves than they are about the possibility that they might link up with people from other parts of society—especially workers. That sort of cross-class alliance, if well organized, could make the massive demonstrations of 1989 look like child's play.

Why is this? Simply put, because the sad fate that has befallen Chinese workers in recent years has led to widespread and deep discontent throughout urban Chinese society. This discontent dwarfs that of 1989, when the largest protest movement in the history of the People's Republic of China took place. The bloody images we saw on television in 1989 showed us that protesting intellectuals can be suppressed. Today, though, given that income disparities between society's haves and have nots are becoming ever more conspicuous, that China's urban unemployment rate is the highest it has been since the Communist Party took power in 1949, and that workers' protests are erupting all over the country, one wonders what might happen if activists from campuses and factories begin to make common cause. The possibility of truly grave social unrest at the hands of millions of angry workers is all too clear to the country's leaders; at a May 1998 national conference convened to address the problem, President Jiang Zemin and Premier Zhu Rongji acknowledged that the fate of China's entire reform process could well hinge on the Party-state's ability to meet the basic needs of the country's troubled urban workforce.[2]

Some Chinese workers have clearly benefited from the economic reforms, but most—in state-owned and private enterprises alike—are working under harsher and more exploitative conditions, and must cope with far greater uncertainty, than before. Unlike repression in Tibet, of Chinese Christians, or of outspoken intellectual dissidents, the increasing misery of Chinese workers is not a much-discussed subject in the United States, where issues of economic and redistributive justice tend not to be linked with human rights. Moreover, to concentrate on the exploitation of workers in China or elsewhere is to recognize that we as consumers are indirectly implicated. The U.S. buys vast quantities of Chinese goods—a little research in almost any clothing store, K-Mart, or Target will bear this out. Indeed, low-paid Chinese workers desperately need U.S. shoppers; the United States has only a fifth of China's population but it outconsumes China by 53-to-1.[3]

All of this can be rather discomforting. It is far easier emotionally and intellectually to concentrate on the repression of individuals or groups calling for political and religious freedoms than it is to fundamentally scrutinize the effects of the global market system that the U.S. is actively working to promote. Nevertheless, it is undeniable that in today's increasingly interconnected global economy, work conditions in one country are linked to patterns of consumption and the rights of workers in other countries. I do not mean to suggest that the United States is to blame for the plight of China's workers but instead to call attention to a "category" of human suffering downplayed in U.S. media celebrations of China's market reforms, and thereby to observe that capitalism is creating new problems in China at the same time that it is helping to eliminate old ones.

THE TRANSFORMATION OF THE SOCIALIST ECONOMY

Although China has already transformed into a hybrid economy with collective and domestic- and foreign-invested private firms accounting for a growing percentage of enterprises and industrial output, state-owned enterprises, or SOEs, which represent the socialist part of China's economy, still dominate major sectors such as coal, metals, chemicals, textiles, printing, tobacco, fertilizers, motor vehicles, electronics, and defense. At present, there are roughly 300,000 SOEs in China, a third of which are industrial, and altogether these employ some 110 million people, or some 65 percent of the country's urban workforce. The percentage of the economy comprised by the state-owned sector will continue to shrink relative to other sectors of the economy in the coming years, but by any measure it will remain massive for some time to come.

At the 15th Congress of the Communist Party held in September 1997— the first since the death of Deng Xiaoping six months earlier—the Party leadership made it abundantly clear that it had subscribed to what Dorothy J. Solinger refers to as the "ideology" of "globalization" and "an attendant neoliberal economic ideology with the deregulation and privatization" that it "dictates."[4] In the name of greater economic efficiency the 15th Party Congress approved policies that will dismantle most of the socialist sector of the economy in a rapid fashion that guarantees unprecedented rates of unemployment for workers in state-owned enterprises. With the exception of some thousand or so key industries that are to be retained by the state, hundreds of thousands of smaller SOEs face the prospect of merger, privatization, or even bankruptcy. The reason the Communist leadership wants to speed up the transformation process by undertaking the massive project of converting the state-owned enterprises is plain enough: it no longer wishes to pay the wages and other costs associated with these outmoded and noncompetitive industries. As was the case in the former Soviet Union and in the former Communist countries of Eastern Europe, after 1949 China's state-run factories were not autonomous enterprises operating in a free-market economy but part of a planned national economy. Moreover, they were originally designed as cradle-to-grave social welfare institutions, so chronic unprofitability and high rates of worker redundancy were tolerated by a Communist Party whose legitimacy depended in great part on its ability to assure that all people had access to the indestructible "iron rice bowl," which, in addition to a guaranteed job, provided medical care, subsidized housing, food, and pensions.

There is no question that most of China's state-owned enterprises are highly inefficient and that the Party-state is in a very difficult position. In 1996, for the first time, state firms as a whole lost more money than they took in. During the first three quarters of 1997 some 46.8 percent of them were operating at a loss. In some cases such enterprises operate with World War II–era technology that is as inefficient as it is highly polluting. Moreover, the state-owned sector's share of industrial output is dropping rapidly; whereas in 1978 it accounted for 80 percent of output, by 1995 it had fallen to under 50 percent. Because they are so unprofitable, SOEs tend to fall behind in their tax payments to the state. Between 1978 and 1995 tax

Fig. 11.1. Jobless men sit beneath a revolutionary statue in the northeastern city of Shenyang, where thousands of workers have been laid off from state-owned enterprises. (Photo by Mark Henley)

revenues fell from 35 percent of GDP to 11 percent, largely owing to the poor performance of state enterprises. Despite this, SOEs still absorb the lion's share of loans granted to enterprises by China's state-owned banks. In the mid-1990s, though SOEs accounted for under 35 percent of industrial output value, they were gobbling up nearly 75 percent of national industrial investment.[5] By selling off the majority of the state-owned enterprises or by allowing them to be privatized or simply to declare bankruptcy, the Party will rid itself of a massive financial burden and, it hopes, free up savings that will encourage the growth of a truly competitive, market-driven economy. What this means is that the "bottom line"—profitability—is going to play an increasingly important role in determining which industries survive and which do not.[6]

What it also means, of course, given that well over half the urban workforce is employed in SOEs, is that the social costs associated with the economic restructuring are going to be extremely painful. In his speech at the 15th Party Congress in September 1997 Jiang Zemin admitted as much, though he also argued—with a logic similar to that put forth by the World Bank and the IMF—that these painful market reforms will ultimately be in the Chinese people's best interest: "With the deepening of enterprise reforms, technological progress and readjustment of the economic structure, it would be hard to avoid the flow of personnel and lay-offs. It will cause temporary difficulties to some workers. But, fundamentally speaking, it is conducive to economic development, thus conforming to the long-term interests of the working class."[7] In speaking about "temporary difficulties," Jiang was euphemistically referring to the fact that in a society in which jobs in a state-owned firm were once prized and in which employment was once assumed to be for life, tens of millions of workers are going to be "downsized" out of their jobs. Furthermore, given the welfare functions that have traditionally come with jobs in state-owned enterprises, for a great many people "unemployment" means not only the loss of work but also the smashing of the socialist "iron rice bowl," which previously assured their housing, education, medical care, and pensions.

Between 11 and 12 million urban workers lost their jobs in 1997 and massive cuts are to continue over the next several years. Spurred on by the policy laid out at the 15th Party Congress, enterprises all over the country have been announcing layoff plans. A week after that Congress one of China's largest state-run enterprises, Aviation Industries of China, announced that it will lay off a quarter of its workers, or some 150,000 people, over the next two years. In early 1998 the railway system announced plans to drop over a million workers from its payroll over the next three years, the extremely hard-hit textile industry stated that it will lay off 1.2 million workers in that same period of time, and authorities in charge of the iron and steel sector pledged to halve its workforce, meaning that some 700,000 workers will lose their jobs by the year 2000. The situation is worst in rust-belt cities in the northeastern provinces of Liaoning, Jilin, and Heilongjiang, where up to a third of urban workers have been laid off, as well as in the inland provinces of Henan, Hubei, and Anhui, which have not enjoyed the same economic boom as the coastal regions. Another extremely hard-hit province is Sichuan, whose population alone is roughly four times that of the entire country of Canada. In Sichuan 11 percent of the state-owned enterprise workers have been laid off; at the end of June 1997 China's official figure for all workers laid off from SOEs was 17.8 million and 2.75 million were in Sichuan. In addition the province has 9.25 million surplus rural laborers.[8]

China's total unemployment figures are difficult to establish and vary widely, depending on the method of counting. For example, according to official statistics, the urban jobless rate at the end of 1997 was 3.1 percent, but this figure did not include workers dismissed by SOEs because technically most of them have only been "temporarily" laid off (though few are likely to be rehired) and are receiving token pay rather than their full paychecks. But according to a recent finding by the State Statistical Bureau, only half of these people receive the monthly stipends they are promised, which averages about U.S. $17 a month, not nearly enough to live on.[9] Official reports allow for at least 11.5 million of these people. Using the highly conservative 3.1 percent national urban unemployment rate and then factoring in the vast number of unemployed in the countryside, in June 1998 Chinese officials arrived at a total, nationwide combined urban and rural under- or unemployment rate of 17 percent, which translates into 125–150 million people. This is a mind-boggling total, considering that the entire population of the United States is 260 million![10]

The logic of Chinese capitalism is leading not only to dramatic "downsizing" but in many cases to harsher and less egalitarian work environments in state-owned enterprises as well. According to sociologists Zhao Minghua and Theo Nichols, who conducted extensive surveys of work conditions in three state-owned cotton mills in Henan Province in 1993 and 1994, management has gained greater power and workers are experiencing more exploitation under the current labor conditions than was the case under the former socialist labor system. Workers in cotton mills once had permanent job status but now are hired on short-term contracts. In other words, their jobs are no longer "for life" but instead depend on their work performance and/or the performance of their enterprise in the marketplace. Moreover, there are two classes of workers in the cotton mills. Those who were once permanent employees of the mills and who therefore possess urban "residence permits" (*hukou*)[11] receive higher wages and better benefits and welfare than peasant contract workers from the countryside, who do not have urban residence permits. Rural workers are often forced to work harder than urban workers. This can take the form of either having to work more shifts or working in the oldest workshops with the worst machinery.[12]

Because managers are now evaluated according to the profitability of their firms, they are forcing workers to meet higher production quotas and to work longer hours (sometimes up to sixteen hours at a stretch), and despite laws setting minimum pay for overtime hours, surveyed workers complain about never being paid at the overtime rate. And workers are facing stricter work attendance requirements. Said one woman: "Nowadays, it's not good to work in a cotton mill or to be a worker at all. Just imagine, you can't even take a day's leave without big cuts in your wages. It wasn't like this before. Now they don't care about your problems, even when your kids are sick, when you yourself are sick, or your relatives are dying." Management has adopted detailed standards for evaluating workers' performances that are so difficult to understand that most workers do not know how their wages are computed or what payment they will receive from one month to the next. Not surprisingly, tension between management and workers in state-owned factories is increasing. According to a man laid off from his machinery factory: "Workers have changed from being the masters to the slaves of the enterprise. The director has become the patriarch of the family. I dare say this view represents 100 percent of the workers in my factory."[13]

Workers in SOEs who still have their jobs thus often face highly exploitative conditions that have prompted foreign researchers to compare the very enterprises once glorified for treating workers as the "masters of society" to "sweatshops." But as a rule people employed in state-owned enterprises are not the most harshly treated workers in Chinese society. Sociologist Ching Kwan Lee concedes that workers in SOEs face an increasingly "despotic factory regime," but she also explains that these workers routinely use a variety of methods to express their noncompliance that usually do not lead to serious punishment. One tactic the dispirited workers in the state-owned enterprises that Lee studied in Guangzhou Province have long used to register their unhappiness is "goldbricking," or putting little effort into their work. If workers in privately owned factories, who often have no work contracts whatsoever, engaged in similar slow-down techniques, they might well be summarily dismissed from their jobs and have their last paychecks withheld.[14]

Dorothy J. Solinger has shown that workers connected to the state are generally at an advantage compared with those in other sectors of the economy. Workers employed in other sectors of the economy sometimes earn more money than their counterparts working for the state, but to do so they have to sacrifice the greater welfare and other protective guarantees that are legally mandated for SOEs. According to Solinger, those who work in the private sector often "struggle in a world that harkens back to the long-gone, gruesome days of Charles Dickens' early industrialization."[15] Workers employed in state-owned enterprises work under harsher conditions than before; face very uneven wages, depending on their residence status; and cannot always count on their managers to uphold the laws with regard to overtime pay, holidays, and the like, but the fact is that those laws do exist and are far more often followed in SOEs than in non-state enterprises. In short, while things are getting worse for workers in state-owned enterprises, conditions for those still employed by them are generally more secure than for workers employed in other sectors of the economy.

THE FOREIGN-INVESTED SECTOR

The worst industrial work conditions in China are to be found in foreign-invested factories in the southern part of the country, where some 17 million low-skilled people toil in sweatshops funded by investors from Taiwan, Hong Kong, and South Korea, attracted to China by the cheap labor. Most of the goods produced in these sweatshops are sold outside China. Unlike high-skill operations in China funded by U.S., Japanese, and German multinationals, which tend to employ U.S.-style "human resource management" techniques and collective bargaining, factories that make low-skill goods like shoes, toys, and clothing for export to the United States and other developed countries usually do not allow collective bargaining.[16] In a March 1998 special report prepared for the National Labor Committee, a New York–based nongovernmental organization (NGO)

dedicated to the exposure of human rights and labor abuses by corporations, Charles Kernaghan documented appalling work conditions in Hong
Kong-, Taiwanese-, and South Korean–owned garment factories in southern China that produce clothing for the U.S. market on subcontract for
companies such as Ann Taylor, Ralph Lauren, Liz Claiborne, The Limited,
J. C. Penney, K-Mart, and Wal-Mart.

In his report Kernaghan explains how subcontracting enables U.S. companies to hide what they are doing by making it extremely difficult for
concerned consumers to learn which factories are making the items they
are buying. To address this situation the National Labor Committee is
working with a coalition of religious, human rights, consumer, and student groups across the country to force corporations to disclose exactly
where their products are made, by whom, and under what work conditions, in the belief that U.S. consumers, once armed with accurate information, will take it upon themselves to force the companies they buy from
to provide better wages, benefits, and so forth to the hidden and far away
laborers who make the things they profit from selling in the United States.
It was pressure of this sort that forced TV talk-show personality Kathie
Lee Gifford to promise to investigate labor conditions in the Central
American factories that produce clothing under her label. In a further sign
that many U.S. citizens care about these problems, in July 1998 university
students from across the country formed a nationwide organization,
United Students Against Sweatshops (USAS), to put pressure on university administrators to guarantee that clothing bearing university logos is
produced in factories that protect workers' rights. Also, in May 1999
the Washington, D.C.,–based International Labor Rights Fund (ILRF)
launched a campaign on human rights principles for U.S. businesses with
operations in China.

Most of the workers in the Hong Kong-, Taiwanese-, and South
Korean–owned garment factories detailed in Kernaghan's report are
young women, seventeen to twenty-five years old. Females dominate the
low-skill workforce in these factories because they tend to receive lesser
educations than men and because much of the work is considered to be
"women's work." Most of them are only semi-literate and have no knowledge of their legal rights, making them highly vulnerable in the face of
exploitative bosses. Usually they live in crowded dormitory rooms, have
little free time, and are paid shockingly low wages. Unsafe or unsanitary
work conditions, a total lack of benefits, sexual harassment, and physical
and psychological battering often come with the job as well. According to

one report from 1994, 18 percent of workers in twenty factories in Guang-dong province reported that they have been regularly beaten or insulted.[17] At Kang Yi Fashion Manufacturers, a factory in Shenzhen that makes clothing for Ann Taylor and Preview, three hundred women work four-teen hours a day, six days a week, at wages that range from 14 to 23 cents an hour. At times the women were paid two to three weeks late. Charles Kernaghan reports that the women live in dormitories six to ten to a room. At the Liang Shi Handbag Factory in Dongguan City, Guangdong, which makes Kathie Lee handbags for Wal-Mart, a portion of the proceeds from which are donated to children's charities in the United States, "the typical workweek stretches 60 to 70 hours, with 10 hour shifts six or seven days a week." There are no fire exits in the building; women workers are forced to share small beds and have no work contracts and no benefits. At the You Li Fashion Factory in Shigang Village, Guangzhou, which makes clothing marketed under the Esprit label, women face similarly long hours and low wages. Furthermore, according to the researcher who supplied Charles Kernaghan with his information, the dorm rooms were "dark, dirty, and foul smelling," and the women who lived there "feel they are under con-stant surveillance, watched 24 hours a day, both at work and in the dorm."[18]

In the strictest factories (most of which are owned by Korean and Tai-wanese firms) workers can go to the toilet only at certain times. They can-not marry or even date while they are employed there, and female work-ers are not allowed to get pregnant. As should now be all too clear, work under such conditions amounts to indentured servitude. Yet many of these workers are producing for U.S. consumers. In addition to the cases cited previously, Australian researcher Anita Chan has also documented Chi-nese working conditions that should interest U.S. shoppers. In 1996 she visited the largest footwear factory in the world, a Taiwanese-run enter-prise in Guangdong Province in south China that employs 40,000 workers who produce shoes for, among others, Adidas, Nike, and Reebok. After working eighty hours of overtime a month, workers there make between U.S. $80 and U.S. $90 per month, which is barely above the newly imple-mented minimum wage standard.[19] Said one U.S. businessman who prof-its from the Chinese labor system: "We have a factory in China where we have 250 people. We own them; it's our factory. We pay them $40 a month, and they work 28 days a month. They work from 7 a.m. to 11 p.m. with two breaks for lunch and dinner. They all eat together, 16 people to a room, stacked on four bunks to a corner. Generally, they're young girls that come from the hills."[20] Since they work without contracts, and because there are countless other poor women who would willingly work for the same low wages, these workers have little choice but to put up with these conditions. If they complain, they can be fired on the spot and replaced by another poor woman from the countryside almost immediately.

Many of the conditions that obtain at these sweatshops violate the Chinese labor code that went into effect in January 1995. Among other things, that code spells out minimum wages based on local conditions, guarantees workers a minimum of one day off a week, limits the amount of overtime to no more than three hours beyond the standard eight-hour day, provides premium pay for overtime, and clearly defines beating, threatening, and harassing workers as criminal acts.[21] Despite the Communist Party's official position on these matters, having committed itself to a path of market-driven growth in which foreign investment is highly coveted, there is a built-in contradiction between its laws and its development strategy that works against workers' interests. As Anita Chan has written, any conscientious government official "who tries to protect workers' rights will suffer the risk of being criticized for undermining the country's investment climate."[22]

This can happen because foreign factory owners faced with challenges to work conditions in their factories can and do threaten to move their enterprises to other places in China or out of the country altogether. Poor Asian countries such as China, Indonesia, and Vietnam set legal minimum wages at the lowest possible rates, which will enable them to compete with one another "to sell their workers' labor in the international labor market while maintaining their workers' physical survival." These wages often become the maximum amount foreign investors are willing to pay.[23] One example of this cited in Charles Kernaghan's report involves Wal-Mart, which quickly cut its ties to a garment factory in north China, where it had been paying 800 workers between 37 and 50 cents an hour for 60-hour workweeks, as well as medical and retirement benefits, so that it could benefit from even more "choice" conditions at garment factories in the south where the wages are lower, government oversight is less, and there are no benefits.

OFFICIAL VERSUS INDEPENDENT TRADE UNIONS

What, if any, means do workers toiling in these privately owned sweatshops have of protecting themselves? And how about the millions of people laid-off by "downsizing" state-owned enterprises? The Party-state responsible for the policies that have brought about these conditions continues to maintain that workers are the "masters of society," but is the state taking actions to make that claim anything other than a bad joke? As mentioned previously, a national labor code went into effect in 1995 establishing basic workers' rights regarding wages, benefits, and overtime pay, but there continue to be widespread violations of the law. While the new labor code does not include the right to strike, it is significant that it doesn't criminalize strikes either. However, the state discourages strikes and attempts to persuade disgruntled workers to articulate their grievances through the All-China Federation of Trade Unions (ACFTU) and its subordinate branches. The ACFTU is an official union that was formally created in 1950 as an umbrella organization representing the interests of the Communist Party to the workers and the interests of the workers to the Communist Party. Since its founding shortly after the Communist Revolution, the ACFTU, in other words, has been a tool of the Party-state.

During the demonstrations of spring 1989, there was a short-lived attempt on the part of some workers to establish autonomous workers' unions outside the structure of the ACFTU. The unofficial workers' group called itself the Beijing Workers' Autonomous Association and declared that its goal was "to set up a nationwide non-Communist union along the lines of Poland's Solidarity trade union."[24] Highly threatened by such talk, the director of the ACFTU accused the leaders of the autonomous workers' union of seeking "to make the unions a political force to oppose the Communist Party and socialist system." Later that year, after the June 4th Massacre, the government issued regulations stating: "No social organization, including societies, associations, federations, research units, foundations, cooperatives and chambers of commerce, will be considered legal unless it is registered with the appropriate authorities."[25] In 1992, the Communist Party promulgated the Trade Union Law, which re-affirmed the ACFTU as the only legal trade union organization in China. All efforts to establish trade unions outside the purview of the ACFTU are considered illegal and are crushed.

All of this is not to say that the ACFTU is utterly worthless as a representative of workers' interests; many union officials are genuinely concerned about abuses of workers, and in the state-owned sector the union has successfully negotiated some improvements, including a shortened workweek (from forty-eight to forty-four hours). Moreover, since 1994 the ACFTU has been engaged in an intensive effort to organize branch unions in all foreign-invested enterprises so as to prevent the very kinds of abuses documented in Charles Kernaghan's March 1998 report. Nevertheless, as Anita Chan, Jude Howell, and others studying Chinese labor conditions argue, the ACFTU's close connections to the Communist Party make it increasingly ineffective as a representative of workers' interests. Clearly, given the continuing sweatshop conditions, simply establishing union branches in the foreign-owned enterprises in southern China is not automatically leading to improved conditions there. As an arm of the Party-state, the ACFTU supports the Party's economic reform agenda and especially the policy of opening China to foreign investment. Thus, the ACFTU can seek a highly confrontational stance in its negotiations with management only at the risk of driving foreign investors out of China. The ACFTU is caught by the contradictions inherent in its position: if it pursues workers' interests, it goes against the interests of the Party-state; but if it merely serves as a go-between between foreign investors and Chinese labor, it often fails to protect Chinese workers.

Given the ACFTU's compromised status as an advocate for workers, it is no surprise that polls and interviews indicate workers' skepticism about the value of the union. Asked if she would ever go to the ACFTU for help if her rights had been violated, for example, one woman stated: "It would really be pointless asking the union to help. All they do is issue a few souvenirs on holidays and organize leisure events. They don't really have much to do with us and certainly are not the people to ask if you've got problems at work." Asked the same question, another woman captured the essence of the matter: "The thing is that looking after workers' rights is a sensitive issue at the moment and the union can't do anything to protect us."[26] Anger with the government is mounting. A recent article in *China Labour Bulletin*—a bi-monthly newsletter published in Hong Kong and edited by exiled labor leader Han Dongfang (on whom see endnote 24)—makes this clear:

> The government frequently claims to anyone who will listen that the current rate of unemployment is below 4%. But if you look at your own family's living conditions or at those of your friends and neighbours and think of what the real standard of living is for most of us, it is not hard to see why most Chinese workers are cynically indifferent to the images of our society as portrayed by government statistics. It is perfectly clear to all of us that not only is the government failing to fulfill its responsibilities, but hardest to bear, they are shamelessly lying in order to cheat us of the truth.[27]

Many workers, especially women and older, unskilled people, have little chance of improving their conditions or of finding new work once they've been laid off. There's a widespread feeling that they've been betrayed, and most of the fury is being directed at their management and by extension the Party-state. This anger obviously stems from everything addressed previously: the worsening work environment; a deeply held belief among China's workers that they are entitled to an "iron rice bowl"; and frustration at not being able to defend their interests through independent unions. Another factor stoking worker resentment is their perception, oftentimes accurate, that while they are suffering inept and corrupt factory managers are doing just fine. Nor is this something honest managers can tolerate. In a recent discussion about how to invigorate state-owned enterprises, for example, the manager of a textile factory in Taiyuan did not mince words: "Some people have not observed the principle of seeking truth from facts, and have been telling lies, but they are getting promoted. Some people have ruined their enterprises but have been transferred afterward to other places to take up new posts, leaving the hopeless mess to the government."[28]

To be sure, the market reforms carried out over the last decade have created tens of millions of new jobs, and a sizable number of workers in both the state-owned and private sectors are doing better in the new economy—making more money, enjoying more options and greater responsibility—than would have been imaginable just ten years ago. But most of the people who are getting ahead are young male college graduates. So, while the reforms have delivered great prospects to the new elite in China's coastal cities, they have also resulted in a far greater income gap than before. The situation is particularly bleak for women since they are being laid off in far higher numbers than men and face serious discrimination in searching for jobs; this is especially true for women over thirty-five in a society in which youthful beauty is often part of the job description. An unemployed woman of forty-three who lives in the city of Tianjin recently summed it up this way: "If you're over thirty-five, it's very difficult to find work . . . What can you do? . . . You have young and old ones to look after. You're too old to learn new skills. You're not attractive anymore. Nobody wants us." In 1997 61 percent of China's laid-off workers were female, and in some provinces the number was as high as 75 percent. According to the results of a recent survey conducted by the women's department of the ACFTU, "about 71.6% of the 413 managers in 14 provinces and cities . . . said they would not hire women, even if they were better qualified than men."[29] Under these circumstances increasing numbers of women are entering the sex trade (see Evans, this volume). For example, a survey recently conducted by the Chinese Conscience and Care Action Organization found that a large number of unemployed women in Sichuan province have begun prostituting themselves; 40 percent of "hostesses" in some cities are urban residents who have been waiting for jobs or who have just been "downsized."[30]

The severity of the unemployment situation for dismissed urban workers is compounded by the fact that many of China's cities have become home to large numbers of peasants who have migrated from the countryside in search of a better livelihood (see Oakes, this volume). This internal labor movement constitutes the "largest labor migration in history."[31] Many of China's coastal cities have provincial ghettos, entire neighborhoods peopled by poor immigrants from the same rural region. These migrant laborers are forced to accept second- or third-class social status as compared with their registered, and therefore legal, urban neighbors. Though rural workers are forced to take society's most undesirable jobs, they nevertheless represent an unwelcome source of competition to urban dwellers fallen on hard times, and it should come as no surprise that tensions between city dwellers and rural migrants are on the rise. As the *New York Times* has reported, this tension has been exacerbated since the Communist Party has recently begun lecturing workers to lower their expectations and learn from poor peasant migrants who are willing to work hard and expect to pull themselves up by their bootstraps.[32]

Such moralistic lectures not withstanding—or perhaps because of them—the Communist Party's nightmare scenario is already coming true: workers are rising up in protest. In 1992 there were some five hundred strikes involving hundreds of thousands of workers.[33] Since then the number of labor disputes has been doubling at an annual rate. In the first half of 1997 labor disputes soared by 59 percent compared to the same period in 1996. In March 1997 some of the "worst labour unrest since the 1949 Communist revolution" took place in the city of Nanchong in Sichuan Province. More than 20,000 workers from a silk factory marched through the streets to protest the fact that they hadn't been paid in six months. The workers took their manager hostage, forced him into the painful and humiliating "airplane position" inflicted on so many people during the Cultural Revolution of the 1960s and '70s, then paraded him through the streets in the rain. This happened when they learned that the same manager who had not paid them in six months was preparing to leave on an "official" inspection tour of Thailand at company expense. At one point during the disturbances there was a bomb attack on city hall. The dispute was so severe that the central government was forced to pay the workers off and then imposed a news blackout to prevent similar strife elsewhere. The blackout did not solve the problem: On July 7 thousands of angry workers from three recently bankrupt textile factories in the city of Mianyang in Sichuan took to the streets to demand new jobs. More violence and arrests followed. In October 1997 a thousand workers in the city of Zigong, also in Sichuan Province, clashed with police. The workers were protesting the low pay they received from the Radio Factory that employed them, as well as the lack of reimbursement for health insurance claims turned in over the last two years. Anti-riot police broke up the demonstration and there were more arrests.[34]

Sichuan Province, ravaged by layoffs at its many state-owned industries, is clearly a hotbed, but throughout 1998 and 1999 similar kinds of labor disputes have been reported from other interior provinces as well, including Shanxi, Henan, Hubei, and Gansu.[35] The situation is so tense in some places that the police don't dare interfere in strikes for fear of sparking wider confrontations. For example, when 4,000 unpaid pensioners blocked a railroad in the northeastern city of Fushun in April 1999, the police did not attempt to move them. The workers left only after a city official promised they would receive the back pay they were due.[36] Labor strife is most serious in the northeast and in poorer interior provinces, where the state offers fewer tax incentives for capitalists and foreign investment is low. The markets in those smaller provincial cities in the interior are being flooded with high quality goods from coastal cities like Shanghai, and as that happens local workers are finding that their factories simply cannot compete.[37] What that means is more plant closures and additional joblessness. In many cases what follows is a family decision to send one or two of its members to one of the big coastal cities to look for work along with all the others in the "floating population." In addition to the other problems mentioned previously, China is thus experiencing a resurgence of the exploitative and socially aggravating regional income disparities that the Communist Party had gone a long way toward overcoming after gaining power in 1949.

As the pace of the layoffs has picked up, outspoken political dissidents have begun to pay more attention to the plight of China's workers, linking their own calls for democracy and human rights to demands that the Communist Party allow workers to form trade unions independent of the

Fig. 11.2. Looking for work in Dandong, Liaoning Province. (Photo by Mark Henley)

ACFTU. For example, in December 1997, as layoff announcements multiplied in the wake of the 15th Party Congress, four veteran dissidents sent a signed letter to foreign news organizations calling on the Chinese government to permit workers to defend their own interests. The four letter writers (Wang Xizhe, who lives in New York; Lu Siqing, who lives in Hong Kong; and Qin Yongmin and Xu Wenli, who live in China) timed their letter to correspond with China's October 1997 signing of the United Nation's International Covenant on Economic, Social, and Cultural Rights (ICE-SCR),[38] that stipulates "the right of everyone to form trade unions and join the trade union of his choice." The letter writers admitted that workers will inevitably face hardships during the economic reforms and blamed the beleaguered state of China's state-owned enterprises on the socialist policies of the pre-reform era, but they also made clear that workers must have the right to defend themselves and that they believe the Chinese government committed itself to that position by signing the ICESCR.[39] While this open letter was extraordinary because of the international attention it received, it represents only one action by an increasingly large community of dissidents who are putting workers' rights at the top of their agenda. And while it is true that the Chinese government is cracking down on attempts to form independent trade unions, there is no question that by signing the ICESCR it has handed labor activists a normative standard to rally around. The pages of *China Labour Bulletin* are full of information about worker attempts to take advantage of their legal right (under the ICESCR) to form labor unions and to get permits to march in the streets.

CONCLUSION: THE LIKELIHOOD OF GREATER CONFLICT TO COME

Increasing labor unrest and calls by activists for independent labor unions represent perhaps the greatest political threat to the Chinese Communist Party today. The Party knows its legitimacy is badly undermined by the economic pain being felt by so many who once were its strong backers and that it cannot control millions of angry and disoriented workers who feel they have little to lose. Given that Party leaders delayed fundamental restructuring of the state-owned sector for years out of fear that reforms would lead to serious social instability, one might question why the Party launched the program of massive layoffs before designing a reliable social safety net to assist the millions of workers who were destined to (and since have) lost their jobs. Clearly, the Party found itself in a no-win situation. That it went ahead with the restructuring despite its fear of social instability shows just how fearful the Party was that insolvent SOEs would derail the economic reforms to which its own political fortunes are pinned. It also makes clear that Party leaders were willing to gamble that continued economic growth could produce enough new (even if not necessarily better) jobs at a fast enough pace over the next several years to mitigate the worst effects of the "downsizing."

When the Asian financial crisis began to be felt in China in early 1998, however, this assumption no longer appeared safe. Since then foreign investment has slowed because cash-starved Asian investors can no longer afford to build in China. In addition, export-reliant Chinese factories have only been able to watch (and, of course, "downsize") as lower-paid workers in even poorer southeast Asian countries have demonstrated an ability to produce goods for export to the world's wealthy consumer societies at prices lower than what China can manage—at least for now.[39]

When these negative developments started to occur, China's Communist Party leadership was suddenly faced with the prospect that economic growth would not produce enough new jobs in the near term to substantially ameliorate the crisis of joblessness after all. Officials who are sincerely concerned about the welfare of the workers therefore moved quickly to find ways to soften the hurt, and the Party leadership began frantically pursuing a number of strategies to forestall further labor unrest. Among the things the Party has recently done are: pass new regulations that make it harder to lay off workers who have been working in SOEs for over twenty years; increase subsidies to some SOEs to keep them temporarily afloat (a tactic that has been criticized by some neoliberal economists in the West); attempt to reassign workers new jobs; offer tax breaks for laid-off workers who set up their own businesses; and establish retraining, pension, and unemployment insurance programs.[41] Perhaps most important, economic leaders decided the state had to undertake a multibillion dollar spending program to make up for the drop off in China's growth rate due to the Asian economic crisis. In hopes of boosting the country's gross domestic product to at least 8 percent through the end of the century (planners consider a growth rate of 9 percent necessary to relieve unemployment pressure significantly) China's economic decision makers determined to spend tremendous sums on public works projects that could employ laid-off workers and therefore also pump money into the economy. Even small drops in the economy's growth rate can make a big difference; in human terms, each percentage-point fall in gross domestic product means the loss of roughly 5 million jobs.

The programs put in place to assist laid-off workers have had some positive results to be sure, but as of May 1999, the government's New Deal–style attempt to stimulate the economy was barely holding the line, and further economic slow-down has been predicted for the second half of the year.[42] No wonder, then, that the Communist Party tolerated angry mobs throwing stones at the U.S. embassy to protest NATO's destruction of the Chinese embassy in Belgrade in early May 1999 but put its foot down when protesters began to organize boycotts on U.S. products. With the economy slipping (by the third quarter of 1999 the Chinese government admitted that it expected the economy to expand just 7.0 percent for the year), China needs to "grow" its foreign exports now more than ever; it can scarcely afford to watch its trade ties with the affluent United States suffer.

As the situation grows tenser, it is not surprising that the Party is taking a very hard line against activists agitating for independent trade unions. This has been the case for several years now. For example, shortly after Qin Yongmin signed the much-publicized open letter calling for independent trade unions in December 1997, he found that authorities were tapping his phone and intercepting his mail; they then advised him to leave China immediately for the United States. But Qin refused to leave China: "I'd rather give up my personal security and even my life to support the final realization of a legal opposition party and free workers' unions."[43] Since then he has been watched closely by security forces and detained at least one time. The same has been true for Xu Wenli, another co-signer of the December 1997 letter calling for independent trade unions. In April 1998 agents of the Public Security Bureau ransacked his home and confiscated his computer, fax and copy machines, and political books. He was detained for twenty-four hours. These two cases have received considerable attention, but countless other less well-known labor activists are being treated to similar harassment and, in some cases, lengthy prison sentences.[44]

What all this makes obvious is that the Communist Party is terrified by the prospect of a Polish-style trade union movement capable of translating specific worker grievances into a larger political tide of opposition. Even as it attempts to appear more open and tolerant with regard to democratic and human rights by "freeing" high-profile dissidents like Wei Jingsheng and Wang Dan into exile and signing the ICESCR and the International Covenant on Civil and Political Rights (ICCPR), the Party is doing everything in its power to crush all signs of an independent labor movement. In April 1998 it set up a new high-level Office on Maintaining Social Stability, whose top priority is "to ensure that increasingly frequent labor disturbances in different cities will not escalate into a national crisis." The person in charge of this office is Wei Jianxing, a member of the Politburo Standing Committee and president of the ACFTU. As president of the ACFTU, one might expect Wei to be well known for his support of workers' rights, but in fact he is most famous for the draconian "Strike Hard" law and order campaign, which encourages frequent use of the death penalty to crack down on criminal offenses.[45]

The creation of the Office on Maintaining Social Stability and the appointment of Wei Jianxing to oversee its operation (it coordinates social control efforts by the police, the Ministry of State Security, the People's Armed Police, and departments handling propaganda and trade unions, among others) clearly appears to be part of the solution to Party leaders, but it also points to greater problems ahead. The Party has committed itself to further economic reforms that will lead to greater pain for workers just as the Asian economic crisis is slowing China's growth; the workers are not allowed to set up their own unions to defend themselves but must instead work through the ACFTU; but the ACFTU is a stooge of the Party, and its leader is a law and order man at the forefront of the state's effort to keep the lid on an explosive situation.

While it is easy to see why the Communist Party is deathly afraid of the torrent of anger that its market-oriented reform policies have unleashed, it is hard to imagine how its confrontational approach will lead to anything other than greater antagonism if conditions for workers do not improve. The quotation from exiled labor-leader Han Dongfang that begins this article indicates that the leaders of China's working class understand this clearly and intend to press their case when the government is most desperate to prevent social and political instability, so did the May 1, 1999 (International Labor Day), application by activists Gao Hongmin and Xu Yonghai, requesting permission to establish a "China Free Labor Union," led and administered by workers themselves. Approval of the application was not granted. In late May, three more labor-rights activists (Yue Tianxing, Guo Xinmin, and Wang Fengshan) went on trial in Gansu Province, charged with, among other things, subverting state power by organizing laid-off workers. In early July 1999 the three activists were sentenced to ten-, two-, and two-year prison terms, respectively.[46]

NOTES

For their helpful suggestions about this article and/or reading recommendations, I am grateful to: Bama Athreya, Joshua Howard, Lionel Jensen, Padraic Kenney, Dorothy Solinger, David Welker, and Marcia Yonemoto. Of course, I alone am responsible for all errors and weaknesses that remain.

1. Tang Xinmin and Ray Zhang, "China Per-Capita GNP to Hit 800 Dollars by 2000," *China News Digest*, June 2, 1997 (Global News, no. GL97–078). *China News Digest* can be found on the Internet at: <http://www.cnd.org/CND-Global/>. Also see "Red Alert," *Economist* (October 24, 1998), collected in Suzanne Ogden, ed., *Global Studies China*, 8th ed. (Guilford, Conn.: Dushkin/McGraw Hill, 1999), 130–134.

2. *Foreign Broadcast Information Service*, "China: Zhu Rongji on Helping Laid-Off Workers," document no.: FBIS-CHI-98-139; document date: May 19, 1998.

3. Advertisement, *Daily Camera*, Boulder, Colorado, May 13, 1999, 3B.

4. Dorothy J. Solinger, "Virtual Globalization and Outcomes for Membership: The Chinese Case," unpublished manuscript, courtesy of the author, 1998, 22.

5. Edward S. Steinfeld, "Beyond the Transition: China's Economy at Century's End," *Contemporary History* (September 1999): 275.

6. Solinger, "Virtual Globalization and Outcomes for Membership: The Chinese Case," 30–33; Ray Zhang and Wan Guochen, "Laid-off Workers Lack Qualifications for Re-Employment," *China News Digest*, December 19, 1997 (Global News, no. GL98-059); Neil C. Hughes, "Smashing the Iron Rice Bowl," *Foreign Affairs*, vol. 77, no. 4 (July/August 1998): 67–77, esp. 71–74.

7. Jiang Zemin, "Hold High the Great Banner of Deng Xiaoping Theory for an All-Round Advancement of the Cause of Building Socialism with Chinese Characteristics into the 21st Century," *Beijing Review*, vol. 40, no. 40 (October 6–12, 1997).

8. Wu Fang and Ray Zhang, "State-Run Enterprise Announced Lay Off Plan for Better Efficiency," *China News Digest*, October 6, 1997 (Global News, no. GL97-068); Joyce Barnathan, et al., "Can China Avert Crisis?" *Business Week* (March 16, 1998): 45–49; Erik Eckholm, "Joblessness: A Perilous Curve On China's Capitalist Road," *New York Times*, January 20, 1998, A1; Solinger, "Virtual Globalization and Outcomes for Membership: The Chinese Case," 24; Judy M. Chen, "A Ricebowl in Pieces: The Unemployment Crisis Bites," *China Rights Forum* (Spring 1998): 38–40. *Foreign Broadcast Information Service*, "China: Sichuan Leader on Reemployment of Jobless," document no.: FBIS-CHI-98-231, document date: August 19, 1998; "Analysis of the ICESCR," *China Labour Bulletin*, no. 40 (January–February 1998): 9.

9. "Employment: Threats to Women's Economic Independence," *China Rights Forum* (Spring 1999): 51.

10. The government is reluctant to give widespread public attention to higher unemployment numbers, but accurate information can easily be found in China. For example, the *Beijing Economic Daily* (*Beijing Jinji Ribao*) recently ran an article in which a joint survey undertaken by the International Labor Organization and the Ministry of Labor indicated gigantic numbers of "hidden," as opposed to "registered," unemployed. The article disclosed that when both urban and rural "hidden" unemployed are counted, the overall jobless rate for the country is over 25 percent. See *Foreign Broadcast Information Service*, "China: Article Analyzes Causes of Unemployment," document no. FBIS-CHI-98-072, document date: March 13, 1998. On China's unemployment figures, see Solinger, "Virtual Globalization and Outcomes for Membership: The Chinese Case," 26–27; Cui Ying and John Lin, John, "Number of Jobless Swells to 150 Million," *China News Digest*, June 19, 1998 (Global News, no. GL98-089).

11. The household registration system, or *hukou*, was established in 1950 and by the early 1960s made it virtually impossible for peasants to move to urban areas. This was a method of controlling population movement within the country, which involved the granting of subsidized housing, cheap transportation, essentially free medical care, food, water, gas rations, and free schooling to urbanites. Because virtually no one could afford to live in the city without such assistance, it served, and

with some modifications still does serve, as a means of keeping migrants out of the city or of controlling them once they were there.

12. Zhao Menghua and Theo Nichols, "Management Control of Labor in State-Owned Enterprises: Cases from the Textile Industry," in *Adjusting to Capitalism: Chinese Workers and the State,* Greg O'Leary, ed. (Armonk, N.Y.: M. E. Sharpe, 1998), 76; Dorothy J. Solinger, "Job Categories and Employment Channels among the 'Floating Population,' " also in O'Leary, *Adjusting to Capitalism: Chinese Workers and the State,* 21–22; Tamara Jacka, *Women's Work in Rural China: Change and Continuity in an Era of Reform* (Cambridge: Cambridge University Press, 1997), 178.

13. The woman's quote is from Zhao Menghua and Theo Nichols, "Management Control of Labor in State-Owned Enterprises: Cases from the Textile Industry," 78, 86. The man's quote is from Ching Kwan Lee, "The Labor Politics of Market Socialism," *Modern China,* vol. 24, no. 1 (January 1988): 18.

14. Charles Kernaghan, *Behind the Label: "Made in China,"* special report prepared for the National Labor Committee, New York, N.Y., March 1998, 71–78; Ching Kwan Lee, "The Labor Politics of Market Socialism," 9; Jacka, *Women's Work in Rural China: Change and Continuity in an Era of Reform,* 179.

15. Solinger, "Job Categories and Employment Channels among the 'Floating Population,' " 24.

16. Anita Chan, "Labor Relations in Foreign-funded Ventures, Chinese Trade Unions and the Prospects for Collective Bargaining," in O'Leary, *Adjusting to Capitalism: Chinese Workers and the State,* 124–129.

17. Jude Howell, "Trade Unions in China: The Challenge of Foreign Capital," in O'Leary, *Adjusting to Capitalism: Chinese Workers and the State,* 154–155; Anita Chan and Robert A. Senser, "China's Troubled Waters," *Foreign Affairs,* vol. 76, no. 2 (March/April 1997): 106; Jacka, *Women's Work in Rural China: Change and Continuity in an Era of Reform,* 179.

18. Kernaghan, *Behind the Label: "Made in China,"* 33.

19. Anita Chan, "Labor Standards and Human Rights: The Case of Chinese Workers under Market Socialism," *Human Rights Quarterly* 20 (1998): 893–895.

20. Kernaghan, *Behind the Label: "Made in China,"* 9.

21. Chan and Senser, "China's Troubled Waters," 112.

22. Chan, "Labor Relations in Foreign-Funded Ventures, Chinese Trade Unions and the Prospects for Collective Bargaining," 136.

23. Chan, "Labor Standards and Human Rights: The Case of Chinese Workers Under Market Socialism," 894.

24. The Beijing Workers Autonomous Federation, which at its height reached 20,000 members, was headed by a young railroad worker named Han Dongfang, who was later arrested. Once in prison, Han went on a hunger strike. In April 1991, after his case became internationally known, he was released from prison. Currently, Han lives in Hong Kong, but he is not allowed to travel into China. Han Dongfang is editor of *China Labour Bulletin* and a leading activist working on Chi-

nese labor issues. On the comparison with Poland's Solidarity, see Elizabeth J. Perry, "Casting a Chinese 'Democracy Movement': The Roles of Students, Workers, and Entrepreneurs," in *Popular Protest & Political Culture in Modern China,* Jeffrey N. Wasserstrom and Elizabeth J. Perry, eds. (Boulder: Westview Press, 1992), 156.

25. Elizabeth J. Perry, "Labor's Battle for Political Space: The Role of Worker Associations in Contemporary China," in Deborah S. Davis, et al., *Urban Spaces in Contemporary China* (Cambridge: Woodrow Wilson Center Press and Cambridge University Press, 1995), 320.

26. Chan and Senser, "China's Troubled Waters," 113; Xiong Bo and Yin De An, "Workers Lose Confidence in the Communist Party," *China News Digest,* May 9, 1997 (Global News, no. GL97-068); "Equal Protection in Political and Public Life," *China Rights Forum* (Spring 1999): 49.

27. "Analysis of the ICESCR," *China Labour Bulletin,* no. 40 (January–February 1998): 8.

28. *Foreign Broadcast Information Service,* "Article: Consult Masses on SOE Reforms," document no.: FBIS-CHI-1999-0408; document date: February 11, 1999.

29. Elisabeth Rosenthal, "In China, 35+ and Female = Unemployable," *New York Times,* October 13, 1998, A1; "Employment: Threats to Women's Economic Independence," *China Rights Forum* (Spring 1999): 51.

30. Chen, "A Ricebowl in Pieces: The Unemployment Crisis Bites," 39.

31. Greg O'Leary, "The Making of the Chinese Working Class," in O'Leary, *Adjusting to Capitalism: Chinese Workers and the State,* 63.

32. Erik Eckholm, "Joblessness: A Perilous Curve on China's Capitalist Road." For a valuable, full-length study of labor migration in China, see Dorothy J. Solinger, *Contesting Citizenship in Urban China: Peasant Migrants, the State, and the Logic of the Market* (Berkeley: University of California Press, 1999).

33. Perry, "Labor's Battle for Political Space: The Role of Worker Associations in Contemporary China," 321.

34. Matt Forney, "We Want to Eat," *Far Eastern Economic Review* (June 26, 1997): 14–16; Zhao Hua and Wan Guochen, "20,000 Workers Gather to Protest Rear-Pay in Sichuan," *China News Digest,* June 23, 1997 (Global News, no. GL97–087). Liu Weijun and Ray Zhang, "Protesters Clash with Police in Sichuan," *China News Digest,* October 15, 1997 (Global News, no. GL97–141).

35. See, for example, the list of strikes in the "News Update" section at the back of any recent issue of *China Rights Forum,* a quarterly journal published by Human Rights in China. On Human Rights in China, see the article by Xiao Qiang in this volume.

36. Craig S. Smith, "Workers in China Organize to Oppose Restructurings," *Wall Street Journal,* June 7, 1999.

37. I am grateful to Joshua Howard for pointing out this phenomenon to me.

38. The ICESCR was originally passed by the United Nations in December 1966.

Along with the International Covenant on Civil and Political Rights (ICCPR), also passed by the United Nations in 1966, the ICESCR was intended to convert the Universal Declaration of Human Rights, adopted by the UN General Assembly in 1948, into treaties with legal teeth.

39. Erik Eckholm, "Chinese Democracy Campaigners Push for Free Labor Unions," *New York Times*, December 24, 1997, A3.

40. Barnathan, et al., "Can China Avert Crisis?," 45; Nicholas R. Lardy, "China and the Asian Contagion," *Foreign Affairs*, vol. 77, no. 4 (July/August 1998): 82, 88.

41. For a very clear discussion of efforts to ameliorate the unemployment crisis in three Chinese cities, see Dorothy J. Solinger, "The Impact of Openness on Integration and Control in China: Migrants, Layoffs, Labor Market Formation in the Antinomies of Market Reform in Guangzhou, Shenyang and Wuhan," unpublished manuscript, courtesy of the author, December 1998.

42. Barry Naughton, "China's Economy: Buffeted from Within and Without," *Current History* (September 1998): 27–275; Yin De An and Zhu Junhua, "Economists Cast Doubts on 'China's New Deal,' " *China News Digest*, April 24, 1998 (Global News, no. GL98–058); "Red Alert," *Economist* (October 24, 1998); "China Admits Only Partial Success From Massive Stimulus Package," Agence France Presse, May 19, 1999.

43. Erik Eckholm, "Chinese Dissident Refuses to Leave for Exile in U.S.," *New York Times*, January 15, 1998.

44. On Xu Wenli, see Erik Eckholm, ""China Arrests Another Prominent Democracy Advocate," *New York Times*, April 4, 1998.

45. Zhang Kewen and Yin De An, "CCP Special Office Set Up to Curb Social Unrest," *China News Digest*, April 27, 1998 (Global News, no., GL98–059); "ACFTU Chief Heads New Office to Police Workers," posted on the *China Labour Bulletin* Web page, updated May 18, 1998, <http://www.china-labour.org.hk>.

46. Luo Zhenyuan and Wu Yiyi, "Activists Seek Independent Union," *China News Digest*, May 3, 1999 (Global News, no. GL99–057). Sue Bruell and Yin De An, "Labor-Rights Activists Go to Trial," *China News Digest*, May 31, 1999 (Global News, no. GL99–071). "Gansu Labour Activists Sentenced," *China Labour Bulletin*, press release, July 5, 1999 (posted on the *China Labour Bulletin* Web page, updated July 21, 1999, <http://www.china-labour.org.hk>.

SUGGESTED READINGS

Anita Chan, *China's Workers under Assault* (Armonk, N.Y.: M. E. Sharpe, 1999).

Kevin Bales, *Disposable People: New Slavery in the Global Economy* (Berkeley: University of California Press, 1999).

Tamara Jacka, *Women's Work in Rural China* (Cambridge: Cambridge University Press, 1997).

Nicholas R. Lardy, *China's Unfinished Economic Revolution* (Washington, D.C.: Brookings Institution, 1998).

Lee, Ching Kwan, *Gender and the South China Miracle: Two Worlds of Factory Women* (Berkeley: University of California Press, 1998).

Maurice Meisner, *The Deng Xiaoping Era: An Inquiry into the Fate of Chinese Socialism, 1978–1994* (New York: Hill and Wang, 1996).

Barry Naughton, *Growing Out of the Plan: Chinese Economic Reform, 1978–1993* (Cambridge: Cambridge University Press, 1995).

Greg O'Leary, ed., *Adjusting to Capitalism: Chinese Workers and the State* (Armonk, N.Y.: M. E. Sharpe, 1998).

Dorothy J. Solinger, *China's Transition from Socialism: Statist Legacies and Market Reforms* (Armonk, N.Y.: M. E. Sharpe, 1993).

———, *Contesting Citizenship in Urban China: Peasant Migrants, the State, and the Logic of the Market* (Berkeley: University of California Press, 1999).

Andrew Walder, *Communist Neo-Traditionalism: Work and Authority in Chinese Industry* (Berkeley: University of California Press, 1986).

12

Reading Out-of-Print:

Popular Culture and Protest on China's Western Frontier

Jay Dautcher

Ethnic minorities are like untamed mustangs. No matter how well you feed them, they may run off at any time.
—Han official after the demonstrations in Yining of February 6, 1997 (*Pingguo ribao* [Apple Daily], Hong Kong, February 18, 1997)

Some people dance in front of the leaders, and fill their hands with fine foods. What if, one day, they find their hands empty? I wonder what will happen to those people then?
—Popular Uighur song, circulated in Yining, c. 1996

To understand China as an outsider can be a daunting task. The serious student grapples with centuries of dynastic history, decades of revolution and political upheaval, the global impact of China's re-entry into the world economy, and the unprecedented organizational and ideological transformations that the post-1979 reforms have engendered. Given all that, it is not surprising if ethnic differences within the People's Republic are often overlooked. And after all, since 92 percent of China's population count themselves as Han—making that by far China's dominant ethnic group— aren't we basically correct to view China as a Han nation? In a word, no. Equating China with its Han majority at best provides only half the picture. For if one draws a diagonal line from the northeast corner of China down to the southwest, cutting the country roughly in half, nearly 95 percent of the Han population is located on the right side of that line.[1] To understand that remaining half of China's territory—to enter a land where policies and politics, social stability and social change, education and economic development have everything to do with ethnic differences and inter-ethnic conflicts—we must accept that a serious look at China's ethnic diversity is unavoidable (see Blum, this volume).

In this short article I cannot hope to address the vast range of China's ethnic diversity.[2] What I wish to show in this paper instead is this: That in the global dialogue on China's future, there are many voices within China that are not often heard, neither at home nor abroad. Among these are the voices of China's ethnic minorities, who form a critical part of the country's political landscape. To do this I will concentrate on just one region— Xinjiang (pronounced *shin-jang*)—and on that region's majority ethnic group—the Uighur (pronounced *wee-gur*)—as I discuss my own experiences with trying to "read beyond the headlines." In this chapter I will present three sections. In the first, I provide the reader with some general knowledge about Xinjiang's Uighurs—who are Muslims—focusing on the area I know best, the city of Yining. In the second section, I review official commentary and news accounts about an incident in Yining—a protest march and subsequent period of unrest—in order to point out how the state and local Uighurs understand the meaning of such events quite differently. After showing that official accounts of Uighur society are incapable of providing the kind of context necessary for understanding the isolated and questionable facts they *do* provide, I suggest an alternate source of information and insight. Folklore and popular culture express an unofficial version, in many ways a Uighur version, of Uighurs' lives, their struggles in the present, and their hopes for the future. I intend this cursory review of some such materials—songs and jokes—to demonstrate that for understanding China, an active, inquisitive, and creative approach is useful, even necessary. The ideas and images, the facts and figures delivered daily in our own broadcast and print news media, no matter how serious and convincing they seem, often simply reproduce the official Chinese state version of reality and can rarely if ever take us beyond the headlines.

BACKGROUND INFORMATION ON UIGHURS IN XINJIANG

My own knowledge of Xinjiang derives largely from the twenty-four months of research I conducted there between 1992 and 1996. As an anthropologist interested in the overall impact of China's economic reforms on

Uighur communities, I arranged to live with two families of Uighur merchants. I first spent one year in Urumqi—Xinjiang's main, primarily Han, urban center (population 1.2 million)—and another in the suburban Uighur neighborhoods that skirt the small city of Yining (population 275,000) in the fertile Ili River valley on China's borders with Kazakhstan.

In Yining, my fieldwork experience was enhanced by the fact that I conducted my research and social interaction almost entirely in Uighur—a Turkic language, linguistically unrelated to Chinese, written in Arabic script. Some local men did speak a smattering of Mandarin Chinese, which they picked up in Yining's thriving wholesale markets, where they traded and brokered deals between migrant Han Chinese sellers and visiting Central Asian trader-tourist buyers. Outside of such interactions, however, residents of the Uighur neighborhoods I visited lived their lives entirely within a Uighur-speaking social world and, like the majority of all Uighurs, knew or used few words of Mandarin Chinese. Han individuals reside throughout Xinjiang—through in-migration[3] their numbers have grown from 200,000 in 1949 to over 7 million today—and they generally speak no Uighur. Even among second-generation settlers or settlers who have lived in Xinjiang for decades, those who speak passable Uighur are rare.

Fig. 12.1. Xinjiang with bordering provinces and countries

This almost absolute linguistic divide reflects an even more total division between the social worlds of Uighur and Han. Sharing food, to take just one important example, is an activity that social groups use worldwide to establish and maintain friendly relations. In Xinjiang, however, Uighurs' observance of *halal* dietary laws, which include a strict pork taboo, keep them from ever sharing food in a Han household or from offering their hospitality to a Han guest whose routine consumption of pork makes them ritually impure. Given their inability to exchange either language or food, and in the almost total absence of inter-ethnic marriages and the alliances they create, Uighur and Han occupy parallel worlds. For those individuals at school or at work in ethnically mixed environments at state-run institutions, group events do promote inter-ethnic solidarity, but these events are often ill-conceived. In one work unit I visited, for example, leaders planned a lavish afternoon banquet for a day when all Muslims fast for Ramadan, revealing either an ignorance of minority customs or an agenda of forcing minorities to put their allegiance to the state before their identity as Muslims.

Yining was traditionally one of Xinjiang's largest handicraft production centers and is now the marketing and administrative center for the surrounding Ili River valley region. Most residents who worked outside the home were small-scale merchants (including a significant number of women) or craftsmen, and China's official embrace of free-market commerce has stimulated many Uighur communities with deep roots in a tradition as market traders. Although Uighurs' entrepreneurial strategies are diverse, the local urban economy rests ultimately on a much larger-scale flow of goods. For it is Yining's thriving border trade markets that can be counted on to bring a never-ending stream of both sellers and buyers into the city. Thousands of Han entrepreneurs travel from China's coastal manufacturing regions to remain in Yining for months or years, shipping in from their home provinces train-cars and truckloads of the same consumer goods that China exports around the world. Tourist-traders cross daily over the Kazakhstan border, coming from home cities throughout the former Soviet Union, and hurry to load their own trucks and buses with bales of goods—socks, gym suits, children's shoes—before their three-day visas expire.

While many of my male friends spent their days trading in the marketplace, relaxing in the open-air pool halls, or picnicking by the riverside, their wives generally stayed at home, busy with a number of laborious tasks, perhaps whitewashing the walls of their flat-roofed adobe houses or tending the gardens and grapevines that decorate their courtyards. Sisters or female neighbors might gather to bake several weeks' worth of flat bread at a time in their large beehive ovens or set off in colorful dresses for the markets to buy green peppers and strips of mutton, perhaps with money contributed to the household economy by their young children out selling apricots at Sunday bazaar. But not all market items are to meet the practical needs of the household. Islamic religious pamphlets for sale by peddlers were a popular and well-selling item while I was in Yining. These mimeographed booklets were bought regularly by Uighur men and women in their twenties and thirties, usually those interested in increasing their limited practice of prayer to the full recitation of five daily prayers but who were deprived of adequate lessons when younger due to a long-standing ban on religious schooling.

Although the rhythms of their daily lives were centered around local markets and the streets of their neighborhoods surrounding the urbanizing center of Yining, kinship ties linked their families eastward, into the networks of villages scattered across the fertile Ili River valley, and also westward across the border into the former Soviet Union, where tens of thousands of Uighurs fled in the early 1960s to escape famine and persecution.

My experiences in Yining were mainly among the suburban and urban middle class, whose small incomes allowed them to enjoy relative prosperity after decades of poverty; but most of Xinjiang's 7 million Uighurs are rural peasants, and their situation is quite bleak. Unlike Han farmers who settle in Xinjiang, who are free to raise cash crops for sale on open markets, Uighurs generally remain legally obliged to raise grain and sell it to the state at fixed low prices, an activity for which they rely almost entirely on hand-tools and family labor. In rural villages, per capita incomes remain under U.S. $100 per year for many of these peasants. In urban areas, one detailed study concludes that Uighurs' struggle for equal access to education, employment, and compensation is largely unsuccessful.[4] Given these disparities, it is striking, at least at first glance, that Uighur unrest in Yining, as it is elsewhere in Xinjiang, has been over three much less tangible social goods: freedom of association, of religious faith, and of cultural expression.

OFFICIAL TRANSCRIPTS OF UIGHUR RELIGIOUS PROTESTS: "HOLY WAR" OR WHOLLY INACCURATE?

As we turn now to a discussion of the period of unrest I mentioned earlier, we will examine more carefully the conflicting descriptions of what are the issues of contention between Uighurs and the state. On or around February 6, 1997, the city of Yining erupted in the largest incident of inter-ethnic violence in Xinjiang since 1949. Official reports about the incident, however, not only conflict with each other but diverge sharply from reports emanating from other sources. What is clear, however, is that the events that followed thrust the Uighur cause into the international spotlight to an unprecedented degree. This is owing in great part to the fact that some unofficial reports indicated casualty figures ranging from one hundred to three hundred. Yet some official reports said no casualties occurred. What exactly transpired? Let's look at the headlines (with my emphasis in italics).

In the view of an official spokesman for the Yining city television station, it was not a demonstration, what happened was *"just an act of beating, smashing and looting by some drug addicts, looters and 'social garbage.'"*[5] According to the director of the Yining police department's administrative office, about two hundred demonstrators from an *"illegal religious organization . . . took off all their clothes and shouted slogans like 'Don't sleep. Don't eat. Don't work.'"*[6] In June 1997, Xinjiang's Communist Party Chairman blamed the event on *"a handful of separatists and religious elements . . .* [who] *whipped up religious fanaticism and preached a 'holy war.'"*[7] By September, officials from Tibet and Xinjiang *"vowed to impose ethnic and religious harmony at all costs."*[8]

On the other hand, Agence France Press (AFP) reported on February 15, 1997, that about one thousand Uighur students had been arrested on February 4 and 5 for *criticizing a government decision to appoint all mullahs* [local religious leaders] *through administrative channels. Demonstrations began a few days later in response.*[9] The Eastern Turkistan Information Center reported on February 10, 1997, that "the *riot began when Chinese police attempted to arrest two Uighur talips (religious school students) from the mosque during religious service.* Angered by such an insult to their religious rights, worshipers refused to surrender the students. A fight broke out and the policemen opened fire killing two Uighurs in the mosque."[10]

One Hong Kong newspaper in a February 10 article cited official sources as saying: *"Armed police did not fire a shot."* Yet the next day, an Associated Press (AP) wire service cited a Yining police officer as saying that Uighurs ignited the violence, demanding independence, beating people to death, and burning three cars. "In response, he said, *police fired in the air* and arrested up to 500 people."[11]

What happened after the initial event is even less clear. One foreign reporter learned from residents in Ili that around one hundred protesters were executed within the first week after the riots occurred. The same reporter adds, *"A police spokesman in Yining not only refused to confirm the executions, but also denied that the riots had even taken place. 'Nothing happened here last week,' he said."*[12]

The more one reads official statements on ethnic relations and social unrest, the more it becomes apparent that they are constructed on a scaffold of questionable assumptions and ideologically loaded terms that serve state interests well—since they deny the very possibility of questioning the legitimacy of state authority—but do little to reveal the truth of events as experienced by local participants. The following stock phrases of official jargon are taken from stories about the February 6 incident. Consider them not for what they say, but for what they do not say.

"AUTHORITIES LAUNCHED A CRACKDOWN ON UNDERGROUND RELIGIOUS ACTIVITIES"

Such phrases as this, reproduced in virtually every official account of unrest in Xinjiang, suggest a simple contrast between legal and illegal religious activities, yet almost never do they explain exactly which religious activities are illegal. China's citizens are by law not guaranteed any of the rights outlined in China's Constitution *until those rights are implemented in specific Party policies.* And the right to religious freedom by law permits only the propagation of atheism, making it potentially illegal for parents to promote religious belief among their children. In practice, to be sure, much of family life from 1978 to the present has generally remained outside the reach of the basic-level state apparatus, but the state can and does use such technicalities whenever it wishes. One substantial aspect of illegal activity in Ili consisted of parents sending children to learn to recite the Koran at small informal prayer schools. An even more important form was the *mexrep* groups, young men who gathered for moral education and community service. The local state had staked out a strong position against the *mexrep* groups, and anything they did was seen as criminal activity against the state. In the following sections, I will return to discuss the importance of *mexrep* groups in greater detail.

"UNAUTHORIZED CONSTRUCTION OR RENOVATION OF 133 MOSQUES"

Is there such a thing as *authorized* construction of mosques? What requirements are there? Must the state contribute to its funding? Are private donations permitted openly, or must they be, can they be, channeled through the state? Given the chaotic nature of laws and building codes in China, it is not unlikely that mosque builders thought their activities to conform with state requirements.

Even more important, the seemingly simple contrast between authorized and unauthorized activities makes little sense to anyone familiar with the actual progress of both legal reforms and economic development in post-1979 China. Under reforms, the government has indeed issued dozens and dozens of new laws where for decades only Party policy applied, but these are often little more than vague formulations that summarize and express Party policies. Furthermore, there are vast areas of public and private life—civil, criminal, economic, and administrative—where no laws really apply. To claim that a simple action, erecting a particular building on a particular site, for example, is either legal or illegal ignores the reality that a hefty portion of all construction in China, all commerce in China, all manufacturing in China, has for the last ten years taken place outside of or on the gray fringes of the domain of the strictly legal. That an activity is "illegal" might in practice mean one of three things; (1), a law exists that says it is illegal; (2), a relevant law exists that does not say that it *is* legal; or (3) no law yet exists regarding the activity whatsoever.

UNDERSTANDING RELIGION IN XINJIANG

If religious sentiments and activities are somehow related to the unrest, and news reports unclear as to their exact nature, where can we look for clarification? Xinjiang has scholars who research local religious phenomena; perhaps we can learn from their expertise. In 1991 the Xinjiang Academy of Social Sciences organized a closed conference for its approximately 110 scholars. Among the papers presented by scholars of religion, consider the following, briefly excerpted as follows.

1. "On New Topics in Religious Studies in Xinjiang," by Sang Rong
   "*How to make religious work*[13] *better serve Xinjiang's economic construction and opening and reform . . . is a primary topic of research . . .* In some regions of Xinjiang there has appeared for some time the phenomenon of . . . *a loss of control over religious work, this is* [due to] *foreign enemies, seeking to split national unity under the guise of religion.*"

2. "On the Serious Problem of the Existence of Religious Faith among Xinjiang's Youth," by Nuermaimaiti (Nurmemet)

"For several years we have gone down to conduct first-hand research, and arrived at these conclusions . . . *Youths of under 18 years of age are participating in religious activities . . . and lack a scientific* [i.e., atheistic] *world view* . . . Middle and elementary school students also attend *illegal scripture schools* to study [the Koran], seriously *disrupting the normal progress of state education* . . . scripture schools imbue youths with unhealthy, even extremely reactionary thoughts, *causing some students to take part in illegal activities* [which] seek to split the nation and damage ethnic unity."

Note that there are no "legal" religious schools for young children in Xinjiang and no opportunities for Muslim parents to arrange for a specialist to educate their children into the religion. Merely attending an afternoon scripture class is an activity without legal protection. As such, it does not merely "cause students to take part in illegal activities"; in itself it constitutes an "illegal" activity. Uighurs in their sixties and seventies told me that, as children, they all attended such schools, usually only for several months, in order to learn to recite the Arabic language prayers all Muslims use.

If news coverage is so unreliable and provides insufficient context to understand the information it does provides, and if local scholars are trapped—and I believe most of them are trapped, and not willing co-conspirators—within the narrow ideological confines of official discourse, where can we turn to see another point of view?

UNOFFICIAL TRANSCRIPTS: UIGHUR FOLKLORE AND POPULAR CULTURE

The songs, jokes, puns, and poems that circulate orally in Yining, animating daily marketplace conversations and late-night gatherings, express—in my opinion—many of the deepest concerns of the people who enjoy repeating them, concerns and attitudes that might otherwise remain hidden. The same is true for materials originating in this oral tradition but which are circulated on cassette tapes, either dubbed singly for resale or copied in small batches to be bought and sold in the marketplace. I first describe the production and circulation of these materials, then discuss in detail some of their content. The song lyrics and jokes presented sometimes speak clearly for themselves, and sometimes they require that one read more deeply into them. Whether my interpretations are convincing or not, the reader alone can judge.

THE PRODUCTION OF CULTURAL EXPRESSION IN CHINA

Since 1949, the Han leaders of China's centralized government have sought to maintain positive relations with ethnic minorities in various ways, including by promoting their many forms of expressive culture. To accomplish this, a vast state bureaucracy is dedicated to training minorities in, and supporting the performance of, minority dance, music, theater, and fine arts. While the state sees its actions as benevolent, if also self-serving,[14] state support for minority culture has had two negative effects. The first negative effect is that the culture bureaucracy is run by Han Party members, so that officially sanctioned forms of minority culture tend to express mostly what Han leaders decide are suitable expressions of minority identity. Song lyrics, television programs, costumes, and choreography are purged of any symbols, motifs, or ideas that threaten the ideology of Party-state supremacy. That an ideological bias is imposed by the state is not an accident. During the long revolution that led to the Communist takeover in 1949, folk performing genres popular among Han themselves, like storytelling and vaudeville comedy sketches, were widely used by the Party as vessels to deliver propaganda to masses of illiterate peasants. State leaders merely continued this approach with minorities, filling their cultural forms with pro-Han and pro-state content.

In Xinjiang, for example, typical themes of the songs, dances, and theater sketches appearing daily on state-run television are how much Uighur peasants love the People's Liberation Army and how grateful minorities are to the Party for nurturing them. In the late-Dengist period when I was in Xinjiang, the state showed every sign of trying to maintain strict control over the world of "official" minority culture. The second negative effect of state support for minority culture is that the state only allows sanctioned performers and cultural organizations to have access to print and broadcast media and to performance venues. As a result, for decades foreign observers have had difficulties locating unofficial cultural expressions, sometimes even to the point of suggesting such unofficial culture did not exist.

But no matter how repressive a totalitarian regime is, folklore—items that circulate orally and that can exhibit variation at each retelling—remains an avenue of commentary available to all. In Xinjiang I was not surprised to find folklore a rich source of local commentary on all aspects of Uighurs' experience. What did surprise me, however, was the noticeable growth of unofficial popular culture—items circulating as mass-produced commodities in a market economy—that Uighurs used to represent publicly their feelings and ideas. The cassette tapes of music, poetry, and jokes; the videotapes of variety performances and comedy sketches; and the T-shirts and posters produced locally throughout Xinjiang are examples of the popular culture that has exploded everywhere in China in the 1990s. The values expressed in these popular cultural forms promise—the state might say threaten—to remain a primary source of ideological heterogeneity in China in the future.

POPULAR CULTURE IN YINING

In Yining, local Uighurs all seemed to share a strong interest in folk and popular music. Perhaps the most common form of recreation I found

Fig. 12.2. A Uighur tape merchant in a village outside Yining waits for customers, who pay to dub single copies from his collection of published and privately recorded Uighur songs, jokes, and poetry. (Photo by Jay Dautcher)

Fig. 12.3. Uighur-owned booth selling audio cassettes and videotapes of Uighur popular and folk cultural performances. (Photo by Jay Dautcher)

among men was the *olturax* (literally, "sitting together"). Men from the suburban neighborhoods would gather several times weekly in the afternoon or evening at a local restaurant or at one person's house and sit together for four or six hours, sometimes much longer. Plates of spicy mutton and vegetable dishes would be served, and the men would drink strong *akh'arakh* liquor by the glass, using a single glass among them and drinking in rotation. After an hour or two of chatting, joking, and swapping good-natured insults, someone would fetch a long-necked *dotar*, and the singing would begin. Often everyone would take a turn, strumming the two nylon strings and singing a favorite song, before the more skilled musicians present took over, singing ancient songs of cruel tyrants and clever heroes, along with newer songs that commented obliquely on Han domination in Xinjiang. After singing for an hour or two, the men would return to swapping stories and jokes, and then back again to music, and in this way pass long hours in each other's company.

Songs like those presented here are recorded by local amateur or semi-professional Uighur artists, produced by small-scale Uighur entrepreneurs in batches of several thousands, and circulated throughout Xinjiang to be resold in small private shops, retailing for around U.S. $1.00. One local radio station managed to receive the approval of authorities to embrace all-Uighur programming, broadcasting Uighur music, reading from Uighur novels and poetry, and hosting Uighur call-in talk programs. Not only did my household keep this station tuned in during its entire transmission, roughly 6:00 A.M. until 6:00 P.M., but virtually every Uighur butcher, bread-baker, or clothing merchant in the bazaars whose stall possessed a radio would tune in all day. Han pedestrians passed by, deaf to words all Uighur ears could hear. Even songs whose political messages seemed only faintly disguised, such as the following, managed somehow to make it past state censors.

> *Better to live briefly and like a hawk,*
> *than to live like a crow for a hundred years.*
> *Better to be dung, to be used for fertilizer,*
> *than to live without doing something for one's people.*
>
> *Days will pass, months will pass, years, too, will pass.*
> *The time of your life will be used up.*
> *But if the book of your life is written in gold dust,*
> *future generations will remember you.*

I remember one day hearing a long promotional segment for a newly released cassette that included this eventually popular song.

Coming into the world, you met only with hardship,
did you foresee that Destiny itself would betray you?
When nothing good appears, you make not a sound?
Won't you say something, you kind-hearted, peaceful Uighurs?

Some people, crying "Uighur," raise a shout,
some people, being Uighur, prepare to rout.
Doesn't your conscience burn, doesn't it drive you at all?
Tell me, my kind-hearted, peaceful Uighurs.

Some people would tell you that your fortune is tied to destiny,
as they prepare to put the pincers to your gullible heart.
If you don't pay such treatment back, will you ever attain the prosperity you hope for?
Tell me, my kind-hearted, peaceful Uighurs.

Here the singer seems to taunt and mock Uighurs for being too docile, and indeed on several occasions I heard Uighurs lament what they see as their

overly docile nature, which allows the Han Chinese to dominate their territory.

Certain sentiments are widespread in the subtext of these tunes: resentment against the Chinese state and against a never-ending stream of Han
migrant settlers, bitterness about events that seem to them out of their control, and the perception that their identity as a historical group, together
with their cultural and social existence, is threatened by the unchecked
power of the Chinese Party-state. These sentiments cannot easily find open
expression in those media regulated by the state, but they do find
extremely widespread expression in folklore and some areas of popular
culture. For example, consider again the Uighur song excerpted on the first
page of this chapter. As one Uighur informant explained to me, certain
Uighur individuals prosper through collaboration with the state, for example, serving as top Party officials. They are well fed for dancing the dance,
in other words, professing allegiance to the Party-state. But one day will
come, when the present regime is gone, and without its protection,
Uighurs who today serve the Han state will be left with nothing.

Another song popular while I was there, "The Hen That Wouldn't Lay
(*Tughmas tohu*)," contains the following lyrics:

> The hen that never lays, she lords it over the rest of the roost,
> It's the wandering hen without a home, who lays eggs one after the other.
> The hen that never lays, she eats all the finest grain.
> She never lays, those who do lay, sit locked out, and wait in vain.
>
> One day I got to thinking, there are people like that, too,
> like that barren hen, despised by all.
> Is there any good in such people, who give nothing to the world?
> Like the barren hen, lording it over others, their days are numbered.

To confirm my own interpretation, I asked a friend what he thought it
meant. He looked at me, "What do people do with a hen that won't lay? It's
not doing any good, so they kill it to eat the meat." He went on to explain,
the state has demonstrated that it cannot provide for Uighurs, who live in
poverty. This state only lays eggs for the Han, only provides for them. The
song is asking, What should the Uighurs do? He answered his own question, saying that many Uighurs recognize that such a state will never serve
their interests, and one day they will surely do away with it.

Mexrep groups, which I mentioned earlier, were responsible for organizing the youth sports league. These informal groups are referred to

locally only as "the youths who play *mexrep*" (*mexrep oynaydighan balilar*) or "the thirty lads" (*ottuz yigit*), the symbolic number of young men in each group. My experiences in Yining suggest to me that these *mexrep* organizers are seen by many Uighurs as central to whatever events transpired on February 6. Careful searching of Chinese news service articles uncovered only a single mention of their role in the protest activities, but this one mention is revealing. Less than six months after the rioting, Amudun Niyaz, the Uighur chairman of the Xinjiang Regional People's Congress, visited Uighur peasant villages on the outskirts of Yining. He spoke briefly to his media escort, condemning terrorist activity and separatism; then, as reported in Xinjiang's main daily newspaper,

> at nightfall . . . [he] took part in the *maixilaifu* [i.e., *mexrep*], a traditional Uighur recreation, at a vineyard in Turpan Yuzi township. Young men and women, dressed in colorful ethnic costumes, sang, danced, and told jokes and stories; a merry and tranquil atmosphere prevailed throughout the evening.
>
> Amudun Niyaz said: *Maixilaifu* is a popular activity among the Uighurs. However, a handful of national separatists, in order to realize their ulterior motive, have manipulated this recreation to establish illicit ties, using *maixilaifu* as a ground for disseminating speeches, undermining national unity and motherland unification, and for carrying out illegal religious activities. This is absolutely not permissible. We must expose such tricks and conspiracies by refusing to participate in their kind of "*maixilaifu*."[15]

While the state tries to distinguish between good *mexrep*s and bad *mexrep*s, how do Uighurs themselves see the meaning of these groups and their activities? To explain the situation as Uighur informants explained it to me, let me begin with the following joke, also recorded by a local talent, the Yining comedian Jür'ät Ehmät, and released on cassette in Yining in 1995.

> A young man shows up late for a gathering of his friends:
> *"Hey man, you're late, that's a fine!," they say, and pour him three shots of liquor. So, he drinks the first two one right after the other, but the third one, he spills a little bit on the ground, and one of his friends says:*
> *"Hey, you spilled liquor at me, another fine!," and he pours another three shots. Again the fellow downs the first two, but spills a little bit of the third.*
> *"You spilled it again, another fine!," his friend says, pouring another three shots. Well, the guy can barely get them down—three fines, nine shots total—the guy is wasted, he stumbles outside, and on the street he bumps into a cop.*
> *"Hey, you, you're disturbing the peace, I'm going to have to fine you," the cop says.*
> *"Awww, just shut up and pour!"*

This depiction of a typical *olturax* exposes a basic tension in the lives of many Uighur residents of Yining. In private spaces such as informal social gatherings, men spoke to each other often of a code of behavior (*kha'idä*, or "rules") that must be obeyed, and transgressors were regularly forced to submit to the authority of the group, perhaps through the person of an informal leader. Out in the street, a different authority reigns, the authority of the state and its agents, as represented by the policeman. Recorded on the cassette tape, an all-male audience explodes in laughter at the exact moment the man confuses the two codes of behavior. Caught in the collision of two worlds, his willingness to conform to the code of behavior of his private social world places him in direct opposition with the state's efforts to regulate urban spaces and bring them under the control of its authority.

How is this basic tension related to the violence of the popular unrest of February 6 and the military crackdown that followed? Discussions with Uighur informants suggest that *mexrep*s are at heart organizations that seek to lure men away from the lifestyle of heavy drinking and that generally accompanies participation in *olturax*. Participation in a *mexrep* group entails certain concrete behavioral changes, such as a commitment to abstain from alcohol and an increased effort to maintain a regular prayer schedule. After *mexrep* groups began to surge in popularity in villages throughout the entire Ili river valley area in 1994–1995, rural stores became completely dry, shopkeepers were afraid to put alcoholic beverages on shelves for fear of boycotting, and a substantial source of revenue for local governments was lost. It was widely rumored that the state was extremely upset that a movement without any visible public presence could generate such a pronounced shift in lifestyle patterns.

But beyond these concrete behavioral changes, there was a deeper point of *mexrep* participation, as one friend active in a *mexrep* group explained to me. This was to make men move away from their concern with the familiar code of honor used in all-male face-to-face gatherings like the *olturax*—such as forcing each other to continue drinking at each passing of the glass or forbidding any one person to depart the gathering before all were ready—and to promote a code of behavior grounded in the life of the wider community. When men sit at *olturax*, it is typically the ritual interactions of the *olturax* itself that are the subject of moral discussion. At *mexrep*, men open up their attention to their own and their fellow participants' behavior in their entire private and public lives, and consider its effects on families, local communities, and on the Uighur ethnic group as a whole.

So why is the state concerned? Since the 1950s the Communist Party has regularly and quite openly announced its goal of shaping the consciousness of China's citizens to conform with the Party's own socialist ideals. An implicit corollary has always been that no other organized efforts to shape worldview, outside of Party control, can be tolerated. This desire to monopolize the production of ideological messages—to achieve hegemony, some would call it—explains the state's concern to bring all association groups, religious or secular, under its regulation.

Before I conclude, let me present one more joke, also widely circulated in Yining and again recorded by a native of Ili at a private party in the city suburbs.

These kids today, some of them don't know anything about rules of behavior (khaidä). In our neighborhood there's this kid Rehmetulla, who doesn't know the first thing about the rules of Islam. So one day I'm going to Friday prayers, I put on my clothes, perform my ablutions, and I go out to the street corner. Standing on the corner is Rehmetulla, and so I say:

"Hey, Rehmetulla, come on, we'll go over to Friday prayers," and he says:

"Friend, but I don't know the rules." So I say:

"But you're a Muslim just like me, so let's go to the mosque and you just do whatever I do, okay?," and he says, "Okay." So he got ready, and we went into the mosque. After everyone in the mosque was finished performing the first two prayers, it's time to perform the Salaam, so I look to my right and I say, "Peace be upon you, Rehmetulla," and he looks at me and says "And upon you, peace."

Readers can be excused for not "getting" the joke, of course. For Friday prayers in Yining, as elsewhere in the Muslim world, men gather at mosques in groups of a hundred or more to pray together. The Salaam is a specific point within the sacred space of prayer when each man wishes peace upon his neighbors, and they in turn wish him peace, *using the exact same phrase.* In the profane world of everyday life, on the other hand, men greet each other with the same phrase, "Peace upon you," but the reply is always inverted—"And upon you, peace." Anthropologists have found that reversal is among the features that commonly mark the distinction between the sacred and the profane, between the ritual and the mundane. The taped audience laughs when Rehmetulla treats the sacred language of prayer—ultimately, an exchange between man and God—as an everyday social interaction. Even on its surface, the joke reveals tensions in Uighur communities about the meaning of being a Muslim, tensions within male cohorts about the degree to which one practices Islam, and it reveals a concern with knowing the basic rules of performing a Muslim life. When I was in Ili, neighbors and friends often expressed their concerns about children being deprived of the ability to learn to pray.

CONCLUSION

As we sit in our living rooms or at our breakfast tables, the political scientists and think-tank analysts we see editorializing in print and broadcast media are always eager to appear confident in their analyses. Equipped with facts and figures, it is their very job to appear as experts, feeding a society that has over a period of decades become increasingly organized around the idea that ordinary citizens must hand responsibility for collective decision making over to such "experts". If I am doubtful that this will prove successful, it is not because I feel expertise is unattainable, but because I think our vision of what counts as "hard" data is often too narrow. Quantitative investigations of economic productivity, political participation, or consumer behavior provide easy answers to questions, but

Fig. 12.4. Uigher men gather at a private home in Yining to record a joking session for market release in cassette form. (Photo by Jay Dautcher)

Fig. 12.5. The artwork on this cassette cover is typical of locally produced cassettes, which alternate between popular songs and joke-telling.

what if the questions themselves are questionable? The qualitative examination of trends in Chinese society, the careful scrutiny of the ephemera of everyday life, whether the latest joke or the most fashionable hairstyle, may not seem as solid a basis for understanding China as "hard" numbers, but their importance cannot be overlooked. Forms of language and expressions of values such as found in popular culture and folklore can, if we know how to read them correctly, tell us much about power relations between the government and China's citizens; about the social inequality between Han and Uighur; between urban elite, urban poor, and rural peasants; between men and women.

Taken together, the materials presented here show us that Xinjiang's 7 million Uighurs, like the other tens of millions of China's ethnic minorities, not only could, but already do, have much to say about China's search for a future and that they have many ways of speaking past the barriers of silence imposed on them.

NOTES

Roberto Gonzales and Timothy Weston read and commented insightfully on drafts of this article, and I thank them, though I alone bear responsibility for all its shortcomings. Tim Weston deserves additional thanks for his valuable editorial support. Field research on which this article is based was made possible through a dissertation grant from the Committee for Scholarly Communication with China, through the support of the Xinjiang Academy of Social Sciences, which hosted me for two years in China, and through the untold generosity of Uighur friends, families, and communities.

1. Rose Maria Li, "Migration to China's Northern Frontier, 1953–1982," *Population and Development Review,* vol. 15, no. 3 (September 1989).

2. For an introduction to China's minorities, see June T. Dreyer, *China's Forty Millions* (Cambridge, Mass.: Harvard University Press, 1976). For a more recent look at the condition of China's minorities, see Stevan Harrell, ed., *Cultural Encounters on China's Ethnic Frontiers* (Seattle: University of Washington Press, 1995).

3. In the language of social science, decades of Han relocation into Xinjiang might be described as "in-migration." The reasons for migration have varied over the past fifty years: some transfers have been voluntary, some forced by the state, some prompted by the state through rewards offered to Han settlers. But the term *in-migration* connotes, I think, the idea that for purposes of analysis, such events can be considered outside of their social-political contexts and meanings, an idea I find highly questionable. Social scientists long spoke of "depopulation" in the Americas, when what they meant was genocide. Are Han "colonizing" Xinjiang or merely "migrating" there? A fuller treatment of such questions is desirable but falls outside the scope of this article.

4. Ji Ping, "Frontier Migration and Ethnic Assimilation: A Case of Xinjiang Uygur Autonomous Region of China," Ph.D. diss., Brown University, 1990.

5. *Ming pao,* February 11, 1997, A6, as excerpted in BBC-SWB.

6. Associated Press, February 11, 1997.

7. Human Rights Watch Asia, *China: State Control of Religion* (New York, 1980), 39, citing FBIS, June 10, 1997.

8. "Beijing Defends Its Hard Line on Tibet, Xinjiang," AFP (Agence France Press) Wire Report, September 17, 1997. What kind of "harmony" can be imposed through coercion, and at what cost? Answers to such questions are, of course, never asked, let alone answered.

9. To lend credibility to this account, an Amnesty International document, *People's Republic of China: Secret Violence: Human Rights Violation in Xinjiang,* notes that regulations issued in Xinjiang on September 16, 1990, require that all religious workers be "licensed" by "patriotic religious organizations" themselves officially recognized by the Party. During one campaign, more than 12,000 religious personalities in the southern district of Kashgar alone underwent individual scrutiny in a state-run appraisal process, which weeded out any persons whose activities were deemed threatening and which was meant to intimidate the remainder.

10. Taken from the Internet: http://www.uygur.com/enorg/wunn/wunn 021097.html

11. Associated Press, February 11, 1997. To put the value of such claims in context, I was present in Lhasa on December 10, 1988, when a Dutch woman was wounded

by gunfire from military troops who were responding to a crowd of Tibetan protesters. That evening in our hostel several U.S. and European citizens standing near her when she was shot recounted how a Lhasa Television crew recorded police firing into the air and pleading with protesters to return home—images destined for China's national television news, perhaps—at the same time as a squad leader shot his pistol at the nearest protester, hitting him in the forehead and signaling a volley of shots that killed seven persons. Personal knowledge of such happenings generates many feelings, among them skepticism of official news coverage.

12. Gilles Campion, "Mass Trials, Executions Follow Moslem Riots in China," AFP, February 12, 1997.

13. The phrase "religious work" refers mainly to the Party supervision of religious activity and secondarily to the activities of religious leaders themselves.

14. Consider the Han cadre's comment on the first page of this article that "ethnic minorities are like untamed mustangs. No matter how well you feed them, they may run off at any time." His statement reflects Party leaders' belief that restive minorities can be appeased with rewards—whether prosperity under reforms or support for the arts—and will allow themselves to be corralled in (physically) and herded about (ideologically) as state leaders wish. It hints, too, at other biases that have informed state minority policies for decades, such as that without Han cultural values, minorities are without culture at all, like wild animals, and that they are therefore rightfully domesticated by benevolent masters.

15. " 'Determined Efforts Must Be Made to Eliminate 'Vermin' and Eradicate Poisonous Weeds,' Says Amudun Niyaz during Inspection of Ili Prefecture," *Xinjiang ribao* (Xinjiang Daily), July 28, 1997, 1. Appears as "Xinjiang Official Says 'Poisonous Weed' Separatists Must Be Eliminated," in BBC-SWB, August 13, 1997.

SUGGESTED READINGS

For readers seeking a broader understanding of current events in Xinjiang, in addition to the sources cited in my endnotes, I recommend a book by Justin Jon Rudelson, *Oasis Identities: Uyghur Nationalism along China's Silk Road* (New York: Columbia University Press, 1997), based on the author's field research in Turpan. To better appreciate the historical backdrop for today's conflicts, see Andrew Forbes, *Warlords and Muslims in Chinese Central Asia: A Political History of Republican Sinkiang 1911–1949* (Cambridge/New York: Cambridge University Press, 1986). Also, the writings of Sven Hedin (1865–1952) and Aurel Stein (1862–1943)—based on their first-hand investigations in the region in the first half of this century—make for fascinating reading. A recommended starting point is Stein, *On Ancient Central Asian Tracks,* Jeannete Mirsky, ed. (New York: Pantheon Books, 1964).

Readers interested in searching for Web sites on Uighurs and Xinjiang or in searching library indexes for the literally thousands of books and articles available on the history, politics, and culture of Xinjiang should realize that spellings of key terms vary widely: Uighur is at times spelled Uyghur, Uigur, or Uygur, and many books on Xinjiang employ the place name Sinkiang, or Chinese Turkestan. To complement Uighur-run Web sites on the Internet, a valuable source is Amnesty International, whose wide-ranging publications methodically document cases where China's state security apparatus imprisons and executes Uighurs—and others of all ethnicities throughout China—accused of political activism.

13

China's Market Reforms:

Whose Human Rights Problem?

Tim Oakes

We have a factory in China where we have 250 people. We own them; it's our factory. We pay them $40 a month, and they work 28 days a month. . . . Generally, they're young girls that come from the hills.
— Irwin Gordon, president, Ava-Line Co.,
cited in *Business Week*, August 21, 1996

INTRODUCTION: JIANG'S TRAVELS

Of all the arresting images garnered by the press during Chinese president Jiang Zemin's autumn 1997 visit to the United States, one was particularly evocative of just how much China has changed since the years of Mao's Cultural Revolution. The *New York Times* front-page photo of the Chinese president ringing the bell at the New York Stock Exchange to begin the day's trading on Halloween ranks as one of those crystalline moments in photojournalism, where gestalt history itself is captured in a single image.[1] Interestingly, for those who applauded Jiang's gesture, this was not some dyed-in-the-wool communist interloper, disingenuously wearing the capitalist mask for a bit of Wall Street trick-or-treating. Rather, China's turn to the market is regarded as a genuine step toward the ultimate realization of a truly global capitalism, and Wall Street has already been salivating at the prospect. No one wants to miss out on what promises to be a future cornucopia of riches. Investors await the waking of the "hibernating dragon" with the unusual patience of a smitten lover rather than the cold calculations of the profit-minded. At the same time, the market is thought by many supporters of the Clinton administration's policy of "constructive engagement" to offer the surest way of achieving political reform within China itself. The point being that where political diplomacy has failed, capitalism and the market will triumph. Whereas the idea of "human rights" has seemingly run into significant translation difficulties, the U.S. press happily notes that down deep, we all speak the same language: the vernacular of money.

It is not surprising, then, that the *New York Times* would contrast the New York and Washington phases of Jiang's travels as capturing the intriguing dualistic character of the Chinese–U.S. relationship. While Jiang was said to have experienced some "discomfort" in Washington, with all the congressional snubs over human rights and democracy, and the perhaps ineffectual pestering of President Clinton over the same topics, the Chinese president was said to be far more "at home" in New York, where his visit to the Stock Exchange served as prelude to an elegantly hosted dinner for some two hundred CEOs representing the most powerful corporations in the country.[2] Indeed, the *Times* went so far as to print a series of photos showing President Clinton stooping to provide a stool for Jiang, so that the two could be seen at the same level. Here, an interesting message suggested itself: Clinton bows before Jiang, who bows before Wall Street. Jiang's political intransigence over the question of human rights and other "Western values" was striking only for its contrast to his uninhibited worship before that other temple of Western values. While the "dialogue" over China's human rights record has gone nowhere on the political front, "constructive engagement" has been a clear success as far as U.S. business is concerned.[3]

"Human rights" nevertheless remains primarily a political issue in the U.S. mind. Most people equate the issue of human rights in China with images of student demonstrators gunned down, Tibetans tortured, and ordinary citizens imprisoned for having dissenting views. These images convey a totalitarian China in need of the liberalizing influence of the market. "Constructive engagement," along with the more general process of China's entry into the global marketplace, will, the argument goes, erode the Party's authoritarian base and replace it with the democracy-building civil institutions of a rising middle class. It is rarely questioned, however, whether the assumed building of capitalism in China might in fact present a set of new human rights problems of its own. While Beijing aggressively pursues a place among the world's most powerful market economies, persistent poverty in the countryside presents one of the most troubling—but for U.S. citizens generally unnoticed—human rights problems in China. As China's strategies for modernization and development increasingly garner accolades from the World Bank and international financial analysts, the plight of some 160 million impoverished farmers and another 100 million who have already fled the countryside to float through China's booming cities in search of work, raises serious questions about just what kind of "liberal" society China's market-reforms might be producing.

In this light, it is significant to note that Jiang's travels represent not simply a pilgrimage to the Mecca of global capitalism in New York, but a shoring-up of his Party's legitimacy as the undisputed authority in guiding China's transformation from an isolated enclave of command socialism to a global superpower.[4] Jiang's opening of the day's trading at the Stock Exchange made clear that it is not in spite of his Party's policies that China is being wooed by Wall Street but rather *because* of them. Those policies have not only enabled the growth of a limited market economy in China but have also been responsible for an increasing gap between the rich and the poor. And so, the issue of poverty in rural China has also found a place on Jiang's itineraries. On a 1996 visit to the interior province of Guizhou, for example, Jiang stopped by a miserable mountain hamlet to pass out some blankets and cotton padded jackets. He made a point of assuring his impecunious hosts that "the Party hasn't forgotten you," and that "socialism does not equal poverty."

In this latter claim, Jiang was repeating the words of the late Deng Xiaoping himself, who spoke them nearly two decades earlier in an effort to assure a weary China emerging from the chaos of the Cultural Revolution that the Party would from now on be committed to improving the people's living standards rather than embroiling them any further in Mao's continuous revolution. How ironic that Jiang should speak them again, in an effort to assuage the fears of the poor that the Party had now abandoned the one role that yielded its very legitimacy in their eyes: its commitment to economic and social justice for all of China. That China's market-reforms and modernization strategy represent any kind of socialism would be a claim lost on the majority of China's rural poor. A group of Shanghai reporters covering President Jiang's trip to Guizhou took some time to visit a few more poor villages on their own. Confronted at each stop with the abject poverty of this rocky, mountainous region of poor soil, heavy erosion, and incompetent officials, they rhetorically asked their local guides if Guizhou even *had* a communist party. "How could the Party allow this to happen?" one asked. "This is a travesty of socialism!"[5]

Indeed. In rural Guizhou, the ironies of China's turn to the marketplace become cruelly apparent. China's increasingly prominent position in the global economy is being achieved by the systematic exploitation of a huge reserve of underemployed rural labor. China pursues its place in the pageant of modern nations by mobilizing a "surplus population" of rural workers rendered desperate for wage labor by market reforms that have made agriculture a losing venture for most. The situation is eerily similar to that described by Marx himself a century and a half earlier, when industrializing Britain modernized on the backs of a readily exploitable labor force made redundant by the capitalization of the rural economy. That the Communist Party in China now plays the role of the capitalist boss profiting from the exploitation of a willing "disposable industrial reserve army," as Marx put it, is profoundly ironic.[6] It may be premature to assume—as do the proponents of "constructive engagement"—that the appearance of capitalism in China will result in the rise of a "liberal market economy," complete with an independent middle class and the autonomous institutions of "civil society." For we see less the emergence of an independent liberal capitalism in China than the deepening involvement in the econ-

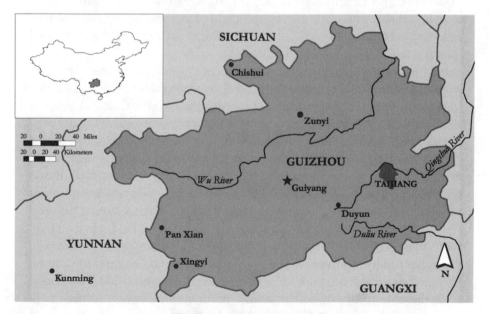

Fig. 13.1. Guizhou Province

omy of the Party-state itself and the resulting entrenchment of power in the hands of a political elite that continues to hold the reins of economic power as well (see the essays by Xiao and Rosemont, this volume).

In this paper, then, I want to explore the ironies of China's pursuit of market reforms and suggest that U.S. critics of China's human rights abuses often miss the broader implications of their self-righteous rhetoric. Market liberalization has generated a glaring income gap within China, the most visible manifestation of which is the "floating population" of peasant laborers, the *mingong*. From their vantage point, China's modernization resembles the worst sort of capitalism that Marx himself could have imagined. China's "human rights problem," then, is not necessarily one associated with the political nature of totalitarianism or communism, per se, but with the political-economic nature of capitalism and uneven development. It is a problem that has historically plagued the West to a much greater degree than China. Do workers have the right to a proper livelihood? Do they have the right to enjoy the fruits of their labor? These questions have befuddled liberal theorists in the West for generations. Yet these are the "rights" whose absence weigh most heavily on the majority of China's rural population. The failure among some of China's critics in the United States to articulate the human rights issue in these broader terms

Fig. 13.2. Farming the thin, rocky soil of Guizhou. (Photo by Tim Oakes)

speaks, I believe, to their unwillingness to see in China an increasingly sharp reflection of the darker sides of our own capitalist modernity and, more important, our complicity in abuses that have been the standard fare of capitalist development around the world.

CAPITALISM WITH CHINESE CHARACTERISTICS

Officially, what China is pursuing in its market reforms is "socialism with Chinese characteristics." This idea has been enshrined in Beijing with the recent addition of "Deng Xiaoping Theory" to the standard lexicon of "Marxist-Leninist-Mao Zedong Thought," which has provided the rhetorical justification for the Communist Party's policies since the late 1950s. "Deng Xiaoping Theory" principally offers a somewhat after-the-fact ideological explanation for the *ad hoc* modernization strategy pursued by China's leadership; the "theory" claims that the country's productive forces must be developed and advanced before China can progress beyond the "primary stage of socialism."[7] Developing China's productive forces—that is, making them more efficient, profitable, and competitive in the global marketplace—is a project best suited for the "invisible hand" of the market, and this means that a certain degree of social inequality must be tolerated as the temporary result of market forces rewarding those willing to take risks. This mobilization of the market, along with its economic opportunities and risks, reached a new level during the 15th Party Congress, when Jiang proposed a new model of public ownership for China's ailing state-owned enterprises.[8] In this regard, his pilgrimage to Wall Street makes even more sense. Jiang's model for revamping the last holdout sector of economic inefficiency in China is basically one of a corporation, collectively owned by investing stockholders, which must answer primarily to the needs of its investors rather than those of its workers (see Weston, this volume).

With China increasingly following a corporate model of enterprise ownership, one inherent quality of the post-Mao reforms now stands out clearer than ever. The reforms have been driven primarily by the promise of increased incomes and increased personal material wealth for the Chinese. Progress is no longer being measured in terms of production, as in Mao's day, but rather in terms of consumption. In a way, one could say the Party is now buying its legitimacy, offering the promise of a personal fortune to anyone willing to practice "socialism with Chinese characteristics," a phrase that appears increasingly meaningless. As one Nanjing University professor put it, "Nobody knows what the concept means. It is only rhetoric, and it can mean anything but socialism."[9] The socialist revolution has formally been diverted from an ostensibly political project of equality and social justice to an overtly economic project of energizing China's latent productive resources at any cost. The Party, rather than proletarians, is now the vanguard of profitability. Equality and equity are no longer explicit goals for a developing country still mired in the "primary stage of socialism." Similarly, the whole concept of democracy is thought of not as a hegemonic political ideology—as Mao might have viewed it—but as a "luxury" currently unaffordable to the incipient consumers of China. "Only people who have enough food on their dinner table can afford democracy," states one restaurant owner in an article by Yin Xiaohuang. "Look at the Russians: the root of their problem is that there is too much freedom but too little bread."[10]

It is little wonder that such an approach to modernization should be so pleasing to the international capitalist community. "Deng Xiaoping Theory" provides something of a model for the austerity programs that were implemented in Latin America and, now, Russia. It also mirrors the political climate within the United States itself, where the market's magic is increasingly called upon to fulfill the functions of a shrinking government. In China, as in the United States, economic growth—the gratification of material desires—is the key to the ideology of market liberalization. And in both countries, the social costs of marketization are increasingly blamed on the shortcomings of the poor themselves. As China replaces the cult of Mao with the cult of the commodity, it resembles the United States more and more.

The important point here, however, is not simply that China has abandoned its revolutionary ideals in an effort to catch up with the materialism of the developed world. Rather, what is most striking about the enshrining of "Deng Xiaoping Theory" is the deepening involvement of the Party-state in the development of China's productive resources, and, indeed, the justification of that involvement in the hollow rhetoric of "socialism with Chinese characteristics." In China, at least one political scientist has suggested, capitalism itself requires a redefinition, one that accounts for the fact that the Party-state, rather than an independent middle class, continues to dominate the social means of production.[11] The Party-state, in other words, has proved remarkably adaptable to the needs of global integration by disciplining its labor force to the imperatives of capitalist development.

Deng's reforms have created a system that still requires strong centralized political control "and indeed a state that is prepared to act in a brutally repressive fashion to enforce the intensive exploitation of the working population that yields the capital accumulation necessary for rapid economic growth."[12]

This role of the state as a bureaucratic capitalist entity has been masked by an ideology of wealth as the just reward for one's willingness to take risks and work hard in the new "socialist marketplace." Similarly, the state's approach to the continuing and worsening problems of poverty and class polarization is to assert that one's poverty is most likely a result of ignorance and an inability to grasp the principles of the commodity economy. China's peasants are routinely blamed for their "small farmer mentality" and their "subsistence orientation."[13] More recently, however, there has been a greater focus on the problem of poverty, indicated, for example, by Jiang's 1996 visit to Guizhou. But the newly invigorated project of poverty alleviation in China has been aimed almost exclusively at short-term schemes to increase peasant incomes and help them learn the value of the commercial economy rather than at addressing the underlying structural conditions that perpetuate rural poverty. It is to these rural problems that we now turn.

THE GROWING INCOME GAP

China's post-Mao market reforms began in the countryside; between 1979 and 1982 all of the country's rural collectives were disbanded and individual households began taking up most of the responsibilities for agricultural production. This had the immediate effect of mobilizing a considerable amount of the countryside's latent productive forces, and the years 1979 to 1984 saw an agricultural boom that—combined with a significant increase in peasant savings—resulted in a stunning decline in rural poverty. This unprecedented achievement was halted, however, and even reversed somewhat in the late 1980s.[14] Since then, there has been little change in the proportion of rural poor in China. The stunning gains of the initial phase of rural reforms have now faded considerably. Since the brief boom of the early 1980s, the income gap between poor and rich regions of China has been widening (see figure 13.3).

Between 1985 and 1991, eight interior provinces saw an actual fall in real income per capita, while the majority of provinces saw only marginal

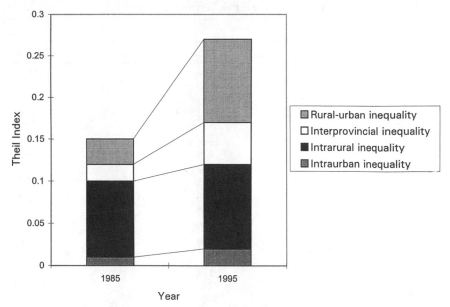

Fig. 13.3. Income inequality in China

gains.[15] Rural China's income boom has been a very limited phenomenon spatially, affecting a few eastern coastal regions containing less than one-fifth of the country's population. As indicated in table 13.1, income inequality grew substantially through the first half of the 1990s. Moreover, while urban income disparities are notable, they pale in comparison to the enormous disparities in rural incomes. It is in the countryside, where roughly two-thirds of China's population lives, that the greatest inequalities are found. Disparities in rural income have a number of causes (see figure 13.4). Perhaps the greatest cause of intrarural disparities within both poor and rich regions of the countryside is the amount and composition of household labor power. Interregional disparities, however, are primarily caused by differential access to off-farm income and to markets for agricultural products.[16] High rural incomes in coastal regions are largely a result of both a much higher density of rural industries and the proximity of rural residents to large urban markets where consumers display relatively high purchasing power.

What caused the mid-1980s stall in improving rural livelihoods overall was the increasing difficulty in earning viable income from agriculture alone; the high dependence on agriculture for the majority living in

Table 13.1   China: Urban and Rural Per Capita Income (%)

	1992		1996	
Region	Urban	Rural	Urban	Rural
China	100	100	100	100
Coastal regions				
Shanghai	149	284	176	252
Guangdong	172	167	171	165
Beijing	126	201	157	185
Zhejiang	129	173	145	180
Tianjin	110	167	126	156
Jiangsu	105	135	107	157
Fujian	112	125	105	129
Shandong	97	102	103	108
Guangxi	104	93	102	88
Hainan	115	108	101	91
Hebei	92	87	93	107
Liaoning	96	127	86	112
Interior regions				
Xizang (Tibet)	126	106	135	70
Yunnan	104	79	102	64
Hunan	104	94	98	93
Xinjiang	97	94	98	67
Anhui	89	73	92	83
Sichuan	99	81	91	75
Hubei	93	86	88	97
Guizhou	94	66	84	66
Qinghai	89	77	82	61
Shaanxi	85	71	80	60
Henan	79	75	79	82
Jilin	81	103	79	110
Jiangxi	75	98	78	97
Heilongjiang	80	121	76	113
Ningxia	90	75	75	73
Shanxi	80	80	75	81
Gansu	84	62	71	58
Nei Monggu	74	86	71	83

Source: *Zhongguo Tongji Nianjian* (China Statistical Yearbook) (Beijing: Zhongguo Tongji Chubanshe, 1997).

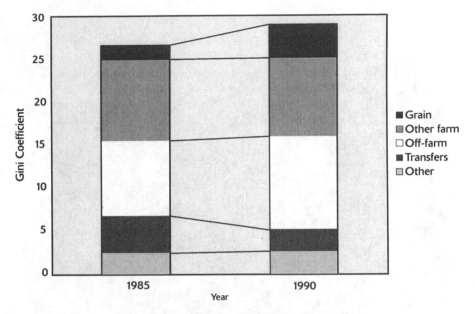

Fig. 13.4. Contributions to income inequality

Fig. 13.5. Preparing a field for spring rice planting, high on a mountainside, an hour's walk from home. (Photo by Tim Oakes)

Fig. 13.6. Hand transplanting of rice seedlings. (Photo by Tim Oakes)

China's interior has been the most significant factor in their inability to take full advantage of the market reforms. The most common explanation for the increasingly poor profitability of agricultural production in China is that the prices of agricultural products, in the increasingly marketized rural economy, have not kept pace with the prices of agricultural inputs. Faced with rising production costs, more and more farmers have been going into debt.[17] In the early 1980s, the state rapidly raised its grain procurement prices in an effort to boost rural incomes and invigorate stagnant grain production. At the same time, it maintained tight control over the price of inputs by steadily increasing its subsidy of fertilizer prices. The result was a doubling of fertilizer applications and record grain harvests in 1982, 1983, and 1984.[18] These were the so-called "golden years" of the rural reforms, in which many grain farmers saw their incomes soar beyond belief.

In 1985, however, the government both dropped its quota grain procurement policy and effectively reduced its official grain purchase price, while at the same time liberalizing the fertilizer market, thereby reducing substantially the amount of fertilizer sold to farmers at state-subsidized prices. Insofar as the result was a massive shift away from grain production, the government achieved its objective of stimulating agricultural diversification and commercial orientation. Yet for farmers in regions with undeveloped agricultural markets, diversification into economic crops was an unrealistic option. With little choice but to continue their dependence on grain income, these farmers saw their income gains of the early 1980s rapidly offset by the nearly 20 percent annual price increase for fertilizer, while the government purchase price for grain changed little. The late 1980s also saw a government-induced slowdown in the development of rural industries, due to the perception that they were competing for scarce resources with the inefficient large-scale state industries. In regions where this growth might have offset declining agricultural incomes by providing alternative employment sources for struggling farm households, there was a sharp decline in rural industrial growth rates.[19]

Simultaneous with this liberalizing of the agricultural economy, there has been a substantial shift in the nature of state assistance to poor farmers. Chinese socialism under Mao never had a formal state welfare system in the countryside. Assistance to the needy in the rural sector was the responsibility of the local collective, through which poor households were guaranteed a basic grain ration (one that they, in fact, "purchased" from the collective on credit). The state's approach to the problem of rural poverty under collectivization was less concerned with providing assistance to the poor than with reducing the numbers needing assistance by instituting projects aimed at increasing the self-sustenance abilities of collectives.[20] Assistance to poor households, in fact, was primarily provided by broader kinship networks and filial obligations among the local population. Thus, by the end of collectivization, only a tiny fraction of the rural population was being supported by collectives.

The state did, however, alleviate the threat of hunger or starvation in regions of chronic poverty through its control of interregional grain transfers. The state's grain procurement policy was understandably a source of much tension and discontent among grain-surplus collectives.[21] It is well known, for instance, that the state enforced an artificially low price for this grain in order to maintain a high investment rate for its heavy industrialization program, and this was a major cause of the overall stagnation of the rural sector during the Maoist era. But up to one-third of the state's procurement grain was resold to grain-deficit rural regions at subsidized prices. Indeed, China's remarkable success in reducing its mortality rate by more than half in less than two decades—three times as fast as comparable countries—can largely be attributed to the success of its egalitarian grain redistribution policies.[22]

The state's grain resale policy to poor and deficit regions was terminated

Fig. 13.7. Village schoolhouse, Guizhou. (Photo by Tim Oakes)

in 1985. Households in these regions must now make up for their deficits by purchasing grain on the open market, at prices that have more than doubled in the past decade.[23] At the same time, with the disbanding of rural collectives, whatever local-level assistance these organizations did provide has largely disappeared in poor regions. Whereas collectives previously functioned more or less as banks, doling out the (admittedly meager) fruits of agricultural production after local welfare needs were met, village governments must now rely on extracting their revenues from households in the form of fees and taxes that are as unpopular as they are evaded. The result has been a breakdown in collective services in poor regions, with education, health care, and poverty relief suffering the most. Once a public good available to all regardless of income, health care is now, for many farm families, feared as a catastrophic expenditure that could drive them into a cycle of unrecoverable debt (see figure 13.8). In regions where a significant amount of off-farm income has contributed to sharp rises in rural incomes, villages have not had any trouble generating the necessary revenue to provide basic assistance to poor families. Indeed, in many regions, such as the Pearl River Delta, wealthy villages have rebuilt many collective welfare institutions, using revenues generated by

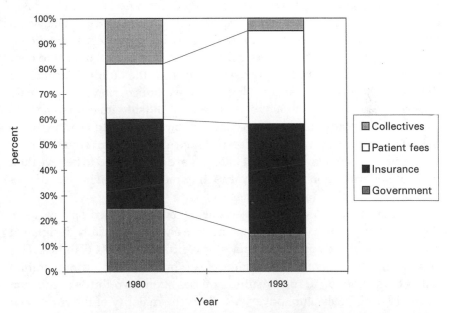

Fig. 13.8. Sources of health care financing

local industries to build schools, recreational facilities, pension programs, and assistance programs to poor families.[24] Yet in the areas where such a "safety net" is needed most, rural households remain atomized and isolated from any broader system of social security.

The state's response to these problems has primarily been directed at regional-based poverty alleviation efforts that concentrate on introducing income-raising schemes for poor households rather than addressing the more fundamental problem of inadequate collective resources for health care, education, and social security. In strikingly Dickensian fashion, the state also encourages those who have "gotten rich first" to not forget their less fortunate neighbors. In 1985, Deng Xiaoping himself urged rich regions to "spare a little to help the poor areas." That the state must resort to invoking the charitable compassion of the newly rich only emphasizes its unwillingness to deal with the more fundamental causes of rural poverty. Instead, poverty alleviation is marshaled as a campaign to enlist the rural poor into contributing to China's capitalist development. Poverty projects thus focus on low-interest loans for such potentially income-enhancing projects as fruit orchards and the provision of plastic sheeting for fields.[25] In regions where markets are limited and agricultural prices remain depressed, such schemes are bound to fail. Illustrating the "jump into the sea of commerce" (*xiahai*) mentality encouraged even in the poorest regions, poverty relief funds distributed to one Guizhou village for health care and education needs were used not to purchase medicine, reduce patient fees, pay teachers' salaries, or provide scholarships to poor students. Rather, the funds were used to improve the building facades for the hospital and school. As the village head explained, they thought making the village more "attractive" to potential outside investors eager to cash in on the ready supply of unemployed farmers would be more beneficial.[26] With the government endorsing special investment zones all over the country, it is little surprise that villagers are encouraged to believe their path to modernization is found in attracting mobile capital instead of providing basic services for themselves.

Official poverty alleviation projects also tend to be based on a regional approach to poverty, concentrating on some eighteen officially designated poor regions of the country, comprising a fifth of China's counties. This approach, based on the conveniences of bureaucratic administration rather than attention to rural realities, misses about two-thirds of the total number living in absolute poverty.[27] Thus, the majority of the rural poor fall outside of official state alleviation programs and must instead rely on conventional sources for sustenance and credit. Not surprisingly, the overall demand for credit vastly outweighs supply. Part of the problem is that banks are unwilling to lend to poor farmers who are now seen as a high credit risk. Instead, the vast majority of rural credit is reserved for industrial enterprises, and in poor regions where rural industrial development is impractical, banks instead lend to urban applicants or even to other regions altogether.[28] For instance, in 1984, when bank lending was deregulated throughout China, Guizhou banks exported over 700 million *yuan* to other provinces in loans, an amount equivalent to 80 percent of that year's total financial revenue for the province. Amazingly, state officials blame this problem not on lending priorities themselves but on the inability of locals to demonstrate their qualifications to borrow.[29] As far as the government is concerned, it is primarily the fault of the farmers that they can't acquire the credit they need to "take off" into the brave new world of "market socialism."

As with the rural market reforms in general, then, the state treats the whole issue of poverty as a problem requiring more marketization, more deregulation, and more efforts to "liberate the mind" of the peasant farmer who lacks "entrepreneurial spirit" and displays an "excessive adherence to the old ways."[30] The result has been not only the widening regional income gap discussed previously but increasing class stratifica-

Fig. 13.9. Village Party secretary's house, Guizhou. (Photo by Tim Oakes)

Fig. 13.10. Most of the houses in the Party Secretary's village (see fig. 13.9) resemble this one. (Photo by Tim Oakes)

tion within rural society in general. To be sure, rural society under Mao saw its own brand of social stratification, based not on income but on access to the redistributive power of the socialist state. Thus, a privileged class of rural cadres emerged during collectivization, cultivating a web of patron–client relationships that have, in many ways, remained in place during the reform era. But the post-Mao era's focus on income generation at the expense of investment in basic social services has resulted in the rapid formation of a rural class structure based on differential access to the means of production. In rural Guizhou, Yunnan, and Guangxi, for example, many households cannot raise enough grain to feed themselves for an entire year. Unable to get credit for the purchase of fertilizers (or, indeed, wary of becoming indebted to relatives or usurers), they must scrape together enough cash each year to make up their grain deficit on the open market. Households lucky enough to have had their children before the single-child family policy was initiated may have the surplus labor power to earn a wage in a nearby town or city (or even a distant coastal city), but for many mountainous villages, additional income-earning opportunities are negligible. One sociologist has estimated that between 5 and 15 percent of the households in these poor regions are caught in this trap of perpetual poverty. Another 10 to 20 percent, on the other hand, have become relatively prosperous and are able to afford all the fertilizer they want, while the remainder of farming households are "getting by."[31]

In China's more prosperous agricultural regions (for example, the grain-rich basins of Hubei and Hunan), rural cadres who became powerful under collectivization through clientelist networks of favors and obligations, have emerged as a new class of nouveaux riche. Despite the government's intention at the outset of rural reforms not to disband completely the collective assets that had been built up under Mao, these have nevertheless fallen under the private control of rural cadres and other households that happened to have the resources to acquire them and the skills to manage them. Thus, assets previously owned by the collective—such as fish ponds, fruit orchards, grasslands, or small-scale rural industries—are now under private control. In the wake of the state's close regulation of rural life under collectives, cadres have stepped in as powerful brokers of local access to scarce inputs and services. "The peasantry still remains dependent upon the goodwill of village and higher-level cadres to get access to fertilizers, credit, new housing sites, and licenses to engage in business, and they frequently need to resort to currying these cadres' favour through gifts and shows of deference."[32] Thus, rural society is in fact stratified by two complementary hierarchies of power. One is still based on differential access to larger channels of resource distribution, while the other is based solely in control of economic assets.

IMPACTS OF FISCAL DECENTRALIZATION

The ease with which local officials occupy new spaces of political and economic power is symptomatic of the broader state's ability to maintain
bureaucratic control while pursuing an agenda of fiscal deregulation and
marketization. China's decentralization of fiscal policy has created both
new opportunities and new difficulties for rural officials. As suggested
earlier, the central government's redistributive effectiveness has declined
considerably, especially with respect to addressing the basic needs of poor
regions. According to one report, "the center is severely strained in its fiscal resources, and its transfers are generally insufficient or ineffective in
raising the growth of capital investment in these poor regions to match the
national level."[33] Since 1980, the trend toward local self-financing has been
a driving force behind widening regional economic disparities. As indicated in table 13.2, the central government's share of the budget has
dropped precipitously, matched by similar declines in revenue as a proportion of GDP. Poor provinces such as Guizhou are faced with growing
fiscal responsibilities and increasingly inadequate revenues. In 1995, for
example, Guizhou's provincial revenues only amounted to 45 percent of
expenditures. At the same time, the center's ability to address regional economic disparities through budgetary manipulation has declined. Of the
center's budgetary transfers to provinces, only quota subsidies are based
on need, and by 1990 these accounted for only 15 percent of total transfers.
Over half of the transfers were earmarked grants, the overwhelming
majority of which were absorbed as price subsidies in grain, oil, and cotton for relatively prosperous urban populations.[34]

In Guizhou, the provincial government has been unable to keep up with
its increasing fiscal responsibilities.[35] By the 1990s, Guizhou was no longer

Table 13.2   China: Expenditure and Revenue (%)

| *Central and Local Shares of Government Expenditure 1955–1995* | | | | | | |
	1955	*1959*	*1965*	*1971*	*1984*	*1990*	*1995*
Central	78.1	47.6	62.2	59.5	46.6	39.8	29.2
Local	21.9	52.4	37.8	40.5	53.4	60.2	70.8
Government revenue as % of GDP					21.6	17.9	10.7

Source: *Zhongguo Tongji Nianjian* (China Statistical Yearbook) (Beijing: Zhongguo Tongji Chubanshe, 1996).

able to transfer its diminishing subsidies to counties and instead was extracting a surplus from them to finance provincial outlays. This has resulted not only in inadequate attention at the local level to agricultural investment and rural poverty but in a proliferation of damaging fees and surcharges on rural households and industries as counties scramble to meet their remittance quotas. One report charges that "in Guizhou, since 1988, the entire rural sector has acquired net remitter status, so that the rural sector may be supporting the urban sector."[36] Poor counties have thus seen very little growth in expenditures, while even relatively wealthy counties are strapped with heavy revenue sharing burdens that dampen whatever comparative advantages they've been able to muster in the reform era.

In an effort to arrest fiscal decline and increase central revenue shares, a new tax-sharing arrangement was introduced by the Ministry of Finance in 1994. This shifted the bulk of turnover taxes (value added tax, business tax, and product tax) to the center and created a new consumption tax on luxury goods, including alcohol and tobacco, also to be remitted directly to the center. This recentralization of revenues has in fact been an ongoing trend throughout the reform era.[37] These developments only exacerbate the financial difficulties of poor regions. Most of the revenue expansion for many counties in Guizhou has come from turnover taxes, and the loss of these indirect revenues in the rural sector will put significant stress on counties to find new sources of income. At the same time, many of the counties in southwest China, where the country's greatest concentrations of rural poverty are found, were able to capitalize on a comparative advantage in tobacco and liquor production in the 1980s. They now face the loss of most of these revenues to the center.

In Guizhou's Taijiang county (see figure 13.1), the need to generate revenue and fulfill provincial remittance quotas led the local government to pursue coastal trading companies for setting up labor-intensive, export-oriented textile factories. By 1994, there were at least three of these operating in the county and dozens throughout the province, all taking advantage of the low wages peasant workers (all of them women) were willing to accept and (paradoxically) the tax concessions county governments made in order to make the deals more lucrative. One Taijiang factory was set up by a Jiangsu company to produce tie-dyed silk cloth to be exported to Japan. It employed about one hundred women, recruited from the countryside, who sat all day tying up thousands of tiny dot patterns on silk. They were paid rmb 6 for every 10,000 ties, and although the manager said they could typically produce 5,000 ties per day, workers on the shop floor told me that the most anyone earned was between rmb 30 and 40 ($3.50–$4.70) per month. This was low pay even by local standards (where the average monthly pay in 1992 was rmb 165).[38] Another Taijiang factory employed a similar number of rural women earning similar wages making embroidered cloth for export to Southeast Asia. I visited a number of factories throughout the region, and in all cases women lived in crowded factory-provided dormitory rooms and were responsible for their own food. Employment averaged about one hundred persons per factory, and wages seldom exceeded RMB¥ 50 ($5.90) per month. Because of special regional policies developed to attract this kind of economic activity, local governments were in fact collecting few tax revenues from these factories.

When asked in 1994, an officer at the Taijiang county government justified these exploitative ventures by stressing that they only represented a first step in modernization. He likened them to a window through which more coastal companies could see the county's investment potential. He said that Taijiang's rural households still had few opportunities to earn a cash income and that these factories would help generate a "commercial consciousness" in the countryside. All that was needed, in other words, was for the peasants to start *wanting* to earn money, and then the county's budget problems would amazingly disappear. He did not believe that future development might be truncated by using Guizhou's countryside purely as a source of cheap labor for enhancing the profitability of coastal companies dabbling in international trade. But by 1996, the county's attitude had changed considerably. The county had refused to renew any leases for the coastal-run factories, citing insufficient pay and poor working conditions. For Taijiang, the previous goal of attracting external investment at any cost had clearly backfired. "We lost money and the workers were treated badly," an officer admitted. Furthermore, the county no longer had any funds available for promoting its own indigenous industrial development in crafts production. The county's annual appropriation for new commercial schemes had been cut due to provincial budgetary difficulties, and what funds they did receive in the form of central development grants were being swallowed up by day-to-day administrative expenditures and salaries for cadres and teachers.

If Taijiang's attempts to cultivate a rural industrialization project backfired, in wealthier regions such schemes can be highly lucrative for local revenue generation. In this regard, county speculation in rural industries is often referred to as "tax farming." The point is that local bureaucracies have grown increasingly involved in income-generating developments.

Far from a liberalized market economy, what has instead been emerging in the countryside is bureaucratic capitalism in a society where political power remains largely the exclusive preserve of a well-entrenched cadre elite. While rural industries, by 1990, constituted one-fourth of China's GNP and employed over a fifth of China's rural workforce (92 million peasant-workers), the wealth they have generated, beyond contributing to the cash incomes of farmers, has not always contributed to improving local social services and welfare. One study of village industry in Sichuan, for example, found that cadres were the dominant shareholders in village factories and that their increasing wealth had become a polarizing force in village communities. Furthermore, benefits of employment and ancillary activities (such as establishing marketing enterprises for factory products in distant cities) were distributed primarily along kinship lines rather than according to the needs of the community on whose land the factory had been built. As one villager put it, "People look at the factory and think the village is very rich. But it has nothing to do with us. Those in the factory have become rich. Most of them are relatives of the cadres and big bosses from outside."[39]

THE FLOATING POPULATION

For Marx, the "floating population" (*liudong renkou*) was that component of the surplus population that, having become redundant due to productivity gains in one sector of the economy, formed a readily available workforce prepared to meet the needs of the next cycle of capital expansion.[40] In China, the *liudong renkou* refers more specifically to those living "temporarily" in a place other than where they are officially registered. The bulk of these people are migrants from the countryside—Marx's "latent surplus population"—who, having become redundant due to the liberalization of the agricultural economy, "follow capital" to wealthier regions where they might sell their labor. Having introduced reforms resulting in increased inequalities and social polarization in the countryside, the state has offered those rural families with sufficient labor power a way out by allowing them to contribute a body or two to the growing pool of cheap labor, China's foremost international comparative advantage. Indeed, many interior local governments actively promote out-migration as their primary strategy for reducing poverty.[41] The unleashed army of underemployed labor has fueled the recent rapid growth of rural and urban

industries and contributed immensely to urban infrastructural developments. In an effort to curb massive migrations to China's booming eastern
coastal cities such as Shanghai and Guangzhou, the government has advocated a policy of urbanization in "small and medium" cities throughout
the interior. While the state remains committed to restricting the pace of
urbanization, much as it did during the Maoist era, conditions in the countryside are severely undermining these efforts. Although the state officially promotes the idea of *litu bulixiang* ("leave the soil, but don't leave the
countryside") through the development of rural industries, China's cities
have benefited in many ways from the army of workers willing to sell their
labor for almost nothing and live in the harshest of conditions while contributing to one of the most rapid urban redevelopment projects in Asia.

Liberalization of migration restrictions began in the early 1980s when
the state allowed rural residents to establish permanent businesses in
small towns.[42] The Chinese state, it should be kept in mind, has always
been wary of the costs of rapid urbanization, and although it needed to
establish outlets for surplus rural labor, it did not want to bear the costs of
additional workers in the cities, where they might require more housing,
improved infrastructure and transportation facilities, along with other
social services that had always been strictly rationed to official urban residents. For this reason, labor mobility reforms began in small towns, where
costs for social services had always been minimal anyway. In 1983, peasants engaged in nonagricultural work in small towns were allowed to
obtain residence status as long as they did not claim any state-supplied
benefits and had secured private accommodation. Officially, these were
known as "households with self-supplied food grain." By 1985, the state
had legalized "temporary residence" throughout all urban centers. At the
same time, the ban on urban enterprises hiring from the countryside was
lifted. The annual quota of official conversions from agricultural to nonagricultural residency status (*nongzhuangfei*) was also raised. This allowed
cities more flexibility in hiring cheap rural labor. Legally, urban migrants
must apply for a "temporary residence permit" (*zhanzhuzheng*) within
three days of arriving in a city. If they plan to stay and work, they must
also apply for a "permit to live elsewhere" (*jizhuzheng*). There is a fee associated with each of these permits, and most reports indicated that roughly
half of the migrant population actually obtains them. Nevertheless, they
remain a significant source of revenue for cities.

Significantly, while the state has enabled greater labor mobility, it has
not relinquished its institutional control over migrant workers; the contin-

uing presence of China's household registration system offers the state a mechanism for manipulating the rural surplus population to meet the needs of capital accumulation and rapid economic growth, yielding what one geographer has called a "two-class urban system."[43] Migrants are treated essentially as "guest workers" in their own country. Many cities have set up their own procedures for managing migrants. In a number of urban places "Blue Cards" (*lanka*) are sold to those who have already been "temporary residents" for some time and have made significant investments in the urban locality. A "Blue Card" is often very expensive and grants all the privileges normally reserved for formal residents, such as schooling, health care, greater opportunities for higher wage employment, and so on. This is tantamount to selling urban residency, and that's exactly what many cities are set on doing, particularly municipal governments that are strapped for cash. By 1994, 3 million urban residence registrations had been sold, generating some rmb 25 billion in revenues for cities. As one political scientist has argued, migrants, in effect, become commodities—in terms of both their labor and their desire for urban residency. Urban citizenship, once an inalienable birthright under Mao, is now for sale.[44]

However, the urban institutional reaction to this phenomenon is quite varied, depending on the city and the particular bureaucracy involved.[45] Units responsible for generating income and not concerned with public order tend to view migrants positively. Those responsible for maintaining order *and* generating revenue tend to have conflicting attitudes toward migrants. These units are given the primary responsibility of controlling the flow of migrants. For example, public security is responsible for maintaining order, yet it also stands to gain by imposing fines, issuing licenses, and even accepting bribes or engaging in extortion. Thus, the marketized environment has bred an unusual amount of tolerance among public security officials toward migrants. Labor and construction bureaus are supposed to protect urban jobs, but they can also help businesses prosper by turning a blind eye to those that hire mostly migrants at greatly reduced wages and without obligations to provide other services like housing or health care for them. Even within single bureaucratic units, upper levels tend to be more concerned with order whereas lower levels are with making money. In Beijing, city officials ordered the demolition of the large semipermanent courtyard houses that had emerged in the migrant squatter settlement known as Zhejiang Village. Local Fengtai district officials, however, refused to comply. Fengtai earns some 40 percent of its revenues from Zhejiang Village. Faced with the insubordination of its lower officials, the city ultimately called on the army to get the job done.

Some officials and scholars in China have proposed eliminating the entire household registration system. Now, however, it's a source of income for many components of the urban state. Having been marketized, household registration has become too valuable to the state and its goals of rapid modernization and development. In this light, the rural reforms themselves have been a huge success for the state in both freeing up a surplus population of desperate laborers and guaranteeing them a future of destitution if they remain on the farm. While urban residents clearly display ambivalence regarding their daily encounters with the unwashed masses from the countryside, many official organs seek to remind the public of how urban living is improved by migrants' willingness to perform the disagreeable tasks shunned by the more "refined" (see Weston, this volume). Marx reserved special scorn for this kind of attitude toward the poor; one can only imagine what he would have thought hearing it from leaders in China's Communist Party itself.[46]

CONCLUSION: CLINTON'S TRAVELS

If China is practicing a kind of capitalism, with the Communist Party overseeing a progression of increasing inequalities that in turn are sending wave upon wave of workers to the front lines of the global assembly line, then it is perhaps not so unusual that the most powerful capitalist state in the world should offer its blessings. President Clinton's reciprocal visit to China in 1998 was significant in symbolizing the U.S. administration's faith in the economic and political success of "constructive engagement." But the critics of Clinton's travels entirely missed the mark as they scrambled to proclaim their righteous indignation over what they saw as a United States endorsement of China's human rights abuses. Clinton's decision to take part in a welcoming ceremony at Tian'anmen Square invited a predictable heaping of scorn on the president over the demise of democracy in China and opened the floodgates for another wave of vitriol in the United States Congress over China's human rights abuses in general. I do not mean to belittle the genuine need for concern over China's lack of democratic political freedoms (see Xiao, this volume). But my suspicion is that the trumpeting by the United States of the human rights cause too often diverts our attention from the commonalities between China and the United States and the forces that increasingly link us together.

Those commonalities are found in the mutual commitments of Jiang and Clinton to open the labors of their countrymen to the questionable rewards of the global marketplace. The Clinton administration has conveniently deluded itself with the fantasy that it is sewing the seeds of liberal democracy in China via capitalist development. Farmers in Guizhou, and workers in Flint, know better. China's reform policies have simply allowed the channels of global capital accumulation to feed the Party-state's insatiable appetite for power (see Xiao, this volume). *This* is a human rights problem that the Clinton administration *and its critics alike* seem unwilling to acknowledge openly. It makes even the mainstream U.S. media squeamish. Little surprise, then, that there was little reporting of a protest march in Hong Kong that took place the morning of President Clinton's arrival in the former colony, the last stop on his nine-day China tour.

As Clinton prepared to meet Jiang Zemin at Hong Kong's new airport, demonstrators marched through Kowloon, burning a U.S. flag and calling for U.S. companies to improve working conditions in their factories in China (see Weston, this volume). Labor activist Han Dongfang was quoted saying, "We criticize Bill Clinton for talking about human rights and doing nothing about it." Had he been referring to Clinton's failure to not attend the Tian'anmen ceremony, his group's protest march may have generated more interest in the U.S. press. Certainly, it would have caught the attention of those U.S. politicians eager to proclaim, once again, their own commitments to "freedom and democracy." But he was referring to the human rights of workers, rights about which the United States and China alike remain clearly ambivalent. As they marched, the demonstrators chanted, "Workers' rights are human rights!" and carried flags that read: "Stop US businesses in China from creating a workshop of sweat and blood."[47]

U.S. businesses, of course, have had plenty of help in their expropriation of China's surplus labor value. Organized labor—that pesky thorn in the side of U.S. corporate interests—remains conveniently illegal in China, courtesy of the Communist Party (see both Weston and Xiao, this volume). As the Chinese state itself increasingly emulates the profit-seeking behavior of a global corporation, we are faced with the glaring fact that human rights are not merely a civil or political problem. Certainly, they are not just a Chinese problem. They are more profoundly a capitalist problem, a political-economic problem of globalization, the responsibility for which the United States itself must be indicted with at least as much stricture as that which we more conveniently reserve for nondemocratic states such as China.

NOTES

Thanks to Lionel Jensen, Tim Weston, and an anonymous reviewer for their helpful comments on an earlier draft of this paper. Fieldwork for parts of this paper occurred in 1993–1994 and 1996 with the generous assistance of the National Science Foundation and the Committee on Scholarly Communication with China.

1. John Kifner, "Mao's Heir Finds Path: Wall Street," *New York Times*, November 1, 1997. The image of Jiang ringing the bell at Wall Street was echoed a year and a half later when Prime Minister Zhu Rongji visited the Nasdaq-Amex market and presented a wooden bull to the chairman of the National Association of Security Dealers. See Joseph Kahn, "China Leader Concentrates on Capitalism in New York," *New York Times*, April 14, 1999.

2. Seth Faison, "US Hosts' Urging Seems to Toughen Chinese on Rights," *New York Times*, November 2, 1997.

3. That U.S. business interests have come to dominate U.S. policies toward China became even clearer during Prime Minister Zhu Rongji's trip to the United States in April 1999, the result of which was the decision of the Clinton Administration—under pressure from both Zhu Rongji and U.S. business interests—to quicken approval of China's entry into the World Trade Organization. See David Sanger, "How Push by China and US Business Won over Clinton," *New York Times*, April 15, 1999.

4. This aspect of Jiang's visit to the United States was made explicitly clear in a state-produced film titled *Across the Pacific*. Drawing on images of him ringing the bell at Wall Street, standing at Clinton's side and fielding questions from the U.S. press, speaking English at Harvard, dressed to the nines at a White House banquet, the film portrayed Jiang as a world statesman of a rank befitting the leader of an up-and-coming superpower. See Erik Eckholm, "Before Clinton Visit, Propaganda Movie Stars Chinese President," *New York Times*, June 18, 1998.

5. Many thanks to an official in the Guizhou provincial government, who shall remain anonymous, for relating this information (personal interview, Guiyang, November 9, 1996).

6. Karl Marx, *Capital: A Critique of Political Economy*, Ben Fowkes, trans. (New York: Vintage, 1977 [1867]), 784.

7. See Jiang Zemin, "Upholding the Banner of Deng's Theory," *Beijing Review*, vol. 40, no. 34 (August 25–31, 1997): Internet edition (http://www.chinanews.org/bjreview/); and Wen Li, "Jiang's Speech Held As the Political Declaration of the Present CPC Leadership," in *Beijing Review*, vol. 40, no. 34, Internet edition.

8. Li Ji, "Enterprise Ownership with Chinese Characteristics," *Beijing Review*, vol. 40, no. 37 (September 15–21, 1997): Internet edition (http://www.chinanews.org/bjreview/).

9. Yin Xiaohuang, "China's Gilded Age," *Atlantic Monthly* (April 1994): 42.

10. Yin Xiaohuang, "China's Gilded Age," 44.

11. David Goodman, "The People's Republic of China: The Party-State, Capitalist Revolution, and New Entrepreneurs," in *The New Rich in Asia*, Richard Robison and David Goodman, eds. (London: Routledge, 1996), 226.

12. Maurice Meisner, "The Other China," *Current History*, vol. 96, no. 611 (September 1997): 264.

13. Wang Xiaoqiang and Bai Nanfeng, *The Poverty of Plenty*, Angela Knox, trans. (New York: St. Martin's Press, 1991), 38.

14. By official count, the proportion of the rural population living in poverty declined from 27 percent (or roughly 200 million people) in 1979 to 12.3 percent (or 102 million) in 1985. By 1988, however, official figures indicated 14.8 percent of the rural population living below poverty line; economist Carl Riskin puts the actual number for 1988 somewhat lower at 12.7 percent. See Carl Riskin, "Rural Poverty in Post-Reform China," in *The Third Revolution in the Chinese Countryside*, Ross Garnaut, Guo Shutian, and Ma Guonan, eds. (Cambridge: Cambridge University Press, 1996), 69. See also Barry Naughton, *Growing Out of the Plan: Chinese Economic Reform, 1978–1993* (Cambridge: Cambridge University Press, 1996), 142.

15. Ke Bingshen, "Regional Inequality in Regional Development," in *The Third Revolution in the Chinese Countryside*, Garnaut, Guo, and Ma, eds., 247–248.

16. Ke Bingshen, "Regional Inequality in Regional Development," 251, and Riskin, "Rural Poverty in Post-Reform China," 73.

17. Elizabeth Croll, *From Heaven to Earth: Images and Experiences of Development in China* (London: Routledge, 1994), 137; Yin, "China's Gilded Age," 48.

18. On fertilizer applications, see Zhang Wenbao and Zuo Changsheng, "Fertiliser Price," in *The Third Revolution in the Chinese Countryside*, Garnaut, Guo, and Ma, eds., 102.

19. Croll, *From Heaven to Earth: Images and Experiences of Development in China*, 145; David Zweig, "Rural Industry: Constraining the Leading Growth Sector in China's Economy," in *China's Economic Dilemmas in the 1990s: The Problems of Reforms, Modernization, and Interdependence*, U.S. Congress Joint Economic Committee, ed. (Washington, D.C.: United States Congress, 1991), 422.

20. Althar Hussain and Stephen Feuchtwang, "The People's Livelihood and the Incidence of Poverty," in *Transforming China's Economy in the Eighties, Vol. I: The Rural Sector, Welfare, and Employment*, Althar Hussain and Thierry Pairault, eds. (Boulder, Colo.: Westview, 1988), 38; Riskin, "Rural Poverty in Post-Reform China," 72.

21. See Jean Oi, *State and Peasant in Contemporary China: The Political Economy of Village Government* (Berkeley: University of California Press, 1989).

22. Hussain and Feuchtwang, "The People's Livelihood and the Incidence of Poverty," 60–68.

23. Croll, *From Heaven to Earth: Images and Experiences of Development in China,* 145.

24. Zhou Daming and Zhang Yingqiang, "Rural Urbanization in Guangdong's Pearl River Delta," in *Farewell to Peasant China: Rural Urbanization and Social Change in the Late Twentieth Century,* Gregory Guldin, ed. (Armonk, N.Y.: M. E. Sharpe, 1997), 71–122.

25. Croll, *From Heaven to Earth: Images and Experiences of Development in China,* 154.

26. Pan Nianying, *Bainian Gaopo* (A Century in Gaopo) (Guiyang: Renmin Chubanshe, 1997), 205–206.

27. Riskin, "Rural Poverty in Post-Reform China," 72.

28. Croll, *From Heaven to Earth: Images and Experiences of Development in China,* 154; Riskin, "Rural Poverty in Post-Reform China," 71; Jonathan Unger, " 'Rich Man, Poor Man': The Making of New Classes in the Countryside," in *China's Quiet Revolution: New Interactions Between State and Society,* David Goodman and Beverly Hooper, eds. (Melbourne: Longman Cheshire, 1994), 49. See also: Jonathan Unger and Jean Xiong, "Life in the Chinese Hinterlands under the Rural Economic Reforms," *Bulletin of Concerned Asian Scholars,* vol. 22, no. 2 (June 1990): 4–17.

29. Wang and Bai, *The Poverty of Plenty,* 71.

30. Wang and Bai, *The Poverty of Plenty,* 38.

31. Unger, " 'Rich Man, Poor Man': The Making of New Classes in the Countryside," 49.

32. Unger, " 'Rich Man, Poor Man': The Making of New Classes in the Countryside," 56. See also Anita Chan, Richard Madsen, and Jonathan Unger, *Chen Village under Mao and Deng* (Berkeley: University of California Press, 1992), chapter 10; Jean Oi, "Rational Choices and Attainment of Wealth and Power in the Countryside," in *China's Quiet Revolution,* Goodman and Hooper, eds., 64–79.

33. Hanson C. K. Leung and Kam Wing Chan, "Chinese Regional Development Policies: A Comparative Reassessment," presented at the Annual Meetings of the Canadian Asian Studies Association, Winnipeg (April 1986), 44.

34. *Guizhou Nianjian* (Guizhou Yearbook) (Guiyang: Renmin Chubanshe, 1996), 60; Christine Wong, Christopher Heady, and Wing T. Woo, *Fiscal Management and Economic Reform in the People's Republic of China* (Hong Kong: Oxford University Press, 1995), 96.

35. Between 1988 and 1994, Guizhou received annual fixed quota subsidies of rmb 740 million, representing a significant proportional decline in central transfers as the provincial budget expanded. As indicated in a 1995 Asian Development Bank report, in the early 1980s subsidies financed nearly 60 percent of Guizhou's total budget. By 1993, this figure was down to less than 20 percent. In 1995, 70 percent of total fixed capital investments were financed by the province, a significant

increase over the 1992 figure of 48 percent. See Wong, Heady, and Woo, *Fiscal Management and Economic Reform in the People's Republic of China*, 92; Christine Wong, ed., *Financing Local Government in the People's Republic of China* (Manila: Asian Development Bank, 1995); *Guizhou Nianjian*, 60; *Guizhou Tongji Nianjian* (Guizhou Statistical Yearbook) (Beijing: Zhongguo Tongji Chubanshe, 1993), 102.

36. Wong, *Financing Local Government*, 11.

37. Whereas in 1980 the center collected only 19 percent of state revenues, by 1994, it was collecting nearly 58 percent. See *Zhongguo Tongji Nianjian* (China Statistical Yearbook) (Beijing: Zhongguo Tongji Chubanshe, 1995), 21.

38. *Guizhou Tongji Nianjian*, 95.

39. Yang Minchuan, "Reshaping Peasant Culture and Community: Rural Industrialization in a Chinese Village," *Modern China*, vol. 20, no. 2 (1994): 169–170.

40. Karl Marx, *Capital: A Critique of Political Economy*, 794–796.

41. Elisabeth Croll and Huang Ping, "Migration for and against Agriculture in Eight Chinese Villages," *China Quarterly*, no. 149 (March 1997): 128–146.

42. For a comprehensive analysis of migration and urbanization policies during China's reforms, see Kam Wing Chan, *Cities with Invisible Walls* (Hong Kong: Oxford University Press, 1994).

42. Kam Wing Chan, "Post-Mao China: A Two-Class Urban Society in the Making," *International Journal of Urban and Regional Research*, vol. 20, no. 1 (1996): 134–150.

44. Dorothy J. Solinger, *Contesting Citizenship in Urban China* (Berkeley: University of California Press, 1999). See also Lisa Hoffman and Liu Zhongquan, "Rural Urbanization on the Liaodong Peninsula," in Guldin, *Farewell to Peasant China: Rural Urbanization and Social Change in the Late Twentieth Century*, 175–176; and Bruce Jacobs, "Shanghai: An Alternative Centre?," in *China's Provinces in Reform: Class, Community and Political Culture*, David S. G. Goodman, ed. (London: Routledge, 1997), 183.

45. This argument is put forth in Solinger, *Contesting Citizenship in Urban China*, 57–99.

46. Marx, *Capital: A Critique of Political Economy*, 800–801.

47. Associated Press, "Hong Kong Protest Faults Clinton," *New York Times*, July 2, 1998.

SUGGESTED READINGS

Anita Chan, Richard Madsen, and Jonathan Unger, *Chen Village under Mao and Deng* (Berkeley: University of California Press, 1992).

Cheng Tiejun and Mark Selden, "The Origins and Social Consequences of China's Hukou System," *The China Quarterly* 139 (1994): 644–668.

"China: From Communism to Capitalism." Special issue of *Current History*, vol. 98, no. 629 (September 1999).

Maurice Meisner, *The Deng Xiaoping Era: An Inquiry into the Fate of Chinese Socialism, 1978–1994* (New York: Hill and Wang, 1996).

Barry Naughton, *Growing Out of the Plan: Chinese Economic Reform, 1978–1993* (Cambridge: Cambridge University Press, 1996).

Dorothy J. Solinger, *Contesting Citizenship in Urban China* (Berkeley: University of California Press, 1999).

Edward Steinfeld, "The Asian Financial Crisis: Beijing's Year of Reckoning," *Washington Quarterly*, vol. 21, no. 3 (1998): 37–51.

Jonathan Unger and Jean Xiong, "Life in the Chinese Hinterlands under the Rural Economic Reforms," *Bulletin of Concerned Asian Scholars*, vol. 22, no. 2 (April-June 1990): 4–17.

Wang Feiling, "Floaters, Moonlighters, and the Underemployed: A National Labor Market with Chinese Characteristics," *Journal of Contemporary China*, vol. 7, no. 19 (1998): 459–475.

Wang Xiaoqiang and Bai Nanfeng, *The Poverty of Plenty*, Angela Knox, trans. (New York: St. Martin's Press, 1991).

David Zweig, "Internationalizing China's Countryside: The Political Economy of Exports from Rural Industry," *China Quarterly* 128 (1991): 716–741.

14

Border Crossings:

Chinese Writing, in Their World and Ours

Howard Goldblatt

> Novelists are totally unethical beings: when the truth of fact and the needs of
> fiction conflict, the novelist will always favour the latter.
> —David Lodge, The Practice of Writing

Novels and poems. Why do we read them? How do we read them? A puz-
zling question, perhaps, but the range of answers can be instructive when
dealing with the literary output of China and with its reception in the
West. Historically, that is, throughout the twentieth century, the socio-
political intentions and applications of Chinese literature have frequently
overshadowed the belletristic for a "foreign" audience; read more as a
window onto contemporary events and society than for its aesthetic or
entertainment values, modern and contemporary fiction and verse have
tended to follow, and sometimes subvert, the political and ideological
twists and turns of the nation. Whether because of the nature of the writing or because China, like so many countries, appears so culturally remote
to Western readers, those few novels, stories, and poems that migrate
beyond China's geographical and linguistic borders attract an audience
made up primarily of those who wish to "learn about China" in a more
reader-friendly format than a textbook. Take, for instance, the following
comments from a *New York Times* review of Mo Yan's "breakthrough"
novel, *Red Sorghum*, "In 'Red Sorghum,' Mo Yan introduces Western readers to the unfamiliar culture of provincial China through dozens of vivid
characters. By the end, they and Mo Yan have put Northeast Gaomi Township securely on the map of world literature,"[1] or on Jia Pingwa's *Turbu-*

lence, "The Chinese countryside, home to nearly a billion peasants, is described in ways that are both instructive and moving."

That "instructive" precedes "moving" is in itself instructive, for that implies a predetermined, and probably nonliterary, motivation for coming to the Chinese novel in the first place. Novels as textbooks, fiction as sociology, facts over imagination. That, in spite of the verity that "literature is not the best way to learn about other lands and cultures, especially when the literature appears in our own culture's forms, that is, when the literature is familiar in form . . . bent on telling a story in a way we like our stories told."[2] At the risk of seeming overly idealistic, it seems to me that writing from another culture, at its best, tells us not so much about that particular culture as it does about the similarities and dissimilarities of individuals who are nurtured in that culture with those from other societies; a fine point, perhaps, but significant, in that human truths tend not, I believe, to be restricted by spatial or temporal borders, while the various ways to those truths and how they are articulated and experienced give them greater universal meaning.

Sometimes, of course, the works of Chinese authors are praised for their artistic achievements, if not always on their own terms, as illustrated in *Kirkus Reviews:*

> Balzac and Zola would have recognized a kindred spirit in our author, whose extraordinary pictures of the extremes to which human beings drive one another and themselves seem scarcely inferior to their own.

or, as the novelist Amy Tan states on the cover of *Red Sorghum:*

> Having read *Red Sorghum*, I believe Mo Yan deserves a place in world literature. His imagery is astounding, sensual and visceral. His story is electrifying and epic. I am convinced that this book will successfully leap over the international boundaries that many translated works face . . . and that his voice will find its way into the heart of the American reader, just as Kundera and García Márquez have.

This essay has been undertaken in part to supply a "non-Other" context, however superficial or preliminary, to contemporary writing from China, and in part as an introduction for readers who come to that writing in translation, for whatever reason. As a translator first and a critic second, my personal biases will become transparently obvious. That I tend to deal with works and authors I have translated is not as self-serving as it may seem; in a field of endeavor that has attracted few practitioners, I am fortunate to have been free to select and work on much of the best and most appealing fiction written in Chinese, and I cite it here for the reasons that drew me to it, not for the results of the translation. In the role of cultural mediator, for that is what a literary translator becomes, the responsibilities toward authors, texts, and readers are themselves mediated by the pleasures obtained from wrestling with words, concepts, and images from one culture and clothing them in new garb for another.

FROM THERE . . .

Much has changed in Chinese literature since the days of political and ideological extremism ended in the mid 1970s. Writers, who had been hobbled by Maoist demands for socialist-realist literary production for nearly three decades, began to enjoy a bit more freedom in the choice of subject matter and modes of writing, a phenomenon that has continued to the present, with a brief but tragic interruption in June 1989. Poets and novelists, in line with Dengist liberalization/reform policies and a bit of double-edged neglect during the economic boom, have continually pushed the envelope, taking on increasingly controversial topics and experimenting with a variety of writing styles.[3]

While cognizant of the risk of essentialism when characterizing the corpus of writing that has emerged from China over the past decade, I think it is constructive to identify some of its most prominent features, especially in regard to fiction, which is still the most commercially popular, the most engaging, and perhaps the liveliest genre. Foremost among these features is a move away from mimetic realism, that which strives to imitate the real world, toward new forms of expression. The critic David Wang agrees:

> The best contemporary Chinese fiction cannot be classified as realistic in a traditional sense. For those used to seeing modern Chinese fiction as a supplement to social history or as a predictable Jamesonian "national allegory" of sociopolitics, the fiction produced since the late eighties may tell a different story. It shows that literature in the post–Tian'anmen period has not harked back to the old formulas of reflectionism. Precisely because of their refusal either to remain silent or to cry out in an acceptably "realist" way, the new writers see life as an ongoing process, a conglomeration of possibilities and impossibilities. Precisely because of their inability to believe in the one true path through realism to modernism and then postmodernism, or in any

melodramatically predictable path through history, contemporary Chinese writers promise new and lively beginnings for the end-of-the-century Chinese imagination.[4]

These "lively beginnings" are most notably anchored in China's past. In encountering novels and stories from fin-de-siècle China, one is struck by an obsession with history and with memory, individual and collective. That is so, I think, for a variety of reasons: First, successful and widely read contemporary writers, most of them in their thirties and forties, are fascinated by China's past, having lost so much of their recent history through the political process. Second, as the cultural critic Rey Chow has stated, "the weight of history bears upon the writing of 'fiction' in such a way as to force one to reflect critically on the space in which the Chinese intellectual has had to live. This is a space without fresh air."[5] Recapturing that past and subjecting it to renewed scrutiny is at the core of some of the most successful fiction in the post-Mao era.

Prominent among this group of writers is Mo Yan, whose re-creations of early twentieth-century Chinese history, especially the war years, in such powerful and panoramic novels as *Red Sorghum* evoke a sense of futility and loss.[6] By merging myth and reality, biographical and historical incidents, heroic and mundane activities, Mo Yan makes a case for cultural degeneration while drawing attention to the way the past is reconstructed, a narrative process that has been characterized as "one that oscillates and mediates between remembered history and imaginative reconstruction." Referring to his hometown and, perhaps, by extension, all of China, as "the most beautiful and most repulsive, most unusual and most common, most sacred and most corrupt, most heroic and most bastardly, hardest-drinking and hardest-loving place in the world" (4), he cries out against China's blind rush to modernity, the human cost of which appears to be civility and morality: "Now I stood before Second Grandma's grave, affecting the hypocritical display of affection I had learned from high society, with a body immersed so long in the filth of urban life that a foul stench oozed from my pores" (356). Modernity as a national icon takes a substantial drubbing from this "peasant writer," while historiography, and perhaps history itself, is problematized, to the horror of the literary establishment and the government it represents.

For writers like Mo Yan, and so many of his contemporaries, history is neither circular nor linear but random and shifting, until the boundaries between past and present blur into obscurity. By denying history its traditional authority, they raise fundamental questions about contemporary life, politics, and values. Historical fiction, once a refuge for writers intent on buttressing or criticizing specific politics or ideologies, has become a showcase of human nature, frequently at its most despicable. The past is now open to a plethora of interpretations by China's writers, who refuse to accept official versions and, in the most extreme cases, do not admit the "possibility" of knowing history at all. The sanctity of history, we learn from these Chinese authors, exists in its mystery and in its possibilities, not in either its glorification or manipulation by ideologues.

Often characterized as members of a lost generation, writers such as these, whose childhood and teen years were spent "making (or, for the youngest, playing at) revolution" in the service of Mao, only to be abandoned by him and left to contemplate their enormous losses in education, family cohesion, and the little pleasures of life, turned naturally to the theme of alienation, especially in the wake of the Tian'anmen Massacre of 1989. Coupled with the heady delights of commercialization, this trend has produced a coterie of novelists and poets whose work reveals a place where surface stability uneasily masks a society in turmoil and whose cynicism has alarmed the official literary community while capturing a considerable readership of like-minded urbanites.

Themes (contents), of course, do not tell all the story. As China stumbles along toward modernity and international respect, its writers have become more experimental, more daring, more self-consciously iconoclastic than ever before. Topics and a host of hybrid narrative strategies once considered taboo now inform the works of many of the writers of fin-de-siècle China. Opaque language, self-reflective and disjointed narratives have, along with unthinkable acts and ideas—from cannibalism to perverted sex—become trademarks of the most conspicuous among them. While they are sometimes accused of pandering to Western tastes, either by filling their work with sensationalist descriptions or dissident views, or by consciously striving for writing with a high degree of "translatability,"[7] these writers are nevertheless becoming more defiant and much more self-assured.

It may seem bewildering that they are published at all, given the seemingly subversive nature of much of their writing; indeed, some of their work does disappear from bookstores under withering attacks by conservative critics. Yet so long as they do not openly attack the Party and leadership or call for a new system of government, the limitations of book distribution, contrasted, say, with movies, and, one hopes, the unrelenting pressure of freedom-to-write advocates and the attention of readers around the world conspire to keep iconoclasm alive and visible. While some of these writers must sometimes publish their work first in Taiwan or, less often, in foreign translation, none with whom I am familiar has yet wound up in jail for a novel, a story, or a poem.

The issue of Western influence, not just on the exploration of nontraditional, even corrupting, topics, but on styles of writing as well, has been widely, and emotionally, debated. Few will deny the influence of the magic-realists of Latin America or the more self-conscious collagistic writings of the Czech novelist Milan Kundera and the like on aspiring writers in the wake of the Cultural Revolution, yet those influences have led to transformations more readily suited to the linguistic, semantic, and cultural realities of China. The highly allusive, myth-laden, and enigmatic stories of a clutch of avant-gardists have plumbed the descriptive powers of the Chinese language as authors have set out to shock and alienate a readership more comfortable with a "reality-anchored" style of writing, whether it is "hard-core" realism or grotesque exposé. In speaking of the avant-garde school, the critic Jing Wang has written:

> [I]ts irreverent attitude toward history and culture is decipherable only when seen against the historical context from which it emerged [the economic boom of the late 1980s]. The young heretics' fabrication of a rootless subject, devoid of memory, was not a mindless pursuit. The making of a subject without a core who narrates without a purpose was a highly subversive act. What the avant-gardists sneered at was the sublime subject construed for a decade by humanist writers and intellectuals. Theirs was a socio-politically centered and culturally invested subject invigorated with a teleological and utopian vision toward life . . . Posing as seditious elements in the post-Mao era, the avant-gardists adopted an impious attitude toward history. Those who look in their stories for trenchant critiques of the Cultural Revolution will be disappointed. What they display, instead, is a voracious appetite for the clinical depiction of unmotivated violence, which represents a metonymy, rather than just a metaphor, of the historical cataclysm of the Cultural Revolution.[8]

In the sweep of Chinese literary history of this century, this constitutes an unprecedented change in attitude. In characterizing the goals of writers from the pre-communist period, the critic C. T. Hsia has observed that "what distinguishes this 'modern' phase of Chinese literature alike from the traditional and Communist phases is rather its burden of moral contemplation: its obsessive concern with China as a nation afflicted with a spiritual disease and therefore unable to strengthen itself or change its set ways of inhumanity."[9] As the twenty-first century begins, that no longer holds true, at least not for members of the post–Cultural Revolution generation. One defiantly individualistic novelist, for instance, has claimed tersely: "I can't stand people with a sense of mission."[10] Concurrent with recent changes in the way novelists are writing these days are changes in the way they view their role as artists. No longer interested in placing their pens in the service of society, which seems to be unraveling in the midst of economic reforms intended to fulfill the national dream of becoming rich and powerful, they view the xenophobic zeal of their parents' generation with skepticism at best, contempt at worst. They see themselves as independent artists whose works can, and should, appeal to readers and viewers all over the world.[11] In their truth-telling about contemporary and historical China, they present a picture of a nation that is turning away from its past and demanding new paths to an urbanized, entrepreneurial, less static future; it may turn out that in the long run they are appreciated less in their own country than elsewhere.

In fact, in this era of increasing globalization and information overload, these young writers speak to the rest of the world precisely because they no longer care to speak *for* China. The common thread of misanthropy running through much of their work and the emphasis on skewed, anti-Confucian family relations, including incest, rape, murder, voyeurism, and more, underscore a belief that they are no more responsible for social instability in their country than are entrepreneurs who want only to get rich, students who want only to leave, or petty bureaucrats who want only to enlarge themselves at public expense. Whether their pessimistic views of China turn out to be prophetic, mimetic, or even wrong, it is now as hard to make arguments for a benign Chinese exoticism as it was to evoke visions of a genteel, kimono-clad Japan in the wake of novels by "postmodernists" Murakami Haruki and Murakami Ryu, and even the trendy Banana Yoshimoto, who speaks to the fantasies and perplexities of her thirty-something generation.

In the urban centers of China, where images have eroded the power of ideas and where the pace and nature of MTV, rock concerts, and soap operas dominate culture, darkly cinematic writings are winning over a materialistic and cynical readership that is caught up in a rush to embrace capitalist consumerism and experience as much decadence as they can squeeze into their young lives.

The reader will note that up to this point I have focused on fiction, both because its narrative possibilities, its spatial and temporal sweep, more neatly accommodate the demands of national modernity and more closely capture (or subvert) the *zeitgeist* of the age, and, of course, because a lot more people read novels and stories—and watch the movies that are adapted from them—than go to the theater or curl up with a book of verse. With the exception of small coteries of intellectuals and esthetes who write, read, and view performances of contemporary Chinese plays—many of which are performed only outside the country—drama has fallen on hard times in the People's Republic and, for that matter, other Chinese communities. If the term *avant garde* has a home, it is not in the Chinese novel or short story, but on the stages and in the chap books that struggle to retain a dwindling audience/readership. Gao Xingjian, now a full-fledged expatriate in Paris, is both the best-known and the most prolific dramatist working in Chinese today; his recent plays, extremely opaque and accessible only to the most dedicated viewers and critics, are performed in Europe and America to small but enthusiastic audiences. Several Taiwanese and Hong Kong dramatists, plus a few on the mainland, keep the experiment going, and while their work is occasionally translated into Western languages, it does not travel well.[12]

Poets, on the other hand, do attract readers in the original and in translation. Language, of course, is the supreme barrier, for the highly allusive, concise nature of Chinese is a constant frustration to translators, whose creative talents are strained to the limit. Much in the mold of Western poets such as John Ashbery, whose quest to tease the most out of poetic language has taken him into "slippery syntax, elusive personae, narrative uncertainty, the blending of incongruous dictions,"[13] today's poets from the Cultural Revolution generation are turning more inward, more subjective, and more elusive in their writing. What was once characterized as "misty poetry" has, for many at least, become a dense fog through which beauty pokes here and there without ever forming a recognizable whole.

Only one poet, Bei Dao, has had his work published in the West to any significant degree. And he, like a disproportionate number of poets from the People's Republic, has lived in the West in exile since the bloodshed in Beijing a decade ago.[14] It is, in fact, the plight of the displaced artist that most compellingly informs, and internationalizes, contemporary Chinese poetry, at least that which is published in Western languages. Some poets have begun writing in English; most, however, have continued to write in Chinese while living abroad, becoming more nostalgic and more cynical as their exile deepens.[15]

. . . TO HERE

Writing in the *New York Times* (June 18, 1998), Martin Arnold states that "the sale of foreign translations in the United States is generally like a nearly empty can of shaving cream: a little air and a few bubbles." As recently as 1990, the percentages of all translated titles were nearly 10 percent for France, over 25 percent for Italy, and under 3 percent for the United States; no figures are available for China, although the number is surely quite high. While this points to the growing influence of English-language production throughout the world, it also leads one to speculate that cultural xenophobia is alive and well in the United States.

The implications are clear: The selection criteria—who to introduce, what to translate, and when to do so—are critical, if Chinese writers are to receive even a fraction of the attention they deserve. And it is virtually impossible for contemporary Chinese writing to enter the Western literary mainstream, as have, for instance, the novels of Gabriel García Márquez, Mario Vargas Llosa, Milan Kundera, and others. As Rey Chow points out:

> While the "world" significance of modern Chinese literature derives from its status as minority discourse, it is precisely this minority status that makes it so difficult for modern Chinese literature to be legitimized as "world" literature, while other *national* literatures, notably English, French, and Russian, have had much wider claims to an international modernity in spite of their historical and geographical specificity.[16]

Without a broad and representative corpus of fiction and verse available in translation, Chinese books cannot exert much artistic influence on Western writers. Which takes us back to the prior issue of selection, the one area in which translators can make a difference. But before examining the particulars of what gets translated, and why, it is worth our time to look at some underlying concerns about literary translation in general.

In an essay devoted to an exploration of the latest crop of English-language translations of Chinese fiction, the critic Kam Louie quotes Liu Sola, a well-known (and reasonably well-translated) Chinese novelist who has asserted "the popular proposition that only Chinese can fully appreciate Chinese literature—no matter how skilled the translator, foreigners can never fully understand Chinese writing since they have not experienced the Cultural Revolution, the anti-Japanese War, or the recent reform policies." Complaining, perhaps in contradictory fashion, that "the world has been Westernized to a degree where everything is judged from the perspective of Europe/America," Liu expresses "the frustrations felt by some Chinese writers at the tardy and often reluctant recognition of their works on the international literary scene."[17] While sympathizing with the author's frustrations—who wouldn't?—both Louie and I take strong exception to the claim that cultural interchange is an impossibility, even between China and the West. Beyond Liu's apparent negation of the power of the imagination, what lies at the heart of this debate is the dialectic between national/indigenous peculiarities and universal issues of humanity. Although the concept of a "world literature" may be too laden with economic, even imperialist and hegemonic baggage, too insular a view of cultural boundaries smacks of cultural relativism, wherein the experiences of one community cannot be understood, appreciated, or shared by another.[18] Furthermore, Liu's argument leads too easily, and quite uncomfortably, to similar restrictions on age, gender, class, and more. It is not somewhere we want to go if literature is to remain a viable form of "interchange."

To be sure, the nature and quality of the translated "product" play an important role in the possibility of translinguistic/transcultural exchange. Quality, easily recognized in only the very best and the very worst translations, is too reliant upon subjective criteria for us to consider here. Needless to say, such concerns as fidelity (getting it "right"), understandability, and literariness determine how well a text is rendered from one language into another. On the other hand, the goals and approaches of a translator can be readily determined. Some observers and practitioners of translation insist that a translator is obligated to bring the reader toward the author and not the other way around. To them, a "foreignized text" (a literal translation, for lack of a better word) has become an ideological necessity, a work that happily disrupts cultural codes in the target language, unlike a domesticated (or literary) translation, which is an appropriation of a foreign culture that denies the opportunity of revealing stylistic possibilities in one's own language that are different from the original.

The "literary" school, exemplified by works that read as if they were actually written in the target language, appears to be winning the publishing lottery, because those are the translations that emerge from the editorial offices of commercial and university presses; whether one celebrates that trend or laments it, the fact remains that "readable" translations of "translatable" books are the ones that get published.

So what does the English-language reader of contemporary Chinese writing have to look forward to? I shall end this essay with some answers to that question, based upon my personal experience as a translator. To that end, I shall focus my examination on three recent, and quite disparate, novels on which I have worked.

Over the past two decades, I have been involved in the production of two dozen or more translations of modern and contemporary Chinese fiction, and while the results of those endeavors can in no way reflect all the literary twists and turns in post-Mao China, they fairly represent my own tastes in literature, some of the strictures within which I work, and, most important, the essence of Chinese novels and short stories to which English-language readers have been exposed.[19]

Contemporary writing dates from the early 1980s. The earliest creations of the post–Cultural Revolution period, while dealing with issues of reform in the Dengist era, were not all that different from the socialist-realist writing that had monopolized the first three decades of the People's Republic. Oh, we Western readers were pleased to see that the ideologues were no longer in the spotlight, that reformers were beginning to get their way, and that just plain folk could finally fall in love with something other than a tractor. But the themes and the writing style—hardcore, representational realism—continued to reflect Party and governmental policy; in other words, these novels and many more like them from the early to mid-1980s fulfilled the role of state-sponsored art (if this sounds harsh, it must be remembered that virtually all professional writers at this time were, in fact, on the national payroll and were well paid for their efforts).[20] No breakthrough yet, although more liberal views of sexuality, the autonomy of the individual, and unflattering descriptions of the behavior of Party and government representatives were beginning to appear, however tentatively.

Not until the arrival of members of the generation who were children or teenagers during the Cultural Revolution and who were just beginning their writing careers when the Tian'anmen Massacre of June 4, 1989, occurred did a remarkable change in the very nature of writing take place. Holding themselves blameless for the horrific excesses of the Maoist era and finding great intellectual and creative stimulation from the nascent internationalist climate in (the cities of) China, they began producing works that excited domestic readers as well as those of us who, in order to practice our craft, had been seeing ourselves as unwitting supporters of "socialist art," that is, "portrayals of the social state and social space that corresponds to reality and to the possibilities hidden in reality."[21]

It is now possible to choose works to translate based primarily on aesthetic or other literary criteria, although political and market considerations continue to play a role. While it may be true that more critical or
darker works are chosen over works that paint a rosier picture of historical or contemporary Chinese society, it is also highly likely that those
works are more artistically and intellectually satisfying. I do not think
that literature is well served if the translator's choices are ideologically
motivated.

As post-Deng turned into postmodern, the very ethos of literary writing, at least among a talented coterie of experimental and often self-indul-
gent young men and women, changed dramatically. As I implied earlier,
personal vision supplanted national policy in their fiction, poetry, and
plays, and the tendency was toward an increasingly solipsistic form of
writing, that which refers only to itself (sometimes referred to as "art for
art's sake"). Not surprisingly, that vision is dark, often nihilistic, even, at
times, perverse. And it has struck a resonant chord with readers outside
China. The reasons for this are complex but include, I think, a diminution
of the long-held dreamily exotic view of China in the West (with a concomitant lessening of tolerance toward the positivistic brand of writing
with which we have become familiar), a global fin-de-siècle anxiety (which
informs the sexual and social behavior of characters in recent writing from
China), and a fear that the world has become apocalyptically violent. With
images of June 4, 1989, still fresh in the public consciousness, in recent literature from China, selected and mediated by translators, we see more
currents of commonality than ever before.

The most disturbing Chinese writing to appear in English is laden with
graphic depictions of horrific violence, often in elegiacal proportions. One
critic's comment on the novelist Yu Hua could easily be applied to many
young Chinese writers: "To journey through his fictional universe is to
subject oneself to a harrowing series of depictions of death, dismembered
bodies, and acts of extreme and seemingly gratuitous cruelty."[22] Disori-
enting stories of grotesque brutality, layered with symbolism and often
lacking the traditional markers—time, place, names—that is, stories incor-
porating a sense of universality, bestow upon the numbing violence in
them a true metonymic quality. Savage, homicidal fictions, while seemingly "ready-made for appropriation into the critique of the antihumanis-
tic ravage of the Cultural Revolution," nonetheless have become "a heresy
to the older generation of writers and critics for whom violence [is] a political act and a symptom, albeit an irrational one, of history. The pure con-

sumption of violence as an aesthetic form [is] inconceivable, and not surprisingly, utterly sacrilegious, to survivors of turbulent historical
trauma."[23] But these claustrophobic worlds of depravity and bestiality
(not unlike that of the Polish writer Bruno Schulz, a Jew who was killed in
the Holocaust) epitomizes what David Wang has called a "familiarization
of the uncanny. [B]y turning the world into a realm of fantastic and
uncanny elements or by identifying normalcy with the grotesque and
insane, writers awaken their readers from aesthetic and ideological iner-
tia, initiating them into a new kind of reality."[24]

Violence and evil, with all their metonymic possibilities, are nowhere
more powerfully evoked than in Su Tong's catalogue of horrors with the
innocuous title of *Rice*.

The tale of a thoroughly malign individual who corrupts (or kills) every
person with whom he comes into contact during the course of his self-con-
suming life, the novel portrays a society (pre-war China) bent on self-
destruction and, in the view of many critics, the pervasive dehumanizing
climate of contemporary society. *Rice* is a grim, numbing, disturbing, even
profane work that, with all its exaggerated grotesqueries, is all too believ-
able. One reviewer, having posed the question "Why would anyone read
this book in the first place?," supplies her own thoughtful answer:
"Because Su Tong renders these people so vividly that they possess, for us,
the individuality that they deny one another. Even their rampant misog-
yny . . . tells us how willfully alone each is, how frightened and defensive.
And because when we read about bad things happening to bad people, we
feel bad—and that's good. That's what makes us human."[25] Su Tong's
novel, and many of his stories, paint China's recent history—and by allusive implication, its present—in unrelieved darkness. Fiction with a historical setting, particularly during the Republican era, that is, the first half
of the twentieth century, presents an opportunity to deal obliquely with
contemporary events with a measure of safety; one can, however disingenuously, point to the damning visions in one's writing and imply that
the setting, now past, would be impossible in the socialist context, and that
is precisely how many of them refute the accusations of conservative critics that their work is somehow "unhealthy."

No one has been accused of writing "unhealthy" fiction more than Mo
Yan, until recently a member of the Cultural Section of the People's Liberation Army. With *Red Sorghum* he created sympathetic heroes out of ban-
dits, adulterers, murderers, and anti-Party activists. With his second novel,
The Garlic Ballads, he went further, examining the precarious, even antag-

onistic, relationship between the Chinese peasantry and the Communist government in his most transparently ideological novel. In *Large Breasts and Full Hips*, the focus is on sex, politics, and, echoing *Red Sorghum*, China's frightful modern history. None of these works, each unique in its own right, prepared the reader for what, in my opinion, may be the most astonishing novel to appear from China in this century, *Republic of Wine*.

Hailed by one critic as a "twentieth-century fin-de-siècle masterpiece," this experiment in narrative technique is a multi-layered work of fiction that confronts the Chinese trait of gluttony, a national discomfort with the issue of sex, and a host of human relationships, many of them quite bizarre. Reminiscent of, if not exactly parallel to, Swift's "A Modest Proposal," the novel explodes the myths of a benevolent government ruling over a civilized nation; while it is but the latest in a long tradition of literature dealing with cannibalism in China, the novel views the aberrant behavior as an extreme example of China's vaunted gourmandism in the context of a racy parade of sexual misconduct and ultimately constitutes an attack by Mo Yan on some of China's cultural sacred cows, as well as a reaction by him to the horrors of June 4th at Tian'anmen Square.

Beyond that, *Republic of Wine* is concerned not only with issues of culture and humanity, but with the process of writing as well, a self-conscious "retrospective" of the author's oeuvre. The text includes a series of fictional correspondences between an amateur writer who lives in Republic of Wine and engages "Mo Yan" in discussions of fiction, of the novel in which he appears, and of food, liquor, and sex. The dialogue between the two characters is further enhanced by the inclusion of stories by the amateur, stories that get increasingly bizarre and intriguing as the novel progresses. Finally, it is a novel about liquor, whose paradoxical social functions—an elevation of the spirit as well as the epitome of excess[26]—undergird the structure of the novel as a whole. If I were to be asked the same question the reviewer asked in regard to Su Tong's *Rice*—Why would anyone read this book in the first place?—the answer would have to include the sheer joy of his Rabelaisian humor and gusto, the structural artistry, and the satirical barbs, much, but not all, of which is apparent even in translation.

Su Tong and Mo Yan, pretty heavy stuff. But what about the young novelist who "can't stand people with a sense of mission"? He reigned as China's most popular writer for much of this decade, and the powers that be dislike him as much as the reading public, particularly the young, adores him. Wang Shuo, in whose novels self-indulgence, hedonism, and the pride of sociopathy mock both the establishment and the vaunted reforms of the Dengist era, has been called Beijing's "bad boy" and worse (or better, depending upon your point of view). The characters of his short novel *The Operators*, for instance, are unprincipled young men who sell their services as proxies—for lovers, people in trouble, henpecked husbands—thus thumbing their nose at social norms: anything for a buck. In *Please Don't Consider Me Human*, a satirical farce that mocks the campaign to recoup feelings of national pride in the wake of the loss of the bid to host the 2000 Olympics, a pedicab driver is chosen by a group of Beijing punks to defend the nation's honor by getting castrated in order to participate in an international sporting event as a woman. Wang Shuo, it has been pointed out in the *New York Times*, "romanticizes young alienated rebels in much the same way that Jack Kerouac did. He explores the paradoxes and absurdities of society, as Joseph Heller and Kurt Vonnegut do."[27]

Instead of criticizing the Communists for being autocratic, Wang Shuo does what is far more devastating: he mocks them for being uncool.

In *Playing for Thrills*, Wang Shuo plays with the mystery genre by building a story about a murder that might have occurred and the young hedonist who might have committed it. The "thrill" for Wang Shuo is in describing the Beijing "lower depths" and weaving a tale that mystifies as it delights, sending the reader off with at least as many questions as answers. For some, like mystery mogul Stephen King, who provided a cover blurb for the novel, Wang has written a book for everyone:

> *Playing for Thrills* is perhaps the most brilliantly entertaining "hardboiled" novel of the 90s . . . and maybe of the 80s, as well. It constitutes a genre by itself, call it China noir, and offers guilty pleasures beyond any most readers will encounter in a bound set of Kinsey Milhones or Lucan Davenports. What the hell is this anyway? Jack Kerouac unbound? I don't think so . . . you have to experience this in order to really get it. Most ultimately cool.[28]

. . . AND BEYOND . . .

More translations of contemporary Chinese literature are appearing these days than ever before; whether this means that the readership base is expanding at the same time, that more people from different walks of life are switching to fuller "cans of shaving cream," is impossible to determine. There is, of course, the fluctuation principle to consider, that literary works from China gain popularity every time China is in the news and disappear from bookstore shelves during more quiescent periods; also at play is the coattail effect, in that as the number of people who travel to China to work or visit increases, so, too, do the quantity and diversity of reading material, including literature.

Another encouraging factor is the trend among U.S. trade publishers toward enriching their lists by adding Chinese authors—not just individual books—and promoting them with at least modest enthusiasm. Unhappily, however, as the burgeoning market economy in China holds out the promise for the more enterprising among its population to enjoy unprecedented material comforts, many writers find it increasingly less rewarding to employ their talents in an endeavor that is not well appreciated in a consumer-capitalist climate. Jianying Zha is correct when she writes:

> Every Chinese intellectual is waking up to one common fact: no longer is the government the only thing they must deal with. Now they must reckon with forces of commercialism. They can't kid themselves anymore: the days of huge readerships are gone, along with the feeling that a writer is the beloved and needed spokesman of the people and the conscience of society.[29]

Many promising young novelists appear to have abandoned their quest for artistic perfection for the more lucrative fields of commerce, TV scriptwriting, and the like. In my view, this could actually work to the advantage of belles lettres in and from the People's Republic, in effect a winnowing process that will leave only the most dedicated and talented writers on the scene and will motivate them to further polish their craft in the face of a smaller though more demanding readership, both in China and abroad. At present, no more than a dozen novelists, most in their middle years, are regularly published in the West; they are becoming identifiable on an international basis and are being read as much for their literary talents as for the windows onto contemporary Chinese society they inevitably provide.

It is, of course, an uphill struggle. Yet even with all the perils inherent in the translation process, and the "Third-World" status of literature from China, contemporary literary works, however mediated, can be uniquely satisfying for, and revealing to, readers beyond China's borders; there is no reason why the words of one critic cannot apply to Chinese literary works rendered into foreign languages: "A translation gives us access to the literature of the world. It allows us to enter the minds of people from other times and places. It is a celebration of otherness, a truly multicultural event without all the balloons and noisemakers. And it enriches not only our personal knowledge and artistic sense, but also our culture's literature, language, and thought."[30] And if it is true that "translating authors from other cultures can prevent a literature from becoming too nationalistic or too provincial,"[31] then the literary borders between China and the rest of the world must, and will, remain open for free movement in both directions.

NOTES

1. Wilborn Hampton, "Anarchy and Plain Bad Luck," *New York Times Book Review*, April 18, 1993. Edward Hower is more concise: "*Red Sorghum* is a book that anyone interested in China will have to read." *New York Newsday*, May 2, 1993. Andrew F. Jones has dealt in detail with the marketing of Chinese literature abroad in his essay "Chinese Literature in the 'World' Literary Economy," *Modern Chinese Literature*, vol. 8 (1994), 171–190. In this essay I have not considered the literature from Taiwan, Hong Kong, or any of the other places where fiction, drama, and prose are written in Chinese. The interested reader may consult *The Columbia Anthology of Modern Chinese Literature*, Joseph S. M. Lau and Howard Goldblatt, eds. (New York: Columbia University Press, 1995). More can be found in the Columbia University Press series "Modern Literature from Taiwan" and the Hong Kong translation journal *Renditions*, which also publishes books.

2. Robert Wechsler, *Performing without a Stage: The Art of Literary Translation* (North Haven, Conn.: Catbird Press, 1998), 246.

3. Needless to say, a substantial amount of writing that hews more closely to Party ideals continues to be published in China; it, too, has a loyal readership, as do all the popular genres—detective fiction, science fiction, romance, even pornography—and bad writing generally. Little of it gains serious attention within China and hardly any gets translated.

4. David Der-wei Wang, "Chinese Fiction for the Nineties," in *Running Wild: New Chinese Writers*, David Der-wei Wang and Jeanne Tai, eds. (New York: Columbia University Press, 1994), 242.

5. *Writing Diaspora: Tactic of Intervention in Contemporary Cultural Studies* (Bloomington, Ind.: Indiana University Press, 1993), 74.

6. Available in my translation from Penguin Books (1994); so, too, his second novel, *The Garlic Ballads* (1996).

7. This is the charge leveled against the poetry of Bei Dao (and, by extension, most modern Chinese poets) by the classical Chinese literature specialist Stephen Owen, in "What Is World Poetry?: The Anxiety of Global Influence," in *The New*

Republic (November 19, 1990): 28–32. Domestic critics, too, have stated their concern over a tendency by writers and moviemakers to cater to Western tastes. The journalist Dai Qing has written of Zhang Yimou's film adaptation of Su Tong's *Raise the Red Lantern*, "this kind of film is really shot for the casual pleasures of foreigners." Quoted in Jianying Zha, *China Pop: How Soap Operas, Tabloids, and Bestsellers Are Transforming a Culture* (New York: The New Press, 1995), 94.

8. Jing Wang, ed. *China's Avant-Garde Fiction* (Durham, N.C.: Duke University Press, 1998), 4.

9. "Obsession with China: The Moral Burden of Modern Chinese Literature," in *A History of Modern Chinese Fiction*, 2d ed. (New Haven: Yale University Press, 1971), 533–534.

10. Contemporary fiction writer, Wang Shuo, as quoted in Jianying Zha, *China Pop*, 110.

11. While these writers have taken heart in the rather amazing reception of Chinese films around the world (do, in fact, participate in the scriptwriting), they are puzzled that their books do not generate the same enthusiasm.

12. For a sampling of contemporary drama, the reader may consult *An Oxford Anthology of Contemporary Chinese Drama*, Martha P. Y. Cheung and Janet C. C. Lai, eds. (Hong Kong: Oxford University Press, 1997); and *Theater & Society: An Anthology of Contemporary Chinese Drama*, Haiping Yan, ed. (Armonk, N.Y.: M. E. Sharpe, 1998). Both anthologies provide illuminating introductions.

13. Mark Ford, *Times Literary Supplement*, in review of John Ashbery's *Can You Hear, Bird* (1995).

14. Several anthologies of Bei Dao's poems have been translated into English, including *The August Sleepwalker*, Bonnie S. McDougall, trans. (1990), and *Landscape over Zero*, David Hinton, trans. (1995), both from New Directions. Bei Dao continues to edit the literary quarterly *Jintian* (Today), begun during the heady "Democracy Wall" movement in 1979, which includes fiction, poetry, criticism, and a feature entitled "Rewriting Literary History." The most comprehensive view of contemporary Chinese poetry is provided in Bonnie S. McDougall and Kam Louie, *The Literature of China in the Twentieth Century* (New York: Columbia University Press, 1997).

15. It is not surprising, given the marginalization of Asia generally and China specifically in Western literary studies, that only two contemporary writers from Asia, the Japanese novelist Yasunari Kawabata and the Chinese short-story writer A-cheng, appear in two recent books on exile: *Exile and the Writer*, Bettina L. Knapp (University Park, Pa.: Pennsylvania State University Press, 1991) and *Altogether Elsewhere: Writers on Exile*, Marc Robinson, ed. (Boston and London: Faber & Faber, 1994), both in the former.

16. Chow, *Writing Diaspora*, 101.

17. Kam Louie, "The Translatability of Chinese Culture in Contemporary Chinese Fiction," in *Modern Chinese Literature* (1994): 216.

18. The ideal of a world literature (*weltliteratur*) originated with Goethe, who wrote that "there can be no question of the nations thinking alike, the aim is simply that they shall grow aware of one another, understand each other, and even where they may not be able to love, may at least tolerate one another." This statement has been adopted as a motto of sorts by the literary quarterly *World Literature Today.*

19. In recent years, about a half dozen anthologies of contemporary Chinese literature in English translation have been published in the West; added to that are a couple of dozen novels or single-author story collections and a few books of poetry. Not a large figure, by any stretch of the imagination, but a broad enough cross-section of offerings in Chinese to give English-language readers an idea of the quality and type of available writing and a wide-ranging glimpse of the society that has spawned it. Most have been published by commercial presses, but university presses have added to the number. Worthy of note is the "Fiction from Modern China" series from the University of Hawaii Press. Foreign Languages Press in Beijing also publishes work by contemporary writers.

20. The Hungarian poet Miklós Haraszti writes: "Before socialism, the function of art had been simply to preserve its own autonomy, or, in a wider sense, to preserve the possibility of autonomy within society at large. In the culture of social commitment it has a new function: to enlarge, direct, and give cohesion to an organized public, the nucleus of the future society." This socialist art, he continues, "neither hates nor worships 'reality'; it merely denies reality the chance to be mysterious." *The Velvet Prison: Artists under State Socialism* (New York: Basic Books, 1987), 37, 38.

21. Haraszti, *The Velvet Prison*, 129.

22. Andrew Jones, "Translator's Postscript," Yu Hua, *The Past and the Punishments* (Honolulu: University of Hawaii Press, 1996), 270.

23. Jing Wang, *China's Avant-Garde Fiction*, 4.

24. Wang, "Chinese Fiction for the Nineties," 243.

25. Kelly Cherry, "The Symbol of Plenty and Nothing, *Los Angeles Times*, January 28, 1996.

26. The multiple roles of alcohol, in the novel and in society in general, are treated in great detail in Xiaobin Yang, "The Republic of Wine: An Extravaganza of Decline," *positions: east asia cultures critique*, vol. 6, no. 1 (Summer 1998): 16.

27. Sheryl WuDunn, "The Word from China's Kerouac: The Communists Are Uncool," *New York Times Book Review*, January 10, 1993, 3.

28. Available in paperback in my translation from Penguin Books (1998).

29. Zha, *China Pop*, 46. According to Zha, the joke around Beijing a few short years ago was "there are more people writing novels than reading novels" (135).

30. Wechsler, *Performing without a Stage*, 11.

31. "Introduction," *Theories of Translation: An Anthology of Essays from Dryden to Derrida*, Rainer Schulte and John Biguenet, eds. (Chicago: University of Chicago Press, 1992), 8.

SUGGESTED READINGS

Martha P. Y. Cheung and Janet C. C. Lai, eds., *An Oxford Anthology of Contemporary Chinese Drama* (Hong Kong: Oxford University Press, 1997).

Howard Goldblatt, ed., *Chairman Mao Would Not Be Amused: Fictions from Today's China* (New York: Grove Press, 1995).

Joseph S. M. Lau and Howard Goldblatt, eds., *The Columbia Anthology of Modern Chinese Literature* (New York: Columbia University Press, 1995).

Bonnie S. McDougall and Kam Louie, *The Literature of China in the Twentieth Century* (New York: Columbia University Press, 1997).

Modern Chinese Literature, vol. 8 (1994).

Wang David Der-wei and Jeanne Tai, eds., *Running Wild: New Chinese Writers* (New York: Columbia University Press, 1994).

Jing Wang, *High Culture Fever: Politics, Aesthetics, and Ideology in Deng's China* (Berkeley: University of California Press, 1996).

Jing Wang, ed., *China Avant-Garde Fiction* (Durham, N.C.: Duke University Press, 1998).

Jianying Zha, *China Pop: How Soap Operas, Tabloids, and Bestsellers Are Transforming a Culture* (New York: The New Press, 1995)

Afterword:

EXTRA—Headlines Obscure the Full Story

Timothy B. Weston and Lionel M. Jensen

After NATO led by the United States attacked the Chinese Embassy in Yugoslavia, the mainstream U.S. media started a whole series of performances in an attempt to shape U.S. and world opinion about the bombing. Their goal was to prevent the American people from understanding what had happened. . . . Their intent was to show that the Chinese government is taking advantage of this to [build] anti-American sentiment and has organized and egged on crowds to surround the U.S. Embassy. In the muddied portrait that the U.S. media is putting out, the real victim—China—became the country harming the United States.

—Fu Zhou, "How the U.S. Media Guides Public
Opinion," in People's Daily, May 8, 1999

A *Newsweek* magazine poll revealed that 51 percent of its surveyed Americans deemed China to be unfriendly to the United States. Of those polled, 80 percent say that China must be regarded as an enemy, UPI reported on Sunday. . . . Concerning the bombing of the Belgrade Chinese Embassy, 23 percent felt that it will cause an irreparable rift in Sino–U.S. relations, whereas 69 percent believe it to be only a temporary setback. Sixty-four percent thought the bombing to be accidental and thought that no high-ranking official from the CIA or the Pentagon should be disciplined or fired.

—Sue Bruell and Yin De An, China News Digest,
May 18, 1999

The success or failure of the experiment undertaken in the previous chapters depends upon this ability of this book to engender a new habit of mind in our readers, one that is instinctively critical, bringing Chinese worldview alongside U.S. worldview and recognizing that the two nations' problems are interrelated. This is possible when minds are released from the obligation to make an easy, even cowardly, compromise with national stereotypes and conspiracy theories of world domination. Yet the two previous epigraphs reveal the dogged persistence of the headlines-only representation of the simple, conventional, and nationally antagonistic, making clear that our greatest challenge continues to be the achievement of mutually respectful recognition.

In recent months the U.S. media has devoted considerable attention to China, owing to the NATO bombing of the Chinese embassy in Belgrade in May 1999, to the CCP's commemoration of the fiftieth anniversary of the founding of the People's Republic of China on October 1, 1999 (*Guoqing jie*, "National Day," a day of patriotic significance comparable to Independence Day in the United States) and to the Chinese government repression of Falun Gong. Some of the reporting has been insightful and valuable; nevertheless, we cannot escape feeling that the cumulative effect of the increased media attention has been a stoking of U.S. distrust of China. In these instances, China seems to make it into popular press accounts not because it is understood to be a potential partner of the United States at the dawn of the new millennium, but because it is widely viewed as the likely primary challenger to U.S. global dominance in the twenty-first century. Mainstream journalistic coverage of China in the United States tends to be divided against itself, able to provide with equal facility stories about China's ominousness and stories about its miraculous transformation.

In spring 1999 the U.S. media was covering two stories—those about China's tampering with the 1996 U.S. elections and about China's alleged theft of "top-secret" nuclear weapons intelligence as detailed in the Cox report—both of which have continued to generate coverage even after they were overtaken by the crisis in Sino–U.S. relations that resulted from the NATO bombing of the Chinese embassy in Belgrade. As we head into the 2000 election it is clear that China has once more taken its place as a salient issue on the U.S. political landscape. Beginning in the second and third weeks of May 1999, headlines such as "Chinese Students Are Caught Up by Nationalism," "The Tempest in China," "Public Anger against the U.S. Still Simmers in Beijing," "More Anti-U.S. Protests in Beijing," covered the international and op-ed pages of U.S. dailies.[1] A febrile intensity marked the Chinese protest and, now that so many of China's urban citizens are "hooked up," outrage was instantly conveyed across the globe. Two days after the bombing, the White House Web site was so overwhelmed with electronic mail from irate Chinese registering their cyberprotest that the site crashed.

For a U.S. government so accustomed to decrying the political machinations of the Chinese Communist Party, the tables suddenly had been turned. From the Chinese vantage, the United States was the aggressor and the violator of human rights. In addition to what was portrayed as an intentional injury to the Chinese nation in the form of the bombing and killing of three Chinese journalists, China's national press was full to brimming with stories about NATO's killing of innocent citizens in Kosovo and Serbia. Indeed, the emblem of Serbian defiance in the face of NATO's bombing in Belgrade—T-shirts bearing a target symbol communicating sarcastically, "Here we are, kill us, too!"—appeared on the streets in Chinese cities as well, an expression of outrage at the United States and of solidarity with the people of Serbia at the same time. Though the United States was profoundly apologetic after the bombing and insisted that it was the result of an honest mistake due to NATO's reliance on outmoded maps, these expressions of remorse were deemed insincere and insufficient to mollify Chinese national injury. Many reports from China indicated that the Chinese people interpret the embassy bombing as further evidence of an ongoing U.S. effort to prevent China from becoming a world power. Furthermore, U.S. accusations about China's theft of nuclear secrets are being treated as an added insult to the Chinese people, as a "tissue of half-truths, conjectures, and lies" that are both absurd and racist.

This we know from reading Chinese headlines as well as our own. The U.S. print and broadcast media carried lengthy coverage of the protests at the U.S. embassy in Beijing and of the burning of the consulate in Chengdu, capital of Sichuan province, and moved in the course of May and June toward a portrait of China as enemy. The cover of the June 7 issue of *Time* was a deep Communist red and in its center, framed by a star-shaped aperture, was an Asian eye and below it the rhetorical caption "The Next Cold War?" The journalistic frenzy proffered U.S. citizens numerous photographs of Chinese students carrying signs denouncing U.S. products and the corporations that sell them, a far cry from the last image of Chinese students that saturated the U.S. media when Tian'anmen Square was host to the Goddess of Democracy. But even these images fail to capture the dimensions of the anti-U.S. sentiment that swept China in the wake of the destruction of a foreign symbol of Chinese sovereignty. We know from personal communications that U.S. students in China were harassed and intimidated to such an extent that they chose to misrepresent themselves as Australians or New Zealanders. In the course of a flurry of anti-U.S. rallies in the city of Chengdu, foreigners were verbally accosted and, in one instance, German students were hit with bottles and stones when exiting a store.[2] Yet U.S. headlines disclosed national sympathy with Chinese anger as they called for NATO and the United States to "own up to a mistake" while stressing that such efforts to assume responsibility would be difficult because the bombing had "smashed our credibility to smithereens."

As it was learned in the United States that the Chinese government had bused angry students to the U.S. embassy in Beijing and even assisted in the choreography of pelting the U.S. embassy with stones and waste-filled bottles, the sorrow most U.S. citizens felt about the killing of the Chinese journalists in Belgrade gave way to suspicion and hostility. In this way, the legitimacy of passionate popular Chinese protest was ignored, as when the *New York Times* announced in bold type on May 14, 1999: "China's Mood: Real Public Rage Stoked by Propaganda Machine." The Chinese state, the usual suspect, was again to blame and, most important, its citizens were robbed of the complexity of their own responses, something that angered a better-informed Chinese populace even more.

Yet, the bombing placed the Chinese government in a predicament, for it was weary from the outrage that swept the country. On the one hand, the government was anxious over the approaching tenth anniversary of the June 4th Massacre and felt pressure to abide by the constitutional guarantee of free assembly. Thus, repressing citizen protests was ill-advised for it could provoke an even greater, more incendiary action against the CCP. In this sense, the Chinese government was not so much leading the Chinese people as it was following them. And it was certainly to the government's advantage as the anniversary approached to encourage the popular belief that the Party and the people formed an outraged united front of injury against a hostile West. But, on the other hand, it could not afford to encourage the proposals for boycotts of U.S. manufactured goods, for it understood all too well that trade with the United States remains critical to its own political survival. Furthermore, the Chinese government did not want to suggest that angry protest should become a common mechanism for the expression of political sentiment, especially in light of the myriad preparations underway for the fiftieth anniversary of the PRC's founding. The Party was concerned to orchestrate an elaborate celebration of its revolutionary legacy, culminating in a presentation of China's contemporary capitalist prosperity.

Chinese students protesting against the United States and NATO were in a predicament as well, because the bombing offered them a rare opportunity to express their public voice of protest and to represent with pride their identity as Chinese. However, as educated members of the new Chinese elite, many of them hoped to study in the United States and were at the very moment of their protest preparing for the TOEFL examination, successful completion of which would ensure their enrollment at U.S. universities where classmates and siblings were already studying. Indeed, a few weeks after the destruction of China's Belgrade embassy Chinese were standing in the usual long lines outside U.S. government offices in Beijing to apply for visas to the United States. Also, a goodly number of Chinese who had no intention of studying abroad were grooming themselves for jobs in U.S. corporate environments in China. Such people could not simply hate the United States or U.S. citizens. Their feelings were not so simple.

And beyond the Chinese headlines were Chinese Internet chat-room discussions—the backstage—revealing a confusing and complicated mix of emotions, the government's awareness of which no doubt deepened its commitment to a safe and uncontroversial commemoration of China's national holiday. In the days and weeks after the destruction of their nation's embassy Chinese expressed themselves openly (often but not always anonymously) from computers on college campuses and in urban "cyber-cafes." There was no single Chinese response. It is simply incorrect to say that all the demonstrations over the embassy bombing were organized by the Chinese Communist Party or that the Chinese people were "brainwashed" by the Party because most of them believed the NATO bombing was intentional. The following four quotations selected from Chinese Internet pages from May 1999 should make it plain that the feelings expressed then were not controlled by the government in a straightforward manner.[3]

The government is incompetent. When it is hit, it can only cry out, like a dog. Why don't the Chinese people overthrow it!!! The day will come when the computer systems of the Pentagon will by attacked by hackers from all around the world. The many kinds of viruses the hackers bring will make all the computers crash. Anti-American hackers of the world unite! Make that day come soon.

—Anonymous post to popular PRC Web site

Professor Jia said that the day after the Embassy bombing he was on his way to a meeting when his taxi driver said, "The Chinese government is too weak! It if was up to me, I'd drive a truck full of explosives to the U.S. Embassy and blow it up!" Professor Jia felt compelled to ask the taxi driver. "After you have blown up the U.S. Embassy, then what?"

—An interview with Beijing University International Relations Institute Vice Director Jia Qingguo (Professor Jia received a Ph.D. from Cornell University in 1988)

Down with NATO, Down with U.S. Imperialism. NATO can't take the place of the United Nations! Has NATO gone crazy? The U.S. led NATO guided missile attack on China's embassy in Yugoslavia seems as foolish as Nazi Germany's invasion of the Soviet Union and the Japanese attack on Pearl Harbor. A high price will be paid for it in the end.

—Anonymous post to popular PRC Web site

Demonstrating to express your anger is fine. But why do you use violence against American diplomatic establishments? Is it that the only way you can protest is by throwing rocks? Or perhaps you respond, "We are putting into practice Chairman Mao's teaching 'If other people don't bother me, I won't bother them.' " But you forget, what you are protesting is the American attack on the Chinese Embassy and its violation of the sovereignty of another country. But isn't that just what you are doing yourselves? Moreover, just a few days after the event occurred before the situation is clear, how can you know that it was a brazen bombing? Under those circumstances, saying that patriotism means using intemperate words and stoning the U.S. Embassy is too simple. What we are doing is the "slogans plus smashing" of the ten year long Cultural Revolution.

—Anonymous post to popular PRC Web site

But it was easy to miss all of this amid the growing political hysteria in both the United States and China. Chinese headlines were vicious and intemperate in their attacks on the United States, especially emphasizing the U.S. government's control of NATO and its deliberate shelling of the Chinese embassy. The U.S. government and the media gave as good as they got, countering Chinese fury over the bombing with U.S. wrath over Chinese theft of defense secrets. Now, as so often in the past, the United States and China have been mutually demonized like the old stock characters of the Cold War drama. Of course, if the bombing of the embassy was deliberate, then the chasm between the U.S. citizenry and the U.S. government may be as wide as that between the Chinese and the

Chinese Communist Party, something that a number of the essays in this volume have suggested.

In the summer months of 1999 the sharpness of the May conflict began to soften and China again fell below the fold in most U.S. newspapers. But in late September and early October the U.S. media once more was full of news about China—this time of a proud and martial China, and of a Tian'anmen Square entirely transformed from its 1989 incarnation as ground zero of the democracy movement into a staging ground for a seamlessly orchestrated state celebration of past, power, and progress. The ten-year anniversary of Tian'anmen came in the same year as the fiftieth anniversary of the founding of the modern state, and curiously enough, the mechanism that ensured the destruction of the citizens' movement of 1989—the declaration of martial law—was the same as that which secured the parade route for the national holiday celebration.

Once again China was colorfully displayed above the fold. Consumers of Western media could feast on a range and depth of stories occasioned by the glow of the celebrations in the Chinese capital. This was exactly as the planners in Beijing intended for it to be, as this was the biggest *qiantai* (front stage) performance of them all. But the media was not uncritical in its reporting on the fiftieth anniversary and went out of its way to remind its audience of the stories on the *houtai* (backstage), most of which conveyed the less glorious sides of life in contemporary China. The net effect was to produce once again the intense ambivalence that has long characterized our relations with China as well as our representation of it.[4]

The question remains whether the West's (and particularly the United States') search for the underside of China's achievements is engendered by a desire to belittle a government it holds in contempt or is inspired by an undercurrent sense of the democratic aspirations common to citizens of China and the United States. We suspect that this backstage of our intertwined hopes is the real story, present but not fully disclosed in the sometimes violent oscillations of U.S. media accounts and scholarly debates about China.

We can only hope that the Chinese and U.S. popular perceptions of shared strengths and weaknesses will inspire our governments, information organs, and technicians of knowledge to recognize that far too much has been built by China and the United States in the last two decades of their cooperation to be squandered. It is clear that the quickness with which both nations occasionally move to define each other as nemesis reveals a depth of political passion lacking in their relations with other countries.

Let us not take this passion as threat but as evidence of an honest airing of our dislikes and reservations, of the sort that is common to any conversation between well-meaning interlocutors. For most citizens of the United States and China it may prove difficult to hear the sounds of our diverse national reactions over the din of the moment's hysterical headlines, yet they must and the few, but loud, voices of this volume will call them to the task of listening, so that we may all learn of the China and the United States beyond the headlines.

NOTES

1. These headlines were randomly selected from the *New York Times*, the *Denver Rocky Mountain News*, and the *Denver Post* between May 11 and May 19, 1999.

2. We are indebted to Elisa J. Holland for her email reports of the hysterical events of anti-U.S. protest in Chengdu in the weeks following the NATO bombing.

3. We would like to thank David Cowhig of the Environment Science and Technology section of the U.S. Embassy in Beijing for culling these exchanges from Chinese chatrooms and posting them on H-ASIA in the weeks following the bombing. The U.S. Embassy Web page may be accessed at http://www.usembassy-china.org.cn.

4. The negative pole of this ambivalence, that of apprehension, was brilliantly displayed in *The Economist*, the October 2, 1999, issue of which was titled "China—The Fireworks to Come."

Index

agricultural economy, 303–15
Ah Q, 121, 122, 134, 138, 139
air pollution, 181–82, 196, 201–4
Ames, Roger, 135, 136
Asian economy, 172–73, 178–79, 186
"Asian values," 106
autonomous regions (*zizhiqu*), 79, 80, 81

Bei Dao (poet), 334
Beijing Massacre (*liusi,* June 4, 1989), 22, 30, 97, 99, 104, 110, 123, 135, 137, 156, 176, 178, 350, 353
Bernstein, Richard, 23, 26, 27, 28, 125–26, 150, 153

capitalism, 5, 47, 154, 158. *See also* economy; market reforms
Chen Xiaotong, 39, 40
Chen Xitong (former Mayor of Beijing), 38, 39, 40, 41, 42, 53
China, People's Republic of (PRC): as autocracy, 32, 115, 116; Belgrade embassy bombing, 7, 118, 127, 147, 148; constitution, 6, 31, 37, 60, 110, 279; criminal codes, 47, 48, 49, 110; ethnic policies, 73–4, 79, 86; fiftieth anniversary of, 348, 350; fiscal decentralization, 314–15; foreign investment in, 109, 173, 179–80, 184–85, 187, 253–56, 263; foreign policy of, 155; human rights policies of, 99, 100–101, 103, 108; income gap, 259, 261, 302–303, 314; international copyright violation, 38, 148, 151; as "leader of the Third World," xiv; legal/civil statutes, 47, 48, 49, 59, 54, 100–101, 110, 157; modernization, 297–98; Most Favored Nation (MFN) status, xvii, 126, 150, 151, 179; National People's Congress, 41, 104, 106, 110; one-child policy, 75, 182; per capita income, 245–46; press censorship, 105; relationship with Japan, 155; religious policies, 88, 90; taxation, 179, 315
China, Republic of (Taiwan), 119, 148, 164; as "Formosa," 157; investment in PRC, 109; Lee Teng-hui (President), 152; reunification with mainland, 30, 149, 156, 165; "state-to-state" relationship with PRC, 152
China Democracy Party (CDP), 105, 109, 119
China "specialists" (Western), xii, xviii, 3, 18, 20, 21, 27, 28. *See also* intellectuals, U.S.
China-U.S. relations, 3, 8, 18, 30–31, 50, 107, 126–29; anti-U.S. sentiment,

China-U.S. relations (*Continued*)
151, 155, 166, 167; containment
strategy, 18, 25–26; engagement
strategy, 18; exceptionalism and,
121, 125, 139n1; military exercises in
Taiwan Strait (1996), 156; potential
future confrontation, 149–50, 151;
"strategic partnership," 2, 64; U.S.
reaction to Chinese nationalism,
147, 247, 253–55. *See also* popular attitudes and images
China-U.S. similarities, 4–5, 52, 55–56,
59, 61–62, 63, 64, 79, 85, 93, 121,
150–51, 153, 160, 321, 347–48
China-U.S. trade, 18, 38, 174, 179, 180
Chinese Communist Party (CCP), 2, 6,
19, 21, 32, 63, 71, 80, 91, 99, 107, 110,
115, 116, 117, 118, 119; agricultural
policy of, 307–13; Campaign
Against the Six Evils, 228; Central
Committee of, 58; corruption and,
37–38, 40, 42, 43, 45, 47, 48, 49, 50,
51, 52, 53, 54, 55, 57, 58, 59, 61; economic policies, 248, 250, 264; ethnic
minority policies of, 282; Fifteenth
Congress (September 1997), 176;
gender ideology, 217; "infallibility
of," 90; intellectuals and, 132–33; labor policy, 256, 263, 319, 321; labor
reform, 246, 264; Politburo of, 41;
public trust in, 6, 32, 52, 53, 155–56;
reform, role in, 176–77, 301–2; religious policies, 289; unions, position
on, 257, 264–65; women, policies toward, 224
Chinese embassy bombing. *See* NATO
"Chineseness," 159–60, 164, 165
"civil society," 128, 132, 134, 136, 138,
141n16
"clean government," policy of, 38, 45
Clinton, Bill (U.S. President), x, 2, 14,
15, 18, 20–21, 23, 25, 29, 33, 45,

61–62, 109, 176, 320–21; state visit to
China (1998), 2, 19, 20–21, 29–30,
107, 109, 123
"Cold War mentality" (U.S.), 155
Coming Conflict with China. See Bernstein, Richard
communism, xi, 2, 73, 99, 106. *See also*
Maoism; Marxism-Leninism
Communist Revolution (1949), ix, 73,
115
"Confucianism," 19, 129, 130, 133, 134,
135, 153
conspicuous consumption, 183–84
consumerism, 221; in China, 5, 59, 157,
158–9, 160; tension between nationalism and, 159, 164, in U.S., 5, 59;
corporate influence in China, 19, 26,
53–54, 109, 127, 147, 148, 153, 157,
173–74, 247, 254–56, 321; Chinese
corporations, 177
corruption: anti-corruption campaigns, 38, 51, 60; anti-corruption
laws, 48–50, 52; Chinese, 5, 37, 38,
39, 40, 41, 42, 43, 44, 46, 47, 48, 49,
50, 51, 52, 53, 54, 57–58, 59, 61, 64,
179; Chinese terminology for,
45–46; definition of, 43, 44; types of,
47, 48–49, 54, 57; U.S., 5, 45, 61
Cox Report, x, 2, 14, 22. *See also* nuclear espionage
Cultural Revolution (1966–1976), ix,
61, 65n2, 104, 115, 124, 132; suppressed eroticism in, 218; women's
appearance in, 218
currency (*renminbi*), 173, 178–79

Dalai Lama, 7, 23, 30, 81
democracy, 113, 114, 116, 117, 119,
134, 136; Chinese advocacy for,
114–16; Chinese attempts at, 115;
democratization, 6, 20, 21, 32, 116,
119, 133, 185–86

Democracy Movement (1989), 50, 116. *See also* Beijing Massacre

Democracy Wall Movement (1978–1979), ix, 113, 116, 124

Deng Xiaoping (former Vice Premier; 1904–1997), ix, 22, 27, 39, 40, 42, 49, 55, 86, 99, 115, 124, 130; and Southern Tour (*nanxun*), 55, 176

Deng Xiaoping Theory, 300–302

Ding Zilin (dissident), 104, 105

dissidents (*yijian butong zhe*), 29, 30, 31, 101, 103, 104, 105, 106, 109, 114, 122, 123, 127, 138, 161. *See also* individual dissidents' names

drama (literature), 334

economy, 32, 173–74, 179, 246; agricultural, 303–15; corruption and, 52; development of, 157; growth of, 195, 245, 264; income gap, 185; state capitalism, 56, 99; state socialism, 56, 130; stock market, 173. *See also* market reforms

education, 4, 100, 177; women's, 224, 237

environment, 100, 181–82; afforestation, 209; costs of damage, 197; deforestation, 197, 208–10; effects of damage, 197, 212; effects of economic expansion, 197; solutions, 214. *See also* air pollution; farmland; greenhouse gases; water supply

ethnic minorities, 72–93, 169n27, 273–74; classification schemes, 73, 74, 75; cultural expression, 282; derogatory Han terms for, 75; dissent, 174, 188, 274; "ethnic group" (*minzu*), 72–73, 75, 80, 82; exploitation of non-Han people, 161–62; linguistic pluralism and, 85–87; minorities as "entertainment," 83, 159, 161, 162–63; policies toward, 73, 75,

79, 83–84, 93, 161; separatism, 82, 161; Sinification, 79, 80, 84. *See also* Hui; Tibetan; Uighur; Yi

exceptionalism: China, 2, 4, 138, 158–59, 160, 166; U.S., 2, 4, 118, 125, 126, 128, 160; U.S. "manifest destiny," 124, 127–28, 138; U.S./China sharing, 4, 121, 127. *See also* intellectuals (Chinese); popular attitudes and images

exports, 179, 180

Falun Gong (Falun Dafa), 91, 348

Fang Lizhi (dissident), 97, 122, 132–33

farmland, 196–97, 205–8

films, China, 148, 157, 236

films, U.S.: *Battle for China*, 24; *Fifty-Five Days in Peking*, 24; *Fu Manchu* serials, 23, 24, 28, 176; *Good Earth*, 23, 24, 28; *Kundun*, 23, 24; *Manchurian Candidate*, 176; *Mulan*, 24; *Red Corner*, 23, 24; *Seven Years in Tibet*, 23, 24, 161; *Star Wars* series, 23, 24, 25, 33

folklore and popular culture, 274, 281–91

Forbes, Steve, 15, 18

Four Cardinal Principles, 110

Four Modernizations, ix, 113. *See also* Wei Jingsheng

free market. *See* market reforms

Gao Hongmin (labor dissident), 266

gender: ideology, 229; media representation of, 219, 221–23

globalization, 5, 127, 180, 236–37, 247, 333. *See also* market reforms

Gorbachev, Mikhail, 32

Gore, Albert Jr. (U.S. Vice President), 23

Great Proletarian Cultural Revolution. *See* Cultural Revolution

greenhouse gases, 196, 211–12
guanxi. See social relations
Guizhou, 297–98, 310, 314–16
Guo Xinmin (labor dissident), 266

Han (majority ethnic group), 72, 74,
    75, 76, 79, 80, 87, 90, 107, 161,
    162–64, 273; cultural diversity
    among, 84, 162
Han Dongfang (labor dissident),
    266n24, 268, 321
health care, 177
Hong Kong, 119, 164, 174–76; democ-
    racy of, 175–76; investment in PRC,
    53–54, 109; loss of, 149; return of, x,
    149, 156
housing, 178,184
Hui (Chinese Muslims), 76, 80–82. *See
    also* ethnic minorities
human rights (*renquan*), 295–96, 299,
    320–21; abuses, 99, 100, 105, 109,
    163; activists and organizations, 97,
    109, 110, 117; business and, 99, 108,
    109; Chinese, 30–31, 38, 97, 99, 100,
    101, 102, 103–111, 124, 148, 153; Chi-
    nese economy and, 99, 138; Chinese
    exceptionalism and, 104; Chinese
    government policies on, 99,
    100–101, 103, 108; exploitation of
    non-Han people, 161–63; interna-
    tional covenants on (ICCPR,
    ICESR), 99, 102–3, 109, 262, 265; in-
    ternational opinion and, 28, 30–1,
    97, 108–109, 110, 111; Internet and,
    103; movements within China, 102,
    105; tactics, 108–110; Tibetan, 7, 107;
    Universal Declaration of Human
    Rights, 98–99; U.S. policies, 28,
    30–1, 134. *See also* workers, rights
Human Rights in China (HRIC), 97,
    98, 99, 102–3, 108
Huntington, Samuel, 131, 150

industrialization, rural, 315–17
intellectuals, Chinese (*zhishifenzi*), 5,
    30, 73, 103, 104, 107, 122, 126, 127,
    130, 131, 133, 134, 135, 136, 137, 138,
    139, 164, 165, 166, 246; and the CCP,
    132, 133; definitions of, 123, 133; use
    of Chinese intellectual history, 129,
    134; use of Western intellectual his-
    tory, 128, 129, 134, 135, 136, 138;
    U.S. media portrayals of, 121, 165
intellectuals, U.S., xviii, 3, 123
International Monetary Fund (IMF),
    184, 186–87
Isaacs, Harold, 13, 15, 16, 17, 23, 24

Japan, 34n2, 55, 119, 150, 152, 155
Jiang Zemin (state chairman, "presi-
    dent"), x, 2, 19–20, 23, 29, 33, 40, 42,
    51, 109, 118–19, 246, 250; on reform,
    297, 300; state visit to the U.S., 20,
    22, 63–64, 295–97
June 4th Massacre (*liusi*; 1989). *See*
    Beijing Massacre

Kissinger, Henry (former U.S. Secre-
    tary of State), 20, 27, 123
labor: conditions, 247, 251–52, 254–56;
    dissidents, 261–62, 265–66; layoffs,
    176, 261, 262; reform, 246, 264;
    strikes, 261; sweatshops, 180,
    253–55, 315–16, 321. *See also* trade
    unions
Leninism. *See* Marxism-Leninism
Leys, Simon (Pierre Ryckmans), 121,
    122, 123. *See also* Ah Q
Lin Mu (dissident), 104, 105
Li Peng (National People's Congress
    Chairman), 37, 38, 51, 57, 59–60,
    100, 104
literature, 327–43; artistic freedom,
    331–32; avant-garde, 332; commer-
    cialization, 331, 342; of dissent, 337,

339–40; experimental, 331; influence of history and memory on, 330–33, 338; instructive, 328, 329; nihilistic, 338; realism, 329–30, 337; sex in, 340; socialist-realism, 337, 339; violent, 338; Western influence on, 332. *See also* translation

Liu Shaoqi (former Vice Chairman of Central Committee; 1898–1969), 58–59

Li Zehou (intellectual), 134, 135, 136

Lu Siqing (labor dissident), 262

Macao, Return of, 156

Madsen, Richard, 17, 126, 127, 133, 134, 135

Mandarin language (*Putonghua* or *guoyu*), 85–86, 87; effort to maintain the "purity" of, 157

Maoism (Mao Zedong Thought), ix, 21, 32, 49, 110, 113, 156. *See also* communism; Marxism-Leninism

Mao Zedong (former Chairman; 1893–1976), xiii, 63, 86, 99, 124, 134

market reforms, xii, xiii, 45–46, 127, 159, 173,176–77,185–89, 246–47, 250, 276, 299–300, 302, 316; effects of, 171, 259, 265; effects on women, 219, 221, 224–28, 234–37, 239; human rights and, 99, 108, 109; liberalization and, xii, 32, 155; privatization and, xiii, 19, 29, 48, 49; unemployment and, 101. *See also* economy; unemployment; women

Marx, Karl, 298–99, 317

Marxism-Leninism (Stalinism), xv, 21, 32, 49, 110, 113, 130, 156. *See also* communism; Maoism

media: coverage of NATO bombing, 348; gender representation in, 219, 221–23, 227–32, 234; international coverage of China, 347–54

media, China, xiv, 7, 27, 103, 107, 148, 150, 152, 155, 157

media, U.S., xi, xii, xiv, 7, 8, 14, 15, 18, 19, 22, 107, 151, 247, 274, 290, 347–50, 353–54; and intellectuals, 123; demonization of China, xiv, 4, 22–3, 26, 71, 151, 153, 168n11; portrayals of China, xiii, xv, 38, 107, 126, 140n8, 166; portrayals of dissidents, 122

media, U.S., broadcast: CNBC, 147–48; *Frontline*, 61–62; "Misunderstanding China" (documentary), 17, 24

media, U.S., print: *Nation*, 27; *National Review*, 23; *New Republic*, 23, 26; *Newsweek*, 147; *New York Review of Books*, 27; *New York Times*, 20, 25, 62, 113, 123, 136, 147; *Time*, 18, 22; *Weekly Standard*, 26

mexrep groups (*maixilaifu*). *See* Uighur

middle class, Chinese, 85, 158–60, 166

Mo Yan (author), 327–28, 330, 339–40; *Garlic Ballads*, 339; *Large Breasts and Full Hips*, 340; *Red Sorghum*, 327–28, 330, 339; *Republic of Wine*, 340

multiculturalism: Chinese, 71–75, 79, 84–87, 92, 93, 165; U.S., 71, 74, 79, 93

Munro, H. Ross. *See* Bernstein, Richard

nationalism (Chinese), 30, 32, 73, 107, 128, 129, 138, 147, 148, 149, 150, 151, 152, 154, 155, 156, 157, 158, 166, 348–54; Chinese works regarding, 129, 137–38, 150, 151, 152, 153, 154, 155, 158, 167; complexities and ambiguities of, 148, 150, 151, 157, 164; domestic manifestation of, 161–64; international perceptions of, 149; tension between consumerism and, 159, 164; ultra-nationalism, 154, 160, 165

nationalism (Japanese), 150
Nationalist Party (Guomindang, GMD; or Kuomintang, KMT), 73, 130
National Labor Committee (NY), 253–54
NATO (North Atlantic Treaty Organization), xiv; bombing of Chinese embassy in Belgrade, x, 7, 118, 127, 147, 148, 347–48; Chinese response to bombing, 348–53
nuclear espionage, 2–3, 7, 118, 348. *See also* Cox Report

Olympics 2000 bid (Beijing), 113, 127, 156, 168n17
"Orientalism," 14, 125

People's Liberation Army, 177, 188
poetry, 334
politics, U.S., 3, 4, 7–8, 13, 18, 22, 25, 61–63, 125; U.S. election scandal (1996), 348
popular attitudes and images: China toward U.S., xiv, 124, 126–29, 147, 148, 153, 154, 155, 166–67; Henry Higgins/Eliza Doolittle relationship, 124–25, 126, 138, 139; U.S. toward China, xi, xii, xiii–xiv, xv, xvii–xviii, 1, 3–4, 5, 11, 14–15, 16–22, 29, 64, 69–71, 107–8, 147. *See also* films, U.S.; media, U.S.
pornography, 226
poverty, 245, 297, 302; rural, 307–15
"princelings" (*taizidang*), 45–50
prostitution, 225–26, 260

Qing Dynasty (Manchu, 1644–1911), xv, 73, 115
Qin Yongmin (labor dissident), 105, 262

reform: as American "wish-fulfillment," 14, 19–20; anti-corruption campaigns, 38, 51, 60; anti-corruption laws, 52
religion, 276, 277–81, 281, 289; Buddhism, 76, 77, 78, 82–83, 88, 91; Christianity, 76, 77, 78, 88, 89–90; Daoism (Taoism), 76, 88; Islam, 76, 77, 78, 80, 81, 82, 87, 88; traditional practices, 82, 83, 90–91, 93
"rule by law" (*yifa zhiguo*), 38, 42, 60, 101; contrasted with "rule of law," 50, 101

Said, Edward. *See* "Orientalism"
sex crimes, 226–27
"six evils," 228
"Socialism with Chinese Characteristics," 42, 48, 49–50, 130. *See also* economy
social relations, 38, 44, 46, 179
Southern Tour (*nanxun*). *See* Deng Xiaoping
Soviet Union. *See* Union of Soviet Socialist Republics
Splendid China (theme park), 159–60
State-owned Enterprises (SOE), 247–51, 254; working conditions in, 252–53
suicide, 183
Sun Yatsen (Sun Zhongshan, National Father; 1866–1925), 30, 86, 130
superstition, 184
Su Tong, 339, 340; *Rice*, 339
sweatshops. *See* labor

Taiwan. *See* China, Republic of
Taoism (Daoism). *See* religion
Tian'anmen Square protests (1989). *See* Beijing Massacre
Tibet (Xizang), 7, 30, 31, 80, 84, 159, 161, 164; human rights and, 7, 107
Tibetan, 73, 74, 76, 80, 81, 107
trade unions: All China Free Trade

Union (ACFTU), 257–258, 265; autonomous, 257, 262, 265–66; Communist Party position on, 257, 264–65
translation (literature), 328–29, 335, 342–43; problems with, 335–36

Uighur, 76, 80, 81, 274–289; economy, 276–77; folklore and popular culture, 274, 281–91; *mexrep* groups (*maixilaifu*), 279, 286–88; religion, 276, 277–81, 281, 289; separatism, 81; social interaction, 276, 284; unrest, 277–78, 286; women, 276–77
underemployment. *See* unemployment
unemployment, 101, 180, 219, 225, 246, 248, 250–51, 260–61, 264
Union of Soviet Socialist Republics (USSR), xv, 1, 2, 32, 72, 73, 74, 103, 119
United Nations (UN), 104, 109. *See also* human rights
United States: Beijing embassy and, 147, 148; Chinese conception of, 106, 128, 129; Chinese criticism of, 129–30, 151–52; constructive engagement, 296, 320; consumption of Chinese products, 247, 253–55; corporate influence in China; 173–74, 247, 254–56; defense, 175, 188; foreign policy of, 16, 122, 152; as "global hegemon," xiv, 2, 148; government policy, 184, 187, 189; human rights and, 107, 130; job losses, 187–88; media, 171, 174–76, 189; pursuit of China's markets, 296; relationship with Japan, 152. *See also* politics, U.S.
urbanization, 318
U.S. Congress, 62–63, 126, 130. *See also* Cox Report

U.S.-China relations, 3, 8, 18, 30–31, 50, 107, 126–29, 348–54; anti-U.S. sentiment, 151, 155, 166, 167; containment strategy, 18, 25–26; engagement strategy, 18; exceptionalism and, 121, 125, 139n1; "humility" and, 134; military exercises in Taiwan Strait (1996), 156; potential future confrontation, 149–50, 151; "strategic partnership," 2, 64; U.S. reaction to Chinese nationalism, 147, 247, 253–55. *See also* popular attitudes and images
U.S.-China similarities, 4–5, 52, 59, 61–62, 63, 64, 79, 85, 93, 121, 150–51, 153, 160, 321, 347–48
U.S.-China trade, 18, 38; exports, 179,180; protectionist policy, 174

Wang Dan (dissident), 29, 31, 104, 105, 106, 108, 164–65, 265; "Tian'anmen Generation" and, 104
Wang Fengshan (dissident), 266
Wang Shiwei (Party critic; 1906–1947), 124
Wang Shuo, 340–41; *Operators,* 341; *Playing for Thrills,* 341; *Please Don't Consider Me Human,* 341
Wang Xizhe (dissident), 262
Wang Youcai (dissident), 105, 109
water supply, 196, 198–200
Wei Jingsheng (dissident), 108, 110, 113–20, 123, 265; "The Fifth Modernization" and, ix, 113
welfare, 176, 177, 182, 184, 248, 250
Wen Ho Lee (physicist), 2–3. *See also* Cox Report; nuclear espionage
Westernization, 228–29, 236
women: communist ideal, 217, 229, 231, 233; daily life, 276–77; education, 224, 237; effects of economic reform on, 219, 221, 224–28, 234–37,

women (*Continued*)
239; employment, 183, 224, 237,
254–56, 259, 315–16; fashion,
218–19, 231, 236; media representation of, 221–23, 227–32, 234; objects in advertising, 217, 219–21,
227; pornography, 226; prostitution, 225–26; public image of,
217–18, 229, 232, 236; sale into
marriage, 224–25; sexuality, 229,
231–33, 239; social roles, 219, 232,
236; violence against, 223, 225–27,
254–55
workers, 100, 101, 109, 127, 176–78;
benefits, 177, 182; conditions,
180–81; exploitation, 180, 181, 247,
251, 254; housing, 178; migrant, 177,
260, 317–18, 320; private sector,
253–56; rights, 253–54, 256, 263;
rural, 260, 315–18; unrest, 178, 246,

252–53, 259, 261, 263, 265–66; urban,
250, 260; women, 183, 254–56, 259,
315–16;
World Trade Organization (WTO), 7,
127, 148–49, 158, 179–80
Wu, Harry (Wu Hongda), 26, 29, 122

Xinjiang, 274–75, 280; economy, 276;
religion, 280–81; Urumqi, 275; Yin-
ing, 276;
Xizang. *See* Tibet
Xu Wenli (dissident), 105, 262
Xu Yonghai (dissident), 266

Yellow River, 199
Yi, 74, 75, 76, 80, 83
Yue Tianxing (dissident), 266

Zhu Rongji (Premier), 14, 15, 19, 22,
119, 173–74, 176, 180, 184, 246

About the Editors and Contributors

Geremie R. Barmé is senior fellow in the Division of Pacific and Asian History of the Research School of Pacific and Asian Studies at Australian National University and is one of the world's most reliable commentators on contemporary Chinese politics, culture, and society. He is the author of *Shades of Mao: The Posthumous Cult of the Great Leader* (1996), *In the Red: On Contemporary Chinese Culture* (1999) and the co-editor of several works, including: (with John Minford) *Seeds of Fire: Chinese Voices of Conscience* (1989), (with Jonathan Unger) *Chinese Nationalism* (1996), and (with Linda Jaivin) *New Ghosts, Old Dreams: Chinese Rebel Voices* (1992). His academic labors have been meritoriously complemented by writing on the award-winning documentary of the 1989 Tian'anmen demonstrations, "The Gate of Heavenly Peace."

Susan D. Blum is a cultural and linguistic anthropologist specializing in China. She is assistant professor of anthropology at the University of Colorado at Denver. To date, her writings and research have focused on ethnic, national, and personal identity; multilingualism; and language as social action, all based on fieldwork conducted in the city of Kunming in southwest China. She is the author of *Portraits of "Primitives": Human Kinds in the Chinese Nation* (2000), and co-editor of *China Off Center: Self and Society on the Margins of the Middle Kingdom* (2000). Her articles have appeared in *Language and Society, Ethnic Groups,* and *Michigan Discussions in Anthropology.*

Timothy Cheek teaches at the Colorado College where he is associate professor of history and director of the Asian-Pacific Studies Program. He is the author of two books and has edited several others. His research interests are focused on intellectuals, the party-state, and ideology. In addition to co-editing (with Carol Lee Hamrin) *China's Establishment Intellectuals* (1986), (with Merle Goldman and Carol Lee Hamrin) *China's Intellectuals and the State: In Search of a New Relationship* (1987), (with Tony Saich) *New Perspectives on State Socialism in China* (1997), and (with Juan Lindau) *Market Economics and Political Change: Comparing China and Mexico* (1998), he has written *Propaganda and Culture in Mao's China: Deng Tuo and the Intelli-*

gentsia (1997). His articles have appeared in *The Australian Journal of Chinese Affairs*, *The China Quarterly*, and *Chinese Law and Government*.

Jay Dautcher recently completed his doctoral work in the department of anthropology at the University of California, Berkeley. He has lived in China for seven years, including two in Xinjiang. His dissertation, entitled "Folklore and Identity in a Uighur Community in Xianjiang China," is on social relations in a suburban merchant community in Yining, Xinjiang. He is currently An Wang Post-Doctoral Fellow at Harvard University.

Harriet Evans is the author of *Women and Sexuality in China: Dominant Discourses of Female Sexuality and Gender since 1949* (1997). She is senior lecturer in Chinese in the School of Languages at Westminster University in London. She also serves on the faculty of Westminster's Centre for the Study of Democracy and is the course convenor for its innovative program in Contemporary Chinese Cultural Studies. She is a frequent contributor to *The China Quarterly* and the *Times Literary Supplement* and has written a number of essays on Chinese women, sexuality, women's liberation during and after the Chinese revolution, and the scientific construction of gender, which have appeared in such journals as *SIGNS: Journal of Women in Culture and Society* and *Intersections*. She is coeditor (with Stephanie Donald) of *Picturing Power in China: Posters of the Cultural Revolution* (1999).

Howard Goldblatt is professor of Chinese literature in the department of East Asian Languages and Civilizations at the University of Colorado at Boulder and a highly distinguished translator of modern Chinese fiction. He has edited numerous collections and has translated nearly thirty book-length works, including: Chen Jo-hsi, *The Execution of Mayor Yin* (1978); Liu Binyan, *China's Crisis, China's Hope* (1990); Jia Pingwa, *Turbulence* (1991); Su Tong, *Rice* (1995); Ma Bo, *Blood Red Sunset* (1995); Mo Yan, *The Garlic Ballads* (1995) and *Republic of Wine*; Wang Shuo, *Playing for Thrills* (1997); Li Rui, *Silver City*; and Hong Ying, *Daughter of the River* (1998). His translations have received international recognition, including the Translation Center's Robert Payne Award in 1985 for Mo Yan's *Red Sorghum*.

Lionel M. Jensen, associate professor of history and director of the Program in Chinese Studies at the University of Colorado at Denver and a specialist in the intellectual and cultural history of traditional and modern China, is the author of *Manufacturing Confucianism: Chinese Traditions and*

Universal Civilization (1997) and editor of *Early China* 20 (1995). He is also co-editor (with Susan D. Blum) of *China Off Center: Self and Society on the Margins of the Middle Kingdom* (2000). As well, his articles have appeared in *positions: east asia cultures critique, Early China, The Historian,* and *Studies in Chinese History.*

Tong Lam was born and raised in Macao, a Portuguese enclave in south China, and is now a Ph.D. candidate in history at the University of Chicago, where his research interests include the use of narratives in community formation, nationalism, and cultural representations in modern China. He is presently writing a dissertation on the historical emergence of modern conceptions of "society" in China, "Investigating and Representing Chinese 'Society,' 1890–1949."

Tim S. Oakes is assistant professor of geography at the University of Colorado at Boulder and specializes in cultural geography with a concentration on place-based identities and cultural politics. He has lived and conducted fieldwork in China's southwestern province of Guizhou and is the author of *Tourism and Modernity in China* (1998).

Henry Rosemont, Jr., is George B. and Wilma Reeves Distinguished Professor of the Liberal Arts at St. Mary's College of Maryland and Senior Consulting Professor of Fudan University in Shanghai. He is the author of *A Chinese Mirror: Moral Reflections on Political Economy and Society* (1991) and the forthcoming *Confucian Alternatives* (2000) and has edited and/or translated seven works on Chinese thought and culture. In collaboration with Roger T. Ames, he has published an edited translation and annotation of the Lunyu, or Analects, based upon the recently discovered Dingxian text and titled *The Analects of Confucius: A Philosophical Translation* (1998).

Vaclav Smil is professor of geography at the University of Manitoba and his studies of the interactions among environment, energy, economy, and society have yielded more than one hundred articles in twenty edited volumes and in fifty periodicals in science, energy, environment, and Asian studies. As well, he is the author of more than twelve books, including: *Biomass Energies* (1983), *The Bad Earth* (1984), *General Energetics: Energy in the Biosphere and Civilization* (1991), *Global Ecology* (1993), and *China's Environmental Crisis: An Inquiry into the Limits of National Development* (1993). He is considered the leading authority on China's energy and environmental problems.

Jeffrey N. Wasserstrom, associate professor of history at Indiana University, is a specialist in the social and cultural history of twentieth-century China. He is the author of *Student Protests in Twentieth-Century China: The View from Shanghai* (1991), as well as the co-editor of *Popular Protest and Political Culture in Modern China*, 2d ed. (1994), and *Human Rights and Revolutions* (2000). His essays on historical, political, comparative, and theoretical issues have appeared in a variety of academic journals, and he has also written for general periodicals such as *Dissent*, the *Times Literary Supplement*, *Media Studies Journal*, and the *Chronicle of Higher Education*.

Wei Jingsheng is the world's best-known Chinese democracy activist and "dissident" who served more than fifteen years in prisons for his aggressive defense of human rights and democratic freedoms. He has been nominated for the Nobel Peace Prize and has received the Olof Palme Award and the European Parliament's Sakharov Prize for Freedom of Thought. Though sentenced to fourteen years for treason in 1994, Wei was released on medical leave and permitted to immigrate to the United States in November 1997. Now exiled from his home, he travels widely to conferences, symposia, and meetings of nongovernmental organizations laboring on behalf of political reform in China. His prison writings and selected essays have been translated into English and published as *The Courage to Stand Alone: Letters from Prison and Other Writings* (1997).

Timothy B. Weston is assistant professor of history at the University of Colorado at Boulder. His research interests are in the political and intellectual history of modern China. He has published in *Modern China* and is the author of *Beijing daxue yu Zhongguo zhengzhi wenhua, 1898–1920* (Beijing University and China's Political Culture, 1898–1920). Currently, he is working on a book tentatively titled *Intellectuals at the Center: Beijing University and Chinese Political Culture, 1898–1928*.

Xiao Qiang is a native of Beijing and has lived in the United States since 1986, when he began graduate study in astrophysics at Notre Dame University. In 1991 he was appointed the Executive Director of the nonprofit international watch group, Human Rights in China (HRIC).